THE PL...
Translated j...
in Four Volum... ...Meyer

"This, one may think, is how Ibsen might have expressed himself in English."
—*The* (London) *Times*

"Meyer does justice, both in scholarship and understanding, to one of the most fascinating creative artists ever to find the chief expression of his gifts in drama."
—*Washington Post*

"Meyer's translations of Ibsen are a major fact in one's general sense of post-war drama. Their vital pace, their unforced insistence on the poetic center of Ibsen's genius, have beaten academic versions from the field."
—George Steiner, *The New Statesman*

"Crisp and cobweb-free, purged of verbal Victoriana."
—Kenneth Tynan

"Michael Meyer's translation gives back to the lines the poetry and dignity . . . which they certainly lack in the translations we have had for so long."
—*The Listener*

"Mr. Meyer's versions should remain definitive for this generation at least."
—*The Times Educational Supplement*

The Plays of Ibsen

Volume I
  A DOLL'S HOUSE
  EMPEROR AND GALILEAN
  JOHN GABRIEL BORKMAN
  WHEN WE DEAD AWAKEN

Volume II
  HEDDA GABLER
  THE PRETENDERS
  BRAND
  THE PILLARS OF SOCIETY

Volume III
  GHOSTS
  THE WILD DUCK
  THE MASTER BUILDER
  AN ENEMY OF THE PEOPLE

Volume IV
  PEER GYNT
  ROSMERSHOLM
  THE LADY FROM THE SEA
  LITTLE EYOLF

Published by WASHINGTON SQUARE PRESS

Most Washington Square Press Books are available at special quantity discounts for bulk purchases for sales promotions, premiums or fund raising. Special books or book excerpts can also be created to fit specific needs.

For details write the office of the Vice President of Special Markets, Pocket Books, 1230 Avenue of the Americas, New York, New York 10020.

THE PLAYS OF

IBSEN

VOLUME III

GHOSTS ▪ THE WILD DUCK
▪ THE MASTER BUILDER
▪ AN ENEMY OF THE PEOPLE

Translated from the Norwegian
and Introduced by
Michael Meyer

WSP

WASHINGTON SQUARE PRESS
PUBLISHED BY POCKET BOOKS NEW YORK

Ghosts, The Wild Duck and *The Master Builder* were first published as a collection in Great Britain in paperback in 1980 by Eyre Methuen Ltd.

Ghosts was first published in this translation in 1962 by Rupert Hart-Davis Ltd., and subsequently by Eyre Methuen Ltd., in 1973. Copyright © Michael Meyer 1962, 1973. Introduction copyright © Michael Meyer 1962, 1973. Revised, 1980.

The Wild Duck was first published in this translation in 1962 by Rupert Hart-Davis Ltd., and subsequently by Eyre Methuen Ltd., in 1968. Copyright © Michael Meyer 1962, 1968. Introduction copyright © Michael Meyer 1962, 1968. Revised, 1980.

The Master Builder was first published in this translation in 1961 by Rupert Hart-Davis Ltd., and subsequently by Eyre Methuen Ltd., in 1968. Copyright © Michael Meyer 1961, 1968. Introduction copyright © Michael Meyer 1961, 1968. Revised, 1980.

An Enemy of the People was first published in this translation in 1963 by Rupert Hart-Davis Ltd., and subsequently by Eyre Methuen Ltd., in 1974. Copyright © Michael Meyer 1963. Introduction copyright © Michael Meyer 1963. Revised, 1980.

Permission to quote from Emilie Bardach's letters has been kindly granted by Gyldendal Norsk Forlag of Oslo. Mrs. Reginald Orcutt has given her permission for the use of the quotations from Basil King's articles, *Ibsen and Emilie Bardach*.

A Washington Square Press Publication of
POCKET BOOKS, a division of Simon & Schuster, Inc.
1230 Avenue of the Americas, New York, N.Y. 10020

NOTE ON THE REVISED EDITION

In this edition, I have made certain revisions to the text resulting from successive productions of these translations. Occasionally, an actor or actress or director has come up with a better line than the one I originally wrote, and I have happily made the change. I have also made certain adjustments for American usage where a word or phrase would sound out of place to an American audience.

Michael Meyer
London
1985

CONTENTS

HENRIK JOHAN IBSEN: A Chronology

1828   Born at Skien in southeast Norway on 20 March, the second child of Knud Ibsen, a merchant, and his wife Marichen, *née* Altenburg.

1834–5 Father becomes ruined. The family moves to Venstœp, a few miles outside Skien.

1844   Ibsen (aged fifteen) becomes assistant to an apothecary at Grimstad, a tiny seaport further down the coast. Stays there for six years in great poverty.

1846   Has an illegitimate son with a servant-girl, Else Sofie Jensdatter.

1849   Writes his first play, *Catiline* (in verse).

1850   Leaves Grimstad to become a student in Christiania (now Oslo). Writes second play, *The Warrior's Barrow*.

1851   Is invited to join Ole Bull's newly formed National Theatre at Bergen. Does so, and stays six years, writing, directing, designing costumes and keeping the accounts.

1852   Visits Copenhagen and Dresden to learn about the theatre. Writes *St. John's Eve*, a romantic comedy in verse and prose.

1853   *St. John's Eve* acted at Bergen. Failure.

1854   Writes *Lady Inger of Œstraat*, an historical tragedy in prose.

1855   *Lady Inger of Œstraat* acted at Bergen. Failure. Writes *The Feast at Solhaug,* another romantic verse-and-prose comedy.

1856   *The Feast at Solhaug* acted at Bergen. Small success. Meets Suzannah Thoresen. Writes *Olaf Liljekrans*, a third verse-and-prose comedy.

1857   *Olaf Liljekrans* acted at Bergen. Failure. Leaves Bergen to become artistic manager of the Christiania Norwegian Theatre. Writes *The Vikings at Helgeland*, an historical prose tragedy.

1858   Marries Suzannah Thoresen. *The Vikings at Helgeland* staged. Small success.

1859   His only legitimate child, Sigurd, born.

1860–1   Years of poverty and despair. Unable to write.

1862   Writes *Love's Comedy,* a modern verse satire, his first play for five years. It is rejected by his own theatre, which goes bankrupt.

1863   Ibsen gets part-time job as literary adviser to the Danish-controlled Christiania Theatre. Extremely poor. Applies unsuccessfully to Government for financial support. Resorts to moneylenders. Writes *The Pretenders,* another historical prose tragedy. Is granted a travel stipend by the Government; this is augmented by a collection raised by Bjœrnson and other friends.

1864   *The Pretenders* staged in Christiania. A success. He leaves Norway and settles in Rome. Remains resident abroad for the next twenty-seven years. Begins *Emperor and Galilean.*

1865   Writes *Brand,* in verse (as a play for reading, not acting), in Rome and Ariccia.

1866   *Brand* published. Immense success; Ibsen becomes famous throughout Scandinavia (but it is not acted for nineteen years).

1867   Writes *Peer Gynt,* in verse (also to be read, not
        acted), in Rome, Ischia and Sorrento. It, too, is a
        great success; but is not staged for seven years.
1868   Moves from Rome and settles in Dresden.
1869   Attends opening of Suez Canal as Norwegian dele-
        gate. Completes *The League of Youth,* a modern
        prose comedy.
1871   Revises his shorter poems and issues them in a vol-
        ume. His farewell to verse; for the rest of his life he
        publishes exclusively in prose.
1873   Completes (after nine years) *Emperor and Gali-
        lean,* his last historical play. Begins to be known in
        Germany and England.
1874   Returns briefly to Norway for first time in ten
        years. The students hold a torchlight procession in
        his honour.
1875   Leaves Dresden after seven years and settles in
        Munich. Begins *The Pillars of Society,* the first of
        his twelve great modern prose dramas.
1876   *Peer Gynt* staged for first time. *The Vikings at
        Helgeland* is performed in Munich, the first of his
        plays to be staged outside Scandinavia.
1877   Completes *The Pillars of Society.* This makes him
        famous in Germany, where it is widely acted.
1878   Returns to Italy for a year.
1879   Writes *A Doll's House* in Rome and Amalfi. It
        causes an immediate sensation, though a decade
        elapses before it makes Ibsen internationally fa-
        mous. Returns for a year to Munich.
1880   Resettles in Italy for a further five years. First per-
        formance of an Ibsen play in England (*The Pillars
        of Society* for a single matinée in London).
1881   Writes *Ghosts* in Rome and Sorrento. Violently at-
        tacked; all theatres reject it, and bookshops return
        it to the publisher.

1882   Writes *An Enemy of the People* in Rome. Cordially received. *Ghosts* receives its first performance (in Chicago).

1884   Writes *The Wild Duck* in Rome and Gossensass. It, and all his subsequent plays, were regarded as obscure and were greeted with varying degrees of bewilderment.

1885   Revisits Norway again, for the first time since 1874. Leaves Rome and resettles in Munich.

1886   Writes *Rosmersholm* in Munich.

1888   Writes *The Lady from the Sea* in Munich.

1889   Meets and becomes infatuated with the eighteen-year-old Emilie Bardach in Gossensass. Does not see her again, but the experience shadows the remainder of his writing. Janet Achurch acts Nora in London, the first major English-speaking production of Ibsen.

1890   Writes *Hedda Gabler* in Munich.

1891   Returns to settle permanently in Norway.

1892   Writes *The Master Builder* in Christiania.

1894   Writes *Little Eyolf* in Christiania.

1896   Writes *John Gabriel Borkman* in Christiania.

1899   Writes *When We Dead Awaken* in Christiania.

1901   First stroke. Partly paralysed.

1903   Second stroke. Left largely helpless.

1906   Dies in Christiania on 23 May, aged seventy-eight.

Ghosts

Introduction

Ghosts, like *A Doll's House*, was conceived in the Alps and written on the shores of the Mediterranean in an Italian summer. The idea for *A Doll's House* had come to Ibsen in Gossensass and, after brooding upon it in Rome, he had written the bulk of it in an old monastery converted into a hotel just outside Amalfi. Published in December 1879, *A Doll's House* had achieved immediate success in Scandinavia, where it ran into three editions within three months and—unlike so many of his plays—was a success when staged in all the Scandinavian capitals. 'Perhaps no book in all literature had made such triumphal progress', recalled Halvdan Koht, who was a child when it appeared. '*A Doll's House* exploded like a bomb into contemporary life'—though it was to be over a decade before it took its place in the general European repertoire.

After completing it Ibsen returned, in the autumn of 1879, from Italy to Munich, and spent the winter there. Next summer he went to Berchtesgaden on holiday, dressed as a genuine German tourist, with a Tyrolean hat on his head. There was much rain and fog that summer, even more than usual for Berchtesgaden, and when his friend John Paulsen asked him what he was busy with Ibsen replied: 'It is a family history—grey and gloomy as this rainy day.'

He did no actual writing in Berchtesgaden, merely brooding upon the theme and characters. In the autumn of 1880 he

3

returned to Munich and there received a note from the Norwegian Ecclesiastical Department, which was also responsible for education, informing him that his son Sigurd could not graduate in law in Norway without first taking certain elementary Norwegian examinations. Ibsen was furious at this example of what he regarded as typical Norwegian pigheadedness. 'To the black gang of theologians which at present rules the Norwegian Ecclesiastical Department,' he wrote to his publisher, Frederik Hegel of Gyldendal, 'I shall in good time raise a fitting memorial.' The immediate effect was that his son decided to continue his studies in Italy, and on 2 November 1880 Ibsen moved to Rome, where he took a house at 75, Via Capo le Case. From there, on 26 November 1880, he wrote to Edmund Gosse that he was 'busy pondering a new play, which I hope to complete during the summer'.

This play, however, seems not to have been *Ghosts,* for on 18 June 1881 he wrote to Hegel: 'There has been a change in my literary plans for the summer. The work* about which I wrote to you previously has temporarily been shelved, and early this month I started on a theme which has long occupied my thoughts and which at length forced itself upon me so insistently that I could no longer ignore it. I hope to be able to send you the manuscript by the middle of October. I'll tell you the title later; today I shall merely state that I describe it as "a domestic drama in three acts." I need

---

*Possibly *An Enemy of the People,* which Ibsen completed with unwonted speed the following year. Within a month of finishing *Ghosts* he wrote to Hegel: 'I am already busy planning a new four-act comedy which I had thought about before but put aside to make way for *Ghosts,* which was obsessing me and monopolising my thoughts.' Some critics, however, believe that Ibsen had been planning another play which never got written, and Paulsen's remark quoted above suggests that he may have had a more sombre work in mind.

hardly add that this play has no kind of connection with *A Doll's House.*'

On 28 June Ibsen and his family moved to Sorrento, and by 23 September he had completed a first draft of the play, which has unfortunately not survived. A week later he wrote to Hegel: 'I take advantage of a free moment to tell you briefly that on the 23rd instant I finished the draft of my new play and on the 25th began my fair copy. The play is called *Ghosts, a Domestic Drama in Three Acts.* If possible you shall have the whole thing by the end of October.' This 'fair copy' in fact took the form of a new draft, the various stages of which he dated, enabling us to chart its swift progress. Act One took him from 25 September to 4 October; Act Two from 13 to 20 October; and Act Three from 21 to 24 October. On 23 November, writing from Rome, he uttered a mild warning to Hegel: '*Ghosts* will probably cause alarm in some circles; but that can't be helped. If it didn't, there would have been no necessity for me to write it.'

Ghosts was duly published by Gyldendal of Copenhagen on 13 December 1881, and at once aroused a consternation and hostility beyond anything Ibsen had envisaged. At first he accepted this calmly; he knew there were small prospects of getting it performed in either Scandinavia or Germany, but reckoned it would have its effect, like *Brand* and *Peer Gynt,* on the reading public. On 22 December he wrote to one of his German translators, Ludwig Passarge: 'My new play has now come out and has created a violent commotion in the Scandinavian press. Every day I receive letters and newspaper articles, some for, some against. A copy will be sent to you very shortly; but I feel it's quite impossible that this play should be performed in any German theatre at this time; I hardly think they'll dare to stage it even in Scandinavia for some little while. Incidentally, it has been printed in an edition of 10,000 copies, and there is every prospect that a new impression will be required soon'—a forecast that was to prove sadly incorrect.

That Christmas, replying to a toast at the Scandinavian Club in Rome, he remarked that Christmas, which to most people brought joy and peace, to him usually brought battle, since it was at this season that his books appeared; but that to him battle was joy, and peace merely a breathing-space until he could take up the struggle anew.

On 2 January 1882 he wrote in the same mood to Hegel: 'The violent criticisms and insane attacks which people are levelling against *Ghosts* don't worry me in the least. I was expecting this. When *Love's Comedy* appeared, there was just as hysterical an outcry in Norway as there is now. They moaned about *Peer Gynt* too, and *The Pillars of Society* and *A Doll's House,* just as much. The commotion will die away this time as it did before.' But he added: 'One thing worries me a little when I think how big an edition you printed. Has all this fuss damaged the sales of the book?'

It had indeed. The scandal created by the critics in Norway was so great that people were afraid to buy *Ghosts;* it was not a book to have about the house. It attacked the most sacred principles of the age—the sanctity of marriage, the commandment that a man must honour his father and mother—it defended free love, and suggested not only that a woman had the right to leave her husband, but that even incest might under certain circumstances be justifiable. Hegel was forced to take back enormous quantities of the book from the shops; and Ibsen's other books sold noticeably less than usual that Christmas.

In the other Scandinavian capitals it was the same. August Lindberg, the Swedish actor, has described the scene in Stockholm when *Ghosts* appeared in the bookshops. 'People were expecting something from Ibsen after the controversial *A Doll's House,* which had appeared the previous *(sic)* year. There was a rush to the bookshops. But the excitement vanished in silence. Absolute silence. The newspapers said nothing and the bookshops sent the book back to the publisher. It was contraband. Something which could not decently be discussed.' When Lindberg asked his chief at Nya Teatern, Ludvig Josephson, if he would not consider presenting *Ghosts,* Josephson refused point blank. 'The play,' he said, 'is one of the filthiest things ever written in Scandinavia.'

It was, however, in Norway itself that *Ghosts* was attacked most violently. Ibsen had expected the right-wing papers to dislike it, but he was shocked to discover that the radical press denounced it with even greater fervour. The left-wing *Oplandenes Avis* set the tone when it declared that: 'complete silence would, in our opinion, be the most fitting reception for this work.' The reviewer went on to describe it as 'the most unpleasant book we have read for a long while', but drew some comfort from the fact that it was 'in our humble opinion at least, much worse written than the author's previous works'. Ironically enough these words were penned by a prominent novelist, Arne Garborg, who had just published a story entitled *The Freethinker*—a point Ibsen was to remember when he wrote *An Enemy of the People*. Andreas Munch, writing in *Morgenbladet,* dismissed Ibsen as 'a fallen star . . . a spent, quenched meteor', and Ibsen's old admirer Henrik Jæger went round the country lecturing against the play. Even such 'progressive' writers as Alexander Kielland and Jonas Lie, in their private letters, raised their eyebrows. Almost the only Norwegians to defend *Ghosts* publicly were Bjœrnson, Camilla Collett and P. O. Schjœtt, who wrote in *Nyt Tidsskrift:* 'When the dust which ignorant criticism has raised has subsided, which we trust will happen soon, Ibsen's latest drama, with its pure bold contours, will stand not only as his noblest deed but as the greatest work of art which he, or indeed our whole dramatic literature, has yet produced.' In Denmark, Georg

Brandes, faithful to his old friend, praised the poet's courage; but even he confidentially expressed the opinion that he found the play 'dramatically weak'.

In Rome, Ibsen read these reviews with increasing indignation. 'What is one to say of the attitude taken by the so-called liberal press?' he wrote to Brandes on 3 January 1882. 'These leaders who talk and write of freedom and progressiveness and who at the same time let themselves be the slaves of the supposed opinions of their subscribers? . . . Under no circumstances will I ever link myself with any party that has the majority behind it. Bjœrnson says: the majority is always right. As a practising politician he has to say so. But I say: the minority is always right.' He was to develop this theme in his next play, *An Enemy of the People*, using these very words. Three days later he wrote to Sophus Schandorph: 'I was prepared for some such commotion. If for nothing else, certain of our Norwegian reviewers have an undeniable talent for completely misunderstanding and misinterpreting the authors whose books they presume to judge.' After denying that the views expressed by the characters in *Ghosts* were necessarily his own ('In none of my plays is the author so wholly detached and uncommitted as in this'), he went on to deny that *Ghosts* advocated nihilism. 'The play is not concerned with advocating anything. It merely points to the fact that nihilism is fermenting beneath the surface in Norway as everywhere else. It is inevitable. A Pastor Manders will always incite some Mrs. Alving into being. And she, simply because she is a woman, will, once she has started, go to the ultimate extreme.'

On 28 January, he wrote to Otto Borchsenius: 'It may well be that in certain respects this play is somewhat audacious. But I thought the time had come when a few boundary marks had to be shifted. And it was much easier for me, as an elder writer, to do this job than for the many younger writers who might want to do something of the kind. I was prepared for a storm to break over me; but one can't run away from such things. That would have been cowardice. What has most depressed me has been, not the attacks themselves, but the lack of guts which has been revealed in the ranks of the so-called liberals in Norway. They are poor stuff with which to man the barricades.'

On 16 March he wrote to Hegel, telling him of his plans for a new work. 'This time it will be a peaceful play, which can be read by cabinet ministers and wholesale merchants and their ladies, and from which the theatres will not need to shrink. . . . As far as *Ghosts* is concerned, comprehension will seep into the minds of the good people of our country, and that in the not too distant future. But all these fading and decrepit figures who have spat upon this work will some time bring upon their heads the crushing judgment of future literary historians. . . . My book contains the future.'

On 24 June, he wrote to Countess Sophie Adlersparre, who had lectured in defence of *Ghosts:* 'I am entirely in agreement with you when you say that further than *Ghosts* I dare not go. I myself felt that the general state of mind in our country would not admit of it; nor do I feel any urgency to go further. A writer has not the right to set such a distance between himself and his public that there is no longer any understanding between them and him. But I *had* to write *Ghosts;* I couldn't stop at *A Doll's House;* after Nora, I had to create Mrs. Alving.'

Before its publication, towards the end of November 1881, *Ghosts* had been offered to the Royal Theatre in Copenhagen, but had been rejected by the theatre's censor, Erik Bœgh. 'It takes as the main theme of its action,' he wrote in his report, using words that would not have sounded amiss in Pastor Manders's mouth, 'a repulsive pathological phenomenon which, by undermining the morality of our social order, threatens its foundations.' The Christiania Theatre and the Royal in Stockholm also refused to stage it. On 20 May 1882 *Ghosts* received its world premiere in, of all places, Chicago, where it was presented in the original language before an audience of Scandinavian immigrants with the Danish actress Helga von Bluhme as Mrs. Alving, the rest of the parts being played by Danish and Norwegian amateurs. This production—the first on record of any Ibsen play in America—subsequently toured Minneapolis and other cities of the Middle West which contained large Scandinavian populations. But it was to be over a year before the play was performed in Europe, and even when the scandal had died down and it was being acted before respectful audiences it was thirteen years before a new edition was required. It remained a book not to be seen about the house.

But if *Ghosts* shocked the literary and theatrical establishment of Scandinavia, it made an immediate and stimulating impact on the young. Herman Bang, then aged twenty-five, and later to become a celebrated Danish novelist and one of Ibsen's most influential pioneers in France, describes how it excited his generation even before it became a subject of scandal.

The play was distributed to the booksellers towards evening. The keenest buyers ran out in the dark to get it. That evening I visited a young actor who had just read *Ghosts* . . . 'This', he said, 'is the greatest play our age will see'. The debate had already started by the next morning. An extraordinary number of people seemed to have read the play that night . . . One or two restless people who had nothing to lose, having no good name to be smeared by associations with *Ghosts*, gave public readings. People flocked to the obscure places where these readings took place, out by the bridges, far into the suburbs. A group of unwanted actors determined to take it on tour. They wanted to act the play in the provinces.

But, Bang adds, 'good society knew its duty', and the project had to be abandoned. Nevertheless, it 'was performed semi-privately, in I know not what impossible places', and all but achieved a professional production in Copenhagen within weeks of publication, for Theodor Andersen, the head of the Casino Theatre, 'read it twenty times before finally rejecting it'.

In Germany, once the play had been published (which did not happen until 1884), the same pattern was repeated. Bang was in Germany then and tells of a performance of *A Doll's House* at Meiningen, with the celebrated actress Marie Ramlo as guest artist. The theatre was full of young students.

> Frau Ramlo was excellent, but it was not she who held their attention. The young people barely heard her. They read when the curtain was down, and they read when the curtain was up. They read furtively and amazed, as though fearful, read, as the book was passed secretly from hand to hand, a little, humble, yellow, paper-bound volume of a hundred pages bearing the title *Gespenster [Ghosts]*. What a strange evening when all those hundreds of young people read as one the play about the sins of their fathers, and when, as a drama about marriage was being acted behind the footlights, that other drama of parents and their children forced its way up from the auditorium on to the stage. They did not dare to read the book at home, and so they read it secretly here.

Bang adds that young actors and actresses used *Ghosts* as an audition piece long before it was allowed to be played in

Germany, and that 'young beginners acted the play secretly in suburban halls far out on the fringes of civilization, as in Norway'.

At length the Swede August Lindberg, having failed to convince Ludvig Josephson of the need to present it, obtained Ibsen's permission to stage the play himself. He organized a company to tour it through the three Scandinavian kingdoms, and on 22 August 1883 he presented it in the Swedish city of Hälsingborg, on the west coast opposite Elsinore. Lindberg himself played Oswald, having visited a hospital in Copenhagen to study patients who had inherited syphilis and lost their reason, and Mrs. Alving was taken by Hedvig Charlotte Winter-Hjelm, a once-famous actress who had been persuaded out of retirement. The occasion passed off without disturbance, and six days later Lindberg took his company across the Sound and gave ten performances at the Folketeater in Copenhagen. In performance the play aroused none of the hostility which it had caused in its printed form. Ludvig Josephson, his fears allayed, allowed the production to visit Nya Teatern in Stockholm, and on 17 October 1883 Lindberg presented *Ghosts* for the first time in Ibsen's own country at the Mœllergaten Theatre in Christiania. William Archer attended this performance, and wrote:

'I was present, and well remember the profound impression it made on the crowded and enthusiastic audience. By this time the reaction in favour of the play had fairly set in. It happened that on the same evening a trivial French farce, *Tête de Linotte* (known in England as *Miss Featherbrain*) was being played at the Christiania Theatre; and the contrast could not but strike people. They saw a masterpiece of Norwegian literature acted by a foreign (Swedish) company at a minor playhouse, while the official theatre of the capital was given over to a piece of Parisian frivolity. The result was that on the following evening, and for some nights afterwards, demonstrations were made at the Christiania Theatre against the policy of the management in rejecting Ibsen's play. . . . Fru Winter-Hjelm's performance of Mrs. Alving was exceedingly powerful, and Lindberg seemed to me an almost ideal Oswald. In his make-up, I remember, there was a strong suggestion of the portraits of Edgar Allen Poe.'

Lindberg himself has left an interesting impression of the Christiania première as it seemed to someone on the other side of the footlights. 'When the curtain was raised, it felt as though the public held its breath. The scenes of the play unfolded in a silence worthy of a spiritual seance. When the final curtain fell, the silence continued for a good while, before the ovations started.'

Altogether, Lindberg's company performed *Ghosts* seventy-five times during this tour, a remarkable record for those days. He returned with the production to Christiania several times during the next few years; in 1891 Ibsen himself attended a performance, and expressed unqualified approval of Fru Winter-Hjelm's interpretation.

In 1883 the Royal Theatre in Stockholm and the Swedish Theatre in Helsinki both staged the play; and Olaus Olsen's Danish-Norwegian company toured it through the Norwegian provinces. It was not, however, until 1890, nine years after its publication, that *Ghosts* was played by a completely Norwegian company, at the National Theatre in Bergen. Schrœder, who had originally rejected it, steadfastly refused to allow the Christiania Theatre to perform it as long as he remained in charge, and it was not presented there until 1900, when Bjœrn Bjœrnson became director. H. A. T. Dedichen, who attended the opening performance of this production on 5 March, remarked that 'it passed as easily as a letter through the post. . . . The assemblage of the "upper ten" which filled the boxes and stalls sat and marvelled that the play could ever have excited such paroxysms of horror.'

In Germany, surprisingly, *Ghosts* had to wait five years

for its first production, which occurred on 19 April 1886 at the Stadttheater in Augsburg. This was a private performance, the local censor having vetoed the play, and Ibsen himself was present. William Archer, in the 1900 introduction to his translation of the play, noted: 'The acting does not seem to have been altogether fortunate, for one of the leading critics of Germany has related to me how the poet, at the dress-rehearsal, expressed his opinions in an oft-repeated comment, *"O nein!"*. When Regina made her appearance in something that purported to be a Norwegian peasant costume (a ridiculous error which almost all non-Scandinavian Reginas commit), Ibsen's *"O nein!"* was particularly emphatic.'

Later that year, on 21 December 1886, *Ghosts* was more worthily presented at the Court Theatre of Meiningen—a production that, according to Archer, 'is said to have elicited warm praise from Ibsen himself.' A few weeks later, on 9 January 1887, a private performance was given at the Residenz Theater, Berlin, and interest in the play was now so great that there were over 14,000 applications for tickets. A more significant production, however, was that of 29 September 1889 with which the Berlin Freie Bühne opened its first season at the Lessing Theater. Archer, writing in 1900, observed: 'This performance is destined to hold a conspicuous place in German literary history, for the Freie Bühne, which it inaugurated, gave the strongest impulse to the recent renascence of the German drama. . . . Before another ten years had elapsed, [Ibsen's] influence, operating largely through the Freie Bühne, and the movement it set on foot, had practically created a new dramatic literature in Germany.'

On 29 May 1890 Antoine produced *Ghosts* at the Théâtre des Menus Plaisirs in Paris, the first recorded performance of any Ibsen play in France. George Moore was present among the audience, and has left a vivid description of the occasion in his *Impressions and Opinions*. The German censorship now withdrew its veto, and in 1894 no less than three separate productions of *Ghosts* were mounted in different theatres in Berlin, to say nothing of a visit by Antoine with the Théâtre Libre production.

In 1890, *Ghosts* was performed in Vienna and Amsterdam. The following year London was scandalized by J. T. Grein's famous Royalty production, and the play was performed in New York (in German) and Tiflis (in Armenian). In 1892 it was staged in Milan, and in 1894 in New York in (at last) English. By the close of the century, *Ghosts* was known throughout Europe, the United States (where the 1894 New York production visited numerous cities, without undue incident), and even in South America, where the great Italian actor Ermete Novelli and his company toured the play in Italian. In this century it has been the most frequently performed of all Ibsen's plays in England, London alone having seen twenty-eight separate professional productions since 1900, including one in German, one in Italian and one in Yiddish.

As has already been stated, Ibsen's original draft for *Ghosts* has not been preserved, and the differences between his second draft and the final version as we know it are few and insignificant. After Ibsen's death, however, six brief sets of notes presumably relating to *Ghosts* were discovered among his papers, some (nos. 1–4) on two sheets of quarto, some (no. 5) on the back of an envelope, and some (no. 6) on a torn newspaper wrapper. They are undated, but probably belong to the winter and spring of 1881:

1. The play to be a [realistic] picture of life. Faith undermined—but people daren't admit it. The 'Orphanage'—for the sake of others. They want to be happy—but this, too, is only an illusion—Everything is ghosts—

   An important point: She has been a believer and a

romantic—and this can't completely be eradicated by the attitude she has subsequently adopted—'Everything is ghosts'.

To marry for the wrong reasons, even though they be religious or moral, brings a Nemesis on the children.

She, the illegitimate child, can be saved by being married to—the son—but then—?

2. He in his youth was depraved, a debauchee; then she appeared, a woman who had 'seen the light'; she saved him; she was rich. He had wanted to marry a girl who was thought unworthy. His wife bore him a son; then he turned back to the girl; a daughter—

3. These modern women, misused as daughters, as sisters, as wives, not educated according to their talents, barred from their vocation, robbed of their inheritance, their minds embittered—these are the women who are to provide the mothers for the new generation. What will be the consequence?

4. She became passionately religious in her youth; partly because of this, but partly also from affection, she married him, the 'bright genius', the 'prodigal'. They move away from town; he 'gets on', eventually becomes a judge, a model public servant, a model man in every way, religious too. They had a son, then another who died young. Very early in his life the eldest was put to lodge with a clergyman, then sent to a boarding school, was seldom allowed to visit his home. The judge performed his duties for many years, much honoured and respected; she too was honoured as his 'good genius', who had been worthily rewarded for her magnanimity. Then he died; a large part of the fortune into which he unexpectedly came after his marriage has been formed into a trust, and now this memorial is about to be dedicated.

Here the play begins.

5. The main theme must be: the fine flowering of our

spiritual life *via* literature, art, etc.—and by contrast, all mankind wandering blindly on the wrong track.

6. The perfect man is no longer a natural product, he is something cultivated like corn and fruit-trees and the Creole race and thoroughbred horses and breeds of dogs, vines, etc.—

The trouble is that mankind as a whole is a failure. If a human being demands to live and develop according to his nature as a human being, it's regarded as megalomania. All mankind, especially Christians, suffers from megalomania.

We raise monuments to the *dead;* because we feel a duty towards them; we allow lepers to marry; but their offspring—? The unborn—?

Ibsen's contemporaries saw *Ghosts* primarily as a play about inherited physical illness; for some years Oswald, not Mrs. Alving, was regarded as being the chief character. They did not realize that what *Ghosts* is really about is the devitalizing effect of inherited convention. Oswald's syphilis is not the theme of *Ghosts,* any more than Dr. Rank's inherited disease is the theme of *A Doll's House.* To quote Halvdan Koht again: 'Oswald was branded with disease, not because his father was a beast, but because Mrs. Alving had obeyed the immoral ethics of society* . . . *Ghosts* is a play about ethical, not physical debility.' The importance of waging war against the past, the need for each individual to

---

*In view of the oft-repeated complaint that syphilis cannot be inherited from one's father, it is worth pointing out that it can be inherited from one's mother, and that a woman can have syphilis without realizing it or suffering any particular discomfort. In other words, and this is a far more frightening explanation of Oswald's illness than the usual one, Mrs. Alving could have caught syphilis from her husband and passed it on to her son. Dr. Jonathan Miller has pointed out to me that Oswald could also have been infected by smoking his father's pipe. Ibsen knew more about medicine than some of his critics.

find his or her own freedom, the danger of renouncing love in the name of duty—these are the real themes of *Ghosts*, as they are the themes of every play Ibsen wrote from *A Doll's House* onwards. And the targets are the same as those which he had attacked in *A Doll's House* and, before that, in *The Pillars of Society*, and which he was to go on attacking until the end of his life—the hollowness of great reputations, provincialism of outlook, the narrowness of small-town life, the suppression of individual freedom from within as well as from without, and the neglect of the significance of heredity. The problem of the connection between heritage and decadence was much discussed in the Scandinavian group in Rome around 1880. J. P. Jacobsen had translated Darwin's *The Origin of Species* into Danish in 1872, and *The Descent of Man* in 1875, and the French naturalistic novelists, with Zola at their head, had hastened to exploit Darwin's thesis that man, like other animals, must adapt himself to the environment in which he lives. Ibsen, however, greatly disliked being compared with Zola, for whose works he had a low regard.[*] 'Zola,' he once said, 'descends into the sewer to bathe in it; I to cleanse it.'

Ibsen never liked admitting that any of his plays owed a debt to any other writer; he said that in any age writers tended to find similar themes. Half a century earlier, however, a *conte* by a Norwegian author named Mauritz Hansen had been published entitled *The Daughter*, and the similarities between it and *Ghosts* are so striking that it is difficult not to believe that, consciously or unconsciously, the former must have provided a starting-point for the latter. *The Daughter* tells how a dissipated lieutenant-colonel, formida-

---

[*]If indeed he had read any of them. When, six months after the publication of *Ghosts*, a Swedish painter asked him what he thought of Zola, Ibsen replied: 'I don't read books. I leave that to my wife and son.' But he read newspapers in most minute detail, including advertisements.

bly named Hannibal Hedebrandt, has in his youth had an affair with his maid, Else. Then he weds a lady of his own station but, on discovering that Else is with child, marries her off to a caretaker named Œken. Else goes mad and dies, but her daughter Henriette grows up in the Hedebrandt household; she is repelled by her supposed father, the caretaker, who has a wooden leg. It is of course perfectly possible, and I think likely, that Ibsen had read this story in his youth and had forgotten it, and that certain details had forced themselves up out of his unconscious—possibly influenced by the fact that he himself, at the age of eighteen when a chemist's assistant in Grimstad, had had an illegitimate child by a servant girl, also named Else. Ibsen had, moreover, from a very early age, been repelled by the fact of his father having gone bankrupt, and Engstrand's club-foot may possibly represent his father's inability to stand on both feet in the world. (He was to paint a more detailed portrait of his father two plays later, as Old Ekdal in *The Wild Duck*.)

Manders, as has been noted, was immediately motivated by Ibsen's indignation at the Norwegian Ecclesiastical Department's treatment of his son; though his contempt for priests was of long standing, and he had already portrayed unsympathetic specimens in *Love's Comedy* (Pastor Straamand), *Brand* (the Provost), and *The Pillars of Society,* in which Dr. Rœrlund the schoolmaster, though not in fact a priest, is referred to contemptuously as Pastor by Lona Hessel. Regina was based on a maid whom the Ibsens had in Munich. She was of Bavarian birth but had spent some while in Paris, and incorporated various French expressions in the high German she used when speaking to Ibsen and his wife, though among her friends she spoke in the Bavarian dialect.

Mrs. Alving is, so to speak, Nora as a mother, and one wonders whether her creation may not partly have been inspired by that 'happy ending' which Ibsen had found himself compelled to write for *A Doll's House* in order to prevent

German adaptors from doing the same thing less competently. (Since he had no means of stopping anyone from altering the play, copyright protection being very ineffective in those days, he decided it would be better to write an alternative ending himself for such theatres as were stupid enough to want one rather than let other people do it.) In that 'happy ending,' Nora returns to her husband and children; and Mrs. Alving is not unlike a picture of what Nora might well have become in twenty years if she had done that. Like Nora, Mrs. Alving is strangled by convention and a misplaced sense of duty. 'After Nora, I *had* to create Mrs. Alving.' Viewed in this context, Oswald's inherited syphilis may be regarded as a symbol of the dead customs and traditions which we inherit, and which stunt and cripple us and lay waste our life.

In one important technical respect *Ghosts* anticipates Ibsen's later plays, and that is in the density of its dialogue. *The Pillars of Society* and *A Doll's House* are both simply written (and comparatively easy to translate), because for most of the time the characters say what they mean. But in *Ghosts*, Mrs. Alving and Manders especially spend much of the time circling round a subject to which they dread referring directly, and at these moments the dialogue is oblique, sometimes even opaque. This double-density dialogue, when the characters say one thing and mean another, was to be one of Ibsen's most important contributions to the technique of prose drama. He knew that when people talk about something concerning which they feel a sense of guilt, they cease to speak directly and instead talk evasively and with circumlocution; and actors, when they are playing these lines, have to speak the text but act the sub-text, the unspoken thoughts between the lines. One of the greatest problems facing a translator of Ibsen is to convey this meaning behind the meaning; if this is not indicated (as Ibsen himself indicates it), it is practically impossible for an actor to convey that sense of guilt and evasion from which almost all of Ibsen's major characters suffer, and which is so often at crises the mainspring of their actions, or of their failure to act.

Historically, *Ghosts* occupies a position of immense importance. Julius Hoffory remarked in 1888 that much of its effect upon Ibsen's contemporaries was due to the fact that here was a play comparable to those of Aeschylus and Sophocles, but about modern people, a fact easily forgotten by us, to whom it is as much a costume play as the *Agamemnon*. *Ghosts* was the first great tragedy written about middle-class people in plain, everyday prose. Büchner's *Danton's Death* and *Woyzeck* are composed in a high-flown prose which frequently, and splendidly, overlaps the frontier of poetry; and while other playwrights had attempted to do what Ibsen achieved in *Ghosts,* none had succeeded. Time has not dulled its impact (though it sometimes, in England and America at any rate, suffers from being publicised as 'the play which shocked our grandfathers'). Indeed, it gains enormously by not having, as so often in the last century, a declamatory and melodramatic Mrs. Alving. Ibsen's plays needed, and helped to nurture, a new kind of player with the strength of restraint, life-size, not Wagnerian. Bernhardt and Henry Irving rejected his works; Duse and Stanislavsky embraced them.

If there is to be a last word on *Ghosts,* it belongs to C. E. Montague, even though he wrote it over seventy years ago. 'It is strange,' he remarked in *Dramatic Values,* 'there were people once who called *Ghosts* immoral. Was this, you ask now when you see it, the play that launched a thousand ships of critical fury? Why, it is rendingly, scaringly moral. When it is before you, you feel that some truths about conduct, which you had thought you knew pretty well, can only have been known as one knows a beast safely caged in a zoo, since now they are going about glaring at you with fanged mouths open; they have turned terrifyingly real. It is fairly arguable that—as Mr. Archer seems to feel—the fierceness of moral intention in *Ghosts* prevents it from ranking with Ibsen's best work. It has a kind of aghast grimness, a bald, austere hardness of conception and dry, level tensity in the working out that seem more expressive of the strong man rightly angered by preventable wrong than of the artist excited and even, in a sense, delighted by everything in the world, good and bad. Perhaps it was some sense of this that made Brandes say, when the play first came out and the foolish people were howling, that it might or might not be Ibsen's greatest work, but it was certainly his noblest deed. Immoral!'

MICHAEL MEYER

CHARACTERS

MRS. HELEN ALVING, widow of Captain Alving, late Chamberlain to the King
OSWALD ALVING, her son, a painter
PASTOR MANDERS
ENGSTRAND, a carpenter
REGINA ENGSTRAND, Mrs. Alving's maid

The action takes place on Mrs. Alving's country estate by a large fjord in western Norway.

This translation of *Ghosts* was first performed on 6 April 1965 at the Theatre Royal, Stratford East, London, in a presentation by Stage Sixty. The cast was:

MRS. ALVING	Catherine Lacey
OSWALD ALVING	Barry Warren
PASTOR MANDERS	Leonard Rossiter
ENGSTRAND	Daniel Thorndike
REGINA ENGSTRAND	Patricia England

Directed by Adrian Rendle

On 17 March 1968 the translation was televised by the British Broadcasting Corporation. The cast was:

MRS. ALVING	Celia Johnson
OSWALD ALVING	Tom Courtenay
PASTOR MANDERS	Donald Wolfit
ENGSTRAND	Fulton Mackay
REGINA ENGSTRAND	Vickery Turner

Directed by Michael Elliott

ACT ONE

A spacious garden-room, with a door in the left-hand wall and two doors in the right-hand wall. In the centre of the room is a round table with chairs around it; on the table are books, magazines and newspapers. Downstage left is a window, in front of which is a small sofa with a sewing-table by it. Backstage the room opens out into a slightly narrower conservatory, with walls of large panes of glass. In the right-hand wall of the conservatory is a door leading down to the garden. Through the glass wall a gloomy fjord landscape is discernible, veiled by steady rain.

> ENGSTRAND, *a carpenter, is standing at the garden door. His left leg is slightly crooked; under the sole of his boot is fixed a block of wood.* REGINA, *with an empty garden syringe in her hand, bars his entry.*

REGINA *(keeping her voice low):* What do you want? Stay where you are! You're dripping wet!

ENGSTRAND: It is God's blessed rain, my child.

REGINA: The Devil's bloody rain, more like.

ENGSTRAND: Why, Regina, the way you talk! *(Limps a few steps into the room.)* What I wanted to say is—

REGINA: Here, you! Don't make such a noise with that foot. The young master's asleep upstairs.

ENGSTRAND: In bed—at this hour? Why, the day's half gone.

25

REGINA: That's none of your business.

ENGSTRAND: I was out drinking last night—

REGINA: I'm sure.

ENGSTRAND: We are but flesh and blood, my child—

REGINA *(drily)*: Quite.

ENGSTRAND: And the temptations of this world are manifold. But God is my witness; I was at my bench by half past five this morning.

REGINA: Yes, yes. Come on now, clear off. I don't want to be caught having a rendezvous with you.

ENGSTRAND: You don't what?

REGINA: I don't want anyone to see you here. Come on, go away, get out.

ENGSTRAND *(comes a few steps nearer)*: Not before I've had a word with you. This afternoon I'll be through with the job down at the school house, and tonight I'm catching the steamer back to town.

REGINA *(mutters)*: Bon voyage.

ENGSTRAND: Thank you, my child. They're dedicating the new Orphanage here tomorrow, and there'll be celebrations, with intoxicating liquor. And no one shall say of Jacob Engstrand that he can't turn his back on temptation. *(REGINA laughs scornfully.)* Yes, well, there'll be a lot of tip-top people coming here tomorrow. Pastor Manders is expected from town.

REGINA: He's arriving today.

ENGSTRAND: Well, there you are. And I'm not darned well going to risk getting into his bad books.

REGINA: Oh, so that's it.

ENGSTRAND: What do you mean?

REGINA *(looks knowingly at him)*: What are you trying to fool the Pastor into this time?

ENGSTRAND: Hush! Are you mad? Me try to fool Pastor Manders? Oh no, Pastor Manders is much too good a friend to me for that. Now what I wanted to talk to you about is this. I'm going back home tonight.

REGINA: The sooner you go the better.

ENGSTRAND: Yes, but I want to take you with me, Regina.

REGINA *(her jaw drops):* You want to take *me—?* What are you talking about?

ENGSTRAND: I want to take you with me, I say.

REGINA *(scornfully):* Home with you? Not likely I won't!

ENGSTRAND: Oh, we'll see, we'll see.

REGINA: You bet your life we'll see. You expect me to go back and live with you? In that house? After Mrs. Alving's brought me up in her own home, treats me as though I was one of the family? Get out!

ENGSTRAND: What the hell's this? Are you setting yourself up against your father, my girl?

REGINA *(mutters without looking at him):* You've said often enough that I'm no concern of yours.

ENGSTRAND: Oh—you don't want to take any notice of that—

REGINA: What about all the times you've sworn at me and called me a—oh, *mon dieu!*

ENGSTRAND: May God strike me dead if I ever used such a vile word!

REGINA: Oh, I know what word you used.

ENGSTRAND: Yes, but that was only when I wasn't myself. Hm. The temptations of this world are manifold, Regina.

REGINA: Ugh!

ENGSTRAND: And when your mother was being difficult. I had to think up some way to nark her. She was always acting the fine lady. *(Mimics.)* 'Let me go, Engstrand! Stop it! I've been in service for three years with Chamberlain Alving at Rosenvold, and don't you forget it!' *(Laughs.)* She never could forget the Captain had been made a Chamberlain when she was working for him.

REGINA: Poor mother! You killed her soon enough with your bullying.

ENGSTRAND *(uncomfortably):* That's right, blame me for everything.

REGINA *(turns away and mutters beneath her breath):* Ugh! And that leg!

ENGSTRAND: What's that you said, my child?

REGINA: *Pied de mouton!*

ENGSTRAND: What's that, English?

REGINA: Yes.

ENGSTRAND: Ah, well. They've made a scholar of you out here anyway, and that'll come in handy now, Regina.

REGINA *(after a short silence):* And—what was it you wanted me for in town?

ENGSTRAND: Fancy asking such a question! What should a father want from his only child? Aren't I a lonely, for-saken widower?

REGINA: Oh, don't try to fool me with that rubbish. What do you want me up there for?

ENGSTRAND: Well, it's like this. I'm thinking of starting out on something new.

REGINA *(sniffs):* You've tried that often enough. And you've always made a mess of it.

ENGSTRAND: Yes, but this time, you'll see, Regina! God rot me if I don't—!

REGINA *(stamps her foot):* Stop swearing!

ENGSTRAND: Ssh, ssh! How right you are, my child! Now what I wanted to say was this. I've put quite a bit of money aside out of the work I've been doing at this new Orphanage.

REGINA: Have you? Good for you.

ENGSTRAND: Well, there ain't much for a man to spend his money on out here in the country, is there?

REGINA: Well? Go on.

ENGSTRAND: Yes, well you see, so I thought I'd put the

money into something that might bring me in a bit. A kind of hostelry for sailors—

REGINA *(disgusted):* Oh, my God!

ENGSTRAND: A real smart place, you understand—not one of those low waterfront joints. No, damn it, this is going to be for captains and officers and—tip-top people, you understand.

REGINA: And I'm to—?

ENGSTRAND: You're going to help me. Just for appearance's sake, of course. You won't have to work hard, my child. You can fix your own hours.

REGINA: I see!

ENGSTRAND: Well, we've got to have a bit of skirt on show, I mean that's obvious. Got to give them a little fun in the evenings—dancing and singing and so forth. You must remember these men are wandering mariners lost on the ocean of life. *(Comes closer.)* Now don't be stupid and make things difficult for yourself, Regina. What can you make of yourself out here? What good is it going to do you, all this fine education Mrs. Alving's given you? I hear you're going to look after the orphans down the road. Is that what you want to do? Are you so anxious to ruin your health for those filthy brats?

REGINA: No, if things work out the way I—ah well, they might. They might.

ENGSTRAND: What are you talking about?

REGINA: Never you mind. This money you've managed to save out here—is it a lot?

ENGSTRAND: All told I'd say it comes to between thirty-five and forty pounds.

REGINA: Not bad.

ENGSTRAND: Enough to make a start with, my child.

REGINA: Aren't you going to give me any of it?

ENGSTRAND: Not darned likely I'm not.

REGINA: Aren't you even going to send me a new dress?

ENGSTRAND: You just come back to town and set up with me, and you'll get dresses enough.

REGINA *(laughs scornfully):* I could do *that* on my own, if I wanted to.

ENGSTRAND: No, Regina, you need a father's hand to guide you. There's a nice house I can get in Little Harbour Street. They don't want much cash on the nail; and we could turn it into a sort of—well—sailors' mission.

REGINA: But I don't want to live with *you!* I don't want anything to do with you. Come on, get out.

ENGSTRAND: You wouldn't need to stay with me for long, my child. More's the pity. If you play your cards properly. The way you've blossomed out these last few years, you—

REGINA: Yes?

ENGSTRAND: You wouldn't have to wait long before some nice officer—perhaps even a captain—

REGINA: I don't want to marry any of them. Sailors haven't any *savoir vivre.*

ENGSTRAND: Haven't any what?

REGINA: I know sailors. There's no future in marrying them.

ENGSTRAND: All right then, don't marry them. You can do just as well without. *(Lowers his voice.)* The Englishman—him with the yacht—fifty pounds he paid out—and she wasn't any prettier than you.

REGINA *(goes towards him):* Get out!

ENGSTRAND *(shrinks):* Now, now, you wouldn't hit your own father!

REGINA: Wouldn't I? You say another word about mother, and you'll see! Get out, I tell you! *(Pushes him towards the garden door.)* And don't slam the door. Young Mr. Alving's—

ENGSTRAND: Yes, I know. He's asleep. Why do you fuss so much about him? *(More quietly.)* Ah-ha! You wouldn't be thinking of *him,* would you?

REGINA: Out, and be quick about it! You're out of your mind. No, not that way. Here's Pastor Manders. Go out through the kitchen.

ENGSTRAND *(goes right):* All right, I'll go. But you ask *him*—his Reverence. He'll tell you what a child's duty is to its father. I am your father, you know, whatever you say. I can prove it from the parish register.

He goes out through the second door, which REGINA *has opened and closes behind him. She looks quickly at herself in the mirror, dusts herself with her handkerchief, and straightens her collar; then she begins to water the flowers.* PASTOR MANDERS, *in an overcoat and carrying an umbrella, and with a small travelling bag on a strap from his shoulder, enters through the garden door into the conservatory.*

MANDERS: Good morning, Miss Engstrand.

REGINA *(turns in surprise and delight):* Why, Pastor Manders! Has the boat come already?

MANDERS: It arrived a few minutes ago. *(Enters the garden room.)* Very tiresome this rain we're having.

REGINA *(follows him):* A blessing for the farmers, though, sir.

MANDERS: Yes, you are right. We city people tend to forget that. *(Begins to take off his overcoat.)*

REGINA: Oh, please let me help you! There. Oh, it's soaking! I'll hang it up in the hall. Oh, and the umbrella! I'll open it out to let it dry.

She takes the coat and umbrella out through the other door, right. MANDERS *takes his bag from his shoulder and puts it and his hat on a chair. Meanwhile* REGINA *comes back.*

MANDERS: Ah, it's good to be under a dry roof again. Well, I trust all is well here?

REGINA: Yes, thank you, sir.

MANDERS: Everyone very busy, I suppose, getting ready for tomorrow?

REGINA: Oh, yes, there are one or two things to be done.

MANDERS: Mrs. Alving is at home, I hope?

REGINA: Oh, dear me, yes, she's just gone upstairs to make a cup of chocolate for the young master.

MANDERS: Ah, yes. I heard when I got off the boat that Oswald had returned.

REGINA: Yes, he arrived the day before yesterday. We hadn't expected him until today.

MANDERS: He's in good health and spirits, I trust?

REGINA: Oh yes, thank you, I think so. He felt dreadfully tired after his journey, though. He came all the way from Paris in one go—*par rapide*. I think he's having a little sleep just now, so we'd better talk just a tiny bit quietly.

MANDERS: Ssh! We'll be like mice!

REGINA *(moves an armchair near the table):* Now sit down and make yourself comfortable, sir. *(He sits. She puts a footstool under his feet.)* There now. Are you quite comfortable?

MANDERS: Thank you, thank you; yes, very comfortable. *(Looks at her.)* Do you know, Miss Engstrand, I really believe you've grown since I last saw you.

REGINA: Do you think so? Madam says I've rounded out a bit too.

MANDERS: Rounded out? Well, yes, a little perhaps. Not too much.

Short pause.

REGINA: Shall I tell Madam you've come?

MANDERS: Thank you, there's no hurry, my dear child. Er— tell me now, Regina, how is your father getting on out here?

REGINA: Thank you, Pastor, he's doing very well.

MANDERS: He came to see me when he was last in town.

REGINA: No, did he really? He's always so happy when he gets a chance to speak to you, sir.

MANDERS: And you go down and see him quite often?

REGINA: I? Oh yes, of course—whenever I get the chance—

MANDERS: Your father hasn't a very strong character, Miss Engstrand. He badly needs a hand to guide him.

REGINA: Oh—yes, I dare say you're right there.

MANDERS: He needs to have someone near him whom he is fond of, and whose judgment he respects. He admitted it quite openly the last time he visited me.

REGINA: Yes, he said something of the sort to me too. But I don't know whether Mrs. Alving will want to lose me, especially now we've the new Orphanage to look after. Besides, I'd hate to leave Mrs. Alving. She's always been so kind to me.

MANDERS: But my dear girl, a daughter's duty! Naturally we would have to obtain your mistress's permission first.

REGINA: But I don't know that it'd be right and proper for me to keep house for an unmarried man at my age.

MANDERS: What! But my dear Miss Engstrand, this is your own father we're talking about!

REGINA: Yes—but all the same— Oh yes, if it was a nice house, with a real gentleman—

MANDERS: But my dear Regina—!

REGINA: Someone I could feel affection for and look up to as a father—

MANDERS: But my dear good child—!

REGINA: Oh, I'd so love to go and live in the city. Out here it's so dreadfully lonely—and you know, don't you, sir, what it means to be all alone in the world? And I'm quick and willing—I think I can say that. Oh, Pastor Manders, don't you know of a place I could go to?

MANDERS: I? No, I'm afraid I don't know of anyone at all.

REGINA: Oh, but do please think of me if ever you should, dear, dear Pastor Manders.

MANDERS *(gets up):* Yes, yes, Miss Engstrand, I certainly will.

REGINA: You see, if only I—

MANDERS: Will you be so good as to fetch Mrs. Alving for me?

REGINA: Yes, sir. I'll fetch her at once.

> *She goes out left.* PASTOR MANDERS *walks up and down the room a couple of times, stands for a moment upstage with his hands behind his back and looks out into the garden. Then he comes back to the part of the room where the table is, picks up a book and glances at its title page, starts, and looks at some of the others.*

MANDERS: Hm! I see!

> MRS. ALVING *enters through the door left. She is followed by* REGINA, *who at once goes out through the door downstage right.*

MRS. ALVING *(holds out her hand):* Welcome to Rosenvold, Pastor.

MANDERS: Good morning, Mrs. Alving. Well, I've kept my promise.

MRS. ALVING: Punctual as always.

MANDERS: But you know it wasn't easy for me to get away. All these blessed boards and committees I sit on—

MRS. ALVING: All the kinder of you to arrive in such good time. Now we can get our business settled before lunch. But where's your luggage?

MANDERS *(quickly):* My portmanteau is down at the village store. I shall be sleeping there.

MRS. ALVING *(suppresses a smile):* I can't persuade you to spend a night in my house even now?

MANDERS: No, no, Mrs. Alving—it's very kind of you, but

I'll sleep down there as usual. It's so convenient for when I go on board again.

MRS. ALVING: As you please. Though I really think two old people like you and me could—

MANDERS: Bless me, you're joking. But of course you must be very happy. The great day tomorrow—and you have Oswald home again.

MRS. ALVING: Yes, you can imagine how happy that makes me. It's over two years since he was home last. And now he's promised to stay with me the whole winter.

MANDERS: No, has he really? Well, that's nice of him. He knows his filial duty. I fancy life in Paris and Rome must offer altogether different attractions.

MRS. ALVING: Yes, but his home is here; and his mother. Ah, my dear boy; he loves his mother, God bless him.

MANDERS: It would be sad indeed if distance and dabbling in art and such things should blunt his natural affections.

MRS. ALVING: It certainly would. But luckily there's no fear of that. I'll be amused to see whether you recognize him again. He'll be down later; he's upstairs now taking a little rest on the sofa. But please sit down, my dear Pastor.

MANDERS: Thank you. Er—you're sure this is a convenient moment—?

MRS. ALVING: Certainly.

She sits down at the table.

MANDERS: Good. Well, then— (*Goes over to the chair on which his bag is lying, takes out a sheaf of papers, sits down on the opposite side of the table and looks for a space to put down the papers.*) Well, to begin with, here are the— (*Breaks off.*) Tell me, Mrs. Alving, how do *these* books come to be here?

MRS. ALVING: Those books? I'm reading them.

MANDERS: You read writings of this kind?

MRS. ALVING: Certainly I do.

MANDERS: And does this kind of reading make you feel better or happier?

MRS. ALVING: I think they make me feel more secure.

MANDERS: How extraordinary! In what way?

MRS. ALVING: Well, they sort of explain and confirm many things that puzzle me. Yes, that's what's so strange, Pastor Manders—there isn't really anything new in these books—there's nothing in them that most people haven't already thought for themselves. It's only that most people either haven't fully realized it, or they won't admit it.

MANDERS: Well, dear God! Do you seriously believe that most people—?

MRS. ALVING: Yes, I do.

MANDERS: But surely not in this country? Not people like us?

MRS. ALVING: Oh, yes. People like us too.

MANDERS: Well, really! I must say—!

MRS. ALVING: But what do you object to in these books?

MANDERS: Object to? You surely don't imagine I spend my time studying such publications?

MRS. ALVING: In other words, you've no idea what you're condemning?

MANDERS: I've read quite enough about these writings to disapprove of them.

MRS. ALVING: Don't you think you ought to form your own opinion—?

MANDERS: My dear Mrs. Alving, there are many occasions in life when one must rely on the judgment of others. That is the way things are and it is good that it should be so. If it were not so, what would become of society?

MRS. ALVING: Yes, yes. You may be right.

MANDERS: Of course I don't deny there may be quite a lot that is attractive about these writings. And I cannot exactly blame you for wishing to keep informed of these intellectual movements in the great world outside about

which one hears so much. After all, you have allowed
your son to wander there for a number of years. But—

MRS. ALVING: But—?

MANDERS *(lowers his voice):* But one does not have to talk
about it, Mrs. Alving. One really does not need to account to all and sundry for what one reads and thinks
within one's own four walls.

MRS. ALVING: No, of course not. I quite agree with you.

MANDERS: Remember the duty you owe to this Orphanage
which you decided to found at a time when your attitude
towards spiritual matters was quite different from what it
is now—as far as *I* can judge.

MRS. ALVING: Yes, yes, that's perfectly true. But it was the
Orphanage we were going to—

MANDERS: It was the Orphanage we were going to discuss,
yes. But—be discreet, dear Mrs. Alving! And now let us
turn to our business. *(Opens the packet and takes out
some of the papers.)* You see these?

MRS. ALVING: Are those the deeds?

MANDERS: All of them. Ready and completed. As you can
imagine, it's been no easy task to get them all through in
time. I really had to get out my whip. The authorities are
almost painfully conscientious when you want a decision
from them. But here we have them nevertheless. *(Leafs
through them.)* Here is the executed conveyance of the
farmstead named Solvik in the Manor of Rosenvold, with
its newly constructed buildings, schoolrooms, staff accommodation and chapel. And here is the settlement of
the endowment and the trust deed of the institution. Look.
(Reads.) Deed of trust for the Captain Alving Memorial
Home.

MRS. ALVING *(stares for a long while at the paper):* So there
it is.

MANDERS: I thought I'd say Captain rather than Chamberlain. Captain looks less ostentatious.

MRS. ALVING: Yes, yes, as you think best.

MANDERS: And here is the bankbook for the capital which has been placed on deposit to cover the running expenses of the Orphanage.

MRS. ALVING: Thank you; but I think it would be more convenient if you kept that, if you don't mind.

MANDERS: Certainly, certainly. I think we may as well leave the money on deposit to begin with. Admittedly the interest isn't very attractive—four per cent with six months' notice of withdrawal. If we could obtain a good mortgage later—of course it would have to be a first mortgage and of unimpeachable security—we might reconsider the matter.

MRS. ALVING: Yes, well, dear Pastor Manders, you know best about all that.

MANDERS: Anyway, I'll keep my eyes open. But now there's another matter I've several times been meaning to ask you about.

MRS. ALVING: And what is that?

MANDERS: Should the buildings of the Orphanage be insured or not?

MRS. ALVING: Yes, of course they must be insured.

MANDERS: Ah, but wait a minute, Mrs. Alving. Let us consider this question a little more closely.

MRS. ALVING: Everything I have is insured—buildings, furniture, crops, livestock.

MANDERS: Naturally. On your own estate. I do the same, of course. But you see, this is quite a different matter. The Orphanage is, so to speak, to be consecrated to a higher purpose.

MRS. ALVING: Yes, but—

MANDERS: As far as I personally am concerned, I see nothing offensive in securing ourselves against all eventualities—

MRS. ALVING: Well, I certainly don't.

MANDERS: But what is the feeling among the local people out here? You can judge that better than I can.

MRS. ALVING: The feeling?

MANDERS: Are there many people with a right to an opinion—I mean, people who really have the right to hold an opinion—who might take offence?

MRS. ALVING: Well, what do you mean by people who have the right to hold an opinion?

MANDERS: Oh, I am thinking chiefly of people sufficiently independent and influential to make it impossible for one to ignore their opinions altogether.

MRS. ALVING: There are quite a few people like that who I suppose might take offence—

MANDERS: You see! In town, we have a great many such people. Followers of other denominations. People might very easily come to the conclusion that neither you nor I have sufficient trust in the ordinance of a Higher Power.

MRS. ALVING: But my dear Pastor, as long as you yourself—

MANDERS: I know, I know—my conscience is clear, that is true. But all the same, we couldn't prevent a false and unfavourable interpretation being placed on our action. And that might well adversely influence the purpose for which the Orphanage has been dedicated.

MRS. ALVING: If that were so I—

MANDERS: And I can't altogether close my eyes to the difficult—I might even say deeply embarrassing—position in which I might find myself. Among influential circles in town there is a great interest in the cause of the Orphanage. After all, it is to serve the town as well, and it is hoped that it may considerably ease the burden of the ratepayers in respect to the poor. But since I have acted as your adviser and been in charge of the business side I must admit I fear certain over-zealous persons might in the first place direct their attacks against me—

MRS. ALVING: Well, you mustn't lay yourself open to that.

MANDERS: Not to speak of the attacks which would undoubtedly be launched against me in certain newspapers and periodicals, and which—

MRS. ALVING: Enough, dear Pastor Manders. That settles it.

MANDERS: Then you do not wish the Orphanage to be insured?

MRS. ALVING: No. We will forget about it.

MANDERS (*leans back in his chair):* But suppose an accident should occur—you never can tell—would you be able to make good the damage?

MRS. ALVING: No, quite frankly I couldn't.

MANDERS: Well, but you know, Mrs. Alving, this is really rather a serious responsibility we are taking on our shoulders.

MRS. ALVING: But do you think we have any alternative?

MANDERS: No, that's just it. I don't think there is any real alternative. We must not lay ourselves open to misinterpretation. And we have no right to antagonize public opinion.

MRS. ALVING: At any rate you, as a clergyman, must not.

MANDERS: And I really think we must believe that such an institution will have luck on its side—nay, that it stands under special protection.

MRS. ALVING: Let us hope so, Pastor Manders.

MANDERS: Shall we take the risk, then?

MRS. ALVING: Yes, let us.

MANDERS: Good. As *you* wish. (*Makes a note.*) No insurance, then.

MRS. ALVING: It's strange you happened to mention this today—

MANDERS: I've often thought of raising the matter with you—

MRS. ALVING: Because yesterday we almost had a fire down there.

MANDERS: What!

MRS. ALVING: Well, it was nothing much really. Some shavings caught fire in the carpentry shop.

MANDERS: Where Engstrand works?

MRS. ALVING: Yes. They say he's very careless with matches.

MANDERS: He's got so many things to think about, poor man—so many temptations. Thank heaven I hear he has now resolved to lead a virtuous life.

MRS. ALVING: Oh? Who says so?

MANDERS: He has assured me so himself. And he's a good worker.

MRS. ALVING: Oh, yes—as long as he keeps sober—

MANDERS: Yes, that is a grievous weakness! But he is often compelled to yield to it because of his bad leg, he says. The last time he was in town I was quite touched. He came to see me and thanked me so sincerely because I had got him this job here, so that he could be near Regina.

MRS. ALVING: I don't think he sees her very often.

MANDERS: Oh yes, he told me himself. He talks to her every day.

MRS. ALVING: Oh, well. Possibly.

MANDERS: He is so conscious of his need to have someone who can restrain him when temptation presents itself. That is what is so lovable about Jacob Engstrand, that he comes to one like a child and accuses himself and admits his weakness. The last time he came up and talked to me— Tell me, Mrs. Alving, if it were absolutely vital for the poor man to have Regina back to live with him again—

MRS. ALVING *(rises swiftly)*: Regina!

MANDERS: You must not oppose it.

MRS. ALVING: I certainly shall. Anyway, Regina is going to work at the Orphanage.

MANDERS: But don't forget, he is her father—

MRS. ALVING: Oh, I know very well the kind of father he's

been to her. No, I shall never consent to her going back to him.

MANDERS *(rises):* But my dear Mrs. Alving, you mustn't get so emotional about it. You seem quite frightened. It's very sad the way you misjudge this man Engstrand.

MRS. ALVING *(more quietly):* Never mind that. I have taken Regina into my house, and here she shall stay. *(Listens.)* Hush now, dear Pastor Manders, let's not say anything more about it. *(Happily.)* Listen! There's Oswald coming downstairs. Now we will think of nothing but him.

> OSWALD ALVING, *in a light overcoat, with his hat in his hand and smoking a big meerschaum pipe, enters through the door left.*

OSWALD *(stops in the doorway):* Oh, I'm sorry—I thought you were in the study. *(Comes closer.)* Good morning, Pastor.

MANDERS *(stares):* Why—! Most extraordinary!

MRS. ALVING: Well, Pastor Manders, what do you think of him?

MANDERS: I think—I think—! But is this really—?

OSWALD: Yes, this is the Prodigal Son, Pastor.

MANDERS: Oh, but my dear young friend—!

OSWALD: Well, the son, anyway.

MRS. ALVING: Oswald is thinking of the time when you used to be so strongly opposed to his becoming a painter.

MANDERS: Many a step which to human eyes seems dubious often turns out— *(Shakes his hand.)* Anyway, welcome, welcome! My dear Oswald—! I trust you will allow me to call you by your Christian name?

OSWALD: What else?

MANDERS: Excellent. Now, my dear Oswald, what I was going to say was this. You mustn't think I condemn the artistic profession out of hand. I presume there are many who succeed in keeping the inner man untarnished in that profession too.

OSWALD: Let us hope so.

MRS. ALVING *(happily):* I know one person who has remained pure both inwardly and outwardly. Just look at him, Pastor Manders.

OSWALD *(wanders across the room):* Yes, yes, mother dear, please.

MANDERS: Unquestionably—there's no denying that. Besides, you have begun to acquire a name now. The newspapers often speak of you, and in most flattering terms. Well—that is to say, I don't seem to have read about you quite so much lately.

OSWALD *(by the flowers upstage):* I haven't done so much painting lately.

MRS. ALVING: Even painters have to rest now and then.

MANDERS: I suppose so. To prepare themselves and conserve their energies for some great work.

OSWALD: Yes. Mother, shall we be eating soon?

MRS. ALVING: In about half an hour. He still enjoys his food, thank heaven.

MANDERS: And his tobacco, I see.

OSWALD: I found father's pipe upstairs in the bedroom, so I—

MANDERS: Of course!

MRS. ALVING: What do you mean?

MANDERS: When Oswald appeared in that doorway with that pipe in his mouth, it was just as though I saw his father alive again.

OSWALD: Oh? Really?

MRS. ALVING: Oh, how can you say that? Oswald takes after me.

MANDERS: Yes; but there's an expression at the corner of his mouth, something about his lips, that reminds me so vividly of Alving—at any rate now when he's smoking.

MRS. ALVING: How can you say that? Oswald has much more the mouth of a clergyman, I think.

MANDERS: True, true. Some of my colleagues have a similar expression.

MRS. ALVING: But put away that pipe, my dear boy. I don't want any smoke in here.

OSWALD (obeys): I'm sorry. I only wanted to try it. You see, I smoked it once when I was a child.

MRS. ALVING: What?

OSWALD: Yes. I was quite small at the time. I remember, I went upstairs to see father in his room one evening. He was so happy and cheerful.

MRS. ALVING: Oh, you don't remember anything from that time.

OSWALD: Oh, yes, I remember very clearly, he picked me up and sat me on his knee and let me smoke his pipe. 'Puff away, boy,' he said, 'puff hard.' And I puffed as hard as I could. I felt myself go pale and the sweat broke out on my forehead in great drops. And that made him roar with laughter—

MANDERS: How very strange.

MRS. ALVING: My dear, it's just something Oswald has dreamed.

OSWALD: No, mother, I didn't dream it. Surely you must remember—you came in and carried me back into the nursery. Then I was sick and I saw you crying. Did father often play jokes like that?

MANDERS: In his youth he was an extremely gay young man—

OSWALD: And yet he managed to achieve so much. So much that was good and useful; although he died so young.

MANDERS: Yes, you have inherited the name of an industrious and worthy man, my dear Oswald Alving. Well, I hope this will spur you on.

OSWALD: Yes, it ought to, oughtn't it?

MANDERS: In any case it was good of you to come home and join us in honouring him.

OSWALD: It was the least I could do for father.

MRS. ALVING: And the best thing of all is that I'm going to have him here for so long.

MANDERS: Yes, I hear you're staying the winter.

OSWALD: I am here for an indefinite period, Pastor. Oh, but it's good to be home!

MRS. ALVING *(warmly):* Yes, Oswald. It is, isn't it?

MANDERS *(looks at him sympathetically):* Yes, you went out into the world early, my dear Oswald.

OSWALD: I did. Sometimes I wonder if it wasn't too early.

MRS. ALVING: Oh, nonsense. It's good for a healthy lad; especially if he's an only child. It's bad for them to stay at home with their mother and father and be pampered.

MANDERS: That is a very debatable point, Mrs. Alving. When all is said and done, the parental home is where a child belongs.

OSWALD: I agree with you there, Pastor.

MANDERS: Take your own son. Well, it will do no harm to talk about it in his presence. What has been the consequence for him? Here he is, twenty-six or twenty-seven years old, and he's never had the opportunity to know what a real home is like.

OSWALD: I beg your pardon, sir, but there you're quite mistaken.

MANDERS: Oh! I thought you had spent practically all your time in artistic circles.

OSWALD: I have.

MANDERS: Mostly among young artists.

OSWALD: Yes.

MANDERS: But I thought most of those people lacked the means to support a family and make a home for themselves.

OSWALD: Some of them can't afford to get married, sir.

45

MANDERS: Yes, that's what I'm saying.

OSWALD: But that doesn't mean they can't have a home. Several of them have; and very good and comfortable homes at that.

MRS. ALVING *listens intently and nods, but says nothing.*

MANDERS: But I'm not speaking about bachelor establishments. By a home I mean a family establishment, where a man lives with his wife and children.

OSWALD: Quite. Or with his children and their mother.

MANDERS *(starts and claps his hands together):* Merciful heavens! You don't—?

OSWALD: Yes?

MANDERS: Lives with—with the mother of his children?

OSWALD: Yes, would you rather he disowned the mother of his children?

MANDERS: So you are speaking of unlegalized relationships! These so-called free marriages!

OSWALD: I've never noticed anything particularly free about the way such people live.

MANDERS: But how is it possible that—that any reasonably well brought up man or young woman can bring themselves to live like that—openly, for everyone to see?

OSWALD: But what else can they do? A poor young artist—a poor young girl. It costs a lot of money to get married. What can they do?

MANDERS: What can they do? I'll tell you, Mr. Alving, what they can do. They should have kept away from each other in the first place—that's what they should have done.

OSWALD: That argument won't get you far with young people who are in love and have red blood in their veins.

MRS. ALVING: No, that won't get you very far.

MANDERS *(takes no notice):* And to think that the authorities tolerate such behaviour! That it is allowed to happen

46

openly? *(Turns to* MRS. ALVING.*)* Wasn't I right to be so
concerned about your son? In circles where immorality is
practised openly and is, one might almost say, accepted—

OSWALD: Let me tell you something, sir, I have been a regular Sunday guest in one or two of these irregular house-
holds—

MANDERS: On Sundays!

OSWALD: Yes, that's the day when one's meant to enjoy
oneself. But I have never heard an offensive word there,
far less ever witnessed anything which could be called immoral. No; do you know when and where I have encountered immorality in artistic circles?

MANDERS: No, I don't, thank heaven.

OSWALD: Well, I shall tell you. I have encountered it when
one or another of our model husbands and fathers came
down there to look around a little on their own—and did
the artists the honour of visiting them in their humble bis-
tros. Then we learned a few things. Those gentlemen
were able to tell us about places and things of which we
had never dreamed.

MANDERS: What! Are you suggesting that honourable men
from this country—?

OSWALD: Have you never, when these honourable men returned home, have you never heard them hold forth on the
rampancy of immorality in foreign countries?

MANDERS: Yes, of course—

MRS. ALVING: I've heard that, too.

OSWALD: Well, you can take their word for it. Some of them
are experts. *(Clasps his head.)* Oh, that beautiful life of
freedom—that it should be so soiled!

MRS. ALVING: You mustn't get over-excited, Oswald. It
isn't good for you.

OSWALD: No, you're right, mother. It isn't good for my
health. It's that damned tiredness, you know. Well, I'll
take a little walk before dinner. I'm sorry, Pastor. I know

you can't see it from my point of view. But I had to say what I felt.

He goes out through the second door on the right.

MRS. ALVING: My poor boy—!

MANDERS: Yes, you may well say that. So it's come to this.

MRS. ALVING *looks at him but remains silent.*

MANDERS *(walks up and down):* He called himself the prodigal son. Alas, alas!

MRS. ALVING *still looks at him.*

MANDERS: And what do you say to all this?

MRS. ALVING: I say that Oswald was right in every word he said.

MANDERS *(stops dead):* Right? Right! In expressing those principles!

MRS. ALVING: Here in my loneliness I have come to think like him, Pastor Manders. But I have never dared to bring up the subject. Now my son shall speak for me.

MANDERS: I feel deeply sorry for you, Mrs. Alving. But now I will have to speak to you in earnest. I am not addressing you now as your business manager and adviser, nor as your and your late husband's old friend. I stand before you now as your priest, as I did at the moment when you had strayed so far.

MRS. ALVING: And what has the priest to say to me?

MANDERS: First I wish to refresh your memory, Mrs. Alving. The occasion is appropriate. Tomorrow will be the tenth anniversary of your husband's death. Tomorrow the memorial to him who is no longer with us is to be unveiled. Tomorrow I shall address the whole assembled flock. But today I wish to speak to you alone.

MRS. ALVING: Very well, Pastor. Speak.

MANDERS: Have you forgotten that after barely a year of

48

marriage you stood on the very brink of the abyss? That
you abandoned your house and home—that you deserted
your husband—yes, Mrs. Alving, deserted, deserted—
and refused to return to him, although he begged and en-
treated you to do so?

MRS. ALVING: Have you forgotten how desperately unhappy
I was during that first year?

MANDERS: Yes, that is the sign of the rebellious spirit, to demand happiness from this earthly life. What right have we
to happiness? No, Mrs. Alving, we must do our duty!
And your duty was to remain with the man you had
chosen, and to whom you were bound by a sacred bond.

MRS. ALVING: You know quite well the kind of life Alving
led at that time; the depravities he indulged in.

MANDERS: I am only too aware of the rumours that were cir-
culating about him; and I least of anyone approve his conduct during his youthful years, if those rumours contained
the truth. But a wife is not appointed to be her husband's
judge. It was your duty humbly to bear that cross which a
higher will had seen fit to assign to you. But instead you
rebelliously fling down that cross, abandon the erring
soul you should have supported, hazard your good name,
and very nearly ruin the reputations of others.

MRS. ALVING: Others? *An* other's, you mean?

MANDERS: It was extremely inconsiderate of you to seek refuge with me.

MRS. ALVING: With our priest? With an old friend?

MANDERS: Exactly. Well, you may thank God that I possessed the necessary firmness—that I was able to dissuade
you from your frenzied intentions and that it was granted
to me to lead you back on to the path of duty and home to
your lawful husband.

MRS. ALVING: Yes, Pastor Manders, that was certainly your
doing.

MANDERS: I was merely a humble tool in the hand of a higher

purpose. And that I persuaded you to bow to the call of duty and obedience, has not that proved a blessing which will surely enrich the remainder of your days? Did I not foretell all this? Did not Alving turn from his aberrations, like a man? Did he not afterwards live a loving and blameless life with you for the remainder of his days? Did he not become a public benefactor, did he not inspire you so that in time you became his right hand in all his enterprises? And a very capable right hand—oh, yes, I know that, Mrs. Alving, I give you credit for that. But now I come to the next great error of your life.

MRS. ALVING: And what do you mean by that?

MANDERS: Once you disowned your duties as a wife. Since then, you have disowned your duties as a mother.

MRS. ALVING: Ah—!

MANDERS: All your days you have been ruled by a fatal spirit of wilfulness. You have always longed for a life unconstrained by duties and principles. You have never been willing to suffer the curb of discipline. Everything that has been troublesome in your life you have cast off ruthlessly and callously, as if it were a burden which you had the right to reject. It was no longer convenient to you to be a wife, so you left your husband. You found it tiresome to be a mother, so you put your child out to live among strangers.

MRS. ALVING: Yes, that is true. I did.

MANDERS: And in consequence you have become a stranger to him.

MRS. ALVING: No, no! That's not true!

MANDERS: It is. It must be. And how have you got him back? Think well, Mrs. Alving! You have sinned greatly against your husband. You admit that by raising the monument to him down there. Confess too, now, how you have sinned against your son. There may still be time to bring him back from the paths of wantonness. Turn; and save what may still be saved in him. *(With raised forefinger.)* For verily, Mrs. Alving, as a mother you carry a heavy burden of guilt. This I have regarded it as my duty to say to you.

 Silence.

MRS. ALVING *(slow and controlled):* You have had your say, Pastor; and tomorrow you will speak publicly at my husband's ceremony. I shall not speak tomorrow. But now I shall say a few words to you, just as you have said a few words to me.

MANDERS: Of course. You wish to excuse your conduct—

MRS. ALVING: No. I simply want to tell you what happened.

MANDERS: Oh?

MRS. ALVING: Everything that you have just said about me and my husband and our life together after you, as you put it, had led me back on to the path of duty—all that is something of which you have no knowledge from your own observations. From that moment you, who used to visit us every day, never once set foot in our house.

MANDERS: You and your husband moved from town shortly afterwards.

MRS. ALVING: Yes. And you never came out here to see us while my husband was alive. It was only the business connected with the Orphanage that compelled you to visit me.

MANDERS *(quietly and uncertainly):* Helen—if this is intended as a reproach, I must beg you to consider the—

MRS. ALVING: The duty you owed to your position, yes. And then I was a wife who had run away from her husband. One can never be too careful with such unprincipled women.

MANDERS: My dear . . . Mrs. Alving, you exaggerate grotesquely.

MRS. ALVING: Yes, yes, well, let us forget it. What I wanted to say was that when you judge my conduct as a wife, you are content to base your judgment on common opinion.

MANDERS: Yes, well; what of it?

MRS. ALVING: But now, Manders, now I shall tell the truth. I have sworn to myself that one day you should know it. Only you.

MANDERS: And what is the truth?

MRS. ALVING: The truth is that my husband died just as dissolute as he had always lived.

MANDERS (gropes for a chair): What did you say?

MRS. ALVING: Just as dissolute, at any rate in his desires, after nineteen years of marriage, as he was before you wedded us.

MANDERS: You call these youthful escapades—these irregularities—excesses, if you like—evidence of a dissolute life!

MRS. ALVING: That is the expression our doctor used.

MANDERS: I don't understand you.

MRS. ALVING: It doesn't matter.

MANDERS: I cannot believe my ears. You mean your whole married life—all those years you shared with your husband—were nothing but a façade!

MRS. ALVING: Yes. Now you know.

MANDERS: But—but this I cannot accept! I don't understand—I cannot credit it! But how on earth is it possible—how could such a thing be kept secret?

MRS. ALVING: I had to fight, day after day, to keep it secret. After Oswald was born I thought things became a little better with Alving. But it didn't last long. And now I had to fight a double battle, fight with all my strength to prevent anyone knowing what kind of a man my child's father was. And you know what a winning personality Alving had. No one could believe anything but good of him. He was one of those people whose reputations remain untarnished by the way they live. But then, Man-

ders—you must know this too—then came the most loathsome thing of all.

MANDERS: More loathsome than this!

MRS. ALVING: I had put up with him, although I knew well
what went on secretly outside the house. But when he offended within our four walls—

MANDERS: What are you saying? Here!

MRS. ALVING: Yes, here in our own home. In there— *(Points
to the first door on the right.)* —it was in the dining-room
I first found out about it. I had something to do in there
and the door was standing ajar. Then I heard our maid
come up from the garden to water the flowers in there.

MANDERS: Oh, yes?

MRS. ALVING: A few moments later I heard Alving enter the
room. He said something to her. And then I heard—
(Gives a short laugh.) —I still don't know whether to
laugh or cry—I heard my own servant whisper: 'Stop it,
Mr. Alving! Let me go!'

MANDERS: What an unseemly frivolity! But it was nothing
more than a frivolity, Mrs. Alving. Believe me.

MRS. ALVING: I soon found out what to believe. My husband
had his way with the girl. And that relationship had consequences, Pastor Manders.

MANDERS *(petrified)*: And all this took place in this house! In
this house!

MRS. ALVING: I had endured much in this house. To keep
him at home in the evenings—and at night—I had to make
myself his companion in his secret dissipations up in his
room. There I had to sit alone with him, had to clink my
glass with his and drink with him, listen to his obscene
and senseless drivelling, had to fight him with my fists to
haul him into bed—

MANDERS *(shocked)*: I don't know how you managed to endure it.

MRS. ALVING: I had to, for my little son's sake. But when the final humiliation came—when my own servant—then I swore to myself: 'This must stop!' And so I took over the reins of this house; both as regards him and everything else. For now, you see, I had a weapon against him; he dared not murmur. It was then that I sent Oswald away. He was nearly seven and was beginning to notice things and ask questions, the way children do. I couldn't bear that, Manders. I thought the child could not help but be poisoned merely by breathing in this tainted home. That was why I sent him away. And so now you know why he was never allowed to set foot in his home while his father was alive. No one knows what it cost me.

MANDERS: You have indeed been sorely tried.

MRS. ALVING: I could never have borne it if I had not had my work. Yes, for I think I can say that I have worked! All the additions to the estate, all the improvements, all the useful innovations for which Alving was praised—do you imagine he had the energy to initiate any of them? He, who spent the whole day lying on the sofa reading old court circulars? No; let me tell you this too; I drove him forward when he was in his happier moods; and I had to bear the whole burden when he started again on his dissipations or collapsed in snivelling helplessness.

MANDERS: And it is to this man that you raise a memorial.

MRS. ALVING: There you see the power of a guilty conscience.

MANDERS: A guilty—? What do you mean?

MRS. ALVING: I always believed that some time, inevitably, the truth would have to come out, and that it would be believed. The Orphanage would destroy all rumours and banish all doubt.

MANDERS: You certainly made no mistake there, Mrs. Alving.

MRS. ALVING: And then I had another motive. I wanted to

make sure that my own son, Oswald, should not inherit anything whatever from his father.

MANDERS: You mean it was Alving's money that—?

MRS. ALVING: Yes. The annual donations that I have made to this Orphanage add up to the sum—I have calculated it carefully—the sum which made Lieutenant Alving, in his day, 'a good match'.

MANDERS: I understand—

MRS. ALVING: It was the sum with which he bought me. I do not wish that money to come into Oswald's hands. My son shall inherit everything from me.

OSWALD ALVING *enters through the second door on the right; he has removed his hat and overcoat outside.*

MRS. ALVING *(goes towards him):* Are you back already? My dear, dear boy!

OSWALD: Yes; what's one to do outside in this eternal rain? But I hear we're about to have dinner. How splendid.

REGINA *(enters from the kitchen with a parcel):* A parcel has just come for you, madam. *(Hands it to her.)*

MRS. ALVING *(with a glance at PASTOR MANDERS):* Copies of the songs for tomorrow's ceremony, I suppose.

MANDERS: Hm—

REGINA: Dinner is served, madam.

MRS. ALVING: Good. We'll come presently. I just want to— *(Begins to open the parcel.)*

REGINA *(to OSWALD):* Shall it be white port or red port, Mr. Oswald?

OSWALD: Both, Miss Engstrand.

REGINA: *Bien*—very good, Mr. Oswald.

She goes into the dining-room.

OSWALD: I'd better help her open the bottles— *(Follows her into the dining-room. The door swings half open behind him.)*

MRS. ALVING (*who has opened the parcel*): Yes, that's right. It's the copies of the songs, Pastor Manders.

MANDERS (*with folded hands*): How I am to make my address tomorrow with a clear conscience, I—!

MRS. ALVING: Oh, you'll find a way—

MANDERS (*quietly, so as not to be heard in the dining-room*): Yes, there mustn't be any scandal.

MRS. ALVING (*firmly, in a low voice*): No. But now this long, loathsome comedy is over. From the day after tomorrow, it will be as if the dead had never lived in this house. There will be no one here but my boy and his mother.

From the dining-room is heard the crash of a chair being knocked over. At the same time REGINA *says sharply, but keeping her voice low.*

REGINA: Oswald! Are you mad? Let me go!

MRS. ALVING (*starts in fear*): Ah!

She stares distraught at the half open door. OSWALD *coughs and begins to hum. A bottle is uncorked.*

MANDERS (*indignantly*): What is going on, Mrs. Alving? What was that?

MRS. ALVING (*hoarsely*): Ghosts. The couple in the conservatory-walk.

MANDERS: What are you saying! Regina—? Is she the child—?

MRS. ALVING: Yes. Come. Not a word.

She grips PASTOR MANDERS*'s arm and walks falteringly towards the door of the dining-room.*

ACT TWO

The same room. The mist still lies heavily over the land-scape. PASTOR MANDERS *and* MRS. ALVING *enter from the dining-room.*

MRS. ALVING *(still in the doorway):* I'm glad you enjoyed it, Pastor Manders. *(Speaks into the dining-room.)* Aren't you joining us, Oswald?

OSWALD *(offstage):* No, thank you. I think I'll go out and take a walk.

MRS. ALVING: Yes, do. It's stopped raining now. *(Closes the door of the dining-room, goes over to the hall door and calls)* Regina!

REGINA *(offstage):* Yes, madam.

MRS. ALVING: Go down to the ironing-room and give them a hand with the garlands.

REGINA: Very good, madam.

> MRS. ALVING *makes sure that* REGINA *has gone, then closes the door.*

MANDERS: He can't hear anything from in there, can he?

MRS. ALVING: Not when the door is shut. Anyway, he's going out.

MANDERS: I am still stunned. I don't understand how I managed to swallow a mouthful of that excellent meal.

MRS. ALVING (*restless but controlled, walks up and down*):
Neither do I. But what is to be done?

MANDERS: Yes, what is to be done? Upon my word, I don't
know. I'm so sadly inexperienced in matters of this kind.

MRS. ALVING: I am convinced that no harm has been done
yet.

MANDERS: No, heaven forbid! Nevertheless, it's a most im-
proper situation.

MRS. ALVING: It's only a casual whim of Oswald's. You can
be certain of that.

MANDERS: Well, as I said, I don't know about these things;
but I'm sure—

MRS. ALVING: She must leave the house. And at once. That's
obvious—

MANDERS: Yes, naturally.

MRS. ALVING: But where to? We can't just—

MANDERS: Where to? Home to her father, of course.

MRS. ALVING: To whom, did you say?

MANDERS: To her—oh, no, but Engstrand isn't her—! But,
dear God, Mrs. Alving, how can this be possible? Surely
you must be mistaken.

MRS. ALVING: Unfortunately I know I'm not mistaken. In
the end Johanna had to confess to me; and Alving
couldn't deny it. So there was nothing to be done but hush
the matter up.

MANDERS: Yes, I suppose that was the only thing to do.

MRS. ALVING: The girl left my service at once, and was
given a considerable sum of money to keep her mouth
shut. The remaining difficulties she solved for herself
when she got to town. She renewed an old acquaintance
with Engstrand, let it be known, I dare say, how much
money she had, and spun him a story about some for-
eigner or other who'd been here with a yacht that summer. Then she and Engstrand got themselves married in a
hurry. Well, you married them yourself.

MANDERS: But how can that be true? I remember clearly how Engstrand came to me to arrange the wedding. He was completely abject, and accused himself most bitterly of having indulged with his betrothed in a moment of weakness.

MRS. ALVING: Well, he had to take the blame on himself.

MANDERS: But to be so dishonest! And to me! I certainly would never have believed that of Jacob Engstrand. I'll speak to him seriously about this. He can be sure of that. And the immorality of it! For money! How much was it you gave the girl?

MRS. ALVING: Fifty pounds.

MANDERS: Just imagine! To go and marry a fallen woman for a paltry fifty pounds!

MRS. ALVING: What about me? I went and married a fallen man.

MANDERS: Good God Almighty, what are you saying? A fallen man!

MRS. ALVING: Do you think Alving was any purer when I accompanied him to the altar than Johanna was when Engstrand married her?

MANDERS: But the two things are utterly different—

MRS. ALVING: Not so different. Oh, yes, there was a big difference in the price. A paltry fifty pounds against an entire fortune.

MANDERS: But how can you compare two such different situations? After all, you were obeying the counsels of your heart, and of your family.

MRS. ALVING *(does not look at him):* I thought you understood where my heart, as you call it, had strayed at that time.

MANDERS *(distantly):* If I had understood anything of the kind, I should not have been a daily guest in your husband's house.

MRS. ALVING: Anyway, I didn't follow my own counsel. That is certain.

MANDERS: Well then, you obeyed your nearest relatives. Your mother and your two aunts. As was your duty.

MRS. ALVING: Yes, that is true. The three of them worked out a balance-sheet for me. Oh, it's incredible how patly they proved that it would be utter madness for me to turn down such an offer. If my mother could look down now and see what all that promise of splendour has led to.

MANDERS: No one can be held responsible for the outcome. And this much at least is sure, that your marriage was celebrated in an orderly fashion and in full accordance with the law.

MRS. ALVING *(by the window)*: All this talk about law and order. I often think that is what causes all the unhappiness in the world.

MANDERS: Mrs. Alving, now you are being sinful.

MRS. ALVING: Yes, perhaps I am. But I can't stand being bound by all these conventions. I can't! I must find my own way to freedom.

MANDERS: What do you mean by that?

MRS. ALVING *(taps on the window frame)*: I should never have concealed the truth about Alving's life. But I dared not do otherwise—and it wasn't only for Oswald's sake. I was such a coward.

MANDERS: Coward?

MRS. ALVING: If people had known, they would have said: 'Poor man, it isn't surprising he strays now and then. After all, his wife ran away from him.'

MANDERS: Perhaps they would not have been altogether unjustified.

MRS. ALVING *(looks hard at him)*: If I were a real mother, I would take Oswald and say to him: 'Listen, my boy. Your father was a degenerate—'

MANDERS: But great heavens above—!

MRS. ALVING: And I would tell him everything I have told you. The whole story.

MANDERS: You scandalize me, Mrs. Alving.

MRS. ALVING: Yes, I know. I know! I scandalize myself. *(Comes away from the window.)* That's how cowardly I am.

MANDERS: You call it cowardice to do your simple duty! Have you forgotten that a child shall love and honour its father and mother?

MRS. ALVING: Let us not generalize so. Let us ask: 'Shall Oswald love and honour Captain Alving?'

MANDERS: Is there not a voice in your mother's heart which forbids you to destroy your son's ideals?

MRS. ALVING: Yes, but what about the truth?

MANDERS: Yes, but what about the ideals?

MRS. ALVING: Oh, ideals, ideals! If only I weren't such a coward!

MANDERS: Don't despise our ideals, Mrs. Alving. Retribution will surely follow. Take Oswald in particular. He hasn't many ideals, I'm afraid. But this much I have discovered, that his father is to him an ideal.

MRS. ALVING: You are right there.

MANDERS: And you yourself have awakened and fostered these ideas of his, by your letters.

MRS. ALVING: Yes. I was bound by a false sense of duty, so I lied to my son, year out and year in. Oh, what a coward, what a coward I have been!

MANDERS: You have established a happy illusion in your son, Mrs. Alving—and you should certainly not regard that as being of little value.

MRS. ALVING: Hm. I wonder. But I shan't allow him to have any relations with Regina. He is not going to make that poor girl unhappy.

MANDERS: Good heavens, no! That would be dreadful.

MRS. ALVING: If I knew that he meant it seriously, and that it would make him happy—

MANDERS: Yes? What then?

MRS. ALVING: But that's impossible. Unfortunately Regina isn't that type.

MANDERS: How do you mean?

MRS. ALVING: If only I weren't such an abject coward, I'd say to him: 'Marry her, or make what arrangements you please. As long as you're honest and open about it—'

MANDERS: Merciful God! You mean a legal marriage! What a terrible idea! It's absolutely unheard-of—!

MRS. ALVING: Unheard-of, did you say? Put your hand on your heart, Pastor Manders, and tell me—do you really believe there aren't married couples like that to be found in this country—as closely related as these two?

MANDERS: I simply don't understand you.

MRS. ALVING: Oh, yes you do.

MANDERS: You're thinking that by chance possibly—? Yes, alas, family life is indeed not always as pure as it should be. But in the kind of case you mean, one can never be sure—at any rate, not absolutely— But in this case—! That you, a mother, could want to allow your own—

MRS. ALVING: But I don't *want* to. I wouldn't allow it for any price in the world. That's just what I'm saying.

MANDERS: No, because you are a coward, as you put it. But if you weren't a coward—? Great God in heaven, what a shocking relationship!

MRS. ALVING: Well, we all stem from a relationship of that kind, so we are told. And who was it who arranged things like that in the world, Pastor Manders?

MANDERS: I shall not discuss such questions with you, Mrs. Alving. You are not in the right spiritual frame of mind for that. But that you dare to say that it is cowardly of you—!

MRS. ALVING: I shall tell you what I mean. I am frightened,

62

because there is in me something ghostlike from which I
can never free myself.

MANDERS: What did you call it?

MRS. ALVING: Ghostlike. When I heard Regina and Oswald
in there, it was as if I saw ghosts. I almost think we are all
ghosts—all of us, Pastor Manders. It isn't just what we
have inherited from our father and mother that walks in
us. It is all kinds of dead ideas and all sorts of old and ob-
solete beliefs. They are not alive in us; but they remain in
us none the less, and we can never rid ourselves of them. I
only have to take a newspaper and read it, and I see ghosts
between the lines. There must be ghosts all over the country. They lie as thick as grains of sand. And we're all so
horribly afraid of the light.

MANDERS: Aha—so there we have the fruits of your reading.
Fine fruits indeed! Oh, these loathsome, rebellious, free-
thinking books!

MRS. ALVING: You are wrong, my dear Pastor. It was you
yourself who first spurred me to think; and I thank and
bless you for it.

MANDERS: I?

MRS. ALVING: Yes, when you forced me into what you
called duty; when you praised as right and proper what
my whole spirit rebelled against as something abominable. It was then that I began to examine the seams of your
learning. I only wanted to pick at a single knot; but when I
had worked it loose, the whole fabric fell apart. And then
I saw that it was machine-sewn.

MANDERS *(quiet, shaken):* Is this the reward of my life's
hardest struggle?

MRS. ALVING: Call it rather your life's most pitiful defeat.

MANDERS: It was my life's greatest victory, Helen. The victory over myself.

MRS. ALVING: It was a crime against us both.

MANDERS: That I besought you, saying: 'Woman, go home

to your lawful husband,' when you came to me distraught and cried: 'I am here! Take me!' Was that a crime?

MRS. ALVING: Yes, I think so.

MANDERS: We two do not understand each other.

MRS. ALVING: No; not any longer.

MANDERS: Never—never even in my most secret moments have I thought of you except as another man's wedded wife.

MRS. ALVING: Oh? I wonder.

MANDERS: Helen—

MRS. ALVING: One forgets so easily what one was like.

MANDERS: I do not. I am the same as I always was.

MRS. ALVING (*changes the subject*): Well, well, well—let's not talk any more about the past. Now you're up to your ears in commissions and committees; and I sit here fighting with ghosts, both in me and around me.

MANDERS: I will help you to exorcise the ghosts around you. After all the dreadful things you have told me today, my conscience will not permit me to allow a young and unprotected girl to remain in your house.

MRS. ALVING: Don't you think it would be best if we could get her taken care of? I mean—well, decently married.

MANDERS: Indubitably. I think it would be desirable for her in every respect. Regina is just now at the age when—well, I don't really understand these things, but—

MRS. ALVING: Regina matured early.

MANDERS: Yes, didn't she? I seem to remember that she was noticeably well developed from a physical point of view when I prepared her for confirmation. But for the present at any rate she must go home. To her father's care—no, but of course, Engstrand isn't—! That he—that *he* could conceal the truth from me like that!

There is a knock on the door leading to the hall.

MRS. ALVING: Who can that be? Come in.

ENGSTRAND (*appears in the doorway in his Sunday suit*):
Begging your pardon, madam, but—

MANDERS: Aha! Hm!

MRS. ALVING: Oh, is it you, Engstrand?

ENGSTRAND: There weren't any of the servants about, so I
took the liberty of giving a little knock.

MRS. ALVING: Yes, yes. Well, come in. Do you want to
speak to me about something?

ENGSTRAND (*enters*): No, thank you, ma'am. It's the Pastor
I really wanted to have a word with.

MANDERS (*walks up and down*): Hm; really? You want to
speak to me? Do you indeed?

ENGSTRAND: Yes, I'd be so terribly grateful if—

MANDERS (*stops in front of him*): Well! May I ask what is the
nature of your question?

ENGSTRAND: Well, it's like this, Pastor. We've been paid
off down there now—a thousand thanks, Mrs. Alving—
and now we're ready with everything—and so I thought
it'd only be right and proper if we who have worked so
well together all this time—I thought we might conclude
with a few prayers this evening.

MANDERS: Prayers? Down at the Orphanage?

ENGSTRAND: Well, of course, sir, if you don't think it's the
right thing to do—

MANDERS: Oh yes, yes, indeed I do, but—hm—

ENGSTRAND: I've been in the habit of holding a little service
myself down there of an evening—

MANDERS: Have you?

ENGSTRAND: Yes, now and then. Just a little edification, as
you might say. But I'm only a poor humble man and
haven't the proper gifts, God forgive me—and so I
thought, seeing as Pastor Manders happens to be out
here—

MANDERS: Now look here, Engstrand, first I must ask you a

65

question. Are you in the correct frame of mind for such a meeting? Do you feel your conscience is clear and free?

ENGSTRAND: Oh, God forgive us, let's not talk about conscience, Pastor.

MANDERS: Yes, that's just what we are going to talk about. Well? What is your answer?

ENGSTRAND: Well—a man's conscience can be a bit of a beggar now and then—

MANDERS: Well, at least you admit it. But now, will you tell me the truth! What's all this about Regina?

MRS. ALVING (quickly): Pastor Manders!

MANDERS (soothingly): Leave this to me—

ENGSTRAND: Regina? Good heavens, how you frighten me! (Looks at MRS. ALVING.) Surely nothing's happened to Regina?

MANDERS: Let us hope not. But what I meant was, what's all this about you and Regina? You call yourself her father, don't you? Hm?

ENGSTRAND (uncertainly): Well—hm—you know all about me and poor Johanna.

MANDERS: Now I want no more prevarication. Your late wife told the whole truth to Mrs. Alving before she left her service.

ENGSTRAND: Well, may the—! No, did she really?

MANDERS: So now you are unmasked, Engstrand.

ENGSTRAND: And she promised and swore on the Bible that she—

MANDERS: Swore on the Bible—?

ENGSTRAND: No, she only promised, but so sincerely.

MANDERS: And all these years you have concealed the truth from me. Concealed it from *me,* who trusted you so implicitly.

ENGSTRAND: Yes, I'm afraid I have, I suppose.

MANDERS: Have I deserved this from you, Engstrand? Haven't I always been ready to assist you with help, both spiritual and material, as far as lay within my power? Answer! Haven't I?

ENGSTRAND: Things would often have looked black for me if it hadn't been for your Reverence.

MANDERS: And this is how you reward me! You cause me to enter false statements in the parish register, and withhold from me over a period of years the information which you owed both to me and to the cause of truth! Your conduct has been completely indefensible, Engstrand. From now on, I wash my hands of you.

ENGSTRAND (*with a sigh*): Yes, of course, sir. I appreciate that.

MANDERS: I mean, how could you possibly justify yourself?

ENGSTRAND: But wouldn't it have made things even worse for poor Johanna if the truth had been allowed to come out? Now just imagine if your Reverence had been in the same situation as her—

MANDERS: I!

ENGSTRAND: Oh, for heaven's sake, I don't mean exactly the same. But I mean, suppose your Reverence had something to be ashamed of in the eyes of the world, as the saying goes. We men mustn't judge a poor woman too harshly, your Reverence.

MANDERS: But I'm not. It's you I'm reproaching.

ENGSTRAND: May I ask your Reverence a tiny question?

MANDERS: Yes, yes, what is it?

ENGSTRAND: Isn't it right and proper for a man to raise up the fallen?

MANDERS: Of course it is.

ENGSTRAND: And isn't it a man's duty to stand by his word?

MANDERS: Certainly it is; but—

ENGSTRAND: That time when Johanna fell into misfortune through that Englishman—or maybe he was an American, or a Russian, as they call them—well, she came up to town. Poor creature, she'd turned up her nose at me once or twice; for she only looked at what was handsome and fine, poor thing; and of course I had this thing wrong with my leg. Well, your Reverence will remember how I'd ventured into a dancing-hall where foreign sailors were indulging in drunkenness and excess, as the saying goes. And when I tried to exhort them to start leading a better life—

MRS. ALVING (*by the window*): Hm—

MANDERS: I know, Engstrand. The ruffians threw you down the stairs. You've told me about it before. Your injury is something to be proud of.

ENGSTRAND: Oh, I take no pride in it, your Reverence. But what I was going to say was, so she came along and poured out all her troubles to me amid weeping and gnashing of teeth. I'll be frank, your Reverence; it nearly broke my heart to listen to her.

MANDERS: Did it really, Engstrand? Well, go on.

ENGSTRAND: Yes, well, so I said to her: 'This American is a vagrant on the sea of life,' I said. 'And you, Johanna, you've committed a sin and are a fallen creature. But Jacob Engstrand,' I said, 'he's got both feet firmly on the ground'—speaking figuratively, you understand—

MANDERS: I understand you perfectly. Go on.

ENGSTRAND: Well, that's how I raised her up and made an honest woman of her so that people shouldn't get to know the wanton way she'd behaved with foreigners.

MANDERS: You acted very handsomely. The only thing I can't understand is how you could bring yourself to accept money—

ENGSTRAND: Money? I? Not a penny!

MANDERS (*glances questioningly at* MRS. ALVING): But—!

ENGSTRAND: Oh yes, wait a moment—now I remember. Johanna did have a few shillings with her. But I wouldn't have any of it. 'Fie!' I said, 'that's Mammon, that's the wages of sin. We'll throw that wretched gold—or notes, or whatever it was—back in the American's face,' I said. But he'd taken his hook and disappeared across the wild sea, your Reverence.

MANDERS: Had he, my dear Engstrand?

ENGSTRAND: Oh yes. And so Johanna and I agreed that the money was to be used to bring up the child, and that's what happened; and I can account for every shilling of it.

MANDERS: But this puts quite a different face on things.

ENGSTRAND: That's the way it was, your Reverence. And I think I can say I've been a real father to Regina—as far as stood within my power—for unfortunately I'm an ailing man.

MANDERS: Now, now, my dear Engstrand—

ENGSTRAND: But this I can say, that I've brought up the child tenderly and been a loving husband to poor Johanna and ordered my household the way the good book says. But it would never have entered my head to go along to your Reverence in sinful pride and boast that for once I too had done a good deed. No, when anything of that kind happens to Jacob Engstrand, he keeps quiet about it. I don't suppose that's always the way, more's the pity. And when I do go to see Pastor Manders I've always more than enough of wickedness and weakness to talk to him about. For I said it just now and I say it again—a man's conscience can be a real beggar now and then.

MANDERS: Give me your hand, Jacob Engstrand.

ENGSTRAND: Why, good heavens, Pastor—!

MANDERS: No argument, now. (*Presses his hand.*) There!

ENGSTRAND: And if I was to go down on my bended knees and humbly to beg your Reverence's forgiveness—?

MANDERS: You? No, on the contrary. It is I who must ask your pardon—

ENGSTRAND: Oh no, really—

MANDERS: Indeed, yes. And I do so with all my heart. Forgive me that I could ever have misjudged you so. And if there is any way in which I can show the sincerity of my regrets and of my good-will towards you—

ENGSTRAND: Would your Reverence really do that?

MANDERS: Most gladly.

ENGSTRAND: Well, in that case there's a real opportunity just now. With the money I've managed to put aside through the blessed work here, I'm thinking of starting a kind of home for sailors in the city.

MANDERS: *You* are?

ENGSTRAND: Yes, a kind of refuge like the one here, in a manner of speaking. The temptations for a sailor wandering on shore are so manifold. But in that house, with me there, it'd be like them having a father to take care of them, I thought.

MANDERS: What have you to say to that, Mrs. Alving!

ENGSTRAND: My means are rather limited, God knows. But if only someone would stretch out a helping hand—

MANDERS: Yes, well, let us consider the matter. Your project interests me very deeply. But go along now and get everything in order and light candles so as to make the place cheerful, and we'll have a little edification together, my dear Engstrand. For now I think you're in the right frame of mind.

ENGSTRAND: Yes, I think I am. Well, goodbye, Mrs. Alving, and thank you for everything. And take good care of Regina for me. *(Wipes a tear from his eye.)* Poor Johanna's child! Hm—it's strange, but—it's just as though she'd grown to be a part of me. It is really, yes. *(Touches his forehead and goes out through the door.)*

MANDERS: Well, what have you to say about that man now, Mrs. Alving? That was quite a different explanation we were given there.

MRS. ALVING: It was indeed.

MANDERS: You see how terribly careful one must be about condemning one's fellows. But then, again, it is a deep

joy to discover that one has been mistaken. Or what do
you say?

MRS. ALVING: I say: you are a great baby, Manders. And
you always will be.

MANDERS: I?

MRS. ALVING *(places both her hands on his shoulders):* And
I say: I'd like to throw both my arms round your neck.

MANDERS *(frees himself quickly):* No, no, bless you! Such
impulses—!

MRS. ALVING *(with a smile):* Oh, you needn't be frightened
of me.

MANDERS *(by the table):* You have such an extravagant way
of expressing yourself sometimes. Now let me just gather
these documents together and put them in my case. *(Does
so.)* There! And now, au revoir. Keep your eyes open
when Oswald comes back. I'll be with you again presently. *(Takes his hat and goes out through the hall.)*

MRS. ALVING *(sighs, looks out of the window for a moment,
tidies the room a little and is about to go into the dining-
room, but stops in the doorway and calls softly):* Oswald,
are you still at table?

OSWALD *(offstage):* I'm just finishing my cigar.

MRS. ALVING: I thought you'd gone for a little walk.

OSWALD: In this weather?

> *There is the clink of a glass.* MRS. ALVING *leaves the
> door open and sits down with her sewing on the sofa by
> the window.*

OSWALD *(still offstage):* Wasn't that Pastor Manders who
left just now?

MRS. ALVING: Yes, he's gone down to the Orphanage.

OSWALD: Hm. *(Clink of decanter and glass again.)*

MRS. ALVING *(with a worried glance):* Oswald dear, you
ought to be careful with that liqueur. It's strong.

OSWALD: It keeps out the damp.

MRS. ALVING: Won't you come in and talk to me?

OSWALD: I can't smoke in there.

MRS. ALVING: You know I don't mind cigars.

OSWALD: All right, I'll come, then. Just one tiny drop more. There. (*He enters with his cigar and closes the door behind him. Short silence.*)

OSWALD: Where's the Pastor gone?

MRS. ALVING: I told you, he went down to the Orphanage.

OSWALD: Oh yes, so you did.

MRS. ALVING: You oughtn't to sit at table so long, Oswald.

OSWALD (*holding his cigar behind his back*): But I think it's so nice, mother. (*Strokes and pats her.*) To come home, and sit at my mother's own table, in my mother's diningroom, and eat my mother's beautiful food.

MRS. ALVING: My dear, dear boy.

OSWALD (*walks and smokes a trifle impatiently*): And what else is there for me to do here? I can't work—

MRS. ALVING: Can't you?

OSWALD: In this weather? Not a glimmer of sunlight all day. (*Walks across the room.*) That's the worst thing about it— not to be able to work—

MRS. ALVING: Perhaps you shouldn't have come home.

OSWALD: Yes, mother, I had to.

MRS. ALVING: I'd ten times rather sacrifice the happiness of having you with me than that you should—

OSWALD (*stops by the table*): Tell me, mother. Does it really make you so happy to have me home?

MRS. ALVING: Does it make me happy?

OSWALD (*crumples a newspaper*): I think it must be almost the same for you whether I'm alive or not.

MRS. ALVING: How can you have the heart to say that to your mother, Oswald?

OSWALD: But you managed so well to live without me before.

MRS. ALVING: Yes. I have lived without you. That is true.

Silence. Dusk begins to gather slowly. OSWALD *paces up and down the room. He has put down his cigar.*

OSWALD *(stops beside* MRS. ALVING*):* Mother, may I sit down on the sofa with you?

MRS. ALVING *(makes room for him):* Yes, of course, my dear boy.

OSWALD *(sits):* There's something I have to tell you, mother.

MRS. ALVING *(tensely):* Yes?

OSWALD *(stares vacantly ahead of him):* I can't keep it to myself any longer.

MRS. ALVING: What? What do you mean?

OSWALD *(as before):* I couldn't bring myself to write to you about it; and since I came home I—

MRS. ALVING *(grips his arm):* Oswald, what is this?

OSWALD: Yesterday and today I've been trying to forget. To escape. But it's no good.

MRS. ALVING *(rises):* Now tell me the truth, Oswald.

OSWALD *(pulls her down on to the sofa again):* Sit still and I'll try to tell you about it. I've complained so much about how tired I felt after the journey—

MRS. ALVING: Yes. Well?

OSWALD: But it isn't that that's wrong with me. It isn't any ordinary tiredness—

MRS. ALVING *(tries to rise):* You're not ill, Oswald!

OSWALD *(pulls her down again):* Sit still, mother. Just keep calm. No, I'm not really ill; not what people usually call ill. *(Clasps his hands to his head.)* Mother, I'm spiritually broken—my will's gone—I shall never be able to work any more!

He throws himself into her lap, with his hands over his face, and sobs.

MRS. ALVING (*pale and trembling*): Oswald! Look at me! No, no, it isn't true!

OSWALD (*looks up at her despairingly*): Never to be able to work again! Never. Never. To be dead while I'm still alive. Mother, can you imagine anything so dreadful?

MRS. ALVING: My poor boy. How did this frightful thing happen to you?

OSWALD (*sits upright again*): Yes, that's just what I can't understand. I've never lived intemperately. Not in any way. You mustn't believe that of me, mother. I've never done that.

MRS. ALVING: Of course I don't believe it, Oswald.

OSWALD: And yet it's happened to me. This dreadful thing.

MRS. ALVING: Oh, but my dear, dear boy, it'll be all right. You've just overworked. You take my word for it.

OSWALD (*heavily*): That's what I thought at first. But it isn't that.

MRS. ALVING: Tell me everything from the beginning.

OSWALD: I shall, yes.

MRS. ALVING: When did you first notice it?

OSWALD: It was soon after the last time I'd been home, and had gone back again to Paris. I began to feel the most violent pains in my head—mostly at the back of my head, it seemed. It was as though a tight iron ring had been screwed round my neck and just above it.

MRS. ALVING: Yes?

OSWALD: At first I thought it was just the usual headaches I used to have so often while I was a child.

MRS. ALVING: Yes, yes—

OSWALD: But it wasn't. I soon realized that. I couldn't work any more. I wanted to begin on a new painting, but it was as though my powers had failed me. It was as though I

74

was paralysed—I couldn't see anything clearly—everything went misty and began to swim in front of my eyes. Oh, it was dreadful! In the end I sent for the doctor. And he told me the truth.

MRS. ALVING: How do you mean?

OSWALD: He was one of the leading doctors down there. I had to tell him how I felt. And then he began to ask me a lot of questions, which seemed to me to have absolutely nothing to do with it. I didn't understand what the man was driving at—

MRS. ALVING: Yes!

OSWALD: In the end he said: 'You've been worm-eaten from birth.' That was the word he used: *vermoulu.*

MRS. ALVING *(tensely):* What did he mean by that?

OSWALD: I didn't understand either, and asked him to explain more clearly. And then the old cynic said— *(Clenches his fist.)* Oh—!

MRS. ALVING: What did he say?

OSWALD: He said: 'The sins of the fathers shall be visited on the children.'

MRS. ALVING *(rises slowly):* The sins of the fathers—!

OSWALD: I nearly hit him in the face—

MRS. ALVING *(walks across the room):* The sins of the fathers—

OSWALD *(smiles sadly):* Yes, what do you think of that? Of course I assured him it was quite out of the question. But do you think he gave in? No, he stuck to his opinion; and it was only when I brought out your letters and translated to him all the passages that dealt with father—

MRS. ALVING: But then he—?

OSWALD: Yes, then of course he had to admit he was on the wrong track. And then I learned the truth. The incredible truth! This wonderfully happy life with my comrades, I should have abstained from. It had been too much for my strength. In other words, I have only myself to blame.

MRS. ALVING: Oswald! Oh, no, you mustn't think that!

OSWALD: There was no other explanation possible, he said. That's the dreadful thing. Beyond cure—ruined for life— because of my own folly. Everything I wanted to accomplish in the world—not even to dare to think of it—not to be *able* to think of it. Oh, if only I could start my life over again, and undo it all!

Throws himself face down on the sofa. MRS. ALVING *wrings her hands and walks to and fro, fighting silently with herself.*

OSWALD *(after a while, looks up and remains half-leaning on his elbow):* If it had been something I'd inherited. Something I wasn't myself to blame for. But this! To have thrown away in this shameful, thoughtless, light-hearted way one's whole happiness and health, everything in the world—one's future, one's life—

MRS. ALVING: No, no, my dear, blessed boy—this is impossible! *(Leans over him.)* Things are not as desperate as you think.

OSWALD: Oh, you don't know—! *(Jumps up.)* And then, mother, that I should cause you all this grief! I've often almost wished and hoped that you didn't care very much about me.

MRS. ALVING: I, Oswald! My only son! The only possession I have in the world—the only thing I care about!

OSWALD *(seizes both her hands and kisses them):* Yes, yes, I know. When I am at home, of course I know it. And that's one of the hardest things to bear. But now you know. And now we won't talk about it any more today. I can't bear to think about it for long. *(Walks across the room.)* Get me something to drink, mother.

MRS. ALVING: Drink? What do you want to drink now?

OSWALD: Oh, anything. You have some cold punch in the house, haven't you?

MRS. ALVING: Yes, but, my dear Oswald—

OSWALD: Oh, mother, don't be difficult. Be nice now! I *must* have something to help me forget these worries. *(Goes into the conservatory.)* Oh, how—how dark it is in here! *(MRS. ALVING pulls a bell-rope, right.)* And this incessant rain. It goes on week after week; sometimes for months. Never to see the sun! In all the years I've been at home I don't remember ever having seen the sun shine.

MRS. ALVING: Oswald! You are thinking of leaving me!

OSWALD: Hm— *(Sighs deeply.)* I'm not thinking about anything. I *can't* think about anything. *(Softly.)* I take good care not to.

REGINA *(enters from the dining-room)*: Did you ring, madam?

MRS. ALVING: Yes, bring in the lamp.

REGINA: Yes, madam, at once. I've already lit it. *(Goes.)*

MRS. ALVING *(goes over to* OSWALD*)*: Oswald, don't hide anything from me.

OSWALD: I'm not, mother. *(Goes over to the table.)* Haven't I told you enough?

REGINA *enters with the lamp and puts it on the table.*

MRS. ALVING: Oh, Regina, you might bring us half a bottle of champagne.

REGINA: Very good, madam. *(Goes.)*

OSWALD *(takes* MRS. ALVING*'s head in his hands)*: That's the way. I knew my mother wouldn't let her boy go thirsty.

MRS. ALVING: My poor, dear Oswald! How could I deny you anything now?

OSWALD *(eagerly)*: Is that true, mother? Do you mean it?

MRS. ALVING: Mean what?

OSWALD: That you wouldn't deny me anything?

MRS. ALVING: But, my dear Oswald—

OSWALD: Ssh!

REGINA *(brings a tray with a half-bottle of champagne and*

two glasses, and puts it down on the table): Shall I open—?

OSWALD: No, thank you, I'll do it myself.

REGINA *goes.*

MRS. ALVING *(sits down at the table):* What did you mean just now, when you said I mustn't deny you anything?

OSWALD *(busy trying to open the bottle):* Let's taste this first.

The cork jumps out. He fills one glass and is about to do likewise with the other.

MRS. ALVING *(puts her hand over it):* Thank you, not for me.

OSWALD: Well, for me, then. *(Empties the glass, refills it and empties it again. Then he sits down at the table.)*

MRS. ALVING *(tensely):* Well?

OSWALD *(not looking at her):* Tell me, mother—I thought you and Pastor Manders looked so strange—hm—quiet—at dinner.

MRS. ALVING: Did you notice?

OSWALD: Yes—hm. *(Short silence.)* Tell me—what do you think of Regina?

MRS. ALVING: What do I think?

OSWALD: Yes, isn't she splendid?

MRS. ALVING: Oswald dear, you don't know her as well as I do—

OSWALD: Oh?

MRS. ALVING: Regina spent too much time at home, I'm afraid. I ought to have brought her here to live with me sooner.

OSWALD: Yes, but isn't she splendid to look at, mother? *(Fills his glass.)*

MRS. ALVING: Regina has many great faults—

OSWALD: Oh, what does that matter? *(Drinks again.)*

MRS. ALVING: But I'm fond of her all the same. And I am responsible for her. I'd rather anything in the world happened than that she should come to any harm.

OSWALD *(jumps up):* Mother, Regina's my only hope!

MRS. ALVING *(rises):* What do you mean by that?

OSWALD: I can't bear all this misery alone.

MRS. ALVING: But you have your mother to bear it with you.

OSWALD: Yes, that's what I thought. And that's why I came home to you. But it won't work. I can see it; it won't work. I can't bear this life here.

MRS. ALVING: Oswald!

OSWALD: Oh, I must live differently, mother. That's why I have to leave you. I don't want you to see.

MRS. ALVING: My poor, sick boy! Oh, but Oswald, as long as you're not well—

OSWALD: If it was just the illness, I'd stay with you, mother. You're the best friend I have in the world.

MRS. ALVING: Yes, I am, Oswald, aren't I?

OSWALD *(walks around restlessly):* But it's all the remorse, the gnawing, the self-reproach. And then the fear! Oh— this dreadful fear!

MRS. ALVING *(follows him):* Fear? What fear? What do you mean?

OSWALD: Oh, don't ask me any more about it. I don't know. I can't describe it.

MRS. ALVING *crosses right and pulls the bell-rope.*

OSWALD: What do you want?

MRS. ALVING: I want my boy to be happy. He shan't sit here and brood. *(To* REGINA *who appears in the doorway.)* More champagne. A whole bottle.

REGINA *goes.*

OSWALD: Mother!

MRS. ALVING: Do you think we don't know how to live here, too?

OSWALD: Isn't she splendid to look at? The way she's made! And so healthy and strong!

MRS. ALVING *(sits at the table):* Sit down, Oswald, and let's talk calmly together.

OSWALD *(sits):* You don't know this, mother, but I have done Regina a wrong. And I've got to put it right.

MRS. ALVING: A wrong?

OSWALD: Well, a little thoughtlessness—whatever you care to call it. Quite innocently, really. When I was home last—

MRS. ALVING: Yes?

OSWALD: She asked me so often about Paris, and I told her this and that about the life down there. And I remember, one day I happened to say: 'Wouldn't you like to go there yourself?'

MRS. ALVING: Oh?

OSWALD: Well, she blushed violently, and then she said: 'Yes, I'd like to very much.' 'Well, well,' I replied, 'that might be arranged'—or something of the sort.

MRS. ALVING: Yes?

OSWALD: Well, of course I forgot the whole thing. But the day before yesterday, when I asked her if she was glad that I was going to stay at home so long—

MRS. ALVING: Yes?

OSWALD: She gave me such a strange look and then she asked: 'But then, what's going to become of my trip to Paris?'

MRS. ALVING: Her trip!

OSWALD: And then I got it out of her that she'd taken the whole thing seriously, that she'd been going around here thinking about me the whole time, and that she'd begun to learn French—

MRS. ALVING: I see—

OSWALD: Mother—when I saw that splendid, handsome, healthy girl standing there in front of me—well, I'd never really noticed her before—but now, when she stood there, so to speak, with open arms ready to receive me—

MRS. ALVING: Oswald!

OSWALD: Then I realized that in her I could find salvation; for I saw that she was full of the joy of life.

MRS. ALVING *(starts):* The joy of life! But how could that help?

REGINA *(enters from the dining-room with a bottle of champagne):* I'm sorry I was so long. I had to go down to the cellar— *(Puts the bottle on the table.)*

OSWALD: And fetch another glass.

REGINA *(looks at him, surprised):* There is Mrs. Alving's glass.

OSWALD: But fetch one for yourself, Regina.

REGINA *starts and throws a quick glance at* MRS. ALVING.

OSWALD: Well?

REGINA *(quietly, hesitantly):* Do you wish me to, madam?

MRS. ALVING: Fetch the glass, Regina.

REGINA *goes into the dining-room.*

OSWALD *(watches her go):* Do you see how she walks? With such purpose and gaiety!

MRS. ALVING: This must not happen, Oswald.

OSWALD: It's already decided. Surely you can see. It's no use trying to stop it.

REGINA *enters with an empty glass, which she keeps in her hand.*

OSWALD: Sit down, Regina.

She glances questioningly at MRS. ALVING.

MRS. ALVING: Sit down.

REGINA *sits on a chair by the dining-room door, with the empty glass still in her hand.*

MRS. ALVING: Oswald, what was it you were saying about the joy of life?

OSWALD: Oh, yes—the joy of life, mother—you don't know much about that here. I never feel it here.

MRS. ALVING: Not when you are with me?

OSWALD: Not when I'm at home. But you don't understand that.

MRS. ALVING: Oh, yes—I think I do now—almost.

OSWALD: The joy of life and the love of one's work. They're practically the same thing. But that you don't know anything about, either.

MRS. ALVING: No, I don't suppose we do. Oswald, tell me more about this.

OSWALD: Well, all I mean is that here people are taught to believe that work is a curse and a punishment, and that life is a misery which we do best to get out of as quickly as possible.

MRS. ALVING: A vale of tears, yes. And we do our best to make it one.

OSWALD: But out there, people don't feel like that. No one there believes in that kind of teaching any longer. They feel it's wonderful and glorious just to be alive. Mother, have you noticed how everything I've painted is concerned with the joy of life? Always, always, the joy of life. Light and sunshine and holiday—and shining, contented faces. That's what makes me afraid to be here at home with you.

MRS. ALVING: Afraid? What are you afraid of here with me?

OSWALD: I'm afraid that everything in me will degenerate into ugliness here.

MRS. ALVING *(looks hard at him):* You think that would happen?

OSWALD: I know it. Live the same life here as down there, and it wouldn't be the same life.

MRS. ALVING *(who has listened intently, rises, her eyes large and thoughtful):* Now I see where it went wrong.

OSWALD: What do you see?

MRS. ALVING: Now I understand for the first time. And now I can speak.

OSWALD *(rises):* Mother, I don't follow you.

REGINA *(who has also risen):* Shall I go?

MRS. ALVING: No, stay. Now I can speak. Now, my boy, you shall know everything. And then you can choose. Oswald! Regina!

OSWALD: Ssh! The Pastor—!

MANDERS *(enters from the hall):* Well, we've had a most splendid and profitable hour down there.

OSWALD: So have we.

MANDERS: We must assist Engstrand with this sailors' home. Regina must go and help him—

REGINA: No thank you, Pastor.

MANDERS *(notices her for the first time):* What! You here! And with a glass in your hand!

REGINA *(puts the glass down quickly):* Oh, *pardon*—

OSWALD: Regina is leaving with me, sir.

MANDERS: Leaving! With you!

OSWALD: Yes. As my wife. If she so wishes.

MANDERS: But, good heavens—!

REGINA: It isn't my doing, sir.

OSWALD: Or she will stay here, if I stay.

REGINA *(involuntarily):* Here?

MANDERS: I am petrified at you, Mrs. Alving.

MRS. ALVING: She will neither leave with you nor stay with you. Now I can speak the truth.

MANDERS: But you mustn't! No, no, no!

MRS. ALVING: I can and I will. And I shan't destroy any ideals, either.

83

OSWALD: Mother, what have you been hiding from me?

REGINA *(listens):* Madam! Listen! People are shouting outside!

She goes into the conservatory and looks out.

OSWALD *(at the window, left):* What's going on? Where's that light coming from?

REGINA *(cries):* The Orphanage is on fire!

MRS. ALVING *(at the window):* On fire!

MANDERS: On fire? Impossible! I've only just left it.

OSWALD: Where's my hat? Oh, never mind! Father's Orphanage—! *(Runs out through the garden door.)*

MRS. ALVING: My shawl, Regina! The whole building's alight!

MANDERS: Terrible! Mrs. Alving, there blazes the judgment of God upon this sinful house!

MRS. ALVING: Perhaps you are right. Come, Regina. *(She and REGINA hurry out through the hall.)*

MANDERS *(clasps his hands):* And not insured either! *(He follows them.)*

ACT THREE

The same. All the doors are standing open. The lamp is still burning on the table. Outside it is dark, with only a faint glow from the fire in the background, left. MRS. ALVING, *with a big shawl over her head, is standing in the conservatory, looking out.* REGINA, *also with a shawl round her, stands a little behind her.*

MRS. ALVING: All burnt. The whole thing. Burnt to the ground.

REGINA: It's still burning in the basement.

MRS. ALVING: Why doesn't Oswald come back? There's nothing to save.

REGINA: Would you like me to go down and take him his hat?

MRS. ALVING: Hasn't he even got his hat?

REGINA *(points to the hall):* No, it's hanging there.

MRS. ALVING: Let it hang. He must come up now. I'll go and look for him myself. *(Goes out through the garden door.)*

MANDERS *(enters from hall):* Isn't Mrs. Alving here?

REGINA: She's just this minute gone into the garden.

MANDERS: This is the most terrible night I have ever experienced.

REGINA: Yes, sir, isn't it a dreadful tragedy?

MANDERS: Oh, don't talk about it? I hardly dare even to think about it.

REGINA: But how can it have happened—?

MANDERS: Don't ask me, Miss Engstrand. How can I know? Are you, too, going to—? Isn't it enough that your father—?

REGINA: What's he done?

MANDERS: Oh, he's completely confused me.

ENGSTRAND *(enters from the hall):* Your Reverence—

MANDERS *(turns, alarmed):* Are you still pursuing me?

ENGSTRAND: Yes, well, God rot me if—oh, good heavens! But this is a terrible business, your Reverence.

MANDERS *(walks up and down):* It is indeed, it is indeed.

REGINA: What is?

ENGSTRAND: Well, you see, it all began with this prayer service. *(Aside.)* Now we've got him, my girl! *(Aloud.)* Fancy me being to blame for Pastor Manders being to blame for something like this.

MANDERS: But I assure you, Engstrand—

ENGSTRAND: But there was no one except your Reverence mucking around with the candles down there.

MANDERS *(stops):* Yes, so you keep on saying. But I'm sure I don't remember ever having had a candle in my hand.

ENGSTRAND: And I saw as plain as plain could be your Reverence take the candle and snuff it with your fingers and throw the wick right down among the shavings.

MANDERS: And you saw this?

ENGSTRAND: Yes, with these eyes.

MANDERS: That I cannot understand. It's not usually my habit to snuff out candles with my fingers.

ENGSTRAND: Yes, it looked a bit careless, I thought. But it can't really be as bad as you say, can it, your Reverence?

MANDERS *(paces uneasily up and down):* Oh, don't ask me.

ENGSTRAND *(walks with him):* And of course you haven't insured it, either?

MANDERS *(still walking):* No, no, no. I've told you.

ENGSTRAND *(still with him):* Not insured. And then to go

86

straight over and set fire to it all. Oh, good heavens, what a tragedy.

MANDERS (*wipes the sweat from his forehead*): Yes, Engstrand, you may well say that.

ENGSTRAND: And that such a thing should happen to a charitable institution which was to have served the city as well as the countryside. The newspapers won't be too gentle with your Reverence, I'm afraid.

MANDERS: No, that's just what I'm thinking. That's almost the worst part of it. All these hateful attacks and accusations—oh, it's frightful to think about.

MRS. ALVING (*enters from the garden*): I can't persuade him to come away from the fire.

MANDERS: Ah, it's you, Mrs. Alving.

MRS. ALVING: Well, now you won't have to make that speech after all, Pastor Manders.

MANDERS: Oh, I'd have been only too happy to—

MRS. ALVING (*in a subdued voice*): It was all for the best. Nothing good would have come of this Orphanage.

MANDERS: You think not?

MRS. ALVING: What do you think?

MANDERS: Nevertheless, it was a terrible tragedy.

MRS. ALVING: We'll discuss it simply as a business matter. Are you waiting for the Pastor, Engstrand?

ENGSTRAND (*in the doorway to the hall*): That's right, madam.

MRS. ALVING: Well, sit down, then.

ENGSTRAND: Thank you, I'm happy standing.

MRS. ALVING (*to* MANDERS): I suppose you'll be leaving with the steamer?

MANDERS: Yes. In an hour.

MRS. ALVING: Would you be kind enough to take all the papers along with you? I don't want to hear another word about this. Now I have other things to think about—

MANDERS: Mrs. Alving—

MRS. ALVING: I'll send you a power of attorney so that you can take any measures you think fit.

MANDERS: I shall be only too happy to shoulder that responsibility. I fear the original purpose of the endowment will now have to be completely changed.

MRS. ALVING: I appreciate that.

MANDERS: Yes, I'm provisionally thinking of arranging for the Solvik property to be handed over to the parish. The freehold cannot by any means be said to be without value. It can always be put to some purpose or other. And the interest from the capital in the savings bank I could perhaps most suitably employ in supporting some enterprise or other which could be said to be of benefit to the town.

MRS. ALVING: As you please. It's a matter of complete indifference to me.

ENGSTRAND: Remember my home for sailors, your Reverence.

MANDERS: Yes, indeed, you have a point there. We shall have to consider that possibility carefully.

ENGSTRAND: Consider? To hell with—oh, good heavens!

MANDERS (with a sigh): And I'm afraid I don't know how long these matters will remain in my hands. Public opinion may force me to withdraw. It all depends on the outcome of the enquiry into the cause of the fire.

MRS. ALVING: What are you saying?

MANDERS: And one cannot possibly predict the outcome.

ENGSTRAND (comes closer): Oh, yes one can. Don't I stand here, and isn't my name Jacob Engstrand?

MANDERS: Yes, yes, but—

ENGSTRAND (more quietly): And Jacob Engstrand isn't the man to fail his blessed benefactor in his time of need, as the saying goes.

MANDERS: But, my dear man, how—?

ENGSTRAND: Jacob Engstrand can be likened to an angel of deliverance, as you might say, your Reverence.

MANDERS: No, no, I really cannot accept this.

ENGSTRAND: Oh, that's the way it's going to be. I know someone who's taken the blame for another man's wickedness once before.

MANDERS: Jacob! *(Presses his hand.)* You are indeed a rare person. Well, you too shall receive a helping hand. For your seamen's home. That you can rely upon.

ENGSTRAND *wants to thank him, but is too moved to speak.*

MANDERS *(hangs his travelling bag on his shoulder):* Well, let's be off. We two shall go together.

ENGSTRAND *(at the dining-room door, says quietly to RE-GINA):* You come with me, my girl. You'll live as tight as the yolk in an egg.

REGINA *(tosses her head): Merci! (Goes into the hall and fetches MANDERS's overcoat.)*

MANDERS: Farewell, Mrs. Alving. And may the spirit of law and order soon enter into this house.

MRS. ALVING: Goodbye, Manders.

She goes towards the conservatory, as she sees OSWALD come in through the garden door.

ENGSTRAND *(while he and REGINA help MANDERS on with his overcoat):* Goodbye, my child. And if ever you find yourself in any trouble, you know where Jacob Engstrand is to be found. *(Quietly.)* Little Harbour Street—hm—! *(To MRS. ALVING and OSWALD.)* And the house for wandering sailors is going to be called Captain Alving's Home. And if I am allowed to run it according to my ideas, I think I can promise you it'll be a worthy memorial to him, God rest his soul.

MANDERS *(in the doorway):* Hm—hm! Come along, my dear Engstrand. Goodbye, goodbye.

He and ENGSTRAND *go out through the hall.*

OSWALD *(goes over towards the table):* What was that he was talking about?

MRS. ALVING: Some kind of home that he and Pastor Manders are going to found.

OSWALD: It'll burn down just like this one.

MRS. ALVING: Why do you say that?

OSWALD: Everything will burn. There will be nothing left to remind people of Father. I, too, am burning.

REGINA *starts and stares at him.*

MRS. ALVING: Oswald! You ought not to have stayed down there so long, my poor boy.

OSWALD *(sits down at the table):* I think you're right.

MRS. ALVING: Let me wipe your face, Oswald. Why, you're soaking wet. *(She dries him with her handkerchief.)*

OSWALD *(stares indifferently ahead of him):* Thank you, mother.

MRS. ALVING: Aren't you tired, Oswald? Wouldn't you like to go upstairs and sleep?

OSWALD *(frightened):* No, no, I won't sleep. I never sleep. I only pretend to. *(Heavily.)* It'll come soon enough.

MRS. ALVING *(looks worried at him):* My dear boy, you really are ill.

REGINA *(tensely):* Is Mr. Alving ill?

OSWALD *(impatiently):* And shut all the doors! Oh, this fear that haunts me—!

MRS. ALVING: Close them, Regina.

REGINA *closes the doors and remains standing by the hall door.* MRS. ALVING *takes off her shawl.* REGINA *does likewise.*

MRS. ALVING *(brings a chair over to* OSWALD's *and sits down beside him):* There, now. I'll sit beside you—

OSWALD: Yes, do. And Regina must stay here too. Regina must always be near me. You'll save me, Regina. Won't you?

REGINA: I don't understand—

MRS. ALVING: Save you—?

OSWALD: Yes. When the time comes.

MRS. ALVING: But Oswald, you have your mother.

OSWALD: You? *(Smiles.)* No, mother, you wouldn't do this for me. *(Laughs heavily.)* You? Ha, ha! *(Looks earnestly at her.)* Though really you're the one who ought to. *(Violently.)* Why don't you speak to me as though I was your friend, Regina? Why don't you call me Oswald?

REGINA *(quietly)*: I don't think Mrs. Alving would like it.

MRS. ALVING: You may do so presently. Come over and sit down here with us. (REGINA *sits quietly and diffidently on the other side of the table.*) And now, my poor, tormented boy, now I shall remove the burden from your mind—

OSWALD: You, mother?

MRS. ALVING *(continues)*: All this remorse and self-reproach you speak of—

OSWALD: You think you can do that?

MRS. ALVING: Yes, Oswald, now I can. You spoke of the joy of life; and that seemed to throw a new light over everything that has happened to me in my life.

OSWALD *(shakes his head)*: I don't understand.

MRS. ALVING: You should have known your father when he was a young lieutenant. He was full of the joy of life, Oswald.

OSWALD: Yes, I know.

MRS. ALVING: It was like a sunny morning just to see him. And the untamed power and the vitality he had!

OSWALD: Yes?

MRS. ALVING: And this happy, carefree child—for he was like a child, then—had to live here in a little town that had no joy to offer him, only diversions. He had to live here with no purpose in life; simply a position to keep up. He could find no work into which he could throw himself heart and soul—just keeping the wheels of business turning. He hadn't a single friend capable of knowing what the joy of life means; only idlers and drinking-companions—

OSWALD: Mother—!

MRS. ALVING: And in the end the inevitable happened.

OSWALD: The inevitable?

MRS. ALVING: You said yourself this evening what would happen to you if you stayed at home.

OSWALD: You mean that father—?

MRS. ALVING: Your poor father never found any outlet for the excess of vitality in him. And I didn't bring any sunshine into his home.

OSWALD: You didn't?

MRS. ALVING: They had taught me about duty and things like that, and I sat here for too long believing in them. In the end everything became a matter of duty—*my* duty, and *his* duty, and—I'm afraid I made his home intolerable for your poor father, Oswald.

OSWALD: Why did you never write and tell me about this?

MRS. ALVING: Until now I have never seen it as something that I could tell you, because you were his son.

OSWALD: And how did you see it?

MRS. ALVING *(slowly):* I saw only one thing. That your father was a depraved man before you were born.

OSWALD *(quietly):* Ah—! *(Gets up and goes over to the window.)*

MRS. ALVING: And day in and day out I dwelt on the thought, that Regina belonged here in this house—just as much as my own son.

OSWALD *(turns swiftly):* Regina—!

REGINA *(jumps up and asks softly):* I?

MRS. ALVING: Yes, now you both know.

OSWALD: Regina!

REGINA *(to herself)*: So mother was one of them.

MRS. ALVING: Your mother was in many ways a good woman, Regina.

REGINA: Yes, but still, she was one of them. Yes, I've sometimes wondered; but—! Well, madam, if you'll allow me I think I'd better leave. At once.

MRS. ALVING: Do you really want to, Regina?

REGINA: Yes, I certainly do.

MRS. ALVING: Of course you must do as you please, but—

OSWALD *(goes over to REGINA)*: Go now? But you belong here.

REGINA: *Merci*, Mr. Alving—yes, I suppose I'm allowed to say Oswald now. But it certainly isn't the way I'd hoped.

MRS. ALVING: Regina, I haven't been open with you—

REGINA: I should say not. If I'd known Oswald was that ill, I— Now that there can never be anything serious between us— No, I'm not going to stay out here in the country and wear myself out looking after invalids.

OSWALD: Not even for someone who is so close to you?

REGINA: No, thank you! A poor girl has got to make the best of her life while she's young. Otherwise she'll be left high and dry before she knows where she is. And I've got the joy of life in me too, Mrs. Alving.

MRS. ALVING: Yes, I'm afraid you have. But don't throw yourself away, Regina.

REGINA: Oh, what will be will be. If Oswald takes after his father, I shouldn't be surprised but what I'll take after my mother. May I ask, Madam, does Pastor Manders know this about me?

MRS. ALVING: Pastor Manders knows everything.

REGINA *(begins to put on her shawl)*: Well then, I'd better get down to the steamer as quick as I can. The Pastor's such a nice man to get along with. And I'm sure I've as much a right to a little of that money as he has—that awful carpenter.

MRS. ALVING: I'm sure you're very welcome to it, Regina.

REGINA *(looks spitefully at her)*: You might have brought me up like the daughter of a gentleman. It'd have been more appropriate considering. *(Tosses her head.)* Oh, what the hell does it matter? *(With a bitter glance at the bottle, still unopened.)* I can still drink champagne with gentlemen.

MRS. ALVING: And if ever you need a home, Regina, come to me.

REGINA: No thank you, Madam. Pastor Manders will take care of me. And if things don't go right, I know a house where I belong.

MRS. ALVING: Where is that?

REGINA: In Captain Alving's home for sailors.

MRS. ALVING: Regina—I can see it. You will destroy yourself.

REGINA: Oh, rubbish. *Adieu! (Curtseys and goes out through the hall.)*

OSWALD *(stands by the window, looking out)*: Has she gone?

MRS. ALVING: Yes.

OSWALD *(mumbles to himself)*: I think it was wrong, all this.

MRS. ALVING *(goes over behind him and places her hands on his shoulders)*: Oswald, my dear boy, has this news upset you very much?

OSWALD *(turns his face towards her)*: All this about father, you mean?

MRS. ALVING: Yes, about your poor father. I'm so afraid it may have been too much for you.

OSWALD: What on earth makes you think that? Of course it came as a great surprise to me. But I can't really feel it makes any difference.

MRS. ALVING *(takes her hands away)*: No difference! That your father was so miserably unhappy!

OSWALD: I feel sorry for him of course, as I would for anyone, but—

MRS. ALVING: Nothing else? For your own father!

OSWALD *(impatiently):* Oh, father, father! I never knew anything about father. I don't remember anything about him,
except that once he made me sick.

MRS. ALVING: This is terrible! Surely a child ought to love its
father whatever may happen?

OSWALD: Even when a child has nothing to thank its father
for? Has never known him? Do you really cling to that old
superstition—you, who are otherwise so enlightened?

MRS. ALVING: Do you really think it's only a superstition—?

OSWALD: Yes, mother, surely you realize that. It's one of
those truisms people hand down to their children—

MRS. ALVING *(shudders):* Ghosts!

OSWALD *(walks across the room):* Yes, that's not a bad word
for them. Ghosts.

MRS. ALVING *(emotionally):* Oswald! Then you don't love
me either!

OSWALD: At least I know you—

MRS. ALVING: Know me, yes. But is that all?

OSWALD: And of course I know how fond you are of me; and
for that I must be grateful to you. And you can do so much
for me now that I'm ill.

MRS. ALVING: Yes, Oswald, I can, can't I? Oh, I could almost bless your sickness for bringing you home to me. I
realize it now. You aren't mine. I must win you.

OSWALD *(impatiently):* Yes, yes, yes. These are just empty
phrases. You must remember I'm sick, mother. I can't be
expected to bother about others. I've enough worry thinking about myself.

MRS. ALVING *(quietly):* I shall be patient and undemanding.

OSWALD: And cheerful, mother!

MRS. ALVING: Yes, my dear boy—I know. *(Goes over to*

him.) Have I freed you from all your anxiety and self-reproach now?

OSWALD: Yes, you have. But who will take away the fear?

MRS. ALVING: The fear?

OSWALD *(walks across the room):* Regina would have done it for the asking.

MRS. ALVING: I don't understand you. What's all this about fear—and Regina?

OSWALD: Is it very late, mother?

MRS. ALVING: It's early morning. *(Looks out into the conservatory.)* The dawn's beginning to show upon the mountains. It's going to be a fine day, Oswald. In a little while you'll be able to see the sun.

OSWALD: I'll look forward to that. Oh, there's still so much for me to look forward to and live for—

MRS. ALVING: Of course there is!

OSWALD: Even if I can't work, there's—

MRS. ALVING: Oh, you'll soon be able to work again, my dear boy. You haven't all these gnawing and oppressing thoughts to brood over any longer now.

OSWALD: No, it was a good thing you managed to rid me of all those ideas. Once I've got over this one thing—! *(Sits on the sofa.)* Let's sit down and talk, mother.

MRS. ALVING: Yes, let's. *(Moves an armchair over to the sofa, and sits close to him.)*

OSWALD: And while we talk the sun will rise. And then you'll know. And then I won't have this fear any longer.

MRS. ALVING: What will I know?

OSWALD *(not listening to her):* Mother, didn't you say earlier tonight that there wasn't anything in the world you wouldn't do for me if I asked you?

MRS. ALVING: Certainly I did.

OSWALD: And you'll keep your promise, mother?

MRS. ALVING: Of course I will, my dearest, my only boy. I've nothing else to live for. Only you.

OSWALD: Yes, well, listen then. Mother, you're brave and strong, I know that. Now you must sit quite still while I tell you.

MRS. ALVING: But what is this dreadful thing you—?

OSWALD: You mustn't scream. You hear? Promise me that. We'll sit and talk about it quite calmly. Do you promise me that, mother?

MRS. ALVING: Yes, yes, I promise. Only tell me.

OSWALD: Well, then, all that business about being tired—and not being able to think about work—that isn't the real illness—

MRS. ALVING: What is the real illness?

OSWALD: The illness which is my inheritance—*(Points to his forehead and says quite quietly)* That's in here.

MRS. ALVING *(almost speechless)*: Oswald! No! No!

OSWALD: Don't scream. I can't bear it. Yes, mother, it sits in here, watching and waiting. And it may break out any time; any hour.

MRS. ALVING: Oh, how horrible—!

OSWALD: Now keep calm. That's the way it is—

MRS. ALVING *(jumps up)*: It isn't true, Oswald! It's impossible! It can't be true!

OSWALD: I had one attack down there. It soon passed. But when I found out what I had been like, this raging fear began to hunt me; and that's why I came back home to you as quickly as I could.

MRS. ALVING: So that's the fear—

OSWALD: Yes—it's so unspeakably repulsive, you see. Oh, if only it had been an ordinary illness that would have killed me—! Because I'm not so frightened of dying; though I'd like to live as long as I can.

MRS. ALVING: Yes, yes, Oswald, you must!

OSWALD: But this is so revolting. To be turned back into a slobbering baby; to have to be fed, to have to be—! Oh—! I can't think about it—!

MRS. ALVING: The child has its mother to nurse it.

OSWALD *(jumps up)*: No, never! That's just what I won't allow! I can't bear to think that I might stay like that for years, growing old and grey. And perhaps you might die and leave me. *(Sits in* MRS. ALVING*'s chair.)* It might not mean that I'd die at once, the doctor said. He called it a softening of the brain or something. *(Smiles sadly.)* I think that sounds so beautiful. I shall always think of cherry-coloured velvet curtains—something delicious to stroke.

MRS. ALVING *(screams)*: Oswald!

OSWALD *(jumps up again and walks across the room)*: And now you've taken Regina from me. If only I had her! She would have saved me. I know.

MRS. ALVING *(goes over to him)*: What do you mean by that, my beloved boy? Is there anything I wouldn't do to save you?

OSWALD: When I had recovered from the attack down there, the doctor told me that when it comes again—and it will come again—then there's no more hope.

MRS. ALVING: How could he be so heartless as to—?

OSWALD: I made him tell me. I told him I had arrangements to make. *(Smiles cunningly.)* And so I had. *(Takes a small box from his inside breast pocket.)* Mother, do you see this?

MRS. ALVING: What's that?

OSWALD: Morphine powders.

MRS. ALVING *(looks at him in horror)*: Oswald—my boy—!

OSWALD: I've managed to collect twelve capsules—

MRS. ALVING *(tries to take it)*: Give that box to me, Oswald.

OSWALD: Not yet, mother. *(Puts it back in his pocket.)*

MRS. ALVING: I can't bear this!

OSWALD: You must bear it. If Regina had been here now, I'd have told her how things were with me—and asked her to do me this last service. I'm sure she would have helped me.

MRS. ALVING: Never!

OSWALD: When the horror was on me and she saw me lying there like a new-born baby, helpless, lost—beyond all hope—

MRS. ALVING: Regina would never have done it.

OSWALD: She would have. Regina was so splendidly care-free. And she would soon have got bored with looking after an invalid like me.

MRS. ALVING: Then thank God that Regina is not here!

OSWALD: Yes, well, so now you will have to do this last service for me, mother.

MRS. ALVING (*screams aloud*): I?

OSWALD: Who else?

MRS. ALVING: I! Your mother!

OSWALD: Exactly.

MRS. ALVING: I, who gave you life!

OSWALD: I didn't ask you for life. And what kind of a life have you given me? I don't want it. Take it back.

MRS. ALVING: Help! Help! (*Runs out into the hall.*)

OSWALD (*goes after her*): Don't leave me! Where are you going?

MRS. ALVING (*in the hall*): To fetch the doctor, Oswald. Let me go!

OSWALD (*also offstage*): You're not going anywhere. And no one's coming here. (*A key is turned.*)

MRS. ALVING (*comes back*): Oswald! Oswald—my child!

OSWALD (*follows her*): If you have a mother's love for me, how can you see me suffer like this?

MRS. ALVING (*after a moment's silence, says in a controlled voice*): Very well. (*Takes his hand.*) I give you my word.

OSWALD: You promise?

MRS. ALVING: If it becomes necessary. But it won't be. No, no, it's impossible.

OSWALD: Yes, let us hope so. And let us live together as long as we can. Thank you, mother.

He sits in the armchair, which MRS. ALVING *has moved over to the sofa. The day breaks. The lamp continues to burn on the table.*

MRS. ALVING *(approaches him cautiously):* Do you feel calm now?

OSWALD: Yes.

MRS. ALVING *(leans over him):* You've just imagined these dreadful things, Oswald. You've imagined it all. All this suffering has been too much for you. But now you shall rest. At home with your own mother, my own dear, blessed boy. Point at anything you want and you shall have it, just like when you were a little child. There, there. Now the attack is over. You see how easily it passed! Oh, I knew it! And, Oswald, do you see what a beautiful day we're going to have? Bright sunshine. Now you can really see your home.

She goes over to the table and puts out the lamp. The sun rises. The glacier and the snow-capped peaks in the background glitter in the morning light.

OSWALD *(sits in the armchair facing downstage, motionless. Suddenly he says):* Mother, give me the sun.

MRS. ALVING *(by the table, starts and looks at him):* What did you say?

OSWALD *(repeats dully and tonelessly):* The sun. The sun.

MRS. ALVING *(goes over to him):* Oswald, how are you feeling?

OSWALD *seems to shrink small in his chair. All his muscles go slack. His face is expressionless. His eyes stare emptily.*

MRS. ALVING *(trembles with fear):* What's this? *(Screams loudly)* Oswald! What is it? *(Throws herself on her knees beside him and shakes him.)* Oswald! Oswald! Look at me! Don't you know me?

OSWALD *(tonelessly as before):* The sun. The sun.

MRS. ALVING *(jumps to her feet in despair, tears her hair with both hands and screams):* I can't bear this! *(Whispers as though numbed.)* I can't bear it! No! *(Suddenly.)* Where did he put them? *(Fumbles quickly across his breast.)* Here! *(Shrinks a few steps backwards and screams)* No; no; no! Yes! No; no! *(She stands a few steps away from him with her hands twisted in her hair, speechless, and stares at him in horror.)*

OSWALD *(still motionless):* The sun. The sun.

Note on the Translation

Unlike its companions among Ibsen's early prose plays, *The Pillars of Society, A Doll's House* and *An Enemy of the People,* all of which are simply and directly written, *Ghosts* is oblique, even sometimes opaque in its dialogue, most noticeably when Mrs. Alving and Manders are speaking together. Like the characters in the later plays, such as *Little Eyolf,* these two spend much of the time circling around a subject they dread referring to directly. Manders is particularly awkward to render. His verbosity and pompousness must not be exaggerated; he has not much more of either than a television cleric (or, for that matter, a television politician). It is hardly necessary to add that he should be played straight, not as a caricature; a glance through the reviews of English and American productions will show how often a 'character performance' in this role has hampered the suspension of disbelief. He should, moreover, be a handsome man; otherwise Mrs. Alving's youthful infatuation with him becomes difficult to credit.

As with the later plays, I have retained certain turns of phrase which look Victorian on the printed page but are effective in the theatre when spoken by an actor or actress in nineteenth-century costume in a nineteenth-century room.

The Norwegian title *Gengangere* corresponds closely to the French *Les Revenants.* It really means 'the ones who walk again,' and Ibsen, even with his very limited knowledge of English—he could hardly write a sentence of it without making some elementary howler—questioned the adequacy of *Ghosts* as an accurate translation of the title. But there is no better alternative, and the word has become so much a part of English and American theatrical history that it seems scarcely desirable to change it now.

My thanks are due to Mr. Casper Wrede for many invaluable criticisms and suggestions.

The Wild Duck

Introduction

On 11th January 1883 Ibsen wrote from Rome to his publisher, Frederik Hegel: 'I am already at work again planning a new play about contemporary life. It will be in four acts, and I hope to be able to get down to the actual writing within a couple of months at most. The Italian air, and the pleasant way of life down here, greatly increase my eagerness to create. I find it much easier to work here than in Germany.'

Ibsen was now fifty-four, and the reception of *Ghosts* in Scandinavia a year earlier might well have deterred a less resilient spirit than his from setting pen to paper for some while. It had been reviled, not merely by the conservative press, which he had expected, but also by the radical press; even such an old admirer as Henrik Jæger had lectured against it, and Hegel had been forced to take back large quantities of the book from booksellers who refused to stock it; indeed, it was thirteen years before the first printing of ten thousand copies was sold out. The theatres of Christiania, Copenhagen and Stockholm had been unanimous in declaring it unfit for public presentation.

So far from being silenced by this reception, however, Ibsen had reacted swiftly with the most buoyant play he had written since *Peer Gynt*. *An Enemy of the People* was immediately accepted by the Christiania Theatre, the management of which seems not to have appreciated, or to have been insensitive to, the fact that its theme was the unworthiness of 'those who do not dare' and its conclusion: 'The strongest man is he who stands most alone.' The play was in its last days of rehearsal when Ibsen wrote to Hegel with plans for its successor.

In the event, it was to be another fifteen months before he began the actual writing of *The Wild Duck,* and a further eleven weeks of intensive revision before he completed it. The slowness and difficulty with which it took shape contrasts markedly with the swiftness and ease with which he had written *An Enemy of the People. The Wild Duck* represented yet another departure into new country. Just as he had abandoned poetic drama as soon as he had mastered it in *Peer Gynt,* so now he threw aside almost contemptuously the new anti-poetic, anti-symbolic form which he had perfected in *A Doll's House, Ghosts* and *An Enemy of the People.* He explained his restlessness and passion for experiment in a letter to Georg Brandes that summer (12th June 1883):

'An intellectual pioneer,' he wrote, 'can never gather a majority about him. In ten years the majority may have reached the point where Dr. Stockmann stood when the people held their meeting. But during those ten years the Doctor has not remained stationary; he is still at least ten years ahead of the others. The majority, the masses, the mob, will never catch him up; he can never rally them behind him. I myself feel a similarly unrelenting compulsion to keep pressing forward. A crowd now stands where I stood when I wrote my earlier books. But I myself am there no longer. I am somewhere else—far ahead of them—or so I hope. At present I am struggling with the draft of a new play in four acts. As time passes, various mad ideas gather in one's head, and one must find some outlet for them. Though since it won't deal with the High Court, or the absolute veto, or even the "pure" flag,* it is hardly likely to arouse any inter-

---

*i.e. without the mark of union with Sweden.

est in Norway. However, I hope it may obtain a hearing in other quarters.'

Ibsen does not seem to have made any progress with *The Wild Duck* during the remainder of 1883, apart from a few pages of rough notes and a provisional list of characters. On 22nd January 1884 he wrote to Laura Grundtvig: 'I have been having one of those periods when I can only with the greatest reluctance sit down to my desk.' On 21st April, however, he was able to send better tidings to his publisher. 'The political complications in Norway,' he wrote to Hegel, 'have prevented me all this winter from working seriously, and with undivided attention, on my new play. But now at last I have managed to free my mind from this chaos, and am writing at full stretch. The first act will be finished this week, and I reckon that by the middle of June I should be able to let you know that the play is ready.'

He completed Act One according to schedule; his manuscript draft of this act is dated 20th–28th April 1884. On 2nd May he began Act Two; but when he was half-way through it, he stopped, and started to rewrite the play from the beginning. By 24th May he had completed Acts One and Two in their new form. Act Three occupied him from 25th–30th May; Act Four from 2nd–8th June; and Act Five from 9th–13th June. The following day, 14th June 1884, he wrote to Hegel:

'I am glad to be able to tell you that yesterday I completed the draft of my new play. It comprises five acts and will, as far as I can calculate, occupy some two hundred printed pages, possibly a little more. It still remains for me to make the fair copy and I shall start on that tomorrow. As usual, however, this will involve not just copying the draft but a comprehensive rewriting of the dialogue. So it will take time. Still, unless some unforeseen obstacle presents itself I reckon the whole manuscript should be in your hands by mid-September. The play doesn't touch on political or social problems, or indeed any matters of public import. It takes place entirely within the confines of family life. I dare say it will arouse some discussion; but it can't offend anyone.'

On 30th June, he left Rome for the little mountain resort of Gossensass in the Tyrol, which was later to prove so fateful to him. There he settled down in his usual strictly methodical manner to revise the play.

'My routine,' he wrote to his wife on 4th July 1884, 'has so far been as follows. Rise at six-thirty; breakfast brought up half an hour later; then I go out while they do the room; then write from nine to one. Then lunch, with a ravenous appetite. In the afternoons, too, I have managed to write a little, or at any rate do groundwork. The second act will be ready in five to six days. I am not drinking any beer; which suits me well. But I am drinking milk, and a little—not much—white wine, with water. A light evening meal at seven-thirty. Up to now I have been in bed each evening by ten, and have been sleeping well.'

Ibsen's wife and son were holidaying in Norway, and his fairly frequent letters to them enable us to date the progress of his revision. He finished Act Two in its final form on 12th July. Act Three took him from 14th July until either 29th or 30th July; Act Four was ready by 17th August. On 27th August he wrote to his son, Sigurd: 'My play is now fast nearing its conclusion. In three to four days it will be ready; then I shall read it through carefully and send it off. I take great joy in working on this play; it grows all the time in little details, and I shall miss it when I have to part from it; though, at the same time, I shall be glad . . . The German sculptor Professor Kopf, from Rome, has with him a thirteen-year-old daughter who is the most perfect model for my Hedvig that could be imagined; she is pretty, has a serious face and manner, and is a little greedy.' Three days later, on 30th August, he wrote to his wife: 'Although I don't know when or where my letters reach you, while you continue to move from town to town, I must nevertheless send you the good news that I have just finished my manuscript. The play will be very rich in content, and bigger than any other of my recent works. I have said everything I wanted to say; and I don't think it could easily have been said better. Now to the business of reading it through, which will take two to three days; then off it goes to Hegel.'

On 2nd September he wrote to Hegel (still from Gossensass): 'I enclose the manuscript of my new play, *The Wild Duck,* which has occupied me daily for the past four months, and from which I cannot now part without a certain feeling of loss. The characters in it have, despite their many failings, grown dear to me as a result of this long daily association. But I cherish the hope that they will also find good friends and well-wishers among the great reading public and, not least, among theatre folk; for they all, without exception, offer rewarding opportunities. But the study and representation of them will not be found easy. . . . This new play occupies, in some ways, a unique position among my dramatic works. Its method differs in certain respects from that which I have previously employed. However, I don't wish to enlarge on that subject here. The critics will, I trust, see this for themselves; at any rate, they will find something to argue about, something to construe. I believe, too, that *The Wild Duck* may possibly tempt some of our younger dramatists to explore new territories, and this I regard as a desirable thing.'

Hegel's firm, Gyldendal of Copenhagen, published *The Wild Duck* on 11th November 1884 in a printing of eight thousand copies. This sold so quickly that a new edition appeared on 1st December. The play received its premiere on 9th January 1885, at Bergen; before the month was out it had also been staged in Christiania, Helsinki and Stockholm, and the following month it was presented in Copenhagen. Germany, surprisingly, had to wait three years to see the play; its German première was on 4th March 1888 at the Residenz-theater, Berlin. Berne, Wiesbaden and Dresden saw it in 1889, and Paris in 1891, when Antoine staged it at the Théâtre Libre (the only Ibsen play, apart from *Ghosts*, which he presented there). William Archer had not yet begun his association with Janet Achurch and J. T. Grein, and it was not performed in London until 1894.

The Wild Duck greatly perplexed Norwegian readers when it first appeared. 'The public does not know what to make of it,' commented the *Christiania Intelligentssedler*. 'One paper says one thing and the other just the opposite.' *Aftenposten* complained: 'One may study and study to find what Ibsen wants to say, and not find it.' *Morgenbladet* found the plot 'as queer as it is thin. . . . The total impression can hardly be other than a strong sense of emptiness and unpleasantness.' *Bergens Tidende* thought the play proved Ibsen's inferiority to Bjœrnson. 'He does not speak from the depths of his heart as does Bjœrnson. He does not make demands of the individual with the same strength, he has no faith in his own ability to ennoble humanity by means of his writings. He states the problems excellently as he sees them, but makes no attempt to show the way beyond them: he chastises as one who has authority, but makes no demand for improvement.' The only newspaper critic in Norway who seemed to appreciate the point of the play was Irgens Hansen in *Dagbladet;* he recognized that Ibsen 'here stands on humanity's ground and speaks humanity's cause, even though it be the cause of a very shabby humanity'.

Across the North Sea, Ibsen's admirers were equally baffled. His earliest English champion, Edmund Gosse, condemned it in the *Fortnightly Review* as 'a strange, melancholy and pessimistic drama, almost without a ray of light from beginning to end . . . There is really not a character in the book that inspires confidence or liking . . .

There can be no doubt that it is by far the most difficult of Ibsen's dramas for a reader to comprehend.' Gosse himself does not seem to have comprehended it very well, for he concluded that 'the ideal spirit of goodness is the untamed bird in its close and miserable garret, captive to circumstances and with no hope of escape'. William Archer also failed to understand it at first, though he later came to admire it greatly, and named it 'Ibsen's greatest play'. Arthur Symons thought it 'a play of inferior quality', and Havelock Ellis dismissed it as 'the least remarkable of Ibsen's plays'. Almost the only critic to see the point of the play during the next ten years was Bernard Shaw, who devoted to it one of his most penetrating passages in *The Quintessence of Ibsenism*:

'After *An Enemy of the People*, Ibsen . . . left the vulgar ideals for dead and set about the exposure of those of the choicer spirits, beginning with the incorrigible idealists who had idealized his very self, and were becoming known as Ibsenites. His first move in this direction was such a tragicomic slaughtering of sham Ibsenism that his astonished victims plaintively declared that *The Wild Duck*, as the new play was called, was a satire on his former works; while the pious, whom he had disappointed so severely by his interpretation of *Brand* . . . began to hope that he was coming back repentant to the fold.'

Shaw concluded: 'The busybody [i.e. Gregers] finds that people cannot be freed from their failings from without. They must free themselves.'

The Wild Duck at first received a mixed reception on the stage. It was admired in Christiania, thanks largely to Arnoldus Reimers's rendering of Hjalmar; but it was hissed in Helsinki. In Stockholm, at that time the most theatrically enlightened of the Scandinavian capitals, it aroused deep interest, not least because the production was so daringly realistic as to include real doors with actual handles and even, which caused a great buzz, a commode in Hjalmar's studio. When it was staged in Rome in January 1892, the audience became so irritated by Gregers's behaviour that they harassed the unfortunate actor who played him with shouts of 'Basta!' and 'Imbecile!' while at the Paris première at the Théâtre Libre some of the spectators showed their displeasure by quacking like ducks. As an illustration of how little people understood the play, Francisque Sarcey, the famous critic of *Le Temps,* thought that Hedvig had shot herself out of grief because the wild duck was dead. And when the play was presented in London in 1894 by J. T. Grein, Clement Scott wrote: 'To call such an eccentricity as this a masterpiece, to classify it at all as dramatic literature, or to make a fuss about so feeble a production, is to insult dramatic literature and outrage common-sense.'

A few people, fortunately, perceived the play's qualities. William Archer, reviewing that same production which had so offended Clement Scott, admitted that the play had, in print, baffled him. 'I came to the theatre,' he declared, 'if not precisely prejudiced against the undertaking, at least with the gravest misgivings as to the probable result . . . Yet, as "the tragedy of the House of Ekdal" unfolded itself, with that smooth, unhasting, unresting movement which is Ibsen's greatest invention in the technical sphere—every word at once displaying a soul-facet and developing the dramatic situation—despite my long familiarity with the play, I felt almost as though a new planet had swum into my ken. I had been told, but had scarcely believed, that *The Wild Duck* was one of Ibsen's most effective stage-plays . . . I was utterly mistaken. The play now proved itself scenic in the highest degree . . . Hardly ever before, as it seemed to me, had I seen so much of the very quintessence of life concentrated in the brief traffic of the stage.'

When the play was revived in London three years later, Bernard Shaw wrote a famous eulogy of it in *The Saturday*

Review. 'Where,' he asked, 'shall I find an epithet magnificent enough for *The Wild Duck?* To sit there getting deeper and deeper into that Ekdal home, and getting deeper and deeper into your own life all the time, until you forget that you are in a theatre; to look on with horror and pity at a profound tragedy, shaking with laughter all the time at an irresistible comedy; to go out, not from a diversion, but from an experience deeper than real life ever brings to most men, or often brings to any man; that is what *The Wild Duck* was like last Monday at the Globe.' Subsequent generations have shared Shaw's opinion, and *The Wild Duck* now shares with *A Doll's House, Ghosts, Hedda Gabler* and *The Master Builder* the honour of being the most frequently staged of Ibsen's plays.

A rich quantity of Ibsen's draft material for the play has survived: nine sets of notes, the unfinished first draft (comprising one and a half acts) and the full second draft, which differs considerably from the final version. The first set of notes, undated but probably written in late 1882 or early 1883, contains a quantity of aphorisms, often rather vapid, but is chiefly of interest in that it shows Ibsen making his first sketches for the characters of Hjalmar and Gregers. Hjalmar seems to have been originally based on a photographer named Edvard Larsen with whom Ibsen had lodged in earlier days, and who had taken the oldest known photograph of him (in 1861–62).

'E.L. . . . is a naïve and pretentious pessimist, devoid of energy, an idle dreamer . . . [His] marriage with a simple wife has, in one way, been a "true" marriage, in that it has caused him to shrink, or at any rate stopped him developing. Now he can't manage without her; or she without him . . . He has to spend the evening with people of quality. It bores and irritates him. He longs to get back to his own narrow, homely surroundings . . . Like A. the printer [Aslaksen of

The League of Youth and *An Enemy of the People*] he has been afforded a glimpse into a higher world; that is his tragedy . . . ''The sixth sense.'' Magnetic [i.e. hypnotic] influence is E.L.'s favourite subject . . . Photographer, failed poet, dreams of a socialist revolution, the revolution of the future, of science. Poison in the breakfast . . . Is a socialist at heart but dares not admit it; he has a family, and so is not free.'

Gregers was at first based on the Norwegian novelist and playwright, Alexander Kielland (1849–1906), whose radicalism Ibsen appears to have regarded as bogus:

'A.K., the sybarite, enjoys an aesthetic indignation at poverty and misery. Enjoys his visits to his old schoolfriend who has come down in the world, without realizing why he enjoys them . . . A.K-d.: to lie tucked up in a soft bed with a well-filled belly and hear the rain pouring down and think of difficult journeys in the wet and cold, is a great pleasure.'

As Ibsen's plans developed, however, Hjalmar and Gregers became more and more different from the E.L. and A.K-d. of these first notes. The Gregers we know has little in common with the character of A.K-d. as sketched here. It is the contrast between the two characters rather than the characters themselves which has survived into the play. The rich man's son visiting his old schoolfellow who has come down in the world seems to have been the idea which first ignited Ibsen's imagination. Gregers gradually developed into a kind of *reductio ad absurdum* of Dr. Stockmann, the hero of Ibsen's preceding play—a living illustration of the danger of a single-minded pursuit of truth if not tempered by common-sense and an understanding of human limitations. Similarly, Ibsen soon found Edvard Larsen inadequate as a model for Hjalmar, and borrowed characteristics from two other Norwegians of his acquaintance, a poet named Kristofer Janson and, especially, a failed artist, Magnus Bagge, from whom Ibsen had taken drawing lessons around

116

1860. Halvdan Koht has said of Bagge that he had 'a constant longing to lift himself above everyday prose'; it was typical of him that when he went to live in Germany he called himself von Bagge. Hjalmar's mode of speech was fairly ordinary at first; it is only in the final (third) draft that it acquires its peculiarly florid quality and its excess of adjectives. He is perhaps the most difficult of all Ibsen's characters to translate, at any rate in the prose dramas.

Hedvig, in Ibsen's early notes, is described as being 'drawn to the sea'. There is a reference to 'the first time she saw a big expanse of water looking down from a height', and a note that 'Human beings are sea-creatures—like the wild duck—not land creatures. Gregers was made for the sea. In time, all people will live on it, when the land becomes swallowed up. Then family life will cease.' Ibsen discarded these ideas from *The Wild Duck,* but returned to them two plays later in *The Lady from the Sea.* Hedvig's impending blindness was an afterthought. There is no reference to it until the final draft; indeed, until that draft she is rather a commonplace child. Hjalmar's 'invention', too, which figures so largely in the play as we know it, is barely touched on in the preliminary drafts. Ibsen, in a letter to Georg Brandes (25th June 1884), described his revisionary work as 'polishing the language and giving a sharper individuality to the characters and dialogue' and, as William Archer remarked: 'Everywhere, on a close comparison of the texts, we see an intensive imagination lighting up, as it were, what was at first somewhat cold and colourless. In this case, as in many others, the draft suggests a transparency before the electricity has been switched on.'

The Wild Duck is full of echoes from Ibsen's own childhood. The family home at Venstœp had contained a library of old books left, like the ones in the Ekdals' loft, by a previous owner of the house known as 'The Flying Dutchman', a Norwegian who had been a prison convict in England and a slave in the Barbary States, and had died the year Ibsen was born. These books had included *Harrison's* (or, as Ibsen originally wrote it, *Harryson's*) *History of London* (1775), which so delighted Hedvig. Hedvig herself seems to have got her name, and probably some of her character, from Ibsen's favourite sister, Hedvig; and old Ekdal contains many traits of the playwright's father, Knud Ibsen, who had been a lieutenant in the militia and a great huntsman before he went bankrupt and brought the family name into disgrace. Ibsen also borrowed certain details from a trial which had caused a sensation during his student days in Christiania, when an army officer accused of embezzlement had tried unsuccessfully to shoot himself. (He was to return to this source for much of his material for *John Gabriel Borkman*.) And, perhaps the most significant echo from Ibsen's past, at the age of eighteen he had, like Haakon Werle, given a servant girl an illegitimate child.

Wherein does the 'method' of *The Wild Duck* differ, as Ibsen told Hegel, from that which he had previously employed? At first sight there is no immediately obvious difference; it seems, like *A Doll's House, Ghosts* and *An Enemy of the People*, to be a realistic play about realistic people, and the method seems to be his old method of raking over apparently dead ashes and exposing the live embers beneath. The symbolism? But Ibsen had used symbolism at least as freely in *Brand*.

Nevertheless, I think there is little doubt that it was the symbolism in *The Wild Duck* to which Ibsen was referring when he wrote of a new method. In *Brand* the symbols are incidental to the play, or at any rate are not fully integrated into it. The ice-church and the hawk are left deliberately imprecise; there is room for intelligent argument about their meaning; perhaps, indeed, they are intended to mean different things to different people. In *The Wild Duck*, however, there is a single and precise symbol, that of the bird itself; and, so far from being incidental to the play, it is the hub and heart of it. *Brand* is a play into which symbols have worked their way; *The Wild Duck* is a play dependent on, and held together by, a symbol; as though the wild duck were a magnet and the characters in the play so many iron filings held together by this centripetal force. This was not a method that Ibsen was to use invariably in his subsequent plays; *Rosmersholm,* for example, and *Hedda Gabler* seem to me to have more in common with *Ghosts* than with *The Wild Duck.* But we find him returning to it in the later plays; the towers and spires in *The Master Builder* and the crutch in *Little Eyolf* serve a similar structural purpose to the wild duck. They are images from which the characters cannot escape, any more than the iron filings can escape the magnet.

Ibsen probably borrowed the image of the wild duck from a poem called *The Sea Bird* by Johan Sebastian Welhaven which describes how a wild duck is wounded and dives down to die on the sea-bed; and Professor Francis Bull suggests that he may also have been influenced by Darwin's account in *The Origin of Species* of how wild ducks degenerate in captivity. Some astonishing theories have been advanced as to what the bird is intended to stand for. Surely Ibsen makes it abundantly clear that he intended it as a double symbol with two precise and obvious references. Firstly, it is, like Hedvig, a by-product of Haakon Werle's fondness for sport which has been rejected by him and is now cared for by the Ekdal family. Secondly, with a more general application, it represents the refusal of most people, once they have been wounded, to go on living and face reality. Both Hjalmar and his father have sought to hide themselves in the 'vasty deep' of illusion, and Gregers, like the 'damned clever dog' trained by his father, hauls them back to the surface. The cynics (Relling and Haakon Werle) watch this operation; so do the two sensible, earthbound women, Gina and Mrs. Sœrby. These women, Ibsen seems to imply, offer the only real refuge: love. Mrs. Sœrby can save Haakon Werle, despite Gregers's cynicism, just as she could have saved Relling, who had also once loved her; Relling knows this, and it is hinted that the loss of her is partly responsible for his having turned into a drunkard. And Gina, if Gregers had not intervened, could have saved Hjalmar. Yet Ibsen leaves a question mark here; is love simply another illusion, like the Ekdals' loft? And if so, then is not the illusion of the loft justified, just as much as the illusion of love?

At the same time, while the wild duck has these two specific significances within the play, it is possible that, consciously or unconsciously, it also reflects Ibsen's impression of himself when he wrote it; one who has forgotten what it means to live wild, and has grown plump and tame and content with his basket; as unlike the author of *Brand* as the duck is unlike the hawk of the earlier play, of which, too, the climax had been a shot fired at (or supposedly at) a bird by a girl of fourteen. How far, Ibsen must have asked himself—and he was to ask the question again, through Allmers in *Little Eyolf* and Rubek in *When We Dead Awaken*—does the artist, like the Ekdals, shut himself off from life? Is his world so very different from their loft with its imitations of reality? Which is the more cowardly refuge, the Ekdals' loft or Brand's ice-church?

Hjalmar and Gregers both represent different aspects of Ibsen; on the one hand the evader of reality, on the other the impractical idealist who pesters mankind with his 'claims of the ideal' because he has a sick conscience and despises himself. How far, one wonders, did Ibsen identify himself with Gregers in that curious episode when the latter, finding that the stove smokes, throws water on it to put out the fire and only makes the stink worse? He had already portrayed these two conflicting aspects of himself in *Brand* and *Peer*

Gynt, and the conflict between Gregers and Hjalmar is as though Brand and Peer Gynt had been brought face to face.

Two main dangers confront anyone who produces *The Wild Duck;* the temptation to play Hjalmar as ridiculous and farcical, and the temptation to play Gregers as spiteful. A perusal of the notices of London productions of the play during the past ninety years reveals how often actors and producers have fallen into these traps. Ibsen foresaw the danger of Hjalmar being made a figure of fun, and warned against it in a letter which he wrote to H. Schrœder, the manager of the Christiania Theatre, on 14th November 1884. 'Hjalmar,' he wrote, 'must not be played with any trace of parody. The actor must never for a moment show that he is conscious that there is anything funny in what he says. His voice has, as Relling observes, something endearing about it, and this quality must be clearly brought out. His sentimentality is honest, his melancholy, in its way, attractive; no hint of affectation. Between ourselves, I would suggest you cast your mind towards Kristofer Janson, who still contrives to give an effect of beauty whatever drivel he may be uttering. There is a pointer for whoever plays the part . . . Where can one find a Hedvig? I don't know. And Mrs. Sœrby? She must be beautiful and witty, *not* vulgar . . . Gregers is the most difficult part in the play, from the acting point of view. Sometimes I think Hammer would be best, sometimes Bjœrn B. . . . I hope you will spare me Isachsen, as he always carries on like some strange actor instead of like an ordinary human being. However, I suppose he might possibly make something out of Molvik's few lines. The two servants must not be cast too casually; Pettersen might possibly be played by Bucher, and Jensen by Abelsted, if the latter is not required for one of the dinner guests. Yes, those guests! What about them? You can't just use ordinary extras; they'd ruin the whole act . . . This play demands ab-

121

solute naturalness and truthfulness both in the ensemble work and in the staging. The lighting, too, is important; it is different for each act, and is calculated to establish the particular atmosphere of that act. I just wanted to pass on these random reflections. As regards everything else, please do as you think best.'

Further evidence of Ibsen's anxiety that his actors should not overstep the boundary dividing comedy from farce is given in an account by P. A. Rosenberg of a conversation which he and some acquaintances had with Ibsen in Copenhagen fourteen years later (3rd April 1898). 'Ibsen spoke also of the Royal Theatre's presentation of *The Wild Duck*, of which strangely enough he did not approve. The rest of us were unanimous in praising Bloch's masterly *mise-en-scène*, Mrs. Henning's enchanting Hedvig, Olaf Poulsen's Old Ekdal and Miss Anthonsen's incomparable Gina. But Ibsen declared it had been played too much for farce. "It must be played as tragi-comedy," he said, "otherwise Hedvig's death makes no sense."'

Gina is misinterpreted almost as frequently as Hjalmar and Gregers. She is, contrary to common supposition, neither a slut nor a whore. There is no evidence that she ever slept with anyone but Werle before her marriage, or that she allowed him to have his way with her more than once. She is a perfectly decent working-class girl who was pestered into bed by her employer. As regards her evasive answer to Hjalmar's question whether he or Werle is Hedvig's father (a question to which we, no more than she, ever know the answer; Hjalmar's mother as well as Werle had weak eyes); the implication of Gina's reply is not clear in the original, but I take it to mean that she is irregular in her periods, had missed one after yielding to old Werle, and he, fearing she might be pregnant, had hastened to match her up with Hjalmar. The child, when it appeared, could thus have belonged to either man.

122

Hedvig is usually played as a pretty girl, and there is nothing in the text that positively contradicts this; but the play is far more moving if she is plain and gawky. Then, when her father rejects her, she has nothing in life to look forward to. If she is the kind of girl whom any young man would admire, her predicament is much less distressing. Hjalmar, as Ibsen reminded Schrœder, must not appear obviously ridiculous; he is not really more self-deluding than a good many husbands. As Bernard Shaw remarked, Hjalmar should, at first, impose on us. William Archer shrewdly added that he 'should be a quite smileless personage. His melancholy is as superficial as his other emotions, but he cultivates it too sedulously to permit of his smiling. Besides, he never sees anything to smile at.'

Gregers must not be seen as a Machiavellian destroyer. He is that much more dangerous figure, a well-meaning and misguided zealot; and he needs to be, as Gina describes him, ugly. Mrs. Sœrby, as Ibsen implied in the letter quoted above, is no more a whore than Gina; she, too, is a perfectly decent woman who, given the chance, will make as excellent a wife to old Werle as Gina has been to Hjalmar. Old Ekdal should not be a nincompoop, but a fine figure of a man, a huge and impressive old soldier. We should believe him when he says he has been a famous hunter, and his reduction to a player of children's games is then much more frightening. Finally, to pick up another point in Ibsen's letter to Schrœder, the servants are, like all Ibsen's servants, sharply differentiated. Pettersen is a butler, used to and imitative of the gentry; Jensen is a hired servant, unaccustomed to waiting in so grand a house.

As a postscript, one may remark how in *The Wild Duck,* as in almost every play he wrote, Ibsen anticipated one of the main discoveries of modern psychology. 'Liberation,' he had noted in his preliminary jottings, 'consists in securing for individuals the right to free themselves, each according to his particular need.' To free *themselves;* how many of Ibsen's contemporaries who regarded themselves as revolutionaries realized that? Ibsen understood that the demand must come from within, and that truth, if it comes from without, is often regarded as an attack on the defensive system which the 'life-lie' represents.

MICHAEL MEYER

CHARACTERS

HAAKON WERLE, a wholesale merchant
GREGERS WERLE, his son
OLD EKDAL
HJALMAR EKDAL, his son, a photographer
GINA EKDAL, Hjalmar's wife
HEDVIG, their daughter, aged 14
MRS. SŒRBY, housekeeper to Haakon Werle
RELLING, a doctor
MOLVIK, sometime student of theology
GRAABERG, a clerk
PETTERSEN, servant to Haakon Werle
JENSEN, a hired waiter
A PALE, FLABBY GENTLEMAN
A BALDING GENTLEMAN
A SHORT-SIGHTED GENTLEMAN
SIX OTHER GENTLEMEN, dinner guests of Haakon Werle
SEVERAL HIRED WAITERS

The first act takes place in Haakon Werle's house, the remaining four acts in Hjalmar Ekdal's studio.

125

This translation of *The Wild Duck* was performed on 7 April 1983 at the Royal Exchange Theatre, Manchester. The cast was:

HAAKON WERLE	John Phillips
GREGERS WERLE	Ian McDiarmid
OLD EKDAL	Espen Skjønberg
HJALMAR EKDAL	Jonathan Hackett
GINA EKDAL	Stephanie Cole
HEDVIG	Sally Cookson
MRS. SŒRBY	Angela Browne
RELLING	Geoffrey Bateman
MOLVIK	Stuart Richman
PETTERSEN	David Bauckham
JENSEN	Paul Butterworth
DINNER GUESTS:	
FLABBY GENTLEMAN	Geoffrey Andrews
BALDING GENTLEMAN	Frank Crompton
SHORT-SIGHTED	
GENTLEMAN	Stuart Richman

and John Keyworth, Peter Pendlebury, Don Poole

Directed by Casper Wrede

ACT ONE

The home of HAAKON WERLE, *a wholesale merchant. A study, expensively and comfortably furnished; bookcases, upholstered furniture. A desk, with papers and ledgers on it, stands in the middle of the room. Lighted lamps with green shades throw a soft light. In the rear wall folding doors stand open; the curtains across the entrance are drawn aside, and within can be seen a large and elegant room, brilliantly lit by lamps and candelabra. Downstage left, a fireplace with coals glowing in it. Upstage of this a double door leads to the dining room.*

> WERLE'S *servant,* PETTERSEN, *in livery, and a hired waiter,* JENSEN, *in black, are arranging the study. In the larger room two or three other* HIRED WAITERS *are moving around putting things in order and lighting more lamps. From the dining room can be heard the buzz of conversation and laughter. Someone taps a knife against a glass; silence; a toast is proposed; cries of 'Bravo!'; then the buzz of conversation begins again.*

PETTERSEN *(lights a lamp on the mantelpiece above the fireplace, and puts a shade over it):* You hear that, Jensen? Now the old man's at it, proposing a toast to Mrs. Sœrby.

127

JENSEN *(moves an armchair forward):* Is it true what they say, that there's something between them?

PETTERSEN: I wouldn't know.

JENSEN: They say he's been a regular old billy-goat in his time.

PETTERSEN: Could be.

JENSEN: Did you say he's giving this party for his son?

PETTERSEN: Yes. He came home yesterday.

JENSEN: I never knew old Werle had a son.

PETTERSEN: Oh yes, he's got a son. The boy spends all his time up at the sawmill, though, out at Hoydal. He's never set foot in town all the years I've worked in this house.

A HIRED WAITER *(in the doorway to the large room):* Pettersen, there's an old fellow here who wants to—

PETTERSEN *(beneath his breath):* What the devil—? Oh, not now!

> OLD EKDAL *enters from the large room, right. He is wearing a threadbare coat with a high collar, and woollen gloves, and carries a stick and a fur hat in his hand and a brown paper parcel under his arm. He has a dirty, reddish-brown wig and small grey moustache.*

PETTERSEN *(goes towards him):* Oh, Jesus! What do *you* want here?

EKDAL *(in the doorway):* Got to get into the office, Pettersen. It's very important.

PETTERSEN: The office has been shut for an hour—

EKDAL: They told me that downstairs, my boy. But Graaberg's still in there. Be a good lad, Pettersen, and let me nip in this way. *(Points at the concealed door.)* I've been this way before.

PETTERSEN: Oh, all right. *(Opens the door.)* But make sure you leave by the proper way. We've got company.

EKDAL: Yes, I know that—hm! Thanks, Pettersen, my boy. You're a good pal.. *(Mutters quietly)* Damn fool!

He goes into the office. PETTERSEN *shuts the door after him.*

JENSEN: Does he work in the office, too?

PETTERSEN: No, he just takes stuff home to copy, when they've more than they can manage. Mind you, he's been quite a gentleman in his time, has old Ekdal.

JENSEN: Yes, he looked as if he might have been around a bit.

PETTERSEN: Oh, yes. He was a lieutenant.

JENSEN: What—him a lieutenant?

PETTERSEN: That's right. But then he went into timber or something of that sort. They say he did the dirty on old Werle once. The two of them used to work together at Hoydal. Oh, I know old Ekdal well. We often have a nip and a bottle of beer together down at Madam Eriksen's.

JENSEN: But he can't have much to spend, surely?

PETTERSEN: I'm the one who does the spending. The way I look at it is, it's only right to lend a helping hand to gentry who've come down in the world.

JENSEN: What, did he go bankrupt?

PETTERSEN: Worse. He went to prison.

JENSEN: Went to prison!

PETTERSEN: Ssh, they're getting up now.

The doors to the dining room are thrown open from inside by WAITERS. MRS. SŒRBY *comes out, engaged by* TWO GENTLEMEN *in conversation. A few moments later, the rest of the company follow,* HAAKON WERLE *among them. Last come* HJALMAR EKDAL *and* GREGERS WERLE.

MRS. SŒRBY *(as she goes through):* Pettersen, have the coffee served in the music room.

PETTERSEN: Very good, Mrs. Sœrby.

She and the TWO GENTLEMEN *go into the large room and out towards the right.* PETTERSEN *and* JENSEN *follow them.*

A PALE, FLABBY GENTLEMAN *(to one with little hair):* Whew—that dinner! Pretty exhausting work, what?

BALDING GENTLEMAN: Ah, it's remarkable what one can get through in three hours, when one puts one's mind to it.

FLABBY GENTLEMAN: Yes, but afterwards, my dear sir! Afterwards!

A THIRD GENTLEMAN: I hear the—er—mocha and maraschino are to be served in the music room.

FLABBY GENTLEMAN: Capital! Then perhaps Mrs. Sœrby will play something for us.

BALDING GENTLEMAN *(sotto voce):* Let's hope it isn't a marching song.

FLABBY GENTLEMAN: No fear of that. Berta won't give her old friends the shoulder.

They laugh and pass into the large room.

WERLE *(quietly, unhappily):* I don't think anyone noticed, Gregers.

GREGERS *(looks at him):* What?

WERLE: Didn't you notice, either?

GREGERS: Notice what?

WERLE: We were thirteen at table.

GREGERS: Thirteen? Oh, really?

WERLE *(glances at* HJALMAR EKDAL*):* We're usually twelve. *(To the others.)* Gentlemen—please!

He and the rest, except for HJALMAR *and* GREGERS, *go out upstage right.*

HJALMAR *(who has overheard their conversation):* You shouldn't have invited me, Gregers.

GREGERS: What? But this dinner is said to be in my honour. So why shouldn't I invite my one and only friend?

HJALMAR: I don't think your father approves. I mean, I never ge: ..ited to this house.

GREGERS: No, so I've heard. But I had to see you and speak with you; I'm not staying very long, you know. Yes, we've lost touch with each other since we were at school, Hjalmar. We haven't seen each other for—why, it must be sixteen or seventeen years.

HJALMAR: Is it as long as that?

GREGERS: I'm afraid so. Well, how is everything with you? You look well. You've filled out a bit; you're quite stout now.

HJALMAR: Oh—I wouldn't say stout. I dare say I'm a bit broader across the shoulders than I used to be. After all, I'm a man now.

GREGERS: Oh, yes. You're as handsome as ever.

HJALMAR *(sadly):* But within, Gregers! There has been a change there. You must know how disastrously my world has crashed around me—and my family—since we last met.

GREGERS *(more quietly):* How is your father now?

HJALMAR: My dear friend, let us not talk about it. My poor unfortunate father lives with me, of course. He has no one else in the world to lean on. But all this is so distressing for me to talk about. Tell me now, how have things been for you up at the sawmill?

GREGERS: Oh, I've been wonderfully lonely. I've had plenty of time to brood over things. Come, let's make ourselves comfortable.

He sits in an armchair by the fire and motions HJALMAR *into another beside him.*

HJALMAR *(softly):* Thank you all the same, Gregers. I'm grateful to you for inviting me to your father's house. I know now that you no longer have anything against me.

GREGERS (*amazed*): What makes you think I have anything against you?

HJALMAR: You did at first.

GREGERS: At first?

HJALMAR: After the great disaster. Oh, it was only natural that you should. It was only by a hairsbreadth that your father himself escaped being dragged into all this—this dreadful business.

GREGERS: And I should hold that against you? Who gave you this idea?

HJALMAR: I know—I know you did, Gregers. Your father himself told me so.

GREGERS: Father! I see. Hm. Was that why you never wrote me a line?

HJALMAR: Yes.

GREGERS: Not even when you went and became a photographer?

HJALMAR: Your father said there would be no purpose in my writing to you about anything whatever.

GREGERS (*thoughtfully*): No, no; perhaps he was right. But tell me, Hjalmar—are you quite satisfied the way things are now?

HJALMAR (*with a little sigh*): Oh yes, indeed I am. I can't complain. At first, you know, I found it a little strange. It was such a different way of life from what I'd been used to. But everything had changed. The great disaster that ruined my father—the disgrace and the shame, Gregers—

GREGERS (*upset*): Yes, yes, of course, yes.

HJALMAR: Naturally, I had to give up any idea of continuing with my studies. We hadn't a shilling to spare—quite the reverse in fact. Debts. Mostly to your father, I believe—

GREGERS: Hm—

HJALMAR: Well, so I thought it'd be best, you see, to make a clean break. Cut myself off from everything that had to do with my old way of life. In fact, it was your father who

132

advised me to do it—and as he was being so very helpful
to me—

GREGERS: Father?

HJALMAR: Yes, surely you must know? How else could I
have found the money to learn photography and equip a
studio and set myself up? That costs a lot of money, you
know.

GREGERS: And father paid for all this?

HJALMAR: Yes, my dear fellow, didn't you know? I understood him to say he'd written to you.

GREGERS: He never said he was behind it. He must have forgotten. We never write to each other except on business.
So it was father—

HJALMAR: Why, yes. He's never wanted people to know
about it; but it was he. And of course it was he who made
it possible for me to get married. But—perhaps you don't
know that either?

GREGERS: I had no idea. (*Shakes him by the arm.*) But my
dear Hjalmar, I can't tell you how happy I feel—and
guilty. Perhaps I've been unjust to father after all—in
some respects. This proves that he has a heart, you see. A
kind of conscience—

HJALMAR: Conscience?

GREGERS: Yes, or whatever you like to call it. No, I can't tell
you how happy I am to hear this about father. Well, and
you're married, Hjalmar! That's more than I shall ever
dare to do. Well, I trust you've found happiness in marriage.

HJALMAR: Oh, indeed I have. She's as capable and good a
wife as any man could wish for. And she's not by any
means uncultured.

GREGERS (*a little surprised*): I'm sure she isn't.

HJALMAR: Yes. Life is a great teacher. Being with me every
day—and we have a couple of very gifted friends who

visit us daily. I can assure you, you wouldn't recognize Gina.

GREGERS: Gina?

HJALMAR: Yes, my dear fellow, don't you remember? Her name's Gina.

GREGERS: Whose name is Gina? I have no idea what you're—

HJALMAR: But don't you remember? She used to work here once.

GREGERS (looks at him): You mean Gina Hansen?

HJALMAR: Of course I mean Gina Hansen.

GREGERS: Who kept house for us when my mother was ill? The year before she died?

HJALMAR: Yes, that's right. But my dear fellow, I'm absolutely certain your father wrote and told you I'd got married.

GREGERS (has got up): Yes, he told me that. But what he didn't tell me was that— (Begins to pace up and down.) Ah, but wait a minute. Perhaps he did after all, now I think about it. But father always writes such brief letters. (Half sits on the arm of his chair.) Look, tell me now, Hjalmar—this is very funny—how did you come to meet Gina—I mean, your wife?

HJALMAR: Oh, it was quite straightforward. As you know, Gina didn't stay long with your father—everything was so upside down at the time—your mother's illness—it was all too much for Gina, so she gave notice and left. It was the year before your mother died. Or was it the same year?

GREGERS: The same year. And I was up at the sawmill. But then what happened?

HJALMAR: Yes, well then Gina went home to live with her mother, a Mrs. Hansen, a very excellent hard-working woman who ran a little café. Well, she had a room to let; a very nice, comfortable room.

GREGERS: And you were lucky enough to find out about it?

HJALMAR: Yes—in fact, it was your father who suggested it. And it was there, you see, that I really got to know Gina.

GREGERS: And the engagement followed?

HJALMAR: Yes. Well, you know how quickly young people become fond of each other—hm—

GREGERS (*gets up and walks up and down for a little*): Tell me—when you were engaged—was that when father got you to—I mean, was that when you began to take up photography?

HJALMAR: Yes, that's right. I was very keen to get married as soon as possible. And your father and I both came to the conclusion that photography would be the most convenient profession for me to take up. And Gina thought so too. Oh, and there was another thing. By a lucky chance, Gina had learned how to retouch photographs.

GREGERS: What a fortunate coincidence.

HJALMAR (*pleased, gets up*): Yes, wasn't it? Amazingly lucky, don't you think?

GREGERS: I certainly do. Father seems almost to have been a kind of fairy godfather to you.

HJALMAR (*emotionally*): He did not forget his old friend's son in his time of need. He's got a heart, you see, Gregers.

MRS. SŒRBY (*enters with* HAAKON WERLE *on her arm*): Not another word, now, Mr. Werle. You mustn't walk around any longer in there with all those bright lights. It's not good for you.

WERLE (*lets go of her arm and passes his hand over his eyes*): Yes, I think you may be right.

PETTERSEN *and* JENSEN *enter with trays.*

135

MRS. SŒRBY *(to the guests in the other room)*: Gentlemen, please! If anyone wants a glass of punch, he must come in here.

FLABBY GENTLEMAN *(comes over to* MRS. SŒRBY*)*: Dammit, madam, is it true that you have deprived us of our sacred privilege, the cigar?

MRS. SŒRBY: Yes. This is Mr. Werle's sanctum, sir, and here there is no smoking.

BALDING GENTLEMAN: When did you introduce this austere edict, Mrs. Sœrby?

MRS. SŒRBY: After our last dinner, sir; when certain persons permitted themselves to overstep the mark.

BALDING GENTLEMAN: And it is not permitted to overstep the mark a little, Madame Berta? Not even an inch or two?

MRS. SŒRBY: No. Not in any direction, my dear Chamberlain.

Most of the GUESTS *have come into the study. The* SERVANTS *hand round the glasses of punch.*

HAAKON WERLE *(to* HJALMAR, *who is standing apart, by a table)*: What's that you're looking at, Ekdal?

HJALMAR: It's only an album, sir.

BALDING GENTLEMAN *(who is wandering around)*: Ah, photographs! Yes, that's rather down your street, isn't it!

FLABBY GENTLEMAN *(in an armchair)*: Haven't you brought any of your own with you?

HJALMAR: No, I haven't.

FLABBY GENTLEMAN: You should have. It's good for the digestion to sit and look at pictures.

BALDING GENTLEMAN: Adds to the fun. We've each got to contribute our mite, haven't we?

A SHORT-SIGHTED GENTLEMAN: All contributions will be gratefully received.

MRS. SŒRBY: I think the gentlemen mean that if one is invited out one should work for one's dinner, Mr. Ekdal.

FLABBY GENTLEMAN: Where the table is so exquisite, that duty becomes a pleasure.

BALDING GENTLEMAN: Yes, by God! Particularly when it's a question of fighting for survival—

MRS. SŒRBY: *Touché!*

They continue amid joking and laughter.

GREGERS *(quietly):* You must join in, Hjalmar.

HJALMAR *(twists uncomfortably):* What should I talk about?

FLABBY GENTLEMAN: Wouldn't you agree, Mr. Werle, that Tokay may be regarded as a comparatively safe drink for the stomach?

WERLE *(by the fireplace):* I'd guarantee the Tokay you drank tonight, anyway. It's an exceptional year, quite exceptional. But of course you would have noticed that.

FLABBY GENTLEMAN: Yes, it had a remarkably *soignée* bouquet.

HJALMAR *(uncertainly):* Is there some difference between the various years?

FLABBY GENTLEMAN *(laughs):* I say, that's good!

WERLE *(smiles):* It's a waste to offer you good wine.

BALDING GENTLEMAN: Tokay's like photography, Mr. Ekdal. It needs sunshine. Isn't that right?

HJALMAR: Oh yes, light is important, of course.

MRS. SŒRBY: But that's like you, gentlemen. You're drawn towards the sun, too.

BALDING GENTLEMAN: For shame! That's not worthy of you.

SHORT-SIGHTED GENTLEMAN: Mrs. Sœrby is displaying her wit.

FLABBY GENTLEMAN: At our expense. *(Threateningly.)* Oh, madame, madame!

MRS. SŒRBY: But it's perfectly true. Vintages do differ greatly. The oldest are the best.

SHORT-SIGHTED GENTLEMAN: Do you count me among the old ones?

MRS. SŒRBY: By no means.

BALDING GENTLEMAN: Indeed? And what about me, dear Mrs. Sœrby?

FLABBY GENTLEMAN: Yes, and me? What vintage are we?

MRS. SŒRBY: A sweet vintage, gentlemen!

She sips a glass of punch. The GENTLEMEN *laugh and flirt with her.*

WERLE: Mrs. Sœrby always finds a way out—when she wants to. Fill your glasses, gentlemen! Pettersen, look after them. Gregers, let us take a glass together.

GREGERS *does not move.*

WERLE: Won't you join us, Ekdal? I didn't get a chance to drink with you at dinner.

GRAABERG, *the book-keeper, looks in through the concealed door.*

GRAABERG *(to* HAAKON WERLE*):* Excuse me, sir, but I can't get out.

WERLE: What, have you got locked in again?

GRAABERG: Yes. Flakstad's gone off with the keys.

WERLE: Well, you'd better come through here, then.

GRAABERG: But there's someone else—

WERLE: Well, let him come, too. Don't be frightened.

GRAABERG *and* OLD EKDAL *come out of the office.*

WERLE *(involuntarily):* Oh God!

The laughter and chatter of the GUESTS *dies away.* HJALMAR *shrinks at the sight of his father, puts down his glass and turns away towards the fireplace.*

138

EKDAL *(does not look up, but makes little bows to either side as he walks, mumbling):* Beg pardon. Come the wrong way. Door locked. Beg pardon.

He and GRAABERG *go out upstage right.*

WERLE *(between his teeth):* Damn that Graaberg!

GREGERS *(stares open-mouthed at* HJALMAR*):* Surely that wasn't—?

FLABBY GENTLEMAN: What's all this? Who was that?

GREGERS: Oh, no one. Just the book-keeper and someone else.

SHORT-SIGHTED GENTLEMAN *(to* HJALMAR*):* Did you know that man?

HJALMAR: I don't know—I didn't notice—

FLABBY GENTLEMAN *(gets up):* What the devil's going on?

He goes over to some of the others, who are talking quietly amongst themselves.

MRS. SŒRBY *(whispers to* PETTERSEN*):* Take something out to him. Something really nice.

PETTERSEN *(nods):* Very good, ma'am.

He goes out.

GREGERS *(quietly, emotionally, to* HJALMAR*):* Then it *was* he!

HJALMAR: Yes.

GREGERS: And you stood aside and denied him!

HJALMAR *(whispers violently):* What could I do?

GREGERS: You denied your own father?

HJALMAR *(in pain):* Oh—if you were in my place—you'd—

The talk among the GUESTS, *which has been carried on in a low tone, now switches over to a forced loudness.*

BALDING GENTLEMAN *(goes amiably over to* HJALMAR *and* GREGERS*):* Hullo, reviving old college memories, what?

139

Don't you smoke, Mr. Ekdal? Want a light? Oh, I'd forgotten—we mustn't—

HJALMAR: Thank you, I won't.

FLABBY GENTLEMAN: Haven't you some nice little poem you could recite to us, Mr. Ekdal? You used to recite so beautifully.

HJALMAR: I'm afraid I can't remember one.

FLABBY GENTLEMAN: Pity. What else can we find to amuse ourselves with, Balle?

The TWO GENTLEMEN *walk into the next room.*

HJALMAR *(unhappily):* Gregers, I want to go. You know, when a man has been as buffeted and tossed by the winds of fate as I have— Say goodbye to your father for me.

GREGERS: I will. Are you going straight home?

HJALMAR: Yes. Why?

GREGERS: In that case I may drop in on you later.

HJALMAR: No, don't do that. You mustn't come to my home. It's a miserable place, Gregers; especially after a brilliant gathering like this. We can always meet somewhere in town.

MRS. SŒRBY *(has come over to them, and says quietly):* Are you leaving, Ekdal?

HJALMAR: Yes.

MRS. SŒRBY: Give my regards to Gina.

HJALMAR: Thank you.

MRS. SŒRBY: Tell her I'm coming out to see her one of these days.

HJALMAR: I will. Thank you. *(To* GREGERS.) Stay here. I don't want anyone to see me go.

He saunters into the other room and out to the right.

MRS. SŒRBY *(to* PETTERSEN, *who has returned):* Well, did you give the old man something?

PETTERSEN: Yes, I put a bottle of schnapps into his pocket.

MRS. SŒRBY: Oh, you might have found something nicer than that.

PETTERSEN: Why, no, Mrs. Sœrby. Schnapps is what he likes best.

FLABBY GENTLEMAN (*in the doorway, with a sheet of music in his hand*): Shall we play a duet together, Mrs. Sœrby?

MRS. SŒRBY: Yes, with pleasure.

GUESTS: Bravo, bravo!

> *She and all the* GUESTS *go out to the right.* GREGERS *remains standing by the fireplace.* HAAKON WERLE *starts looking for something on his desk, and seems to wish that* GREGERS *would go. Seeing that* GREGERS *does not move, he goes towards the door.*

GREGERS: Father, would you mind waiting a moment?

WERLE (*stops*): What is it?

GREGERS: I've got to speak with you.

WERLE: Can't it wait till we're alone together?

GREGERS: No, it can't. We may never be alone together.

WERLE (*comes closer*): What does that mean?

> *During the following scene, piano music can be heard distantly from the music room.*

GREGERS: How has that family been allowed to sink into this pitiable condition?

WERLE: You mean the Ekdals, I presume?

GREGERS: Yes, I mean the Ekdals. Lieutenant Ekdal and you used to be such close friends.

WERLE: Unfortunately, yes. Too close. All these years I've had to pay for it. It's him I have to thank for the stain I have suffered on my name and reputation.

GREGERS *(quietly)*: Was he really the only one who was guilty?

WERLE: Who else?

GREGERS: You and he bought those forests together.

WERLE: But it was Ekdal who drew up that misleading map. It was he who had all that timber felled illegally on government property. He was in charge of everything up there. I was absolutely in the dark as to what Lieutenant Ekdal was doing.

GREGERS: Lieutenant Ekdal seems to have been pretty much in the dark himself.

WERLE: Quite possibly. But the fact remains that he was found guilty and I was acquitted.

GREGERS: Oh, yes, I know nothing was proved against you.

WERLE: An acquittal means not guilty. Why do you rake up these old troubles, which turned me grey before my time? Is that what you've been brooding about all these years up there? I can assure you, Gregers, in this town the whole business has been forgotten long ago, as far as my reputation is concerned.

GREGERS: But what about those wretched Ekdals?

WERLE: What would you have had me do for them? When Ekdal was released he was a broken man, past help. Upon my honour, I did everything I could short of exposing myself to gossip and suspicion—

GREGERS: Suspicion? Oh, I see.

WERLE: I've arranged for Ekdal to do copying for the office, and I pay him a great deal more than the work's worth—

GREGERS *(without looking at him)*: I don't doubt it.

WERLE: You laugh? You don't think it's true? Oh, you won't find anything about it in the books. I don't keep account of that kind of payment.

GREGERS *(smiles coldly):* No, there are certain payments of which it's best to keep no account.

WERLE: What do you mean by that?

GREGERS *(screwing up his courage):* Have you any account of what it cost you to have Hjalmar Ekdal taught photography?

WERLE: Why should I have any account of that?

GREGERS: I know now that it was you who paid for it. And I also know that it was you who so generously enabled him to set himself up.

WERLE: And still you say I've done nothing for the Ekdals? I can assure you, that family's cost me a pretty penny.

GREGERS: Have you accounted any of those pennies in your books?

WERLE: Why do you ask that?

GREGERS: Oh, I have my reasons. Tell me—when you began to take such a warm interest in your old friend's son—wasn't that just about the time he was about to get married?

WERLE: Yes, how the devil—how do you expect me to remember after all these years—?

GREGERS: You wrote me a letter at the time—a business letter, of course—and in a postscript you said—quite briefly—that Hjalmar Ekdal had married a Miss Hansen.

WERLE: Yes, so he did. That was her name.

GREGERS: But what you didn't say was that Miss Hansen was Gina Hansen—our former maid.

WERLE *(laughs scornfully, but with an effort):* No. It didn't occur to me that you were particularly interested in our former maid.

GREGERS: I wasn't. But—*(Lowers his voice.)*—there was someone else in this house who was interested in her.

WERLE: What do you mean? *(Angrily.)* You're not referring to me?

GREGERS *(quietly but firmly):* Yes, I am referring to you.

WERLE: You dare to—you have the impertinence—! That ungrateful—that photographer—how dare he make such insinuations!

GREGERS: Hjalmar has never said a word about this. I don't think he suspects anything.

WERLE: Where did you get it from, then? Who has said such a thing to you?

GREGERS: My unhappy mother told me. The last time I saw her.

WERLE: Your mother! I might have known it. She and you always clung together. She turned you against me from the first.

GREGERS: No. It was all the suffering and humiliation she had to endure before she finally succumbed and came to such a pitiful end.

WERLE: Oh, she didn't have to suffer. Not more than most people, anyway. But one can't do anything with people who are over-sensitive and romantic. I've learned that much. And you nurse these suspicions and go round rooting up all kinds of old rumours and slanders about your own father! At your age, Gregers, it's time you found something more useful to do.

GREGERS: Yes, it's about time.

WERLE: It might enable you to be a little more at peace with yourself than you seem to be now. What good can it do for you to stay up at the sawmill, year after year, drudging away like a common clerk and refusing to accept a penny more than the standard wage? It's absolutely idiotic.

GREGERS: I wish I was sure of that.

WERLE: I understand how you feel. You want to be independent, you don't want to be in my debt. But now there is an opportunity for you to become independent, and be your own master in everything.

GREGERS: Oh? How?

WERLE: When I wrote and told you it was necessary for you to travel here at once—hm—

GREGERS: Yes, what do you want me for? I've been waiting all day to find out.

WERLE: I want to suggest that you become a partner in the firm.

GREGERS: I? Your partner?

WERLE: Yes. It wouldn't mean we'd have to be together all the time. You could take over the business here, and I'd move up to the mill.

GREGERS: You?

WERLE: Yes. You see, I'm not able to work as hard as I used to. I've got to take care of my eyes, Gregers. They've begun to grow a little weak.

GREGERS: They always were.

WERLE: Not like now. Besides—circumstances might make it desirable for me to live up there. For a while, anyway.

GREGERS: I hadn't imagined anything like this.

WERLE: Listen, Gregers. I know there are so many things that stand between us. But we're father and son. It seems to me we must be able to come to an understanding.

GREGERS: You mean, we must appear to come to an understanding?

WERLE: Well, that is something. Think it over, Gregers. Don't you think it might be possible? Well?

GREGERS (*looks at him coldly*): What's behind all this?

WERLE: How do you mean?

GREGERS: You want to use me, don't you?

WERLE: In a relationship as close as ours, one can always be useful to the other.

GREGERS: That's what they say.

WERLE: I should like to have you living at home with me for a while. I'm a lonely man, Gregers. I've always felt lonely, all my life, but especially now that I'm growing old. I need to have someone near me—

GREGERS: You've got Mrs. Sœrby.

WERLE: Yes, I have her. And she's become—well, almost indispensable to me. She's witty and good-humoured; she brightens the house for me. I need that—badly.

GREGERS: Well, then you have things the way you want them.

WERLE: Yes, but I'm afraid it can't continue like this. A woman in her situation may easily find herself compromised in the eyes of the world. Yes; and I dare say it's not very good for a man's reputation, either.

GREGERS: Oh, when a man gives dinners like this, he needn't worry about what people think.

WERLE: Yes, but what about her, Gregers? I'm afraid she won't want to put up with this for much longer. And even if she did—even if, for my sake, she were to set herself above the gossip and the slander— Don't you think then, Gregers—you with your stern sense of right and wrong—that—?

GREGERS (interrupts): Answer me one thing. Are you thinking of marrying her?

WERLE: Suppose I were? Would you be so insuperably opposed to that?

GREGERS: Not in the least.

WERLE: I didn't know if perhaps—out of respect to your late mother's memory—

GREGERS: I'm not a romantic.

WERLE: Well, whatever you are, you've taken a great weight from my mind. I'm delighted that I may count on your agreement to the action I propose to take.

GREGERS (looks at him): Now I see what you want to use me for.

WERLE: Use you? What kind of talk is that?

GREGERS: Oh, let's not be squeamish. Not when we're alone together. *(Gives a short laugh.)* I see. So that's why, at all costs, I had to come along and show myself here. So as to have a nice family reunion in Mrs. Sœrby's honour. Father and son—*tableau!* That's something new, isn't it?

WERLE: How dare you take that tone?

GREGERS: When has there been any family life here? Not for as long as I can remember. But now of course there's got to be a little. It'll look splendid if people can say that the son of the family has flown home on the wings of filial piety to attend his ageing father's wedding feast. What'll become then of all those dreadful rumours about the wrongs his poor dead mother had to put up with? They will vanish. Her son will dissipate them into thin air.

WERLE: Gregers—I believe there's no one in the world you hate as much as you do me.

GREGERS *(quietly):* I've seen you at close quarters.

WERLE: You have seen me with your mother's eyes. *(Lowers his voice a little.)* But you should remember that her vision was sometimes a little—blurred.

GREGERS *(trembling):* I know what you're trying to say. But who was to blame for that? You were! You and all those—! And the last of them you palmed off on to Hjalmar Ekdal, when you no longer—oh!

WERLE *(shrugs his shoulders):* Word for word as though I were listening to your mother.

GREGERS *(not heeding him):* And there he sits, childlike and trusting, caught in this web of deceit—sharing his roof with a woman like that, never suspecting that what he calls his home is built upon a lie! *(Comes a step closer.)* When I look back on your career, I see a battlefield strewn with shattered lives.

WERLE: It seems the gulf between us is too wide.

GREGERS *(bows coldly):* I agree. Therefore I take my hat and go.

WERLE: Go? Leave the house?

GREGERS: Yes. Because now at last I see my vocation.

WERLE: And what is that vocation?

GREGERS: You'd only laugh if I told you.

WERLE: A lonely man does not laugh easily, Gregers.

GREGERS *(points upstage):* Look, father. The gentlemen are playing blind man's buff with Mrs. Sœrby. Goodnight, and goodbye.

> *He goes out upstage right. Sounds of laughter and merriment are heard from the* GUESTS, *as they come into sight in the other room.*

WERLE *(mutters scornfully after* GREGERS*):* Hm! Poor wretch! And he says he's not a romantic!

ACT TWO

HJALMAR EKDAL's *studio. It is quite a large room, and is evidently an attic. To the right is a sloping ceiling containing large panes of glass, which are half-covered by a blue curtain. In the corner upstage right is the front door. Downstage of this a door to the living room. In the left-hand wall are two more doors, with an iron stove between them. In the rear wall are broad double sliding doors. The studio is humbly but comfortably furnished. Between the doors on the right, a little away from the wall, stands a sofa, with a table and some chairs. On the table is a lighted lamp, with a shade. In the corner by the stove is an old armchair. Here and there, various pieces of photographic apparatus are set up. Against the rear wall, to the left of the sliding doors, is a bookcase, containing some books, boxes, bottles containing chemicals, various tools, instruments and other objects. Photographs and small articles such as brushes, sheets of paper and so forth, lie on the table.*

> GINA EKDAL *is seated on a chair at the table, sewing.* HEDVIG *is seated on the sofa with her hands shading her eyes and her thumbs in her ears, reading a book.*

GINA *(glances at her a couple of times, as though with secret anxiety):* Hedvig!

149

HEDVIG *does not hear.* GINA *repeats more loudly.*

GINA: Hedvig!

HEDVIG *(drops her hands and looks up):* Yes, mother?

GINA: Hedvig darling, don't read any more.

HEDVIG: Oh, but mother, can't I go on a little longer? Just a little?

GINA: No, no; put the book away. Your father doesn't like it. He never reads in the evenings.

HEDVIG *(closes the book):* No, father doesn't bother much about reading, does he?

GINA *(puts down her sewing and picks up a pencil and a small notebook from the table):* Can you remember how much we paid for that butter?

HEDVIG: One and sixpence.

GINA: That's right. *(Makes a note of it.)* It's shocking how much butter gets eaten in this house. Then there was the sausages, and the cheese—let me see— *(Writes.)* And the ham—hm— *(Adds it up.)* Mm, that makes nearly—

HEDVIG: Don't forget the beer.

GINA: Oh yes, of course. *(Writes.)* It mounts up. But we've got to have it.

HEDVIG: But you and I didn't have to have a proper meal this evening, as father was out.

GINA: Yes; that helped. Oh, and I got eight shillings for those photographs.

HEDVIG: I say! As much as that?

GINA: Eight shillings!

Silence. GINA *takes up her sewing again.* HEDVIG *picks up a pencil and paper and starts to draw, her left hand shading her eyes.*

HEDVIG: Isn't it lovely to think of father being invited by Mr. Werle to that big dinner?

GINA: He wasn't invited by Mr. Werle. It was his son who

sent the invitation. *(Short pause.)* You know we've nothing to do with Mr. Werle.

HEDVIG: I'm so looking forward to father coming home. He promised he'd ask Mrs. Sœrby for something nice to bring me.

GINA: Yes, there's never any shortage of nice things in that house.

HEDVIG *(still drawing):* I think I'm beginning to get a bit hungry.

OLD EKDAL, *his package of papers under his arm and another parcel in his coat pocket, comes in through the front door.*

GINA: Hullo, grandfather, you're very late tonight.

EKDAL: They'd shut the office. Graaberg kept me waiting. I had to go through the—hm.

HEDVIG: Did they give you anything new to copy, grandfather?

EKDAL: All this. Look!

GINA: Well, that's good.

HEDVIG: And you've another parcel in your pocket.

EKDAL: Have I? Oh, nonsense—that's nothing.

Puts down his stick in a corner.

EKDAL: This'll keep me busy for a long time, this will, Gina.

Slides one of the doors in the rear wall a little to one side.

EKDAL: Ssh!

Looks inside for a moment, then closes the door again carefully.

EKDAL: He, he! They're all asleep. And she's lain down in her basket. He, he!

HEDVIG: Are you sure she won't be cold in that basket, grandfather?

EKDAL: What an idea! Cold? With all that straw? *(Goes towards the door upstage left.)* Are there any matches?

GINA: They're on the chest of drawers.

EKDAL *goes into his room.*

HEDVIG: Isn't it splendid grandfather getting all that stuff to copy again, after so long?

GINA: Yes, poor old father. It'll mean a bit of pocket money for him.

HEDVIG: And he won't be able to spend all morning down at that horrid Mrs. Eriksen's restaurant, will he?

GINA: Yes, there's that too.

Short silence.

HEDVIG: Do you think they're still sitting at table?

GINA: God knows. It wouldn't surprise me.

HEDVIG: Think of all that lovely food father's getting to eat! I'm sure he'll be in a good humour when he comes back. Don't you think, mother?

GINA: Oh, yes. But if only we were able to tell him we'd managed to let that room.

HEDVIG: But we don't have to worry about *that* tonight.

GINA: It wouldn't do any harm. It's no use to us standing empty.

HEDVIG: No, I mean we don't have to worry about it because tonight father'll be jolly anyway. It'll be better if we can save the news about the room for another time.

GINA *(glances across at her):* Does it make you happy to have good news to tell father when he comes home in the evening?

HEDVIG: Yes, it makes things more cheerful here.

GINA: Yes, there's something in that.

152

OLD EKDAL *comes in again and goes towards the door downstage left.*

GINA *(half turns in her chair):* Do you want something out of the kitchen, grandfather?

EKDAL: Er—yes, yes. Don't get up.

He goes out.

GINA: He's not messing about with the fire, is he? *(Waits a moment.)* Hedvig, go and see what he's up to.

EKDAL *returns with a little jug of steaming water.*

HEDVIG: Are you getting some hot water, grandfather?

EKDAL: Yes, I am. Need it for something. Got some writing to do; and the ink's like porridge—hm!

GINA: But grandfather, you should eat your supper first. I've put it in there for you.

EKDAL: Can't be bothered with supper, Gina. I'm busy, I tell you. I don't want anyone to disturb me. Not anyone—hm!

He goes into his room. GINA *and* HEDVIG *look at each other.*

GINA *(quietly):* Where do you think he's got the money from?

HEDVIG: From Graaberg, I suppose.

GINA: No, he can't have. Graaberg always sends the money to me.

HEDVIG: He must have got a bottle on tick somewhere, then.

GINA: Poor grandfather! No one'll give him anything on credit.

HJALMAR EKDAL, *wearing an overcoat and a grey felt hat, enters right.*

GINA (*drops her sewing and gets up*): Why, Hjalmar, are you here already?

HEDVIG (*simultaneously, jumping to her feet*): Oh, father, fancy your coming back so soon!

HJALMAR (*takes off his hat*): Yes, well, most of them had begun to leave.

HEDVIG: As early as this?

HJALMAR: Yes. It was a dinner party, you know. (*Begins to take off his overcoat.*)

GINA: Let me help you.

HEDVIG: Me too.

They take off his coat. GINA *hangs it up on the rear wall.*

HEDVIG: Were there many people there, father?

HJALMAR: Oh no, not many. We were, oh, twelve or fourteen at table.

GINA: And you talked to them all?

HJALMAR: Oh yes, a little. But Gregers monopolized me most of the time.

GINA: Is he still as ugly as ever?

HJALMAR: Well, he's not very much to look at. Hasn't the old man come home?

HEDVIG: Yes, grandfather's in his room, writing.

HJALMAR: Did he say anything?

GINA: No, what should he say?

HJALMAR: Didn't he mention anything about—? I thought I heard someone say he'd been up to see Graaberg. I'll go in and have a word with him.

GINA: No, no—don't.

HJALMAR: Why not? Did he say he didn't want to see me?

GINA: I don't think he wants to see anyone this evening.

HEDVIG *makes signs to* HJALMAR. GINA *does not notice.*

GINA: He's been out and fetched some hot water.

HJALMAR: Oh. He's—?

GINA: Yes.

HJALMAR: Dear God! Poor old father! Bless his white hairs! Let him have his little pleasure.

OLD EKDAL, *wearing a dressing-gown and smoking a pipe, enters from his room.*

EKDAL: So you're home? I thought I heard your voice.

HJALMAR: Yes, I've just got back.

EKDAL: You didn't see me, did you?

HJALMAR: No. But they said you'd been through, and so I thought I'd follow you.

EKDAL: Hm. Decent of you, Hjalmar. Who were all those people?

HJALMAR: Oh, all sorts. There was Mr. Flor—the Chamberlain—and Mr. Balle—he's one, too—and so's Mr. Kaspersen—and Mr.—what's his name, I don't remember what they were all called—

EKDAL (*nods*): You hear that, Gina? People from the palace—and Hjalmar!

GINA: Yes, they're very grand up there nowadays.

HEDVIG: Did the Chamberlains sing, father? Or recite anything?

HJALMAR: No, they just chattered. They tried to get me to recite something. But I said, 'No.'

EKDAL: You said 'No', did you?

GINA: Oh, you might have obliged them.

HJALMAR: No. One can't go round pandering to everyone. (*Begins to walk up and down the room.*) I won't, anyway.

EKDAL: No, no. You won't get round Hjalmar as easily as that.

HJALMAR: I don't see why *I* should have to provide the entertainment on the few occasions when I go out to enjoy myself. Let the others do some work for a change. Those fellows go from one dinner table to the next stuffing themselves every night. Let them work for their food and drink.

GINA: You didn't say all this?

HJALMAR (*hums to himself*): I gave them a piece of my mind.

EKDAL: You said this to their faces?

HJALMAR: Could be. (*Nonchalantly.*) Afterwards we had a little altercation about Tokay.

EKDAL: Tokay, did you say? That's a fine wine.

HJALMAR (*stops walking*): It *can* be a fine wine. But, let me tell you, all vintages are not equally fine. It depends on how much sunshine the grapes have had.

GINA: Oh, Hjalmar! You know about everything!

EKDAL: And they tried to argue about that?

HJALMAR: They tried. But they soon learned that it's the same as with Chamberlains. All vintages are not equally fine.

GINA: The things you think of!

EKDAL (*chuckles*): He he! And they had to put that in their pipes and smoke it?

HJALMAR: Yes. It was said straight to their faces.

EKDAL: You hear that, Gina? He said it straight to the Chamberlains' faces.

GINA: Just fancy! Straight to their faces!

HJALMAR: Yes, but I don't want it talked about. One doesn't repeat such things. It was all very friendly, of course. They're decent friendly people. Why should I hurt them?

EKDAL: But straight to their faces!

HEDVIG (*trying to please him*): What fun it is to see you in tails! You look splendid in tails, father!

HJALMAR: Yes, I do, don't I? And it fits me perfectly; almost as thought it had been made for me. Just a little tight under the arms, perhaps. Give me a hand, Hedvig. (*Takes them off.*) I think I'll put my jacket on. Where's my jacket, Gina?

GINA: Here it is.

She brings the jacket and helps him on with it.

HJALMAR: That's better! Don't forget to let Molvik have the tails back tomorrow morning.

GINA *(puts them away)*: I'll see he gets them.

HJALMAR *(stretches)*: Ah, now I feel more at home. Loose-fitting clothes suit my figure better. Don't you think, Hedvig?

HEDVIG: Yes, father.

HJALMAR: When I loosen my tie so that the ends flow like this—look! What do you think of that?

HEDVIG: Oh, yes, that looks very good with your moustache and those big curls of yours.

HJALMAR: I wouldn't call them curls. Waves.

HEDVIG: Yes, they're such big curls.

HJALMAR: They are waves.

HEDVIG *(after a moment, tugs his jacket)*: Father!

HJALMAR: Well, what is it?

HEDVIG: Oh, you know quite well what it is.

HJALMAR: No, I don't. Really.

HEDVIG *(laughs and whimpers)*: Oh, yes, you do, father. You mustn't tease me!

HJALMAR: But what *is* it?

HEDVIG: Oh, stop it! Give it to me, father! You know! All those nice things you promised me!

HJALMAR: Oh, dear! Fancy my forgetting that!

HEDVIG: Oh, no, you're only teasing, father! Oh, it's beastly of you! Where have you hidden it?

HJALMAR: No, honestly, I forgot. But wait a moment! I've something else for you, Hedvig.

He goes over to the tails and searches in the pockets.

HEDVIG *(jumps up and claps her hands)*: Oh, mother, mother!

GINA: There, you see. Just be patient, and—

HJALMAR *(holds out a card)*: Look, here it is.

HEDVIG: That? That's only a piece of paper.

HJALMAR: It's the menu, Hedvig. The whole menu. Look here. It says *Déjeuner*. That means menu.

HEDVIG: Is that all?

HJALMAR: Well, I forgot the other things. But believe me, Hedvig, they're not much fun really, all those sickly sweet things. Sit over there at the table and read this menu, and then I'll describe to you how each dish tasted. Here you are, now, Hedvig.

HEDVIG *(swallows her tears)*: Thank you.

> *She sits down but does not read.* GINA *makes a sign to her.* HJALMAR *notices.*

HJALMAR *(starts walking up and down)*: Really, it's incredible the things a breadwinner's expected to remember. If one forgets the slightest little thing, there are sour faces all round one. Well, one gets used to it. *(Stops by the stove, where* OLD EKDAL *is sitting.)* Have you looked in there this evening, father?

EKDAL: Yes, of course I have. She's gone into the basket.

HJALMAR: Gone into the basket, has she? She's beginning to get used to it, then.

EKDAL: What did I tell you? Well, now, you see, there are one or two little—

HJALMAR: Little improvements, yes.

EKDAL: We've got to have them, Hjalmar.

HJALMAR: Yes. Let's have a word about these improvements, father. Come along, let's sit on the sofa.

EKDAL: Yes, let's. Er—I think I'll fill my pipe first. Oh, I'd better clean it too. Hm.

> *He goes into his room.*

GINA *(smiles at* HJALMAR*)*: Clean his pipe!

HJALMAR: Oh, Gina, let him. Poor, shipwrecked old man! Yes, those improvements—I'd better get them done tomorrow.

GINA: But you won't have time tomorrow, Hjalmar.

HEDVIG *(interrupts):* Oh, yes he will, mother!

GINA: Don't forget those prints have to be re-touched. They've sent for them so many times.

HJALMAR: Oh, are you on about those prints again? They'll be ready. Have there been any new orders at all?

GINA: No, I'm afraid not. I've nothing tomorrow but those two portraits I told you about.

HJALMAR: Is that all? Well, if one doesn't put one's mind to it—

GINA: But what can I do? I advertise as much as I can—

HJALMAR: Advertise, advertise! You see what good that does. I don't suppose anyone's come to look at the room either?

GINA: No, not yet.

HJALMAR: I might have known it. If one doesn't bother to keep one's eyes and ears open— One must try to make an effort, Gina.

HEDVIG *(goes towards him):* Can I bring your flute, father?

HJALMAR: No. No flute. *I* don't need the pleasures of this world. *(Starts walking again.)* Yes, I'm going to work tomorrow. Don't you worry about that. I'll work as long as there's strength in these arms—

GINA: But my dear Hjalmar, I didn't mean it like that.

HEDVIG: Father, would you like a bottle of beer?

HJALMAR: Certainly not. I want nothing of anyone. *(Stops.)* Beer? Did you say beer?

HEDVIG *(alive):* Yes, father. Lovely, cool beer.

HJALMAR: Well—if you want to, bring in a bottle.

GINA: Yes, do. That's a nice idea.

HEDVIG *runs towards the kitchen door.*

HJALMAR *(by the stove, stops her, looks at her, takes her head in his hands and presses her to him):* Hedvig! Hedvig!

HEDVIG *(happy, crying):* Oh, dear, kind father!

HJALMAR: No, don't call me that. I have been eating at the rich man's table. Gorging my belly at the groaning board. And yet I could—

GINA *(sitting at the table):* Oh, nonsense, nonsense, Hjalmar.

HJALMAR: It's true. But you mustn't judge me too harshly. You know I love you both. In spite of everything—

HEDVIG *(throws her arms round him):* And we love you very, very much, father.

HJALMAR: And if I should, once in a while, be unreasonable—dear God!—remember that I am a man besieged by a host of sorrows. Oh, well. *(Dries her eyes.)* This is not the moment for beer. Give me my flute.

HEDVIG *runs to the bookcase and fetches it.*

HJALMAR: Thank you. Ah, this is better. With my flute in my hand, and you two by my side—ah!

HEDVIG *sits at the table by* GINA. HJALMAR *walks up and down, then begins to play a Bohemian folk dance, with spirit, in a slow and mournful tempo, and sensitively.*

HJALMAR *(stops playing, stretches out his left hand to* GINA *and says emotionally):* Life may be poor and humble under our roof. But it is home. And I tell you, Gina—it is good to be here.

He begins to play again. After a few moments, there is a knock on the front door.

GINA *(gets up):* Hush, Hjalmar. I think there's someone at the door.

HJALMAR *(puts the flute away in the bookcase):* Oh, here we go again.

GREGERS WERLE *(outside on the landing):* Excuse me, but—

GINA *(starts back slightly):* Oh!

GREGERS: Doesn't Mr. Ekdal live here? The photographer.

GINA: Yes, he does.

HJALMAR *(goes over to the door):* Gregers! Are you here? Well, you'd better come in.

GREGERS *(enters):* But I told you I'd visit you.

HJALMAR: But—tonight? Have you left the party?

GREGERS: Yes. I have left the party. And my home, too. Good evening, Mrs. Ekdal. I don't suppose you recognize me?

GINA: Why, yes, Mr. Gregers. I recognize you.

GREGERS: Yes. I'm like my mother. And I've no doubt you remember her.

HJALMAR: Did you say you had left your father's house?

GREGERS: Yes. I've moved to a hotel.

HJALMAR: Oh, I see. Well, since you've come, take off your coat and sit down.

GREGERS: Thank you.

He takes off his coat. He has changed into a simple grey suit of a provincial cut.

HJALMAR: Here, on the sofa. Make yourself comfortable.

GREGERS *sits on the sofa,* HJALMAR *on a chair by the table.*

GREGERS *(looks round):* So this is it, Hjalmar. This is where you live.

HJALMAR: This room is my studio, as you see.

GINA: We usually sit here, because there's more space.

HJALMAR: We had a nicer place before, but this apartment has one great advantage. The bedrooms—

GINA: And we've a spare room on the other side of the passage that we can let.

GREGERS *(to* HJALMAR*)*: Oh, I see. You take lodgers as well?

HJALMAR: No, not yet. It takes time, you know. One's got to keep one's eyes and ears open. *(To* HEDVIG.*)* Let's have that beer now.

> HEDVIG *nods and goes out into the kitchen.*

GREGERS: So that's your daughter?

HJALMAR: Yes, that is Hedvig.

GREGERS: Your only child?

HJALMAR: Yes, she is the only one. Our greatest joy. *(Drops his voice.)* And also our greatest sorrow, Gregers.

GREGERS: What do you mean?

HJALMAR: There is a grave risk that she may lose her eyesight.

GREGERS: Go blind?

HJALMAR: Yes. As yet there are only the first symptoms, and she may be all right for some while. But the doctor has warned us. It will happen in the end.

GREGERS: What a terrible tragedy. What's the cause?

HJALMAR *(sighs)*: It's probably hereditary.

GREGERS *(starts)*: Hereditary?

GINA: Hjalmar's mother had weak eyes, too.

HJALMAR: So my father says. Of course, I can't remember.

GREGERS: Poor child. And how does she take it?

HJALMAR: Oh, you don't imagine we have the heart to tell her? She suspects nothing. Carefree and gay, singing like a little bird, she will fly into the night. *(Overcome.)* Oh, it will be the death of me, Gregers.

> HEDVIG *brings a tray with beer and glasses, and sets it on the table.*

HJALMAR *(strokes her head)*: Thank you, Hedvig.

She puts her arm round his neck and whispers in his ear.

HJALMAR: No, no sandwiches now. *(Glances at* GREGERS.*)* Unless you'd like some, Gregers?

GREGERS: No, no thank you.

HJALMAR *(still melancholy):* Well, you might bring a few in, anyway. A crust will be enough for me. But plenty of butter on it, mind.

HEDVIG *nods happily and goes back into the kitchen.*

GREGERS *(follows her with his eyes):* She looks quite strong and healthy, apart from that, I think.

GINA: Yes, there's nothing else the matter with her, thank God.

GREGERS: She's going to look very like you, Mrs. Ekdal. How old would she be now?

GINA: Almost exactly fourteen. It's her birthday the day after tomorrow.

GREGERS: Quite big for her age.

GINA: Yes, she's certainly shot up this last year.

GREGERS: Seeing how these young people grow up makes one realize how old one's getting oneself. How long have you two been married now?

GINA: We've been married—er—yes, nearly fifteen years.

GREGERS: Good Lord, is it as long as that?

GINA *(suddenly alert; looks at him):* Yes, that's right.

HJALMAR: It certainly is. Fifteen years, all but a few months. *(Changes his tone.)* They must have seemed long to you, those years up at the mill, Gregers.

GREGERS: They seemed long at the time. Looking back on them, I hardly know where they went.

OLD EKDAL *enters from his room, without his pipe but wearing his old army helmet. He walks a little unsteadily.*

EKDAL: Well, Hjalmar, now we can sit down and talk about that—er— What was it we were going to talk about?

HJALMAR *(goes over to him):* Father, we have a guest. Gregers Werle. I don't know if you remember him.

EKDAL *(looks at* GREGERS, *who has got up):* Werle? The son? What does he want with me?

HJALMAR: Nothing. He's come to see me.

EKDAL: Oh. Nothing's wrong then?

HJALMAR: No, of course not. Nothing at all.

EKDAL *(waves an arm):* Mind you, I'm not afraid. It's just that—

GREGERS *(goes over to him):* I only wanted to bring you a greeting from your old hunting grounds, Lieutenant Ekdal.

EKDAL: Hunting grounds?

GREGERS: Yes—up around Hoydal.

EKDAL: Oh, up there. Yes, I used to know that part well, in the old days.

GREGERS: You were a famous hunter then.

EKDAL: Oh, well. Maybe I was. I won't deny it. You're looking at my uniform. I don't ask anyone's permission to wear it in here. As long as I don't go out into the street in it—

HEDVIG *brings a plate of sandwiches and puts it on the table.*

HJALMAR: Sit down now, father, and have a glass of beer. Gregers, please.

EKDAL *mumbles to himself and stumbles over to the sofa.* GREGERS *sits in the chair nearest to him,* HJALMAR *on the other side of* GREGERS. GINA *sits a little away from the table, sewing.* HEDVIG *stands beside her father.*

GREGERS: Do you remember, Lieutenant Ekdal, how Hjalmar and I used to come up and visit you during the summer, and at Christmas?

EKDAL: Did you? No, no, no, I don't remember it. But though I say it myself, I was a first rate shot. I've killed bears too, you know. Nine of them.

GREGERS *(looks at him sympathetically):* And now your hunting days are over?

EKDAL: Oh, I wouldn't say that, my boy. Do a bit of hunting now and again. Not quite the way I used to. You see, the forest—the forest, you see, the forest— *(Drinks.)* How does the forest look up there now? Still good, eh?

GREGERS: Not as good as in your day. It's been thinned out a lot.

EKDAL: Thinned out? Chopped down? *(More quietly, as though in fear.)* That's dangerous. Bad things'll come of that. The forest'll have its revenge.

HJALMAR *(fills his glass):* Have a little more, father.

GREGERS: How can a man like you, a man who loves the open air as you do, bear to live in the middle of a stuffy town, boxed between four walls?

EKDAL *(gives a short laugh and glances at HJALMAR):* Oh, it's not too bad here. Not bad at all.

GREGERS: But what about the cool, sweeping breezes, the free life in the forest, and up on the wide, open spaces among animals and birds? These things which had become part of you?

EKDAL *(smiles):* Hjalmar, shall we show it to him?

HJALMAR *(quickly, a little embarrassed):* Oh, no, father, no. Not tonight.

GREGERS: What does he want to show me?

HJALMAR: Oh, it's only something that— You can see it another time.

GREGERS *(continues speaking to EKDAL):* What I was going to suggest, Lieutenant Ekdal, was that you should come with me back to the mill. I shall be returning there soon.

I'm sure we could find you some copying to do up there too. And there's nothing here to keep you cheerful and interested.

EKDAL (*stares at him, amazed*): Nothing here—?

GREGERS: Of course you have Hjalmar; but then he has his own family. And a man like you, who has always been drawn to a life that is wild and free—

EKDAL (*strikes the table*): Hjalmar, he *shall* see it!

HJALMAR: But father, what's the point of showing it to him now? It's dark.

EKDAL: Nonsense, there's the moonlight. (*Gets up.*) He shall see it, I tell you! Let me come through. Come and help me, Hjalmar.

HEDVIG: Oh, yes, do, father!

HJALMAR (*gets up*): Oh, very well.

GREGERS (*to* GINA): What are they talking about?

GINA: Oh, don't take any notice. It's nothing very much.

> EKDAL *and* HJALMAR *go to the rear wall, and each of them pushes back one of the sliding doors.* HEDVIG *helps the old man.* GREGERS *remains standing by the sofa.* GINA *continues calmly with her sewing. Through the open doors can be seen a long and irregularly-shaped loft, full of dark nooks and crannies, and with a couple of brick chimney-pipes coming through the floor. Through small skylights bright moonlight shines on to various parts of the loft, while the rest lies in shadow.*

EKDAL (*to* GREGERS): You can come right in if you like.

GREGERS (*goes over to them*): What is it, exactly?

EKDAL: Have a look. Hm!

HJALMAR (*somewhat embarrassed*): This belongs to my father, you understand.

GREGERS (*in the doorway, peers into the loft*): Why, you keep chickens, Lieutenant Ekdal.

EKDAL: I should think we do keep chickens! They've gone to roost now. But you should just see them by daylight!

HEDVIG: And then there's the—!

EKDAL: Ssh! Don't say anything yet.

GREGERS: And you've pigeons too, I see.

EKDAL: Why, yes! Of course we've pigeons. They've got their roosting-boxes up there under the roof. Pigeons like to nest high, you know.

HJALMAR: They're not all ordinary pigeons.

EKDAL: Ordinary! No, I should say not! We've tumblers. And a pair of pouters, too. But come over here! Do you see that hutch over there against the wall?

GREGERS: Yes. What do you use that for?

EKDAL: The rabbits go there at night.

GREGERS: Oh, you have rabbits, too?

EKDAL: You're damn right we've got rabbits. You hear that, Hjalmar? He asks if we've got rabbits! Hm! But now I'll show you! This is really something. Move over, Hedvig. Stand here. That's right. Now look down there. Can you see a basket with straw in it?

GREGERS: Yes. And there's a bird lying in the straw.

EKDAL: Hm! A bird!

GREGERS: Isn't it a duck?

EKDAL *(hurt):* Of course it's a duck.

HJALMAR: Ah, but what *kind* of duck?

HEDVIG: It's not an ordinary duck—

EKDAL: Ssh!

GREGERS: It's not one of those Muscovy ducks, is it?

EKDAL: No, Mr. Werle, it's not a Muscovy duck. It's a wild duck.

GREGERS: Oh, is it really? A wild duck?

EKDAL: Yes, that's what it is. That 'bird', as you called it— that's a wild duck, that is. That's our wild duck, my boy.

HEDVIG: My wild duck. I own it.

GREGERS: But can it live up here in this loft? Is it happy here?

EKDAL: Well, naturally she has a trough of water to splash about in.

HJALMAR: Fresh water every other day.

GINA (turns toward HJALMAR): Hjalmar dear, it's getting icy cold in here.

EKDAL: Mm. Well, let's shut up, then. It's best not to disturb them when they're sleeping, anyway. Give me a hand, Hedvig.

HJALMAR and HEDVIG slide the doors together.

EKDAL: Some other time you must have a proper look at her. (Sits in the armchair by the stove.) Ah, they're strange creatures, you know, these wild ducks.

GREGERS: But how did you manage to catch her, Lieutenant Ekdal?

EKDAL: I didn't catch her. There's a certain gentleman in this town whom we have to thank for that.

GREGERS (starts slightly): You don't mean my father, surely?

EKDAL: Indeed I do. Your father. Hm!

HJALMAR: How odd that you should guess that, Gregers.

GREGERS: You told me earlier that you were indebted to my father for so many things, so I thought perhaps—

GINA: Oh, we didn't get her from Mr. Werle himself—

EKDAL: All the same, it's Haakon Werle we have to thank for her, Gina. (To GREGERS.) He was out in his boat, you see, and he shot her. But his eyesight isn't very good. Hm! So he only winged her.

GREGERS: Oh, I see. She got a couple of pellets in her.

HJALMAR: Yes, two or three.

HEDVIG: She got them under her wing, so that she couldn't fly.

GREGERS: Oh, and so she dived to the bottom, I suppose?

EKDAL (sleepily, in a thick voice): Of course. Wild ducks always do that. Dive down to the bottom, as deep as they can go, and hold on with their beaks to the seaweed or whatever they can find down there. And they never come up again.

GREGERS: But your wild duck did come up again, Lieutenant Ekdal.

EKDAL: He had such a damned clever dog, your father. And that dog—he dived down after the duck, and brought her to the surface.

GREGERS *(turns to* HJALMAR*):* And then you took her in here?

HJALMAR: Not at once. To begin with, they took her home to your father's house. But she didn't seem to thrive there. So Pettersen was told to wring her neck.

EKDAL *(half asleep):* Hm. Yes. Pettersen. Damn fool—

HJALMAR *(speaks more softly):* That was how we got her, you see. Father knows Pettersen, and when he heard all this about the wild duck he got him to give her to us.

GREGERS: And now she's thriving in your loft.

HJALMAR: Yes, she's doing extraordinarily well. She's got fat. Well, she's been in there for so long now that she's forgotten what it's like to live the life she was born for; that's the whole trick.

GREGERS: Yes, you're right there, Hjalmar. Just make sure she never gets a glimpse of the sky or the sea. But I mustn't stay longer. I think your father's fallen asleep.

HJALMAR: Oh, never mind about that.

GREGERS: By the bye, you said you had a room to let.

HJALMAR: Yes, why? Do you know anyone who—?

GREGERS: Could I have it?

HJALMAR: You?

GINA: No, but Mr. Werle, it isn't—

GREGERS: Can I have that room? I'd like to move in right away. Tomorrow morning.

HJALMAR: Why, yes, with the greatest pleasure—

169

GINA: Oh no, Mr. Werle, it's not at all the kind of room for you.

HJALMAR: Why, Gina, how can you say that?

GINA: Well, it's dark and poky.

GREGERS: That won't bother me, Mrs. Ekdal.

HJALMAR: Personally I think it's quite a nice room. Not too badly furnished, either.

GINA: Don't forget those two who live down below.

GREGERS: Who are they?

GINA: Oh, one of them used to be a tutor—

HJALMAR: A Mr. Molvik.

GINA: And the other's a doctor called Relling.

GREGERS: Relling? I know him slightly. He had a practice up at Hoydal once.

GINA: They're a real couple of good-for-nothings. They often go out on the spree and come home very late at night, and aren't always—

GREGERS: One soon gets accustomed to that sort of thing. I hope I shall manage to acclimatize myself like the wild duck.

GINA: Well, I think you ought to sleep on it first, all the same.

GREGERS: You evidently don't want to have me living here, Mrs. Ekdal.

GINA: For heaven's sake! How can you think that?

HJALMAR: You're really behaving very strangely, Gina. (*To* GREGERS.) But tell me, are you thinking of staying in town for a while?

GREGERS (*puts on his overcoat*): Yes, now I'm staying.

HJALMAR: But not at home with your father? What do you intend to do?

GREGERS: Ah, if only I knew that, Hjalmar, it wouldn't be so bad. But when one has the misfortune to be called Gregers, with Werle on top of it—Hjalmar, have you ever heard anything so awful?

HJALMAR: Oh, I don't think it's awful at all.

GREGERS: Oh, nonsense. Ugh! I'd want to spit on anyone who had a name like that.

HJALMAR *(laughs):* If you weren't Gregers Werle, what would you like to be?

GREGERS: If I could choose, I think most of all I'd like to be a clever dog.

GINA: A dog?

HEDVIG *(involuntarily):* Oh, no!

GREGERS: Oh, yes. A tremendously clever dog. The sort that dives down after wild ducks when they have plunged to the bottom and gripped themselves fast in the seaweed and the mud.

HJALMAR: Honestly, Gregers, I don't understand a word of all this.

GREGERS: Oh, well, it doesn't mean much really. I'll move in tomorrow morning, then. *(To GINA.)* I shan't cause you any trouble. I do everything for myself. *(To HJALMAR.)* We'll talk about everything else tomorrow. Good night, Mrs. Ekdal. *(Nods to HEDVIG.)* Good night.

GINA: Good night, Mr. Werle.

HEDVIG: Good night.

HJALMAR *(who has lit a candle):* Wait a moment. I'll have to light you down. It's very dark on the stairs.

GREGERS *and* HJALMAR *go out through the front door.*

GINA *(thoughtfully, her sewing in her lap):* Wasn't that a funny thing, saying he'd like to be a dog?

HEDVIG: You know, mother—I think when he said that he meant something else.

GINA: What could he mean?

HEDVIG: I don't know. But I felt as though he meant something different from what he was saying all the time.

GINA: You think so? Yes, it certainly was strange.

HJALMAR *(comes back):* The light was still on. *(Snuffs the candle and puts it down.)* Ah, now I can get a little food inside me at last. *(Begins eating the sandwiches.)* Well, there you are, Gina. If one only keeps one's eyes and ears open—

GINA: How do you mean?

HJALMAR: Well, it's jolly lucky we've managed to let that room at last, isn't it? And, what's more, to a man like Gregers. A dear old friend.

GINA: Well, I don't know what to say about it.

HEDVIG: Oh, mother! You'll see—it'll be such fun!

HJALMAR: You're very awkward. You were aching to let the room, and now we've done it you're not happy.

GINA: Oh, yes I am, Hjalmar. I only wish it had been to someone else. But what do you suppose the old man will say?

HJALMAR: Old Werle? It's none of his business.

GINA: Can't you see? They must have quarrelled again if his son's walked out of the house. You know how things are between those two.

HJALMAR: That may well be, but—

GINA: Now perhaps Mr. Werle'll think you're behind it all.

HJALMAR: All right, let him think so, if he wants to! Old Werle's done a great deal for me, I admit it. But that doesn't make me his vassal for life.

GINA: But, Hjalmar dear, he might take it out of grandfather. Maybe now he'll lose the little bit of money he gets through Graaberg.

HJALMAR: Good riddance—I've half a mind to say. Don't you think it's a little humiliating for a man like me to see his grey old father treated like a leper? But I've a feeling the time is getting ripe. *(Takes another sandwich.)* As sure as I have a mission in life, it shall be fulfilled.

HEDVIG: Oh, father, yes! It must, it must!

GINA: Ssh! For heaven's sake, don't wake him.

HJALMAR *(more quietly):* It shall be accomplished. The day

will come, I tell you—and that's why it's good we've let that room—it makes me more independent. *(Over by the armchair, emotionally.)* My poor old father! Bless his white hairs! Put your trust in your son. He has broad shoulders—well, strong shoulders, anyway. One fine day you will wake up— *(To* GINA.*)* Don't you believe it?

GINA *(gets up):* Of course I believe it. But let's get him to bed first.

HJALMAR: Yes, let's.

They take hold of the old man gently.

ACT THREE

HJALMAR EKDAL's *studio. It is morning. The daylight is shining in through the large window in the sloping ceiling, from which the curtain is drawn back.* HJALMAR *is seated at the table retouching a photograph. Several others lie in front of him. After a few moments,* GINA *enters through the front door, wearing a hat and coat. She has a lidded basket on her arm.*

HJALMAR: Back already, Gina?
GINA: Yes, I've no time to waste.

> *She puts the basket down on a chair and takes off her coat.*

HJALMAR: Did you look in on Gregers?
GINA: I'll say I did. Lovely it looks. He's made it really nice and cosy for himself right from the start.
HJALMAR: Oh, how?
GINA: Manage for himself, he said he would. So he starts lighting the stove. Well, he shoved that damper in so far the whole room got full of smoke. Ugh! It stank like a—
HJALMAR: Oh dear, oh dear.
GINA: That's not all. Then he wants to put out the fire, so he throws all his washing water into the stove. That floor's swimming like a pigsty.
HJALMAR: Oh, I'm sorry about that.

GINA: I've got the caretaker's wife to clean up after him, the pig. But that room won't be fit to live in till this afternoon.

HJALMAR: What's he doing with himself meanwhile?

GINA: He said he'd go out for a bit.

HJALMAR: I went in there too for a moment. After you'd gone.

GINA: So I gathered. I hear you've invited him for lunch.

HJALMAR: Just a little snack, I thought. After all, it's his first day here—we can't very well not. You've got something, I suppose?

GINA: I'll have to find something, won't I?

HJALMAR: Don't skimp it too much. Relling and Molvik may be looking in too, I think. I ran into Relling on the stairs just now, you see, so I couldn't very well—

GINA: Oh, we're having those two as well, are we?

HJALMAR: Good God, a couple more or less, what difference does that make?

OLD EKDAL (*opens his door and looks out*): I say, Hjalmar— (*Notices* GINA.) Oh.

GINA: Do you want something, grandfather?

EKDAL: Oh, no. It doesn't matter. Hm!

He goes inside again.

HJALMAR: All right, all right. I say, Gina, a little of that herring salad for hangovers mightn't be a bad idea. I think Relling and Molvik were out on the tiles again last night.

GINA: Well, as long as they don't come too soon—

HJALMAR: Of course, of course. You take your time.

GINA: Yes, well; and you can get a little work done in the meantime.

HJALMAR: I *am* working! I'm working as hard as I can!

GINA: I only meant, then you'll have it out of the way.

She goes out with her basket to the kitchen. HJALMAR *sits working at the photograph with a brush, slowly and listlessly.*

EKDAL *(pokes his head in, looks round the room and says in a whisper):* Are you working?

HJALMAR: Yes, can't you see I'm struggling away at these pictures?

EKDAL: Oh. Well, never mind. If you're working so hard, I—Hm!

He goes out again. His door remains open.

HJALMAR *(continues silently for a few moments, then puts down his brush and goes across to the door).* Are *you* working, father?

EKDAL *(grumblingly, from the other room):* If you're working, I'm working too. Hm!

HJALMAR: Yes, yes, of course.

He goes back to work.

EKDAL *(after a moment, reappears in the doorway):* You know—I'm not working as hard as all that, Hjalmar.

HJALMAR: I thought you were writing.

EKDAL: Damn it, that Graaberg can wait a day or two. It's not a matter of life and death, is it?

HJALMAR: No. Anyway, you're not a slave, are you?

EKDAL: And then there's that thing in there—

HJALMAR: I was just thinking of that. Did you want to go in? Shall I open the door for you?

EKDAL: That's not a bad idea.

HJALMAR *(gets up):* Then we'd have it out of the way.

EKDAL: That's what I was thinking. We've got to have it ready by tomorrow morning. It is tomorrow, isn't it? Eh?

HJALMAR: Yes, of course it's tomorrow.

HJALMAR *and* EKDAL *each slide back one of the doors. Within, the morning sun is shining in through the sky-*

light. Some pigeons are flying back and forth, while others perch, cooing, on the rafters. Now and then the hens cackle further back in the loft.

HJALMAR: Well now. Get on with it, father.

EKDAL *(goes inside)*: Aren't you going to help?

HJALMAR: You know, I think I— *(Sees* GINA *in the kitchen doorway.)* Me? No, I've no time. I've got to work. Oh—my contraption—

He pulls a cord. A curtain falls in the attic; the lower section of this consists of a strip of old sailcloth, the upper of a piece of fishing net, stretched taut. The floor of the attic is thus no longer visible.

HJALMAR *(goes over to the table)*: Good. Now perhaps I can be allowed to work in peace for a few minutes.

GINA: Is he messing around in there again?

HJALMAR: Would you rather he sneaked off down to Madam Eriksen's? *(Sits.)* Did you want something? You were saying—

GINA: I only wanted to ask whether you think it'd be all right if we eat in here.

HJALMAR: Yes, we haven't any early sittings today, have we?

GINA: Only those two young lovers who want to be taken together.

HJALMAR: Why the devil can't they be taken together some other day?

GINA: It's all right, dear. I've fixed for them to come after lunch, when you'll be having your nap.

HJALMAR: Oh, good. Very well, then, let's eat in here.

GINA: All right. But there's no hurry about laying the table just yet. You can go on using it for a bit longer.

HJALMAR: Surely you can see I'm working as hard as I can!

GINA: I only meant, then you'll be free later.

She goes back into the kitchen. Short pause.

EKDAL *(peers through the net in the loft):* Hjalmar!

HJALMAR: What is it?

EKDAL: Afraid we'll have to move that water-trough after all.

HJALMAR: That's what I've said all along.

EKDAL: Hm—hm—hm.

> *He goes away from the door again.*
> HJALMAR *works for a few moments, then glances towards the attic and half rises.* HEDVIG *comes in from the kitchen.*

HJALMAR *(sits quickly down):* What do you want?

HEDVIG: I only wanted to be with you, father.

HJALMAR *(after a moment):* What are you nosing around for? Have you been told to keep an eye on me?

HEDVIG: No, of course not.

HJALMAR: What's your mother up to now?

HEDVIG: Oh, she's in the middle of the herring salad. *(Goes over to the table.)* Isn't there some little thing I could help you with, father?

HJALMAR: Oh, no. I'd better cope with it alone. While I still can. All will be well, Hedvig. As long as your father's strength holds out—

HEDVIG: Oh, no, father, you mustn't say such dreadful things.

> *She wanders around for a little, then stops by the open doorway and looks into the loft.*

HJALMAR: What's he up to, Hedvig?

HEDVIG: I think he's making a new path up to the water-trough.

HJALMAR: He'll never manage that by himself. And I'm forced to sit here—!

HEDVIG (*comes over to him*): Let me take the brush, father. I know how to do it.

HJALMAR: Oh no, you'll ruin your eyes.

HEDVIG: Nonsense. Come on, give me the brush.

HJALMAR (*gets up*): Yes, well, it won't take more than a minute or two.

HEDVIG: Oh, what does it matter? (*Takes the brush.*) There, now. (*Sits.*) Here's one I can start on.

HJALMAR: But listen—if you ruin your eyes, I won't take the responsibility. On your own head be it. You hear?

HEDVIG (*busy on the photograph*): Yes, yes, I know.

HJALMAR: You're a clever girl, Hedvig. It'll only take a couple of minutes—

He squeezes into the loft past the edge of the curtain. HEDVIG *sits working.* HJALMAR *and* EKDAL *can be heard arguing in the loft.*

HJALMAR (*comes back through the curtain*): Hedvig, get me those pliers from that shelf. And the chisel. (*Turns round towards the loft.*) Now you'll see, father. Just let me show you.

HEDVIG *gets the tools from the bookcase and hands them to him.*

HJALMAR: Ah, thanks. Good thing I came, Hedvig.

He goes from the doorway. They can be heard working and chatting inside. HEDVIG *stands watching them. After a moment, there is a knock on the front door. She does not hear it.*

GREGERS (*enters bareheaded and without an overcoat. He pauses in the doorway*): Hm—

HEDVIG (*turns and goes towards him*): Good morning. Please come in.

GREGERS: Thank you. *(Looks towards the attic.)* Have you got workmen in the house?

HEDVIG: No, that's only father and grandfather. I'll tell them you're here.

GREGERS: No, no, don't do that. I'd rather wait. *(Sits on the sofa.)*

HEDVIG: It's so untidy in here. *(Begins to clear away the photographs.)*

GREGERS: Oh, never mind that. Are those photographs that have to be—er—finished off?

HEDVIG: Yes, just a few I'm helping father with.

GREGERS: Please don't let me disturb you.

HEDVIG: All right.

She arranges the things again and sits down to work.
GREGERS *watches her in silence.*

GREGERS: Did the wild duck sleep well last night?

HEDVIG: Yes, thank you, I think so.

GREGERS *(turns towards the loft):* It looks quite different in there by daylight.

HEDVIG: Oh, yes. It varies a lot. In the morning it looks quite different from what it does in the afternoon. And when it's raining it looks different from when it's fine.

GREGERS: You've noticed that, have you?

HEDVIG: Yes, you can't help seeing it.

GREGERS: Do you like being in there with the wild duck, too?

HEDVIG: Yes, when I'm able to—

GREGERS: But you haven't so much spare time, I dare say. You go to school, of course?

HEDVIG: No, not any longer. Father's afraid I shall ruin my eyes.

GREGERS: Oh. So he reads with you himself?

HEDVIG: Father's promised to read with me, but he hasn't found time for it yet.

GREGERS: But isn't there someone else who could help you a little?

HEDVIG: Yes, there's Mr. Molvik—he's a student who lives downstairs—but he isn't always—er—altogether quite—

GREGERS: Does he drink?

HEDVIG: I think he does.

GREGERS: Oh. Then you've time for all sorts of things. In there, it's like a different world, I suppose?

HEDVIG: Quite, quite different. And there are so many strange things in there.

GREGERS: Oh?

HEDVIG: Yes. There are big cupboards with books in them. And a lot of the books have got pictures.

GREGERS: Ah.

HEDVIG: And there's an old bureau with drawers and bits that slide out, and a big clock with figures that are meant to pop out. But the clock doesn't work any more.

GREGERS: So time has stopped in there with the wild duck.

HEDVIG: Yes. And there are old paintboxes and things like that. And all the books.

GREGERS: And you read books, I suppose?

HEDVIG: Oh, yes, when I get the chance. But most of them are in English, and I can't understand that. But I look at the pictures. There's a great big book called Harrison's History of London—I should think it must be a hundred years old—and that's got heaps and heaps of pictures in it. On the front there's a picture of death with an hour-glass, and a girl. That's horrid, I think. But then there are lots of other pictures of churches and castles and streets and great ships sailing on the sea.

GREGERS: But tell me, where have all these wonderful things come from?

HEDVIG: Oh, there was an old sea captain who used to live here once, and he brought them home. They called him

The Flying Dutchman. It's funny, because he wasn't a Dutchman.

GREGERS: Wasn't he?

HEDVIG: No. But in the end he got lost at sea and left all these things behind.

GREGERS: Tell me—as you sit in there and look at the pictures, don't you feel you want to get out and see the world as it really is?

HEDVIG: Oh, no! I want to stay at home always, and help father and mother.

GREGERS: Help them re-touch photographs?

HEDVIG: No, not only that. Most of all I'd like to learn to engrave pictures like the ones in the English books.

GREGERS: Hm. What does your father say to that?

HEDVIG: I don't think father likes the idea. He's so strange about anything like that. Imagine, he talks about my learning how to plait straw and make baskets! I don't think there can be any future in that.

GREGERS: No, neither do I.

HEDVIG: But father's right when he says that if I'd learned basket-making I could have made the new basket for the wild duck.

GREGERS: Yes, so you could. It was your job really, wasn't it?

HEDVIG: Yes, because it's my wild duck.

GREGERS: Of course it is.

HEDVIG: Oh, yes. I own it. But father and grandfather are allowed to borrow it whenever they want.

GREGERS: Oh? And what do they do with it?

HEDVIG: Oh, they look after it and build things for it, and that kind of thing.

GREGERS: I should think so. The wild duck's the most important thing in there, isn't it?

HEDVIG: Oh, yes. She's a real wild bird, you see. That's

why I feel so sorry for her. She's got no one to care for, poor thing.

GREGERS: No family like the rabbits.

HEDVIG: No. The hens have got friends they used to be chicks with; but she's been separated from all her family. And there's so much that's stran; : about the wild duck. No one knows her. And no one knows where she came from.

GREGERS: And she's been down to the bottom of the vasty deep.

HEDVIG (*glances quickly at him and represses a smile*): Why do you say 'the vasty deep'?

GREGERS: What should I have said?

HEDVIG: You could have said 'the sea bed', or just 'the bottom of the sea'.

GREGERS: Oh, why can't I say 'the vasty deep'?

HEDVIG: Yes, but it always sounds so odd to me when other people talk about 'the vasty deep'.

GREGERS: Why? Tell me.

HEDVIG: No, I won't. It's silly.

GREGERS: Not at all. Tell me now, why did you smile?

HEDVIG: It's because if I suddenly—without thinking— remember what's in there, I always think of it all as being 'the vasty deep'. But that's just silly.

GREGERS: No, you mustn't say that.

HEDVIG: Well, it's only a loft.

GREGERS (*looks hard at her*): Are you sure?

HEDVIG (*astonished*): That it's only a loft?

GREGERS: Yes. You are quite certain about that?

HEDVIG *stares silently at him, open-mouthed.* GINA *comes from the kitchen with cutlery and tablecloth.*

GREGERS (*gets up*): I'm afraid I've come too early.

GINA: Oh, you've got to sit somewhere. Anyway, I'll be ready in a minute. Clear the table, Hedvig.

HEDVIG *clears the table. She and* GINA *lay the cloth, etc., during the following scene.* GREGERS *sits in an armchair and turns the pages of an album.*

GREGERS: I hear you know how to re-touch photographs, Mrs. Ekdal.

GINA *(gives him a quick glance):* Why—yes, I know how.

GREGERS: That was a lucky chance, wasn't it?

GINA: Why lucky?

GREGERS: Since Hjalmar was to become a photographer, I mean.

HEDVIG: Mother can take photographs, too.

GINA: Oh, yes, I've had to teach myself that.

GREGERS: Then it's really you who run the business?

GINA: Yes, when Hjalmar hasn't time himself, I—

GREGERS: His old father takes up a lot of his time, I dare say.

GINA: Yes. And anyway it's no real job for a man like Hjalmar to have to take the portrait of just anyone.

GREGERS: I quite agree. But after all, he has chosen this profession—

GINA: Hjalmar isn't just an ordinary photographer, you know, Mr. Werle.

GREGERS: I'm sure he isn't. But—

A shot is fired inside the loft.

GREGERS *(jumps up):* What's that?

GINA: Ugh, they're shooting again.

GREGERS: Do they shoot, too?

HEDVIG: They go hunting.

GREGERS: What! *(By the door of the loft.)* Are you hunting, Hjalmar?

HJALMAR *(from beyond the curtain):* Are you here? Oh, I didn't know. I was so busy with— *(To* HEDVIG.) Why didn't you tell us?

Comes into the studio.

GREGERS: Do you go shooting in the loft?

HJALMAR *(shows him a double-barrelled pistol):* Oh, only with this.

GINA: You and grandfather'll do yourselves an injury one of these fine days with that popgun.

HJALMAR *(irritated):* This is a pistol, as I think I've told you before.

GINA: I don't see that that improves matters.

GREGERS: So you've turned hunter too, Hjalmar?

HJALMAR: Oh, I just go out after rabbits now and then. Mostly for the old man's sake, you know.

GINA: Men are funny creatures. Always got to have something to diverge themselves with.

HJALMAR *(bad-temperedly):* Quite so. As Gina says, we've always got to have something to divert ourselves with.

GINA: Isn't that what I said?

HJALMAR: Hm. Well— *(To* GREGERS.*)* Yes, you see, as luck would have it the loft's placed in such a way that no one can hear us when we shoot. *(Puts down the pistol on the top shelf of the bookcase.)* Don't touch that pistol, Hedvig. One of the barrels is loaded. Now don't forget.

GREGERS *(peers in through the net):* You've a shotgun too, I see.

HJALMAR: That's father's old gun. It's no use any longer, something's gone wrong with the lock. But it's quite fun to have it around. We can take it to pieces now and then and clean it and grease it and put it together again. Of course it's mostly father who fiddles around like that.

HEDVIG *(to* GREGERS*):* Now you can see the wild duck properly.

GREGERS: Yes, I was just looking at her. She droops a little on one wing, doesn't she?

HJALMAR: No wonder. That's where she was shot.

GREGERS: And she trails one foot a little. Am I right?

HJALMAR: Perhaps just a little.

HEDVIG: Yes, that's where the dog bit her.

HJALMAR: But otherwise there's nothing wrong with her. It's really marvellous when you think she's had a charge of shot in her and has been between the teeth of a dog—

GREGERS *(glances at* HEDVIG*):* And has been for so long at the bottom of the vasty deep.

HEDVIG *(smiles):* Yes.

GINA *(laying the table):* Oh, that blessed wild duck. You make too much of a song and dance about her.

HJALMAR: Hm. Are you nearly ready with that?

GINA: Yes, I shan't be a minute. Hedvig, come and give me a hand.

GINA *and* HEDVIG *go out into the kitchen.*

HJALMAR *(in a low voice):* I think you'd better not stand there watching father. He doesn't like it.

GREGERS *comes away from the loft door.*

HJALMAR: I'd better close up before the others arrive. *(Claps his hands to frighten the birds.)* Shoo, shoo! Get away with you! *(Pulls up the curtain and closes the doors as he speaks.)* I invented these gadgets myself. It's really rather fun to have something like this to fiddle with, and fix when it goes wrong. We've got to have it, because Gina doesn't like rabbits and hens in here.

GREGERS: No, no. It's your wife who runs the studio, I suppose?

HJALMAR: I generally leave the details of the business to her. Then I can lock myself away in the parlour and think about more important things.

GREGERS: What kind of things, Hjalmar?

HJALMAR: I wonder you haven't asked me that before. But perhaps you haven't heard about my invention?

GREGERS: Your invention? No.

HJALMAR: Really? Haven't you? Oh no, I suppose being cut off up there in those forests—

GREGERS: So you've invented something?

HJALMAR: It's not quite finished yet. But I'm working on it. As you can imagine, when I decided to give up my life to the service of photography it wasn't because I wanted to take portraits of the bourgeoisie.

GREGERS: No, that's what your wife said just now.

HJALMAR: I made a vow that if I was going to dedicate my powers to this craft, I would exalt it to the level of both an art and a science. And so I decided to make this astonishing invention.

GREGERS: But what *is* this invention? What's the idea behind it?

HJALMAR: Oh, my dear fellow, you mustn't ask me about details yet. It takes time, you know. And you mustn't think it's vanity that's inspiring me to do this. It isn't for myself that I'm doing this. Oh, no. I have a mission in life that I can never forget.

GREGERS: What kind of mission?

HJALMAR: Have you forgotten that old man with the silver hair?

GREGERS: Your poor father. Yes, but there isn't very much you can do for him, is there?

HJALMAR: I can rekindle his self-respect by restoring to the name of Ekdal the honour and dignity which it once had.

GREGERS: And that's your mission?

HJALMAR: I want to save that shipwrecked soul, yes. Right from the moment the storm broke over him, he was a wreck. And during those terrible investigations he was no longer himself. That pistol over there, Gregers—the one we use for shooting rabbits—has played its part in the tragedy of the House of Ekdal.

GREGERS: Really? That pistol?

HJALMAR: When sentence had been pronounced and he was

about to be taken to prison—he had the pistol in his hand—

GREGERS: You mean—?

HJALMAR: Yes. But he didn't dare. He was a coward. His spirit had been broken. Can you understand it? He, a soldier, who had killed nine bears, and was descended from two lieutenant-colonels—one after the other, of course— Can you understand it, Gregers?

GREGERS: Yes, I understand it very well.

HJALMAR: I can't. But that wasn't the last time that pistol played a part in the history of our family. When he was in his grey garb, under lock and key—oh, it was a terrible time for me, believe me. I kept the blinds drawn over both my windows. When I peeped out I saw that the sun still shone. I couldn't understand it. I saw people in the street, laughing and chatting, about trivial things. I couldn't understand it. I thought the whole world ought to stand still, as though in eclipse.

GREGERS: That is how I felt when my mother died.

HJALMAR: At such a moment, Hjalmar Ekdal held the pistol pointed at his own breast.

GREGERS: You mean you, too, thought of—?

HJALMAR: Yes.

GREGERS: But you didn't fire?

HJALMAR: No. At the critical moment I triumphed over myself. I decided to remain alive. But I can tell you, Gregers, it takes courage under such circumstances to choose life.

GREGERS: Yes, well—that depends on how one—

HJALMAR: Believe me, Gregers, I am right. Anyway, it was better so. Now I shall make my invention; and then, Dr. Relling agrees with me, father may be allowed to wear his uniform again. I shall demand it as my sole reward.

GREGERS: So it's the uniform he—?

HJALMAR: Yes, that's what he longs for most. You can't

imagine how my heart bleeds for him. Every time we have any little family celebration—for example, Gina's and my wedding anniversary, or whatever it may be—the old man appears as the lieutenant he used to be in happier days. But if there's a knock on the door he scampers back to his room as fast as his old legs will carry him, because he daren't show himself to strangers. Oh, it's heart-rending for a son to have to witness such things, Gregers.

GREGERS: How soon do you expect this invention to be ready?

HJALMAR: Good heavens, you can't expect me to work to a schedule. An invention is something that even the inventor himself isn't completely master of. It depends largely on intuition—on inspiration—and it's almost impossible to predict when that's going to come.

GREGERS: But you're making progress?

HJALMAR: Of course I am. I think about it every day. It's always with me. Every afternoon, after I've eaten, I shut myself up in the parlour where I can meditate in peace. But I mustn't be rushed. That won't help at all. Relling says so too.

GREGERS: And you don't think that all that business in the loft distracts you too much, and dissipates your energies?

HJALMAR: No, no, no—quite the contrary. I can't spend all my time brooding over the same exhausting problem. I must have some distraction while I wait for the inspiration to come. Inspiration, you see, comes when it comes.

GREGERS: My dear Hjalmar, I really believe there is something of the wild duck in you.

HJALMAR: The wild duck? How do you mean?

GREGERS: You've plunged to the bottom and are holding on to the seaweed.

HJALMAR: Are you referring to that stroke of fate which crippled father—and me as well?

GREGERS: Not that so much. I wouldn't say you've been

crippled. You've wandered into a poisonous swamp, Hjalmar. You've got a creeping disease in your body, and you've sunk to the bottom to die in the dark.

HJALMAR: Me? Die in the dark? Now really, Gregers, you must stop that talk.

GREGERS: Don't worry. I shall get you up again. I've found a mission in life too, you see. I found it yesterday.

HJALMAR: I dare say, but please leave me out of it. I can assure you that—apart from a certain melancholy, which is easily explained—I'm as contented with life as anyone could wish to be.

GREGERS: That's another effect of the poison.

HJALMAR: Oh, my dear Gregers, do stop talking about diseases and poisons. I'm not used to this kind of conversation. In my house we don't talk about disagreeable matters.

GREGERS: No, I can well believe that.

HJALMAR: Yes—it's not good for me, you see. And you won't find any poisonous fumes here, as you insinuate. In the poor photographer's home the roof is low, I know that well. And the circumstances are narrow. But I am an inventor, Gregers—the breadwinner for my family—and that lifts me above the poverty of my surroundings. Ah, lunch!

> GINA *and* HEDVIG *bring in bottles of beer, a decanter of aquavit, glasses, etc. At the same time,* RELLING *and* MOLVIK *enter from the passage. Neither has a hat or overcoat.* MOLVIK *is dressed in black.*

GINA *(putting the things on the table):* Trust those two to come on time!

RELLING: Molvik thought he could smell herring salad, so there was no holding him. Good morning again, Ekdal.

HJALMAR: Gregers, may I present Mr. Molvik? Dr.—but of course you know Relling.

GREGERS: Yes, we have met.

RELLING: Oh, it's Mr. Werle Junior. Yes, we two have clashed before, up at Hoydal. You moved in here?

GREGERS: I moved in this morning.

RELLING: Molvik and I live underneath, so you haven't got far to go for a doctor or a priest, if you should ever need either of them.

GREGERS: Thank you, I well may. Yesterday we were thirteen at table.

HJALMAR: Oh, don't start that awful business again.

RELLING: Take it easy, Ekdal. You were one of the twelve.

HJALMAR: I hope so, for my family's sake. But now let's sit down, and eat and drink and be merry.

GREGERS: Oughtn't we to wait for your father?

HJALMAR: No, he wants his taken in to him later. Come along now, everybody!

The MEN *sit down at the table and start eating and drinking.* GINA *and* HEDVIG *come and go, waiting on them.*

RELLING: Molvik was as tight as a drum again last night, Mrs. Ekdal.

GINA: Oh? Last night again?

RELLING: Didn't you hear him when I brought him home?

GINA: No, I can't say I did.

RELLING: That's as well. Molvik was *awful* last night.

GINA: Is this true, Molvik?

MOLVIK: Let us draw a veil over the events of last night. It was not a manifestation of my better self.

RELLING (*to* GREGERS): It comes on him like an inspiration. And then I have to go out and paint the town with him. Molvik's daemonic, you see.

GREGERS: Daemonic?

RELLING: Yes, daemonic.

GREGERS: Hm.

RELLING: And people who are born daemonic can't keep a straight course through life. They have to go off the rails now and then. Well, so you're still sticking it out at that ugly black mill, are you?

GREGERS: I have stuck it out until now.

RELLING: And did you manage to enforce that claim you went round pestering everyone with?

GREGERS: Claim? *(Understands him.)* I see.

HJALMAR: Have you been acting as a debt-collector, Gregers?

GREGERS: Oh, nonsense.

RELLING: Oh, yes he has. He went round all the workmen's cottages, shoving something in their faces which he called 'the claim of the ideal'.

GREGERS: I was young then.

RELLING: You're right there. You were very young. And as for that claim of the ideal—you never got anyone to honour it before I left.

GREGERS: Nor since, either.

RELLING: Then I hope you've grown wise enough to reduce your demands a little.

GREGERS: Not when I stand face to face with a man.

HJALMAR: Well, that sounds reasonable enough. A little butter, Gina.

RELLING: And a slice of pork for Molvik.

MOLVIK: Oh no, not pork!

There is a knock on the door of the loft.

HJALMAR: Open the door, Hedvig. Father wants to come out.

HEDVIG *goes across and opens the door a little.* OLD EKDAL *comes out with a fresh rabbit skin. She closes the door behind him.*

EKDAL: Morning, gentlemen. Good hunting today! I've shot a big one.

HJALMAR: Why did you have to skin it before I came?

EKDAL: Salted it too. It's good, tender meat, rabbit meat. Sweet, too. Tastes like sugar. Enjoy your dinner, gentlemen!

He goes into his room.

MOLVIK *(gets up):* Excuse me—I can't—I must—quickly—

RELLING: Drink some soda water, man!

MOLVIK *(hurries out):* Ah—ah!

He goes out through the front door.

RELLING *(to* HJALMAR*):* Let's drink to the old huntsman.

HJALMAR *(clinks glasses with him):* A great sportsman at the end of the road.

RELLING: His hair tempered with grey— *(Drinks.)* By the way, tell me, is his hair grey or white?

HJALMAR: Oh—somewhere between the two. Actually, he hasn't very many hairs left on his head.

RELLING: Well, one can get through the world with a wig, as one can with a mask. You're a lucky man, Ekdal. A beautiful mission to fight for—

HJALMAR: And I do fight for it, believe me.

RELLING: And a clever wife, jogging quietly in and out in her felt slippers, rocking her hips and making everything nice and comfortable for you.

HJALMAR: Yes, Gina. *(Nods to her.)* You are a good companion to have on life's journey.

GINA: Oh, get along with you!

RELLING: And then you have your little Hedvig.

HJALMAR *(moved):* My child, yes. Above all, my child! Hedvig, come to me. *(Strokes her hair.)* What day is it tomorrow, Hedvig?

HEDVIG (*shakes him*): Oh no, father, you mustn't tell them!

HJALMAR: It wounds me like a knife through the heart when I think how poor it must be. Just a little party in the attic—

HEDVIG: But father, that's just what's so wonderful!

RELLING: And just you wait till your father's ready with his great invention, Hedvig.

HJALMAR: Yes, then you'll see! Hedvig, I have resolved to secure your future. You shall never want. I shall make it a condition that you get—er—something or other. That shall be the poor inventor's sole reward.

HEDVIG (*whispers, her arm round his neck*): Oh, dear, kind father!

RELLING (*to* GREGERS): Well, don't you find it pleasant for a change to sit down to a good meal surrounded by a happy family?

HJALMAR: Yes, I think I appreciate these hours at the table more than anything.

GREGERS: Personally I don't like poisonous fumes.

RELLING: Poisonous fumes!

HJALMAR: Oh, for heaven's sake don't start that again.

GINA: By God, you'll find no fumes in here, Mr. Werle! I give the whole place a good airing every day.

GREGERS (*leaving the table*): You can't drive out the stench I mean by opening the windows.

HJALMAR: Stench!

GINA: How do you like that, Hjalmar?

RELLING: I beg your pardon—you couldn't possibly have brought the stench in yourself from those pits up there?

GREGERS: Yes, it's like you to call what I bring with me a stench.

RELLING (*goes over to him*): Listen, Mr. Werle Junior. I've a strong suspicion you're still carrying that 'claim of the ideal' unabridged in your back pocket.

GREGERS: I carry it in my heart.

RELLING: Well, wherever you have the darned thing I'm

damned if I'll let you blackmail anyone with it as long as
I'm in this house.

GREGERS: And if I choose to ignore your warning?

RELLING: Then you'll go headfirst down those stairs. Now
you know.

HJALMAR *(gets up):* But—but, Relling—!

GREGERS: All right, throw me out.

GINA *(goes between them):* Relling, you can't do that. But I
must say, Mr. Werle, after the mess you made with your
stove you're in no position to come and complain to me
about fumes.

There is a knock on the front door.

HEDVIG: Mother, someone's knocking.

HJALMAR: Oh, now that's going to start.

GINA: Let me take care of it.

*She goes over, opens the door and steps back in sur-
prise.*

GINA: Oh! Oh, no!

HAAKON WERLE, *in a fur-lined coat with a fur collar,
takes a step into the room.*

WERLE: I beg your pardon, but I believe my son is living in
this house.

GINA *(swallows):* Yes.

HJALMAR *(goes towards him):* Wouldn't you do us the honour, sir, to—?

WERLE: Thank you, I only want to speak to my son.

GREGERS: Well? I'm here. What is it?

WERLE: I want to speak to you in your room.

GREGERS: Oh? In my room?

Moves towards the door.

GINA: No, for heaven's sake, that's in no state—

WERLE: Out in the passage, then. I want to speak with you alone.

HJALMAR: You can do that here, sir. Relling, come into the parlour.

HJALMAR *and* RELLING *go out to the right.* GINA *takes* HEDVIG *into the kitchen.*

GREGERS (*after a short pause*): Well. Now we're alone.

WERLE: You let drop a few remarks last night about— And since you've now come to lodge with the Ekdals I can only assume that you intend some action directed against me.

GREGERS: I intend to open the eyes of Hjalmar Ekdal. He must see his situation as it really is. That is all.

WERLE: And that is the mission in life you spoke of yesterday?

GREGERS: Yes. It's the only one you have left me.

WERLE: So it's I who have soured your mind, Gregers?

GREGERS: You have soured my whole life. Oh, I'm not just thinking of what happened to my mother. But it's you I have to thank for the fact that I'm continually haunted by a guilty conscience.

WERLE: Oh, so it's your conscience that's queasy, is it?

GREGERS: I ought to have stood up to you when those traps were laid for Lieutenant Ekdal. I ought to have warned him. I knew in my mind what was going on.

WERLE: Then you ought to have spoken out.

GREGERS: I was frightened. I was a coward. I was so miserably afraid of you then. And long afterwards.

WERLE: You seem to have got over that very well now.

GREGERS: Yes, thank God I have. The crimes that have been committed against old Ekdal, by me and by—others—can never be undone. But at least I can free Hjalmar from the conspiracy of silence and deceit which is killing him here.

WERLE: And you think that'd be doing him a service?

GREGERS: I nave no doubt of it.

WERLE: You think this photographer is the kind of man who would thank you for such a proof of friendship?

GREGERS: Yes. He is that kind of man.

WERLE: Well. We shall see.

GREGERS: And besides—if I am to go on living, I must try to find some cure for my sick conscience.

WERLE: Your conscience has been sickly ever since you were a child. There's no cure for it. That's an heirloom from your mother, Gregers. The only thing she left you.

GREGERS (*with a scornful smile*): Haven't you got over your disappointment yet? You miscalculated badly, didn't you, when you thought you'd get rich through her?

WERLE: Don't try to distract me with irrelevancies. Are you still resolved to carry out your intention of guiding Ekdal on to what you suppose to be the right path?

GREGERS: Yes. I am resolved.

WERLE: In that case I might have saved myself the trouble of climbing the stairs. I don't suppose it's any use now asking if you'll come back home?

GREGERS: No.

WERLE: And you won't enter the firm either, I suppose?

GREGERS: No.

WERLE: Very good. But since I am intending to enter into a new marriage, I will arrange for the estate to be divided between us.

GREGERS (*quickly*): No, I don't want that.

WERLE: You don't want it?

GREGERS: No. My conscience won't allow me.

WERLE (*after a moment*): Are you going back to the mill?

GREGERS: No. I have left your service.

WERLE: But what will you do?

GREGERS: I shall simply fulfil my mission. That is all.

WERLE: But afterwards? How will you live?

GREGERS: I have saved a little out of my salary.

WERLE: Yes, but how long will that last?

GREGERS: I think it will see me through.

WERLE: What does that mean?

GREGERS: I think you've asked me enough questions.

WERLE: Goodbye then, Gregers.

GREGERS: Goodbye.

HAAKON WERLE *goes out.*

HJALMAR *(looks in):* Has he gone?

GREGERS: Yes.

HJALMAR *and* RELLING *come in.* GINA *and* HEDVIG *enter from the kitchen.*

RELLING: Well, that's the end of our lunch.

GREGERS: Get your coat, Hjalmar. You and I must take a long walk together.

HJALMAR: Yes, let's. What did your father want? Was it anything to do with me?

GREGERS: Come along. We must have a little talk. I'll go and fetch my coat.

He goes out through the front door.

GINA: I don't like you going out with him, Hjalmar.

RELLING: She's right. Stay here with us.

HJALMAR *(takes his hat and overcoat):* What! When an old schoolfellow feels the need to pour out his heart to me—?

RELLING: But for Christ's sake—don't you see the fellow's mad, twisted, out of his mind?

GINA: There you are! Well, what do you expect? His mother had weird fits like that too, sometimes.

HJALMAR: All the more need for someone to keep a friendly eye on him, then. *(To* GINA.*)* Make sure dinner's ready in good time. Goodbye for now.

He goes out through the front door.

RELLING: What a pity that fellow didn't fall into one of his own mines and drop right down to Hell!

GINA: Mercy on us! Why do you say that?

RELLING *(mutters):* Oh, I have my reasons.

GINA: Do you think young Mr. Werle's really mad?

RELLING: No, worse luck. He's no madder than most people. He's sick all right, though.

GINA: What do you think's wrong with him?

RELLING: I'll tell you, Mrs. Ekdal. He's suffering from a surfeit of self-righteousness.

GINA: Surfeit of self-righteousness?

HEDVIG: Is that a disease?

RELLING: Yes. It's a national disease. But it only very seldom becomes acute. *(Nods to* GINA.*)* Thanks for the lunch.

He goes out through the front door.

GINA *(walks round uneasily):* Ugh! That Gregers Werle. He always was a queer fish.

HEDVIG *(stands by the table and looks searchingly at her):* I think this is all very strange.

ACT FOUR

HJALMAR EKDAL'S *studio. A photograph has just been taken; a camera with a cloth over it, a stand, two or three chairs, a folding table, etc., stand around the room. Afternoon light; the sun is just going down; a little later it begins to grow dark.* GINA *is standing in the open doorway with a small box and a wet glass plate in her hand, talking to someone outside.*

GINA: Yes, definitely. When I make a promise I always keep it. I'll have the first dozen ready by Monday. Goodbye, goodbye.

The other person goes downstairs. GINA *closes the door, puts the glass plate in the box and places the latter in the covered camera.*

HEDVIG *(comes in from the kitchen):* Have they gone?
GINA *(tidying up):* Yes, thank God, I got rid of them at last.
HEDVIG: Why do you suppose father hasn't come home yet?
GINA: Are you sure he's not down with Relling?
HEDVIG: No, he's not there. I've just run down the back stairs to ask.
GINA: And his dinner's getting cold too, I suppose?
HEDVIG: It's funny—father's always on time for dinner.
GINA: Oh, he'll be here soon. You'll see.

HEDVIG: I wish he'd come. Everything seems so strange suddenly.

GINA *(cries out):* Here he is!

HJALMAR EKDAL *comes in through the front door.*

HEDVIG *(runs towards him):* Oh, father! Oh, we've waited and waited for you!

GINA *(gives him a glance):* You've been a long time, Hjalmar.

HJALMAR *(without looking at her):* Yes, I have rather, haven't I?

He takes off his overcoat. GINA *and* HEDVIG *try to help him but he gestures them away.*

GINA: Have you eaten with Werle?

HJALMAR *(hangs up his coat):* No.

GINA *(goes towards the kitchen door):* I'll bring in your food, then.

HJALMAR: No, never mind the food. I don't want any.

HEDVIG *(goes closer):* Aren't you well, father?

HJALMAR: Well? Oh yes, tolerably. We had rather a tiring walk, Gregers and I.

GINA: You shouldn't do that, Hjalmar. You're not used to it.

HJALMAR: But there are a lot of things in life a man's got to get used to. *(Wanders around a little.)* Anyone been here while I was out?

GINA: Only those two sweethearts.

HJALMAR: No new orders?

GINA: No, not today.

HEDVIG: There'll be some tomorrow, father. You'll see.

HJALMAR: Let's hope so. Because tomorrow I intend to start working in real earnest.

HEDVIG: Tomorrow? But don't you remember what day it is tomorrow?

HJALMAR: Ah, that's true. Well, the day after tomorrow,

then. From now on I'm going to do everything myself. I'm going to manage the whole business on my own.

GINA: But why should you do that, Hjalmar? It'll only make you miserable. No, I'll take care of the photography, and you can go on puzzling with your invention.

HEDVIG: And think of the wild duck, father. And all the hens and rabbits and—

HJALMAR: Don't talk to me about all that nonsense. From now on I shall never set foot in that loft again.

HEDVIG: But father, you promised tomorrow we'd have a party—

HJALMAR: Hm, that's true. Well, from the day after tomorrow then. I'd like to wring the neck of that damned wild duck.

HEDVIG (screams): The wild duck!

GINA: I never heard such nonsense!

HEDVIG (shaking him): But father! It's my wild duck!

HJALMAR: That's why I won't do it. I haven't the heart to—I haven't the heart—because of you, Hedvig. But I know in my heart that I ought to do it. I ought not to allow any creature to live under my roof which has been in *his* hands.

GINA: For heaven's sake! Just because grandfather got it from that wretched Pettersen—

HJALMAR (wandering around): There are certain demands— demands a man makes of himself—how shall I put it?—a striving for perfection—one might say the demands of an ideal—which a man may not ignore without danger to his soul.

HEDVIG (goes after him): But father, the wild duck! The poor wild duck!

HJALMAR (stops): I've told you I shall spare it. For your sake. I shall not touch a hair of its—well, as I told you, I shall spare it. I have more important tasks than that to get down to. But you'd better go and take your walk now,

Hedvig. It's getting dark—the light won't hurt your eyes now.

HEDVIG: No, I won't bother to go out today.

HJALMAR: Yes, you must. You screw up your eyes so; all these fumes in here are bad for you. The air under this roof is unclean.

HEDVIG: All right, all right. I'll run down the back stairs and go for a little walk. My coat and hat? Oh, they're in my room. Father, you won't hurt the wild duck while I'm out?

HJALMAR: Not a feather of its head shall be touched. *(Presses her to him.)* You and I, Hedvig—we two—! Well, run along.

HEDVIG *nods to her parents and goes out through the kitchen.*

HJALMAR *(walks around without looking up):* Gina.

GINA: Yes?

HJALMAR: From tomorrow—or let's say the day after tomorrow—I'd like to keep the household accounts myself.

GINA: You want to look after the household accounts too, now?

HJALMAR: Yes. I want to find out where the money comes from.

GINA: Well, heaven knows that won't take you long.

HJALMAR: One would imagine it would. You seem to make it go a remarkably long way. *(Stops and looks at her.)* How do you do it?

GINA: It's because Hedvig and I need so little.

HJALMAR: Is it true that father gets paid very generously for the copying he does for Mr. Werle?

GINA: I don't know if it's so very generous. But then I don't know what that kind of work is worth.

HJALMAR: Well, roughly how much does he get? Come on, tell me!

GINA: It varies. On an average about what it costs us to keep him, and a bit of pocket money over.

HJALMAR: What it costs us to keep him! And you never told me!

GINA: How could I! You were so happy because you thought he got everything from you.

HJALMAR: And all the time he gets it from Mr. Werle!

GINA: Oh, there's more where that comes from.

HJALMAR: I suppose we'd better light that lamp.

GINA *(lights it):* Of course, we don't know if it's the old man himself. It might easily be Graaberg—

HJALMAR: Why drag in Graaberg?

GINA: No, I don't know. I just thought—

HJALMAR: Hm!

GINA: I didn't get this work for grandfather. It was Berta—when she came to live there.

HJALMAR: Your voice has gone funny.

GINA *(puts the shade on the lamp):* My voice?

HJALMAR: And your hands are trembling. Do you deny it?

GINA *(firmly):* Don't beat about the bush, Hjalmar. What's he been telling you about me?

HJALMAR: Is it true—*can* it be true—that there was a kind of relationship between you and Mr. Werle when you were in his service?

GINA: No, it's not true. Not at that time. Oh, he was after me, all right. And Mrs. Werle thought there was something doing; she created a great hullaballoo, and pulled my hair, she did, so I gave my notice and went.

HJALMAR: But it happened afterwards!

GINA: Yes, well, I went home. And mother—she wasn't such a simple soul as you thought, Hjalmar. She kept talking to me about one thing and another. Well, the old man was a widower by then, you see—

HJALMAR: Go on!

GINA: Well, I suppose you'd better know. He wouldn't give in till he'd had his way.

HJALMAR: And this is the mother of my child! How could you keep such a thing from me?

GINA: Yes, it was very wrong. I ought to have told you about it long ago.

HJALMAR: You ought to have told me at once. Then I'd have known what kind of woman you were.

GINA: If I had, would you have married me?

HJALMAR: What do you think?

GINA: Yes, well, that's why I didn't dare to say anything to you at the time. You know how fond I'd grown of you. How could I throw away my whole life?

HJALMAR *(walking about):* And this is the mother of my Hedvig! And to know that everything I see around me— *(Kicks a chair.)*—my entire home—I owe to a predecessor in your favours! Oh, that crafty old seducer!

GINA: Do you regret the fifteen years we have lived together?

HJALMAR *(stops in front of her):* Have you not every day, every moment, regretted the web of concealment and deceit that you've spun around me like a spider? Answer me that! Do you mean to tell me that all this time you haven't been living in anguish and remorse?

GINA: Oh, my dear Hjalmar, I've had enough to think about trying to run the house without—

HJALMAR: Then you never probe your past with a questioning eye?

GINA: You know, I'd almost forgotten the whole dirty business.

HJALMAR: Oh, this soulless, unfeeling complacency! It always fills me with moral indignation. And what is more, you don't even regret it!

GINA: Yes, but tell me, Hjalmar. What would have become of you if you hadn't had a wife like me?

HJALMAR: Like you?

GINA: Yes; I've always been a little more down-to-earth and practical than you. Well, it's natural, I suppose, I'm just that much older.

HJALMAR: What would have become of me!

GINA: Yes. You'd gone a bit off the rails when you met me. You surely won't deny that.

HJALMAR: You call that going off the rails? Oh, you don't understand what it's like when a man is full of sorrow and despair. Particularly a man of my fiery temperament.

GINA: No, no. Perhaps I don't. Anyway, I'm not complaining; you became such a good man once you'd got a house and home of your own. And now it was getting to be so homely and nice here; and Hedvig and I were just thinking we might be able to spend a little on food and clothes.

HJALMAR: Yes, in this swamp of deceit.

GINA: Oh, why did that repulsive little man have to come to our house?

HJALMAR: I too used to think this was a good home. It was a delusion. Where shall I now find the strength I need to transfer my invention into terms of reality? Perhaps it will die with me. And it will be your past, Gina, which will have killed it.

GINA (on the verge of tears): No, you mustn't say things like that, Hjalmar. All our married life I've never thought of anyone but you.

HJALMAR: I ask you—what will become of the breadwinner's dream now? As I lay in there on the sofa brooding over the invention, I had a feeling that it would devour my energies to the last drop. I sensed that the day on which I held the patent in my hands—that day would spell my release. And it was my dream that you should live on as the late inventor's prosperous widow.

GINA (*drying her tears*): Now you mustn't talk like that, Hjalmar. May the good Lord never let me live to see myself a widow!

HJALMAR: Oh, what does it matter? It's all finished now. Everything!

GREGERS WERLE *cautiously opens the front door and looks in.*

GREGERS: May one come in?

HJALMAR: Yes, come in.

GREGERS (*comes forward with a radiant, gratified expression and holds out his hands to them*): Well, my dear friends! (*Looks from one to the other and whispers to* HJALMAR.) Hasn't it happened yet?

HJALMAR: Oh, it has happened.

GREGERS: It has!

HJALMAR: I have just lived through the bitterest moment of my life.

GREGERS: But also, surely, the most sublime.

HJALMAR: Well, we've put that behind us. For the time being, anyway.

GINA: May God forgive you, Mr. Werle.

GREGERS (*greatly amazed*): But what I don't see is—

HJALMAR: What don't you see?

GREGERS: From such a crisis there must spring a mutual understanding on which a whole new life can be founded—a partnership built on truth, without concealment.

HJALMAR: Yes, I know, Gregers. I know.

GREGERS: I felt so sure that when I walked through that door you would be standing there transfigured, and that my eyes would be dazzled by the light. And instead I see nothing but this dull heaviness and misery—

GINA: Oh, I see.

She takes the shade off the lamp.

GREGERS: You don't want to understand me, Mrs. Ekdal. Ah, well. I suppose you need a bit more time. But you, Hjalmar, you? Surely you must have gained a higher understanding now that the crisis is over?

HJALMAR: Yes, of course I have. That is—in a kind of way.

GREGERS: For there is nothing in the world that can compare with the joy of forgiving someone who has sinned and raising her to one's heart in love.

HJALMAR: Do you think that a man can so easily digest the bitter draught that I have just drained?

GREGERS: Not an ordinary man, perhaps. But a man like you—

HJALMAR: Oh yes, I know, I know. But you mustn't rush me, Gregers. It takes time, you see.

GREGERS: There's a lot of the wild duck in you, Hjalmar.

RELLING *has entered through the front door.*

RELLING: So the wild duck's in the air again?

HJALMAR: Yes. Mr. Werle's winged victim.

RELLING: Mr. Werle? Are you talking about him?

HJALMAR: About him and—the rest of us.

RELLING (*aside, to* GREGERS): You bloody fool, why don't you go to Hell?

HJALMAR: What did you say?

RELLING: I was expressing my heartfelt desire to see this quack doctor back where he belongs. If he stays here he's quite capable of wrecking both your lives.

GREGERS: You needn't fear for these two, Dr. Relling. I shan't speak about Hjalmar. We both know him. But in her too, deep in her heart, there is something of honesty and truthfulness.

GINA (*near to tears*): Then you ought to have let me stay as I was.

RELLING: Would it be impertinent to ask exactly what it is you're trying to do in this house?

GREGERS: I want to lay the foundations of a true marriage.

RELLING: Then you don't think their marriage is good enough as it stands?

GREGERS: It's probably as good a marriage as most others, I'm afraid. But it is not yet a true marriage.

HJALMAR: You've never had much faith in ideals, Dr. Relling.

RELLING: Rubbish, my boy! May I ask, Mr. Werle—how many true marriages have you seen in your life? Just roughly.

GREGERS: I hardly think I've seen a single one.

RELLING: Neither have I.

GREGERS: But I've seen so many, many marriages of the opposite kind. And I've had the opportunity to study one at sufficiently close quarters to realize how it can demoralize two human beings.

HJALMAR: The whole moral foundation of a man's life can crumble under his feet. That's the terrible thing.

RELLING: Yes, well, I've never been what you'd call married, so I wouldn't presume to judge. But I do know this, that children are as much a part of any marriage as their parents. So you leave that child alone!

HJALMAR: Ah! Hedvig! My poor Hedvig!

RELLING: Yes, I'll thank you to keep Hedvig out of this. You two are adults; muck about with your own lives, if you enjoy it. But I'm warning you, be gentle with Hedvig, or you may do her irreparable harm.

HJALMAR: Harm?

RELLING: Yes, or she may come to do herself harm—and perhaps others too.

GINA: What would you know about that, Relling?

HJALMAR: There isn't any immediate danger to her eyes, is there?

RELLING: This has nothing to do with her eyes. Hedvig's at a difficult age just now. She's capable of getting up to anything.

GINA: Yes, that's true—I've noticed it already. She's started fooling around with the kitchen stove. She calls it playing with fire. I'm often afraid she'll burn down the house.

RELLING: There you are. You see. I thought as much.

GREGERS (to RELLING): But how would you explain that kind of behaviour?

RELLING (quietly): My boy. Her voice is breaking.

HJALMAR: As long as the child has me— As long as my head is above the ground—

There is a loud knock on the door.

GINA: Quiet, Hjalmar. There's someone on the landing. *(Calls.)* Come in.

MRS. SŒRBY *enters, in an overcoat.*

MRS. SŒRBY: Good evening.

GINA *(goes to greet her):* Berta, is it you?

MRS. SŒRBY: Yes, it's me. But perhaps I've come at an inconvenient moment?

HJALMAR: Of course not. Any messenger from that home is always—

MRS. SŒRBY *(to GINA):* To be honest, I hoped I might find you alone at this hour of the evening, so I looked in to have a chat and to say goodbye.

GINA: Oh? Are you going away?

MRS. SŒRBY: Yes. Tomorrow morning. Up to Moydal. Mr. Werle left this afternoon. *(Casually, to GREGERS.)* He asked to be remembered to you.

GINA: Well, fancy that!

HJALMAR: So Mr. Werle has gone away. And you're going after him?

MRS. SŒRBY: Yes. What have you got to say about that, Ekdal?

210

HJALMAR: I say: take care!

GREGERS: I'd better explain. My father is marrying Mrs. Sœrby.

HJALMAR: Going to *marry* her?

GINA: Berta! So it's happened at last!

RELLING *(with a slight tremor in his voice):* This isn't true, surely?

MRS. SŒRBY: Yes, dear Relling, it's perfectly true.

RELLING: You want to get married again?

MRS. SŒRBY: Yes, I've decided I do. Mr. Werle has obtained a special licence, and we're going to get married quite quietly up at Hoydal.

GREGERS: Well, in that case nothing remains for me but to wish you happiness, as a dutiful stepson.

MRS. SŒRBY: Thank you; if you really mean it. I certainly hope it will bring happiness both to Mr. Werle and to me.

RELLING: Oh, I'm sure it will. Mr. Werle never gets drunk—as far as I know—and I don't think he's in the habit of beating up his wives, as the late lamented horse-doctor used to.

MRS. SŒRBY: Oh, let poor Sœrby rest in peace. He had his good points.

RELLING: But Mr. Werle, we gather, has better ones.

MRS. SŒRBY: At least he hasn't wasted all that was best in him. Men who do that must accept the consequences.

RELLING: I'm going out with Molvik tonight.

MRS. SŒRBY: Don't do that, Relling. Please. For my sake.

RELLING: What else do you suggest? *(To* HJALMAR.*)* Care to join us?

GINA: No, thank you. Hjalmar doesn't go on that kind of spree.

HJALMAR *(aside, irritated):* Oh, be quiet.

RELLING: Goodbye, Mrs.—Werle.

He goes out through the front door.

GREGERS (*to* MRS. SŒRBY): It seems that you and Dr. Relling know each other pretty well.

MRS. SŒRBY: Yes, we've known each other for many years. At one time it even seemed as though our friendship might lead to something more permanent.

GREGERS: Lucky for you it didn't.

MRS. SŒRBY: I know. But I've always been wary of acting on impulse. A woman can't just throw herself away, can she?

GREGERS: Aren't you afraid I might tell my father about this old friendship?

MRS. SŒRBY: You don't imagine I haven't told him myself?

GREGERS: Oh?

MRS. SŒRBY: Anything anyone could truthfully say about me I have already told him. It was the first thing I did when I gathered his intentions.

GREGERS: In that case you've been uncommonly frank.

MRS. SŒRBY: I've always been frank. It's by far the best policy for a woman.

HJALMAR: What do you say to that, Gina?

GINA: Oh, we women are so different. We can't all be like Berta.

MRS. SŒRBY: Well, Gina, I really believe I did the only sensible thing. Mr. Werle hasn't hidden anything from me, either. And perhaps that's what binds us so closely. Now he can talk to me as freely as a child. He's never been able to do that with anyone before. Fancy a strong and vigorous man like him having to spend all his youth and the best years of his life listening to sermons—very often occasioned by quite imaginary offences, from what I've heard.

GINA: Yes, that's true enough.

GREGERS: If you ladies are going to discuss that subject, I had better go.

MRS. SŒRBY: Don't bother. I've had my say. I just wanted

you to know I haven't lied to him or kept anything from
him. I dare say you think I've done very well for myself.
Well, perhaps I have. But I don't think I'm taking more
than I shall be able to give him. I shall never fail him. I
shall serve him and look after him better than anyone,
now that he's growing helpless.

HJALMAR: He? Growing helpless?

GREGERS (to MRS. SŒRBY): Look, I'd rather we didn't discuss that.

MRS. SŒRBY: It's no use trying to hide it any longer, though I
know he wants to. He's going blind.

HJALMAR (starts): Going blind? That's strange. Is he going
blind too?

GINA: It happens to lots of people.

MRS. SŒRBY: It's not hard to imagine what that must mean to
a man like him. Well, I shall try to make my eyes serve
for the two of us as best I can. But I mustn't stay any
longer. I've so much to do just now. Oh, what I wanted to
tell you, Ekdal, was that if there's anything Mr. Werle
can ever do for you, just go and speak to Graaberg.

GREGERS: I hardly think Hjalmar Ekdal will want to accept
that offer.

MRS. SŒRBY: Oh? I haven't noticed in the past that he—

GINA: Yes, Berta. Hjalmar doesn't need to take anything
from Mr. Werle any longer.

HJALMAR (slowly and emphatically): Will you present my
compliments to your future husband and tell him that I intend at the earliest opportunity to visit Mr. Graaberg—

GREGERS: Hjalmar!

HJALMAR: I repeat, to visit Mr. Graaberg and demand from
him an account of the sum I owe his employer. I shall repay this debt of honour— (Laughs.) —debt of honour! But
enough of that. I shall repay it to the last penny, with five
per cent interest.

213

GINA: But my dear Hjalmar, we haven't the money to do that.

HJALMAR: Will you please tell your fiancé that I am working indefatigably at my invention. Will you tell him that my spirit is sustained throughout this exhausting struggle by the desire to be rid of the embarrassing burden of this debt. That is why I have become an inventor. The entire profits shall be used to free me from the money of which your prospective husband has seen fit to disgorge himself.

MRS. SŒRBY: What's been going on in this house?

HJALMAR: Never mind.

MRS. SŒRBY: Well, goodbye. There was something else I wanted to talk to you about, Gina; but it'll have to wait till another time. Goodbye.

HJALMAR *and* GREGERS *bow silently.* GINA *accompanies* MRS. SŒRBY *to the door.*

HJALMAR: Not beyond the threshold, Gina.

MRS. SŒRBY *goes.* GINA *closes the door behind her.*

HJALMAR: There, Gregers. Thank God I've managed to get that debt off my conscience.

GREGERS: Well, you will soon, anyway.

HJALMAR: I think I can claim I behaved correctly.

GREGERS: You behaved exactly as I always knew you would.

HJALMAR: A time comes when a man can no longer ignore the command of his ideals. As the family breadwinner I am continually tormented by this command. I tell you, Gregers, it isn't easy for a man of small means to repay an old debt on which, as one might say, there has settled the dust of oblivion. But there's no other way. I must do what is right.

GREGERS (*puts his hand on* HJALMAR's *shoulders*): My dear Hjalmar. Aren't you glad I came?

HJALMAR: Yes.

GREGERS: Aren't you glad to see yourself as you really are?

HJALMAR *(a little impatiently)*: Of course I'm glad. But there's one thing which troubles my sense of justice. Well, but I don't know whether I should speak so bluntly about your father.

GREGERS: Say what you like. I don't mind.

HJALMAR: Well, then—it offends me to think that it is he, and not I, who is going to make a true marriage.

GREGERS: What are you saying!

HJALMAR: But it's true. Your father and Mrs. Sœrby are entering upon a marriage founded on absolute trust, with complete frankness on both sides. They are keeping nothing from each other. They have confessed their sins, if I may so phrase it, and have forgiven each other.

GREGERS: Well, what of it?

HJALMAR: But that's the whole point. You said yourself that it's only by overcoming all that that you can found a true marriage.

GREGERS: But that's quite different, Hjalmar. You surely don't compare yourself or her with these two—? Well, you know what I mean.

HJALMAR: I can't get away from the fact that there's something here which wounds and offends my sense of justice. Well, it looks as though there's no just power ruling this world.

GINA: Oh, Hjalmar, really! You mustn't speak like that!

GREGERS: Hm—let's not get on to that subject.

HJALMAR: But on the other hand I seem to see the finger of fate at work restoring the balance. He is going blind.

GINA: Oh, we don't know for sure about that.

HJALMAR: Can we doubt it? At least, we ought not to; for there lie justice and retribution. He had blinded a loyal and trusting friend—

GREGERS: I'm afraid he has blinded many.

215

HJALMAR: And now comes the inexorable, the unfathomable, and demands his own eyes.

GINA: Oh, how can you say such a horrible thing? You make me feel quite frightened.

HJALMAR: It is useful to face up to the darker aspects of existence now and then.

HEDVIG, *in her hat and coat, enters happy and breathless through the front door.*

GINA: Are you back already?

HEDVIG: Yes, I didn't want to walk any more. And a good thing too, for I met someone coming out of the front door.

HJALMAR: That Mrs. Sœrby, I suppose.

HEDVIG: Yes.

HJALMAR *(walking up and down):* I hope you have seen her for the last time.

Silence. HEDVIG *looks timidly from one to the other as though to find out what is the matter.*

HEDVIG *(goes nearer him, wooingly):* Father.

HJALMAR: Well, what is it, Hedvig?

HEDVIG: Mrs. Sœrby brought something for me.

HJALMAR *(stops):* For you?

HEDVIG: Yes. Something for tomorrow.

GINA: Berta always brings something for your birthday.

HJALMAR: What is it?

HEDVIG: No, you mustn't know yet. Mother's going to bring it to me in bed tomorrow morning.

HJALMAR: Oh, this conspiracy to keep me outside of everything!

HEDVIG *(quickly):* No, of course you can see it. It's a big letter.

She takes the letter from her coat pocket.

HJALMAR: A letter too?

216

HEDVIG: Only a letter. The present'll come later, I suppose. But fancy—a letter! I've never had a letter before. And there's 'Miss' written on the outside! *(Reads.)* 'Miss Hedvig Ekdal.' That's me!

HJALMAR: Let me see that letter.

HEDVIG *(holds it out to him)*: Here—look!

HJALMAR: This is Mr. Werle's writing.

GINA: Are you sure, Hjalmar?

HJALMAR: Look for yourself.

GINA: How should I know?

HJALMAR: Hedvig, may I open this letter and read it?

HEDVIG: Yes, certainly, if you want to.

GINA: No, Hjalmar, not tonight. It's for tomorrow.

HEDVIG *(quietly)*: Oh, do let him read it, please! It's sure to be something nice, and then father'll be happy, and it'll be nice here again.

HJALMAR: I may open it, then?

HEDVIG: Yes, do, father. It'll be fun to know what's in it.

HJALMAR: Right. *(Opens the letter, takes out a sheet of paper, reads it and looks bewildered.)* What on earth—?

GINA: What does it say?

HEDVIG: Oh, yes, father! Do tell us!

HJALMAR: Be quiet! *(Reads it through again. Then, pale but controlled, he says)* It's a deed of gift, Hedvig.

HEDVIG: I say! What do I get?

HJALMAR: See for yourself.

> HEDVIG *goes over to the lamp and reads the letter under it.*

HJALMAR *(softly, clenching his fists)*: The eyes! The eyes! And this letter!

HEDVIG *(looks up from her reading)*: But I think grandfather ought to have it.

HJALMAR *(takes the letter from her)*: Gina, can you make any sense of this?

217

GINA: You know I don't understand anything. Tell me what it's about.

HJALMAR: Mr. Werle writes to Hedvig that her old grandfather need no longer trouble to copy letters but that he can henceforth draw from the office the sum of five pounds per month—

GINA: Really?

HEDVIG: Five pounds, mother! That's what it says!

GINA: Well, that'll be nice for grandfather.

HJALMAR: Five pounds, for as long as he needs it. That means, of course, for as long as he lives.

GINA: Well, at least he's provided for then, poor old man.

HJALMAR: But there's something else. You didn't read this part, Hedvig. Afterwards, this money is to be paid to you.

HEDVIG: To me? All of it?

HJALMAR: You are assured of this sum for the rest of your life, he writes. Did you hear that, Gina?

GINA: Yes, I heard.

HEDVIG: Imagine all the money I'm going to have! *(Shakes him.)* Oh, father, father, aren't you happy—?

HJALMAR *(avoids her):* Happy! *(Walks about.)* Oh, what vistas, what perspectives begin to unroll before my eyes! It's Hedvig! She's the one he remembers so generously!

GINA: Yes—well, it's Hedvig's birthday.

HEDVIG: But you shall have it all, father! I want to give all the money to you and mother!

HJALMAR: Yes, to mother! There we have it!

GREGERS: Hjalmar, this is a trap which has been laid for you.

HJALMAR: You think this is another trap?

GREGERS: When he was here this morning, he said to me: 'Hjalmar Ekdal is not the man you think he is.'

HJALMAR: Not the man—!

GREGERS: 'You'll see,' he said.

HJALMAR: Meaning that I would let myself be fobbed off with money!

HEDVIG: Mother, what are they talking about?

GINA: Go in there and take your coat off.

> HEDVIG *goes out through the kitchen door, almost in tears.*

GREGERS: Well, Hjalmar, now we shall see which of us is right. He or I.

HJALMAR *(slowly tears the letter in two and puts the pieces on the table).* There is my reply.

GREGERS: I knew it would be.

HJALMAR *(goes over to GINA who is standing by the stove and says in a low voice):* And now let's have the truth. If it was all over between you and him when you—began to grow fond of me, as you put it—why did he make it possible for us to get married?

GINA: I suppose he thought he could have a key.

HJALMAR: Was that all? Wasn't he afraid of a certain possibility?

GINA: I don't know what you mean.

HJALMAR: I want to know if—your child has the right to live beneath my roof.

GINA *(draws herself up; her eyes flash):* You ask me that?

HJALMAR: Answer me! Is Hedvig mine or—? Well?

GINA *(looks at him in cold defiance):* I don't know.

HJALMAR *(trembles slightly):* You don't know!

GINA: How could I? I—couldn't tell—

HJALMAR *(quietly, turning away from her):* Then I have no further business in this house.

GREGERS: Consider, Hjalmar!

HJALMAR *(puts on his overcoat):* There's nothing for a man like me to consider.

GREGERS: You're wrong. There's a great deal to consider. You three must stay together if you are to win the forgiveness that comes with self-sacrifice.

HJALMAR: I don't want to win it! Never, never! My hat!

(Takes his hat.) My home has crashed in ruins about me! *(Bursts into tears.)* Gregers, I have no child!

HEDVIG *(who has opened the kitchen door):* What are you saying! *(Runs over to him.)* Daddy, daddy!

GINA: There, you see!

HJALMAR: Don't come near me, Hedvig! Go—go far away! I can't bear to look at you! Ah—those eyes! Goodbye!

He goes towards the door.

HEDVIG *(clings tightly to him, and screams):* No! No! Don't leave me!

GINA *(cries):* Look at the child, Hjalmar! Look at the child!

HJALMAR: I won't! I can't! I must get away! Away from all this!

He tears himself free from HEDVIG *and goes out through the front door.*

HEDVIG *(with despair in her eyes):* He's leaving us, mother! He's leaving us! He'll never come back again!

GINA: Don't cry, Hedvig. Daddy will come back.

HEDVIG *(throws herself sobbing on the sofa):* No, no. He'll never come back to us again.

GREGERS: Will you believe that I meant it all for your good, Mrs. Ekdal?

GINA: Yes, I believe it. But God forgive you.

HEDVIG *(lying on the sofa):* Oh, I shall die, I shall die! What have I done to him? Mother, you must make him come back home!

GINA: Yes, yes, yes, all right. Calm yourself, and I'll go out and look for him. *(Puts on her overcoat.)* Perhaps he's just gone down to Relling. But you mustn't lie there and cry. Promise me?

HEDVIG *(sobbing convulsively):* Yes, I'll stop. When father comes back.

GREGERS *(to* GINA, *as she is about to go):* Wouldn't it be better to let him fight his bitter battle to the end?

GINA: Oh, that'll have to wait. Now we must think of the child.

She goes out through the front door.

HEDVIG *(sits and dries her tears):* I want to know what all this means. Why won't father look at me any more?

GREGERS: You mustn't ask that till you're grown up.

HEDVIG *(catches her breath):* But I can't go on being unhappy like this all the time till I'm grown up. I know what it is. I'm not really daddy's child.

GREGERS *(uneasily):* How on earth could that be?

HEDVIG: Mummy might have found me. And perhaps father's got to know about it. I've read of things like that.

GREGERS: Well, but even if it were true—

HEDVIG: Yes, I think he should love me just the same. Or even more. After all, we got the wild duck sent to us as a present, but I love it very much.

GREGERS *(changing the conversation):* Yes, that's true. Let's talk for a moment about the wild duck, Hedvig.

HEDVIG: The poor wild duck. He can't bear to look at her any longer, either. Do you know, he wants to wring her neck!

GREGERS: Oh, I'm sure he won't do that.

HEDVIG: No, but he said it. And I think it was such a horrid thing for father to say. I say a prayer for the wild duck every evening. I pray that she may be delivered from death and from all evil.

GREGERS *(looks at her):* Do you always say your prayers at night?

HEDVIG: Oh, yes.

GREGERS: Who taught you to do that?

HEDVIG: I taught myself. Once when father was very ill, and

221

had leeches on his neck. He said death was staring him in the face.

GREGERS: Yes?

HEDVIG: So I said a prayer for him after I'd gone to bed. And since then I've kept it up.

GREGERS: And now you pray for the wild duck too?

HEDVIG: I thought I'd better include her, because she was so ill when she first came to us.

GREGERS: Do you say your prayers in the morning, too?

HEDVIG: Oh, no. Of course not.

GREGERS: Well, why not in the morning?

HEDVIG: In the morning it's light, and then there's nothing to be afraid of any more.

GREGERS: And your father wanted to wring the neck of the wild duck, which you love so much?

HEDVIG: No, he said he ought to, but he'd spare her for my sake. That was kind of him, wasn't it?

GREGERS (a little closer): Yes, but what if you now gave up the wild duck for his sake?

HEDVIG (rises): The wild duck?

GREGERS: Yes. Suppose you sacrificed for him the most precious of your possessions—the thing you love most dearly?

HEDVIG: Do you think that would help?

GREGERS: Try it, Hedvig.

HEDVIG (quietly, her eyes aglow): Yes, I will try it.

GREGERS: Do you think you have the strength to do it?

HEDVIG: I'll ask grandfather to shoot the wild duck for me.

GREGERS: Yes, do that. But not a word to your mother about this!

HEDVIG: Why not?

GREGERS: She doesn't understand us.

HEDVIG: The wild duck! I'll do it tomorrow morning.

GINA *comes in through the front door.*

222

HEDVIG *(goes to meet her):* Did you find him, mother?

GINA: No. But I heard he'd called in to see Relling and they'd gone off together.

GREGERS: Are you sure?

GINA: Yes, the caretaker told me. Molvik went with them too, she said.

GREGERS: Now, when he needs to wrestle with his soul alone!

GINA *(takes off her coat):* Well, men are difficult creatures. God knows where Relling's dragged him off to. I ran over to Mrs. Eriksen's, but they weren't there.

HEDVIG *(trying not to cry):* Oh, suppose he never comes back!

GREGERS: He'll come back. I shall tell him some news to-morrow, and then you'll see how quickly he will come. Don't worry, Hedvig. You can sleep in peace. Good night.

He goes out through the front door.

HEDVIG *(throws her arms, sobbing, round GINA's neck):* Mummy, mummy!

GINA *(pats her on the back and sighs):* Oh, yes, Relling was right. This is what happens when crazy people go round preaching about the commands of the ideal!

ACT FIVE

HJALMAR EKDAL's *studio. A cold, grey morning light. Wet snow lies on the large panes of glass in the roof.* GINA, *wearing an apron, enters from the kitchen with a brush and duster and goes towards the parlour door. At the same moment* HEDVIG *runs in from the passage.*

GINA *(stops):* Well?

HEDVIG: Yes, mother, I think he's down with Relling—

GINA: There you are!

HEDVIG: The caretaker said Relling had two people with him when he came back last night.

GINA: I thought as much.

HEDVIG: But that's no good, if he won't come up and see us.

GINA: You leave it to me. I'll go down and have a word with him.

OLD EKDAL, *in a dressing-gown and slippers and with a lighted pipe, appears in the doorway of his room.*

EKDAL: Hjalmar, I—! Isn't Hjalmar at home?

GINA: No, he seems to have gone out.

EKDAL: What, already? And in this blizzard? Oh, well. Let him. I can go for a walk by myself.

He pushes aside the door of the loft. HEDVIG *helps him. He goes in, and she closes the door behind him.*

HEDVIG *(softly):* Poor grandfather! What will he say when he hears father's leaving us?

GINA: Don't be silly, grandfather mustn't be told about that. Thank God he wasn't here yesterday when all the hullaballoo was going on.

HEDVIG: Yes, but—

GREGERS *enters through the front door.*

GREGERS: Well? Have you found where he is?

GINA: They say he's downstairs with Relling.

GREGERS: With Relling! Has he really been out with those people?

GINA: So it seems.

GREGERS: But he needed so much to be alone, and to collect his thoughts—

GINA: Yes, you may well say that.

RELLING *enters from the passage.*

HEDVIG *(goes towards him):* Is father with you?

GINA *(simultaneously):* Is he there?

RELLING: He certainly is.

HEDVIG: And you didn't tell us!

RELLING: Yes, I'm a beast. But I had to put the other beast to bed first—I refer of course to our daemonic friend—and then I fell asleep—

GINA: What has Hjalmar got to say today?

RELLING: Nothing.

HEDVIG: Doesn't he say anything?

RELLING: Not a damn thing.

GREGERS: No, no. I can understand that so well.

GINA: But what's he doing, then?

RELLING: He's on the sofa, snoring.

GINA: Is he? Yes, Hjalmar's a terrible snorer.

HEDVIG: You mean he's asleep?

RELLING: It certainly sounds like it.

225

GREGERS: It's quite understandable. After the spiritual conflict that's been rending him—

GINA: And he's not used to wandering around outside at night.

HEDVIG: Perhaps it's a good thing he's getting some sleep, mother.

GINA: Yes, I was just thinking that. We'd better not wake him up too soon. Thanks, Relling. I must clean the place up a bit, and then I'll— Come and give me a hand, Hedvig.

GINA *and* HEDVIG *go into the parlour.*

GREGERS *(turns to* RELLING*):* Can you explain this spiritual turmoil in Hjalmar Ekdal?

RELLING: Can't say I've noticed any spiritual turmoil in him.

GREGERS: What! At such a crisis, when his whole life has been given a new moral foundation—! How do you suppose a man of Hjalmar's personality—?

RELLING: Personality—*him?* If he ever had any tendency to the kind of abnormalities you call personality, they were nipped out of him, root and branch, before his voice broke. You take my word for it.

GREGERS: That's surprising, considering the love and care with which he was brought up.

RELLING: By those two twisted, hysterical maiden aunts, you mean?

GREGERS: At least they were idealists—but I suppose you'll laugh at me again for saying that.

RELLING: No, I'm not in the mood for that. I know all about it. I've had to endure vomits of rhetoric about his 'two spiritual mothers'. But I don't think he's got much to be grateful to them for. Hjalmar's tragedy is that all his life he's been regarded by everyone around him as a genius—

GREGERS: Well, isn't he? Deep down inside?

RELLING: I've never noticed any evidence of it. Oh, his father thought so, but—well, *he's* been a bloody fool all his life.

GREGERS: No, he has kept the innocence of a child all his life. That's something you can't understand.

RELLING: All right, have it your way. But when dear little Hjalmar somehow got to University, he was at once hailed as the great white hope there too. Well, he was handsome of course—that helps—you know, peaches and cream, the shopgirl's dream—and with his romantic temperament and throbbing voice and talent for declaiming other people's poetry and ideas—

GREGERS *(indignantly):* Are you talking about Hjalmar Ekdal?

RELLING: Yes. With your permission, that's what this idol you grovel to really looks like when you take him apart.

GREGERS: Well, I don't think I'm completely blind.

RELLING: You're not far off. You're a sick man too, you know.

GREGERS: Yes, you're right there.

RELLING: Oh, yes. Yours is a complicated case. To begin with, you've this tiresome rash of righteousness; and what's worse, you live in a perpetual delirium of hero-worship. You've always got to have something outside yourself that you can idolize.

GREGERS: That's true. I have to seek it outside myself.

RELLING: It's pathetic the way you make a fool of yourself over these supermen you imagine you see all around you. This is just another of those workmen's cottages where you started hawking your ideals. We're all insolvent here.

GREGERS: If that's your opinion of Hjalmar Ekdal, how can you spend so much time with him?

RELLING: I'm meant to be a doctor of sorts, God forgive me. I've got to do something for these wretched cripples I share a roof with.

GREGERS: I see. So Hjalmar Ekdal is sick too?

RELLING: Well, who isn't?

GREGERS: And what medicine are you giving him?

RELLING: My usual one. I feed the life-lie in him.

GREGERS: Life-*lie* did you say?

RELLING: Yes, that's right. The universal stimulant.

GREGERS: And what is the life-lie with which Hjalmar Ekdal is infected, if I may ask?

RELLING: You may not. I don't betray professional secrets to quacks. I wouldn't put it past you to make an even worse mess of him. But my remedy's infallible. I've used it on Molvik for years. I've made him daemonic. That's the serum I've injected into his skull.

GREGERS: Isn't he daemonic, then?

RELLING: What the hell does it mean, daemonic? It's just a bit of claptrap I thought up to keep him alive. If I hadn't done it the poor swine would have succumbed to self-contempt and despair years ago. And what about the old lieutenant? Well, he found the cure himself.

GREGERS: Lieutenant Ekdal? How do you mean?

RELLING: What about that? The great bear-hunter going into that musty old loft to chase rabbits? There isn't a happier sportsman in the world than that old man when they let him potter in there among all that junk. Those four or five withered Christmas trees smell the same to him as the great forests of Hoydal; the chickens are the wild game in the pine-tops; and the rabbits that flop across the floor are bears to challenge the strength and skill of the mighty hunter.

GREGERS: Poor Lieutenant Ekdal! Yes, he's had to abandon his youthful ideals.

RELLING: While I remember it, Mr. Werle Junior, forget that foreign word 'ideals'. Why not use that good old Norwegian word: 'lies'?

GREGERS: Do you suggest the two are related?

RELLING: About as closely as typhus and putrid fever.

GREGERS: Dr. Relling, I will not give up until I have rescued Hjalmar Ekdal from your clutches.

RELLING: So much the worse for him. Deprive the average human being of his life-lie, and you rob him of his happiness. (*To* HEDVIG, *as she enters from the parlour.*) Well, little wild-duck-mother, I'm off downstairs to see if your father's still pondering his great invention on my sofa.

He goes out through the front door.

GREGERS (*goes closer to* HEDVIG): I can see it, Hedvig. You haven't done it.

HEDVIG: What? Oh, that thing about the wild duck. No.

GREGERS: Your strength of purpose failed you when the moment for action came, I suppose.

HEDVIG: No, it wasn't that. It was just that when I woke this morning and remembered what we'd been talking about, I thought it all seemed so strange.

GREGERS: Strange?

HEDVIG: I don't know. Yesterday evening, when you first mentioned it, I thought there was something so beautiful in the idea; but when I'd slept on it and thought about it again, it didn't seem so good.

GREGERS: Oh, no. Of course you can't have grown up in this house without some rot setting in.

HEDVIG: I don't care about that. If only father would come back, I'd—

GREGERS: Oh, if only your eyes could be opened to what really matters in life! If only you had the courage to make your sacrifice truly and joyfully, you'd see—he'd come back to you! But I still believe in you, Hedvig. I believe in you.

He goes out through the front door. HEDVIG *walks around for a little; then she is about to go into the*

229

kitchen when there is a knock on the door of the loft.
HEDVIG *goes over and opens it slightly.* OLD EKDAL
comes out. She closes the door again.

EKDAL: Hm! It's not much fun having to take my exercise
alone.

HEDVIG: Didn't you feel like hunting today, grandfather?

EKDAL: It's bad weather for hunting today. Dark. You can
hardly see your hand in front of your face.

HEDVIG: Don't you ever feel you'd like to shoot something
else besides rabbits?

EKDAL: What's wrong with rabbits? Aren't they good
enough?

HEDVIG: Yes, but what about—well, the wild duck?

EKDAL *(laughs):* Oh, so you're afraid I'll shoot your wild
duck, are you? Don't worry, my child. I'd never do that.

HEDVIG: No, of course, you couldn't. I've heard it's very
difficult to shoot wild ducks.

EKDAL: Couldn't? What do you mean? Of course I could.

HEDVIG: How would you go about it, grandfather? I don't
mean with my wild duck, but with other ones?

EKDAL: I'd shoot them under the breast, Hedvig. That's the
safest place. And you've got to shoot against the feathers,
mind, not with them.

HEDVIG: Do they die then, grandfather?

EKDAL: You bet they die, if you shoot them properly. Well,
I must go in and—hm—clean myself up. You understand—
hm?

He goes into his room. HEDVIG *waits a few moments,
glances towards the door of the parlour, goes over to
the bookcase, reaches up on tiptoe, takes down the
double-barrelled pistol from the shelf and looks at it.*
GINA *enters from the parlour with her duster and
brush.* HEDVIG *quickly puts down the pistol, unnoticed.*

GINA: Don't stand there messing about with your father's things, Hedvig.

HEDVIG *(leaves the bookcase):* I only wanted to tidy up a little.

GINA: Go into the kitchen and see if the coffee's still hot. I'll take the tray when I go down.

> HEDVIG *goes out.* GINA *begins to sweep and clean the studio. After a few moments, the front door is cautiously opened and* HJALMAR *looks in. He is wearing his overcoat but is hatless and unwashed. His hair is tousled and his eyes are dull and tired.*

GINA *(stands with the brush in her hand and looks at him):* Oh. Hullo, Hjalmar—you've come.

HJALMAR *(walks in and answers in a flat voice):* I've come— but only to go at once.

GINA: Yes, yes, of course. But my goodness, look at you!

HJALMAR: At me?

GINA: And your nice winter coat! Well, that's done for.

HEDVIG *(in the kitchen doorway):* Mother, hadn't I better—?

> *Sees* HJALMAR, *gives a cry of joy and runs towards him.*

HEDVIG: Oh, father, father!

HJALMAR *(turns away with a gesture of rejection):* Get away, get away, get away! *(To* GINA.*)* Get her away from me!

GINA *(softly):* Go into the parlour, Hedvig.

> HEDVIG *goes silently out.*

HJALMAR *(feverishly pulls out the drawer of the table):* I must take my books with me. Where are my books?

GINA: What books?

HJALMAR: My scientific books, of course. The technical magazines I need for my invention.

GINA (*looks in the bookcase*): Are these the ones, without any covers?

HJALMAR: Of course they are.

GINA (*puts a heap of magazines on the table*): Shall I get Hedvig to cut the pages for you?

HJALMAR: I don't want them cut.

Short silence.

GINA: So you're really leaving us, Hjalmar?

HJALMAR (*rummaging among the books*): Have I any choice?

GINA: No, no.

HJALMAR (*vehemently*): I can't go on being pierced to the heart every hour of the day!

GINA: May God forgive you for thinking so vilely of me!

HJALMAR: Give me proof—!

GINA: I think you're the one who needs to do the proving.

HJALMAR: With your past! There are certain things a man has a right to demand—one might be tempted to call them demands of the ideal—

GINA: What about grandfather? What's going to become of him, poor old man?

HJALMAR: I know my duty. That helpless old man leaves with me. I shall go into town and make arrangements. Hm—(*Unwillingly.*) Has anyone seen my hat on the stairs?

GINA: No. Have you lost your hat?

HJALMAR: I had it on when I came back last night. Naturally. There can be no doubt about that. But I haven't been able to find it today.

GINA: For mercy's sake, where on earth did you get to with those two scallywags?

HJALMAR: Don't bother me with trivialities. Do you suppose I'm in a mood to recall details?

GINA: Well, I only hope you haven't caught cold, Hjalmar.

She goes out into the kitchen.

HJALMAR *(mutters to himself, half-audibly and furiously as he empties the drawer beneath the table):* You're a scoundrel, Relling! A cad, that's what you are! Oh, you vile seducer! I wish I could hire someone to stick a knife in your back!

He puts some old letters on one side, finds the letter he tore up yesterday, picks it up and looks at the pieces, then puts it quickly down again as GINA *returns.*

GINA *(puts a tray with coffee, etc., on the table):* I've brought you a cup of something warm, in case you feel inclined. And some bread and butter and a bit of cold fish.

HJALMAR *(glances at the tray):* Cold fish? Under this roof? Never! I've had no solid food for nearly twenty-four hours, but no matter. My notes! The first chapter of my memoirs! Where's my diary? Where are all my important papers? *(Opens the parlour door, but shrinks back.)* There she is again!

GINA: But for heaven's sake, the child's got to be somewhere.

HJALMAR: Come out.

He moves aside to make way for her. HEDVIG *enters, frightened.*

HJALMAR *(with his hand on the door-handle, says to* GINA*):* During my last minutes in what *was* my home, I wish to be spared the presence of outsiders.

He goes into the parlour.

HEDVIG *(runs to her mother and asks softly, trembling):* Does he mean me?

GINA: Stay in the kitchen, Hedvig. No, you'd better go to

your room. (*To* HJALMAR, *as she goes in to him.*) Stop rummaging in those drawers. I know where everything is.

HEDVIG (*stands motionless for a moment, anguished and bewildered, biting her lips to keep back her tears. Then she clenches her fists convulsively and says quietly*): The wild duck!

She steals over and takes the pistol from the shelf, opens the loft door a few inches, creeps in and pulls it shut behind her. In the parlour offstage, HJALMAR *and* GINA *begin to argue.*

HJALMAR (*comes out with some notebooks and old loose papers, which he puts down on the table*): Oh, that old bag's no use. There are hundreds of things I've got to lug away.

GINA (*comes after him with the bag*): Well, just take a shirt and a pair of knickers with you. You can come back for the rest later.

HJALMAR: Phew! It's so exhausting, all this packing!

He tears off his overcoat and throws it on the sofa.

GINA: And now your coffee's getting cold, too.

HJALMAR: Hm. (*Automatically takes a mouthful; then another.*)

GINA (*dusting the backs of the chairs*): The big difficulty'll be to find another big loft like this for the rabbits.

HJALMAR: What! Do you expect me to drag all those rabbits along too?

GINA: Well, you know grandfather can't live without his rabbits.

HJALMAR: Well, he'll have to learn. I'm giving up more important things than rabbits.

GINA (*dusting the bookshelves*): Shall I pack the flute?

HJALMAR: No. No flute for me. Give me the pistol, though.

GINA: Are you going to take the pistol?

HJALMAR: Yes. My loaded pistol.

GINA *(looks for it):* It's gone. He must have taken it with him.

HJALMAR: Is he in the loft?

GINA: Yes, of course he's in the loft.

HJALMAR: Hm. The lonely old man!

> *He takes a piece of bread and butter, eats it and empties his cup.*

GINA: If only we hadn't let that room, you could have moved in there.

HJALMAR: What! Live under the same roof as—? Never! Never!

GINA: Couldn't you manage in the parlour for a day or two? You'd be alone there.

HJALMAR: Within these walls? Never!

GINA: Well, how about downstairs with Relling and Molvik?

HJALMAR: Don't mention their names to me! The mere thought of them makes me lose my appetite. No, I must go out into the wind and snow, wandering from door to door seeking shelter for myself and my old father.

GINA: But you've no hat, Hjalmar. You've lost your hat.

HJALMAR: Scum! Vice-ridden scum, that's what they are! We must find a hat. *(Takes another piece of bread and butter.)* Something must be done. I don't intend to die of exposure.

GINA: What are you looking for?

HJALMAR: Butter.

GINA: Coming up right away. *(She goes out into the kitchen.)*

HJALMAR *(shouts after her):* Oh, it doesn't matter. I can eat dry bread.

GINA *(comes back with a butter-dish):* Here, this is meant to be fresh.

She pours him another cup of coffee. He sits on the sofa, spreads more butter on his bread, and eats and drinks for a few moments in silence.

HJALMAR: Would I really not be bothered by anyone if I stayed a couple of days in that room? Anyone at all?

GINA: No, of course not. Why don't you?

HJALMAR: I can't see any hope of getting all father's things moved out all at once.

GINA: And don't forget you've got to break the news to him about your not wanting to live with us any longer.

HJALMAR (*pushes away his coffee cup*): Yes, there's that too. I've got to dig up all those complications again. I must think things over. I must give myself breathing-space. I can't cope with so many different burdens in one day.

GINA: No, of course not. Especially with the weather what it is.

HJALMAR (*touches* WERLE's *letter*): I see that letter's still lying around.

GINA: Yes, I haven't touched it.

HJALMAR: Of course, it's nothing to do with me—

GINA: Well, I certainly don't want to make anything out of it.

HJALMAR: Still, there's no point in letting it get lost. In the confusion of my moving, it might easily—

GINA: I'll see it doesn't.

HJALMAR: Of course, this deed of gift really belongs to father. It's up to him to decide whether it's to be used or not.

GINA (*sighs*): Yes, poor old father!

HJALMAR: Perhaps for safety's sake—where can I find some glue?

GINA (*goes over to the bookcase*): The pot's here.

HJALMAR: And a brush.

GINA: The brush is here, too.

She brings them to him.

HJALMAR *(takes a pair of scissors):* Just a strip of paper along the back— *(Cuts and glues.)* Far be it from me to deprive other people of what belongs to them. Least of all a destitute old man. Or—any other person. There, now! Let that stand for a few minutes. And when it's dry, take it away. I never want to see the thing again. Never!

GREGERS WERLE *enters from the passage.*

GREGERS *(a little surprised):* Oh! Are you here, Hjalmar?

HJALMAR *(gets up quickly):* I was overcome by fatigue.

GREGERS: I see you've had breakfast, however.

HJALMAR: The body makes its demands too, you know.

GREGERS: Well, what have you decided?

HJALMAR: For a man like me, there is no choice. I'm just getting my most important belongings together. But that takes time, you know.

GINA *(a little impatiently):* Well, shall I make the room ready or shall I pack your bag?

HJALMAR *(gives an annoyed glance at GREGERS):* Pack. *And* make it ready.

GINA *(takes the bag):* Well, well. I'll put in a shirt and knick—and the other things.

She goes into the parlour and closes the door behind her.

GREGERS *(after a short silence):* I'd never envisaged it ending like this. Must you really leave your home?

HJALMAR *(wanders around restlessly):* Well, what do you want me to do? I wasn't cut out to suffer, Gregers. I must have peace and calm and comfort around me.

GREGERS: Well, why not? Try! It seems to me that now you

have firm ground to build on. Start afresh! And remember, you have your invention to live for too.

HJALMAR: Oh, don't talk about the invention. That may be further off than you think.

GREGERS: Oh?

HJALMAR: Well, damn it, what *is* there for me to invent? Other people have invented almost everything already! It's becoming more and more difficult every day—

GREGERS: But you've put so much work into it.

HJALMAR: It was that drunkard Relling who started me off on it.

GREGERS: Relling?

HJALMAR: Yes. It was he who first made me conscious that I had the talent to make some invention that would revolutionize photography.

GREGERS: I see. So it was Relling.

HJALMAR: Oh, it's made me so happy thinking about it! Not so much for the sake of the invention itself, but because Hedvig believed in it—believed in it as passionately and trustingly as only a child can believe in a thing. What I mean to say is—I was fool enough to delude myself into thinking she believed in it.

GREGERS: Do you seriously believe that Hedvig hasn't been sincere?

HJALMAR: I can believe anything now. Hedvig's the one who stands in my way. Her shadow is going to shut the sunlight out of my life.

GREGERS: Hedvig? Are you talking about Hedvig?

HJALMAR: I loved that child beyond words. I felt so incredibly happy every time I came back to this humble home and she ran to greet me with those sweet eyes peering at me. Oh, what a credulous fool I was! I loved her so, I loved her so. And I dreamed, I deluded myself into believing that she loved me too.

GREGERS: You call that a delusion?

HJALMAR: How can I know? I can't get anything out of Gina—and anyway, she's so totally insensitive to the idealistic aspect of all these complicated— But to you, Gregers, I feel impelled to open my heart. There's this dreadful doubt in my mind that perhaps Hedvig has never really and truly loved me.

GREGERS: Perhaps you may be given proof that she does. *(Listens.)* What was that? I think I can hear the wild duck crying.

HJALMAR: Yes, that's her quacking. Father's there in the loft.

GREGERS: Is he? *(His eyes shine with joy.)* I tell you, you may perhaps be given proof that your poor, misjudged Hedvig does love you.

HJALMAR: Oh, what proof can she give me? I couldn't believe anything from those lips.

GREGERS: Hedvig is incapable of deceit.

HJALMAR: Oh, Gregers, that's just what I can't be sure of. Who knows what Gina and that Mrs. Sœrby may not have said when they were gossiping up here? And that child keeps her ears open. That deed of gift may not have come as such a surprise to her as she made out. I thought I noticed something odd in her manner.

GREGERS: What on earth has come over you?

HJALMAR: I've had my eyes opened. Just you wait—you'll see. That deed of gift is only the beginning. Mrs. Soerby's always had a soft spot for Hedvig, and now she's in a position to do anything she likes for the child. They can take her from me any moment they want.

GREGERS: Hedvig will never leave you.

HJALMAR: I wouldn't be too sure of that. If they stand there beckoning to her with their hands full of—! And I, who loved her so much, so much! I couldn't imagine any greater happiness than to take her gently by the hand and lead her as a man leads a child who is afraid of the dark

through a large, empty room. I can see it now so clearly—
the poor photographer in his attic has never really meant
very much to her. She was just cunning enough to keep on
good terms with him until the time was ripe.

GREGERS: Oh, Hjalmar, you don't believe that.

HJALMAR: The tragedy is that I don't know what to believe—
and that I never will know. Oh, you're too much of an
idealist, my dear Gregers. If they came to her with their
hands full of gold and cried to the child: 'Leave him! We
can offer you life!'—

GREGERS (*swiftly*): Yes? What do you think she would reply?

HJALMAR: If I were to ask her: 'Hedvig, will you sacrifice
your life for me?'— (*He laughs scornfully.*) Oh, yes!
You'd hear what answer she'd give me!

A pistol shot is heard from the loft.

GREGERS (*cries joyfully*): Hjalmar!

HJALMAR (*enviously*): Oh, now he's started hunting.

GINA (*enters, worried*): Oh, Hjalmar, grandfather's banging
away in there on his own.

HJALMAR: I'll go and have a look.

GREGERS (*alive, excited*): Wait! Do you know what that
was?

HJALMAR: Of course I do.

GREGERS: No, you don't. But I know. It was the proof you
wanted.

HJALMAR: What proof?

GREGERS: A child's sacrifice. She has got your father to
shoot the wild duck.

HJALMAR: Shoot the wild duck?

GINA: What an idea!

HJALMAR: But why?

GREGERS: She wanted to sacrifice for you the most precious
of her possessions, because she thought that then you
would have to love her again.

HJALMAR *(gently, emotionally):* Oh, child, child!

GINA: The things she gets up to!

GREGERS: She only wanted you to love her again, Hjalmar. She couldn't live without it.

GINA *(almost in tears):* There, Hjalmar, you see.

HJALMAR: Where is she, Gina?

GINA *(sniffs):* Sitting outside in the kitchen, I suppose, poor child.

HJALMAR *(walks across and flings open the kitchen door):* Hedvig, come here. Come and talk to me. *(Looks round.)* No, she isn't here.

GINA: She must be in her room, then.

HJALMAR *(outside):* No, she isn't there, either. *(Comes back.)* She must have gone out.

GINA: Well, you didn't want to have her in the house.

HJALMAR: Oh, I wish she'd come home again soon, so that I can tell her! Now everything will be all right, Gregers. Now I think we can start life afresh.

GREGERS *(quietly):* I knew it. Through the child will come resurrection.

OLD EKDAL *appears in the doorway of his room. He is in full uniform, and is busy buckling on his sword.*

HJALMAR *(amazed):* Father! Have you been in there?

GINA: Have you been shooting in your room?

EKDAL *(indignantly, comes closer):* So you go hunting alone now, do you, Hjalmar?

HJALMAR *(confused):* Then it wasn't you who fired that shot in the loft?

EKDAL: Wasn't me? Hm!

GREGERS *(cries to HJALMAR):* Hjalmar! She has shot the wild duck herself!

HJALMAR: What's going on around here?

He runs over to the door of the loft, pulls it open, looks in and cries.

HJALMAR: Hedvig!
GINA *(runs over to the door):* Oh, God! What is it?
HJALMAR *(goes inside):* She's lying on the floor.
GREGERS: Lying on the floor? Hedvig?

He joins HJALMAR *inside.*

GINA *(simultaneously):* Hedvig!

She goes into the loft.

GINA: Oh, no, no, no!
EKDAL *(laughs):* Now she's started hunting too!

HJALMAR, GINA *and* GREGERS *drag* HEDVIG *into the studio. Her right hand is hanging down with the pistol tightly clasped between her fingers.*

HJALMAR *(distraught):* The pistol's gone off! She's shot herself! Call for help! Help!
GINA *(runs out into the passage and calls down):* Relling! Relling! Dr. Relling! Come upstairs! As quick as you can!

HJALMAR *and* GREGERS *lay* HEDVIG *on the sofa.*

EKDAL *(quietly):* The forest has taken its revenge.
HJALMAR *(on his knees beside her):* She's coming round now! She'll be all right!
GINA *(comes back):* Where's the wound? I can't see anything—

RELLING *hurries in.* MOLVIK *follows, with no waistcoat or tie, and with his coat hanging open.*

RELLING: What's happened?
GINA: They say Hedvig's shot herself.

HJALMAR: Come here and help us.

RELLING: Shot herself!

He pushes the table aside and begins to examine her.

HJALMAR *(lying on the floor, gazes up at him in anguish):* It can't be dangerous? Can it, Relling? She's hardly bleeding at all. It can't be dangerous, can it?

RELLING: How did it happen?

HJALMAR: Oh, how do I know?

GINA: She was going to shoot the wild duck.

RELLING: The wild duck?

HJALMAR: The pistol must have gone off.

RELLING: Hm. I see.

EKDAL: The forest has taken its revenge. But I'm not afraid of it.

He goes into the loft and closes the door behind him.

HJALMAR: Well, Relling, why don't you say something?

RELLING: The bullet has entered her breast.

HJALMAR: But she'll be all right?

RELLING: Surely you can see that Hedvig is dead.

GINA *(bursts into tears):* Oh, my child, my child!

GREGERS *(hoarsely):* The vasty deep—!

HJALMAR *(jumps up):* Yes, yes, she must live! Oh, God bless you, Relling, only for a moment! Only long enough for me to tell her how much I loved her—always—always!

RELLING: The bullet entered her heart. Internal haemorrhage. She died instantaneously.

HJALMAR: And I drove her from me like an animal! And she crept into the loft in terror, and died there—because she loved me! *(Sobs.)* I can never atone for this—never tell her—! *(Clasps his hands and cries upwards)* Oh—You up there—if You exist! Why have You done this to me?

GINA: Hush, hush, don't carry on like that. We had no right to keep her—I suppose—

MOLVIK: The child is not dead, but sleepeth.

RELLING: Rubbish!

HJALMAR (*becomes calm, goes across to the sofa and looks down at* HEDVIG, *with folded arms*): How stiff and still she lies!

RELLING (*tries to free the pistol from her fingers*): She's holding on to it so tightly. So tightly.

GINA: No, no, Relling, don't break her fingers. Let the pistol stay there.

HJALMAR: Let her keep it.

GINA: Yes, let her. But the child mustn't lie here like a show. We'll take her into her own room. Help me, Hjalmar.

HJALMAR *and* GINA *pick* HEDVIG *up*.

HJALMAR (*as they carry her out*): Oh, Gina, Gina! How shall we live after this?

GINA: We must help each other. Now she belongs to both of us, you know.

MOLVIK (*stretches out his arms and mumbles*): Praised be the Lord! To dust thou shalt return! To dust thou shalt return!

RELLING (*whispers*): Shut up, man. You're drunk.

HJALMAR *and* GINA *carry the body out through the kitchen door.* RELLING *shuts it behind them.* MOLVIK *slinks out into the passage.*

RELLING (*goes over to* GREGERS *and says*): No one's ever going to make me believe that this was an accident.

GREGERS (*who has stood overcome by horror, shaking convulsively*): No one will ever know how this dreadful thing happened.

RELLING: The powder had burned her dress. She must have pressed the pistol against her breast before she fired.

GREGERS: Hedvig has not died in vain. Did you see how grief set free all that is most noble in him?

RELLING: Most men are noble when they stand by a death-bed. But how long do you think this nobility will last?

GREGERS: For as long as he lives. And it will grow, and grow.

RELLING: In nine months, little Hedvig will be nothing more to him than a theme for a recitation.

GREGERS: You dare say that about Hjalmar Ekdal!

RELLING: Let's talk about it again when the first grasses have withered on her grave. Then you'll hear him gulping about 'the child untimely ripped from her father's bosom'. You'll see him stewing in emotion and self-admiration and self-pity. Just you wait.

GREGERS: If you are right and I am wrong, life is not worth living.

RELLING: Oh, life would be all right if we didn't have to put up with these damned creditors who keep pestering us with the demands of their ideals.

GREGERS *(stares ahead of him):* In that case, I am glad that my destiny is what it is.

RELLING: And what, if I may ask, is your destiny?

GREGERS *(as he goes towards the door):* To be the thirteenth at table.

RELLING *laughs and spits.*

Note on the Translation

The Wild Duck is, after *Little Eyolf,* the most difficult of Ibsen's prose plays to translate. Hjalmar, Gregers and Gina have particularly idiosyncratic mannerisms of speech which are most awkward to render. Hjalmar talks pretentiously, for ever starting sentences he cannot finish, mixing his metaphors, wandering into cliché and indulging in extravagant romanticizing and self-pity. It is always tempting when dealing with a ridiculous character to pare down his absurdities, but it is a temptation that must be resisted; his ridiculousness must be given full play; it is a baroque part for a baroque actor. Gregers is part political fanatic, part evangelist, and has acquired the worst rhetorical characteristics of both. He, like Hjalmar, is full of other people's phrases. Gina is even more of a problem. Her speech is lower-class, and lower-class dialogue is especially difficult to translate because any real equivalent in English has strong regional associations. A Norwegian woman cannot talk Cockney or North Country, and one is forced to compromise with a rough unlocalized speech which necessarily loses some of the richness of the original. In the Norwegian she frequently lapses into Malapropisms (*pigstol* for *pistol, den intricata fordringen* for *den ideala fordringen,* "the ideal demand"), but Malapropisms in English are death to any dialogue except that of farce, and I have not tried to convey them.

The phrase *havsens bund*, which Gregers uses in Act 3 to describe the bottom of the sea, and which Hedvig says is the phrase she always calls to mind when she thinks of the loft, presents considerable difficulties. It has overtones of both infinity and oblivion; Gregers mutters it hoarsely to himself in the last act when he realizes that Hedvig is dead, and in that context it epitomizes the choice she has made. In Norwegian it is an antique phrase, something like "the vasty deep"; an alternative would be "the deep blue sea." The overriding essential is that its significance should be clear when Gregers uses it at the climax of the play.

I again gladly acknowledge my debt to Mr. Casper Wrede for much minute criticism and more valuable suggestions than I can list.

The Master Builder

Introduction

Ibsen wrote *The Master Builder* in Christiania in 1892, at the age of sixty-four. It was the first play he had written in Norway since *The Pretenders* twenty-nine years before.

The previous summer (1891) he had left his home in Munich for a holiday to the North Cape. While he was there, he decided to stay in Christiania over the winter; and as things turned out he stayed there for the remaining fifteen years of his life.

There were several reasons for this decision to settle again in his native country after twenty-seven years abroad. He told Georg Brandes that it would be more convenient for him financially, but Fru Ibsen later said she thought it was because he wanted to die in Norway. During his visit in 1885 he had been unwell, and had then spoken of settling there; and in the beginning of 1890 he had a severe attack of influenza, which may have helped to remind him that he was no longer young. Moreover, he still had the obsessive longing for the sea which twice recently had driven him northwards (in 1885 and 1887). A further reason was that his son Sigurd was now very active in Norwegian politics and was being spoken of as a likely Foreign Minister as soon as Norway should obtain her independence from Sweden. Ibsen was very devoted to his son, and although he did not, in his old age, take much interest in politics he now found himself acclaimed by both the right and the left wing parties. Life in

251

Norway had seemed insufferable to him when he had been impoverished and unsuccessful. Now that he was a national hero, it held certain attractions. So he stayed.

Departing from his usual routine of writing only during the summer and autumn, he began work on a new play the following March (1892). Before the spring was over, however, he scrapped everything he had written, and did not start again until August. We do not know how long he took to complete his new draft, but the unusual number of small mistakes and omissions suggest that he wrote it very rapidly. By 30th October he had finished his revisions and sent his fair copy off to the printer; it contains fewer divergencies from the original draft than in any other of his plays.

The Master Builder was published by Gyldendal of Copenhagen on 12th December 1892. People everywhere were puzzled by it, as they had been puzzled by his two preceding plays, *The Lady from the Sea* and *Hedda Gabler*, but for a different reason. Some new element had entered into Ibsen's work. It had been perceptible in *Hedda Gabler*, but in *The Master Builder* it was more than perceptible; it stuck out for all to see. Even without Freud to suggest the implications of all that talk about towers and spires that made an old man feel giddy and a young girl hear harps in the air, *The Master Builder* seemed primarily to be a play about sexual passion. People speculated as to what new influence could have entered into the aged playwright's life to turn his thoughts so sharply in this direction, and not until after Ibsen's death in 1906 was the answer given.

In that year Georg Brandes published a series of letters which Ibsen had written between October 1889 and December 1890 (i.e. twenty-nine to fifteen months before he began *The Master Builder*) to a young Viennese girl named Emilie Bardach. These revealed that in the summer of 1889, when Ibsen was sixty-one and Emilie eighteen, they had met at Gossensass in the Austrian Tyrol and that some kind of infatuation had resulted; whether this had been mutual or one-sided was not quite clear. They had corresponded for over a year and then Ibsen, gently but firmly, had told her not to write to him any more.

Shortly after these letters appeared a friend of Ibsen, the German literary historian Julius Elias, published an account of a conversation he had had with Ibsen concerning Emilie Bardach which seemed to put the incident into proportion. This conversation had taken place in Berlin in February 1891, over lunch, while Ibsen was waiting for a train:

'An expansive mood came over Ibsen and, chuckling over his champagne glass, he said: "Do you know, my next play is already hovering before me—in general outline, of course. One thing I can see clearly, though—an experience I once had myself—a female character. Very interesting—very interesting." Then he related how he had met in the Tyrol a Viennese girl of very remarkable character, who had at once made him her confidant. The gist of it was that she was not interested in the idea of marrying some decently brought-up young man; most likely she would never marry. What tempted, fascinated and delighted her was to lure other women's husbands away from them. She was a demonic little wrecker; she often seemed to him like a little bird of prey, who would gladly have included him among her victims. He had studied her very, very closely. But she had had no great success with him. "She did not get hold of me, but I got hold of her—for my play. Then I fancy she consoled herself with someone else." '

That seemed to settle the matter. Ibsen's version of Emilie's character, or Elias's report of it, was generally accepted, and Emilie Bardach went down to history while she was still a young woman (she lived until 1st November 1955) as a predatory little monster more or less identical with Hilde Wangel.

In 1923, however, two remarkable articles entitled 'Ibsen

and Emilie Bardach' were published in the American *Century Magazine*. The author was an Ibsen enthusiast named Basil King. In 1908, while travelling in Europe, he had met Emilie, then a woman of thirty-seven, 'gentle of manner, soft of voice, dressed with the distinction of which Viennese women have long possessed the art . . . going to Paris for the spring, to London for the season, and often to Scotland for country house gatherings'. She allowed King to see, and in due course to quote from, the diary she had kept during the time she had known and corresponded with Ibsen. These articles caused no particular sensation at the time, interest in Ibsen being rather low in England and America during the early twenties; there seems, however, no reason to doubt the authenticity of the diary extracts, and they go much further than Ibsen's (or Elias's) account of the incident to explain the stormy and dynamic quality of his last five plays, after the apparent optimism of *The Lady from the Sea*.

Ibsen had come to Gossensass in July 1889. He had holidayed there on several previous occasions, but this was his first visit for five years, and the town had decided to celebrate his return by naming his old look-out on the hill the Ibsenplatz. There was a festal procession, and Ibsen, despite the steep ascent, climbed at the head of it and 'received with friendliness and dignity all the homage that was accorded him'. Emilie Bardach wrote in her diary (5th August 1889):

'The weather is very bad and we cannot make any excursions. The day of the Ibsen fête has been the only fine one; but I washed my hair and could not go. After the concert, however, I made his acquaintance in a way quite delightful.'

On the outskirts of the town there was a valley named the Pflerschtal, with a stream flowing through it and a view of mountains and glaciers. While walking here, Ibsen saw a girl seated on a bench with a book. He came and sat beside her, and learned her name, her parentage, her home residence, and the fact that in Gossensass they lived so near together that his windows looked into hers. A few days later, she ran into him at a dull birthday party. 'It is a pity,' she noted, 'that German gives him so much difficulty, as apart from that we understand each other so well.'

She fell ill and, a few days later, Ibsen came to see her, climbing over the garden gate to do so. 'He remained with me a long while, and was both kind and sympathetic.' A little later: 'We talk a great deal together. His ardour ought to make me feel proud.' Then:

'Ibsen has begun to talk to me quite seriously about myself. He stayed a long time with me on Saturday, and also again this evening. Our being so much together cannot but have some painful influence over me. He puts such strong feeling into what he says to me. His words often give me a sensation of terror and cold. He talks about the most serious things in life, and believes in me so much. He expects from me much, much, much more than I am afraid he will ever find. Never in his whole life, he says, has he felt so much joy in knowing anyone. He never admired anyone as he admires me. But all in him is truly good and noble! What a pity it is that I cannot remember all his words! He begs me so intensely to talk freely to him, to be absolutely frank with him, so that we may become fellow-workers together.'

Next she writes: 'Mama has just gone out, so that I have the room to myself. At last I am free to put down the incredible things of these recent days. How poor and insufficient are words! Tears say these things better. Passion has come when it cannot lead to anything, when both of us are bound by so many ties. Eternal obstacles! Are they in my will? Or are they in the circumstances? . . . How could I compare anything else that has happened to an outpouring like this? It could never go so far, and yet—' She swings off on to Baron A., the only lover who afforded a standard of comparison. 'But how much calmer *he* was, how inarticulate, beside this volcano, so terribly beautiful! Yesterday afternoon, we were alone together at last! Oh, the words! If only they could have stamped themselves on my heart more deeply and distinctly! All that has been offered me before was only the pretence at love. This is the true love, the ideal, he says, to which without knowing it he gave himself in his art. At last he is a true poet through pain and renunciation. And yet he is glad of having known me—the most beautiful! the wonderful! Too late! How small I seem to myself that I cannot spring to him!'

Neither Ibsen's wife nor Emilie's mother suspected what was afoot. But:

'The obstacles! How they grow more numerous, the more I think of them! The difference of age!—his wife!—his son!—all that there is to keep us apart! Did this have to happen? Could I have foreseen it? Could I have prevented it? When he talks to me as he does, I often feel that I must go far away from here—far away!—and yet I suffer at the thought of leaving him. I suffer most from his impatience, his restlessness. I begin to feel it now, even when we are in the salon, quite apart from each other . . .

'It all came to me so suddenly! I noticed for the first time how he began to change his regular ways of life, but I didn't know what it meant. Of course I was flattered at his sympathy, and at being distinguished among the many who surround him, eager for a word . . .'

An early snowstorm came, and the guests at Gossensass began to leave. Emilie realized they would soon have to part. 'And I have nothing to give him, not even my picture, when he is giving me so much. But we both feel it is best outwardly to remain as strangers . . . His wife shows me much attention. Yesterday I had a long talk with his son . . .

'I am reading Ibsen's *Love's Comedy*, but if anyone comes I am seen holding Beaconsfield's *Endymion* in my hands. Nearly everyone has gone. The days we have still to spend can now be counted. I don't think about the future. The present is too much. We had a long talk together in the morning, and after lunch he came again and sat with me. What am I to think? He says it is to be my life's aim to work with him. We are to write to each other often; but what am I to write?'

Ibsen confided his feelings to two ladies. One fainted; another described the scene to Emilie as 'beautiful and terrible as a thunderstorm. She wonders that I do not lose my head. She says that she herself would have been absolutely overcome. This consoles me. I do not seem so weak.'

Did something happen between Ibsen and Emilie on 19th September, and if so was it anything like what Hilde Wangel describes as having happened between her and Solness on another 19th September? Nearly forty years later, in 1927, Emilie told A. E. Zucker that Ibsen had never kissed her; perhaps with Ibsen, as with Solness, these things only happened in his mind. Next day, 20th September, he wrote in Emilie's album: *'Hohes, schmerzliches Glück—um das Unerreichbare zu ringen!'*—'High and painful joy—to struggle for the unattainable!'

A week later, on 27th September, Emilie noted in her diary: 'Our last day at Gossensass. Then nothing but memory will remain. Two weeks ago, memory seemed to Ibsen so beautiful, and now—! He says that tomorrow he will stand on the ruins of his happiness. These last two months are more important in his life than anything that has gone before. Am I unnatural in being so terribly quiet and normal? . . . Last evening, when Mama went to talk to his wife, he came over and sat at our table. We were quite alone. He talked about his plans. I alone am in them—I, and I again. I feel quieter because he is quieter, though yesterday he was terrible.'

That night, at 3 a.m., the express from Verona to Vienna

passed through Gossensass, and Emilie left on it. The same night, she wrote in her diary:

'He means to possess me. This is his absolute will. He intends to overcome all obstacles. I do what I can to keep him from feeling this, and yet I listen as he describes what is to lie before us—going from one country to another—I with him—enjoying his triumphs together . . . Our parting was easier than I had feared.'

Emilie told Zucker in 1927 that Ibsen had, in Gossensass, 'spoken to her of the possibility of a divorce and of a subsequent union with her, in the course of which they were to travel widely and see the world'. The last entry in her diary would seem to bear this out. Once back in Munich, however, Ibsen seemed to resign himself to the impossibility of going through with such a plan. Perhaps he feared the scandal; perhaps he felt a duty towards his sickly and ageing wife, who had stood so firmly by him during the long years of failure; perhaps he reflected that the difference of forty-three years between their ages was too great; perhaps, away from Gossensass, he felt old. Probably all these considerations influenced him. At any rate, his letters from Munich to Emilie in Vienna are no more than those of an affectionate old man to a charming schoolgirl (though we must bear in mind that he is writing in a foreign language which 'gives him much difficulty', that he was always an extremely inhibited letter-writer, and that he must have been very careful not to commit himself on paper).

München, Maximilianstrasse 32.
7th October 1889.

With my whole heart I thank you, my beloved Fräulein, for the dear and delightful letter which I received on the last day of my stay at Gossensass, and have read over and over again.

There the last autumn week was a very sad one, or it

was so to me. No more sunshine. Everything—gone. The few remaining guests could give me no compensation for the brief and beautiful end-of-summer life. I went to walk in the Pflerschtal. There there is a bench where two can commune together. But the bench was empty and I went by without sitting down. So, too, the big salon was waste and desolate . . . Do you remember the big, deep bay-window on the right from the verandah? What a charming niche! The flowers and plants are still there, smelling so sweetly—but how empty!—how lonely!—how forsaken!

We are back here at home—and you in Vienna. You write that you feel surer of yourself, more independent, happier. How glad I am of these words! I shall say no more.

A new poem begins to dawn in me. I want to work on it this winter, transmuting into it the glowing inspiration of the summer. But the end may be disappointment. I feel it. It is my way. I told you once that I only corresponded by telegraph. So take this letter as it is. You will know what it means. A thousand greetings from your devoted—H.I.

The 'poem' may have been *Hedda Gabler,* which he was to write the following year, or it may have been *The Master Builder* itself. He did not in fact write *The Master Builder* until three years later, but he may have conceived it at this stage and then deliberately have put it aside until he could consider it with more detachment.

Emilie's diary, 8th October 1889:

'A few words before I go to bed. I have good news. Today, at last, came Ibsen's long-expected letter. He wants me to read between the lines. But do not the lines themselves say enough? This evening I paid Grandmama a quite unpleasant visit. The weather is hot and stuffy and so is Papa's mood. In other days, this would have depressed me: but now I have something to keep me up.'

We do not know how she replied to Ibsen, for he did not preserve her letter. On 15th October, however, he writes again:

I receive your letter with a thousand thanks—and have read it, and read it again. Here I sit as usual at my desk, and would gladly work but cannot do so.

My imagination is ragingly at work, but is always straying to where in working hours it should not. I cannot keep down the memories of the summer, neither do I want to. The things we have lived through I live again and again—and still again. To make of them a poem is for the time being impossible.

For the time being?

Shall I ever succeed in the future? And do I really wish that I could and would so succeed?

For the moment, at any rate, I cannot—or so I believe. That I feel—that I know.

And yet it must come. Decidedly it must come. But will it? or can it?

Ah, dear Fräulein—but forgive me!—you wrote so charmingly in your last—no, no! God forbid!—in your *previous* letter you wrote so charmingly: 'I am not Fräulein for you'—So, dear Child,—for that you surely are for me—tell me—do you remember that once we talked about Stupidity and Madness—or, more correctly, *I* talked about it—and you took up the role of teacher, and remarked, in your soft, musical voice, and with your far-away look, that there is always a difference between Stupidity and Madness . . . Well, then,

I keep thinking over and over again: Was it a Stupidity or was it Madness that we should have come together? Or was it both Stupidity *and* Madness? Or was it neither?

I believe the last is the only supposition that would stand the test. It was a simple necessity of nature. It was equally our fate. . . . Your always devoted—H.I.

On receipt of this letter, Emilie wrote in her diary: 'I left it unopened till I had finished everything, and could read it quietly. But I was not quiet after reading it. Why does he not tell me of something to read which would feed my mind instead of writing in a way to inflame my already excited imagination? I shall answer very soberly.'

Ibsen to Emilie, 29th October 1889:

I have been meaning every day to write you a few words, but I wanted to enclose the photograph. This is still not ready, and my letter must go off without it . . .

How charmingly you write! Please keep sending me a few lines, whenever you have a half hour not good for anything else.

So you leave my letters unopened till you are alone and quite undisturbed! Dear Child! I shall not try to thank you. That would be superfluous. You know what I mean.

Don't be uneasy because just now I cannot work. In the back of my mind, I am working all the time. I am dreaming over something which, when it has ripened, will become a poem.

Someone is coming. Can write no further. Next time a longer letter. Your truly devoted H.I.

Emilie's diary: 'I wrote to him on Monday, very late at night. Though I was tired, I did not want to put off doing so, because I had to thank him for the books I received on Sunday. The same evening I had read *Rosmersholm*, parts of which are very fine. I have to make so many duty calls, but this and a great many other things I can stand better than I used to. They are only the outward things; my inner world is something very different. Oh, the terror and beauty of having him care about me as he never cared about anyone else! But when he is suffering he calls it *hohes, schmerzliches Glück*—high and painful joy!'

Ibsen to Emilie, 19th November 1889:

At last I can send you the new picture. I hope you may find it a better likeness than the one you have already. A German sketch of my life will appear within a few days, and you will receive it at once. Read it when you have the time. It will tell you my story up to the end of last year.

Heartfelt thanks for your dear letter; but what do you think of me for not having answered it earlier? And yet—you know it well—you are always in my thoughts, and will remain there. An active exchange of letters is on my side an impossibility. I have already said so. Take me as I am.

I am greatly preoccupied with the preparations for my new play. Sit tight at my desk the whole day. Go out only towards evening. I dream and remember and write. To dream is fine; but the reality at times can still be finer. Your most devoted H.I.

On the back of the photograph stood the inscription: *'An die Maisonne eines Septemberlebens'*—'To the May sun of a September life.'

Ibsen to Emilie, 6th December 1889:

Two dear, dear letters have I had from you, and answered neither till now. What do you think of me? But I cannot find the quiet necessary to writing you anything orderly or straightforward. This evening I must go to the theatre to see *An Enemy of the People*. The mere thought of it is a torture. Then, too, I must give up for the time being the hope of getting your photograph. But better so than to have an unfavourable picture. Besides, how vividly your dear, serene features remain with me in my memory! The same enigmatic princess stands behind them. But the enigma itself? One can dream of it, and write about it—and that I do. It is some little compensation for the unattainable—for the unfathomable reality. In my imagination I always see you wearing the pearls you love so much. In this taste for pearls I see something deeper, something hidden. I often think of it. Sometimes I think I have found the interpretation— and then again not. Next time I shall try to answer some of your questions; but I myself have so many questions to ask you. I am always doing it—inwardly—inaudibly. Your devoted H.I.

In her diary, Emilie repeats his words: 'It is some little compensation for the unattainable, for the unfathomable reality.'

Ibsen to Emilie, 22nd December 1889:

How shall I thank you for your dear and delightful letter? I simply am not able to, at least not as I should like. The writing of letters is always hard for me. I think I have told you so already, and you will in any case have noticed it for yourself.

I read your letter over and over, for through it the voice of the summer awakens so clearly. I see—I experience again—the things we lived together. As a lovely creature of the summer, dear Princess, I have known you, as a being of the season of butterflies and wild flowers. How I should like to see you as you are in winter! I am always with you in spirit. I see you in the Ring Strasse, light, quick, poised like a bird, gracious in velvet and furs. In soirées, in society, I also see you, and especially at the theatre, leaning back, a tired look in your mysterious eyes. I should like, too, to see you at home, but here I don't succeed, as I haven't the data. You have told me so little of your home-life—hardly anything definite. As a matter of fact, dear Princess, in many important details we are strangers to each other . . .

More than anything I should like to see you on Christmas night at home, where I suppose you will be. As to what happens to you there, I have no clear idea. I only imagine—to myself.

And then I have a strange feeling that you and Christmas don't go well together. But who knows? Perhaps you do. In any case accept my heartfelt wishes and a thousand greetings. Your always devoted H.I.

On the same day, 22nd December 1889, Emilie wrote to Ibsen, enclosing at last her photograph; it is one of the only two letters from her which survived.

Sunday.

Here is the photograph—very unlike the original—to wish you a happy Christmas. Are you satisfied with it? Do you think it is a good one? I don't think any better picture of me can be expected, but I hope it may give you some small pleasure. Now I must confess that I have had this proof for a fortnight—I kept it back so long in order to send it to you as a Christmas greeting. It was hard to keep it a secret from you for so long, but

I wanted to have some little thing to contribute to the lovely holiday. Should I play no role at all in that! It's bad enough that I am not able to do more. In spite of my *'Nicht Rönnaug'*, a few weeks ago I painted a trifle for you which would have been altogether pointless if it did not recall Gossensass. I used to buy little deer bells there, and since I so often met you on my way home from my study trip to the Strassberg ruins I perpetuated the picture on one of these bells. Then I waited for your son to come here as I would have liked to give it to him to take to you—but he didn't come and it seemed too small a thing to make a business of sending it. I will be silent for a while, then I will be able to tell you better about that. How much longer are you going to make me wait? This detailed letter which is to tell me so much—but no—don't think this is a reproach—I don't mean it like that. I will send a Christmas greeting to your wife—I must write a few words just to her.

Well, once more many tender wishes and regards.
Sincerely,
　　　Emilie.

Ibsen to Emilie, 30th December 1889:

Your lovely and charming picture, so eloquently like you, has given me a wholly indescribable joy. I thank you for it a thousand times, and straight from the heart. How you have brought back, now in midwinter, those brief sunny summer days!

So, too, I thank you from the heart for your dear, dear letter. From me you must expect no more than a few words. I lack the time, and the necessary quiet and solitude, to write to you as I should like . . .

Ibsen to Emilie, 16th January 1890:

How sorry I am to learn that you, too, have been ill. But what do you think! I had a strong presentiment that it was so. In my imagination I saw you lying in bed, pale, feverish, but sweet and lovely as ever . . . How thankful I am that I have your charming picture!

Ibsen to Emilie, 16th February 1890:

Long, very long, have I left your last, dear letter— read and read again—without an answer. Take today my heartfelt thanks for it, though given in very few words. Henceforth, till we see each other face to face, you will hear little from me, and very seldom. Believe me, it is better so. It is the only right thing. It is a matter of conscience with me to end our correspondence, or at least to limit it. You yourself should have as little to do with me as possible. With your young life you have other aims to follow, other tasks to fulfil. And I—I have told you so already—can never be content with a mere exchange of letters. For me it is only half the thing; it is a false situation. Not to give myself wholly and unreservedly makes me unhappy. It is my nature. I cannot change it. You are so delicately subtle, so instinctively penetrating, that you will easily see what I mean. When we are together again, I shall be able to explain it more fully. Till then, and always, you will be in my thoughts. You will be so even more when we no longer have to stop at this wearisome halfway house of correspondence. A thousand greetings. Your H.I.

She replied to him the following day:

Please forgive me for writing again so soon. All these days I had been intending to write to you, for it is part of my nature to feel anxious about persons to whom I am deeply attached, if I do not hear from them for a longish time. Possibly this is a petty characteristic, but it is impossible to control one's feelings. Nevertheless, I mean to control mine, and since I knew how sensitive you are in this respect I came halfway to meet you. Yes, I knew very well that you are an unwilling letter-writer, and from time to time I even felt that you might find my letters a nuisance. All the same, your last letter has shaken me badly, and I have needed all my self-control to conceal my feelings. But I don't want this to prevent you from carrying out your intentions. I certainly do not wish you to write to me frequently and, since you wish it, I shall also refrain. However, I cannot allow myself to prescribe the problems and the moods to which, as you say, I should surrender myself in my young life. What I have so often told you remains unaltered and I can never forget it. Unfortunately the fact remains that I cannot surrender myself completely, nor taste unalloyed enjoyment. Forgive me for drawing you into a conflict with fate. That is ungrateful of me, seeing that you have so often said to me that whatever happens we shall remain good friends, and that I must hold fast to that. And is it friendship not to know if the other is ill or well, happy or wretched? And then can I prevent the thought coming to me that *you* want to avoid seeing me again, and anyhow, if you do not write, how am I to know where we can find each other again? Well, I'll be very, very patient; I can wait, but I shall suffer very much if I don't get a line or a book from you from time to time, or some other proof that you think of me. I am not noble enough to dispense with such little proofs of your interest.

Ought I to be ashamed of my frankness? Will you think less of me for not wishing to give up what has made me so much happier and more contented through all these months? I know you a little and that is why I understand so much that is in you, but I am sure that *your conscience* should never hinder you from continuing to write to me. By so doing you only show your kindness. I will try to understand all other reasons that may prevent you from writing and certainly I don't want you to act against your feelings. What a multitude of things there are to write about, but you do not wish me to write, even though I should not expect an answer.

Tonight I have an invitation to a ball—with friends; I never go out in public. When I am there I shall allow myself to think a little about you because I often find parties like these extremely uninspiring, unless I have something of my own to fall back on. Anyhow, I mean to go, if I can.

With love,
Emilie.

Emilie made no entries in her diary for four days after receiving the news that Ibsen wished to break off their correspondence. Then she writes of balls, singing lessons, domestic duties. Then suddenly: 'What is my inner life after Ibsen's letter? I wrote at once and henceforth will be silent, silent.' Ten days later: 'Will he never write any more? I cannot think about it. Who could? And yet, not to do so is in his nature. In his very kindness there is often cruelty.'

For seven months he did not write to her. During this time, he was struggling with *Hedda Gabler*.* On 29th June

---

*It may be noted that in the first draft of *Hedda Gabler*, in the scene where Hedda shows Lœvborg her honeymoon photographs, the dialogue runs as follows:

he wrote to the Swedish poet Carl Snoilsky that he had been hoping to spend the summer in the Tyrol but had encountered difficulties in the writing of his new play and did not want to leave Munich until he had overcome them. He had in fact been planning to return to Gossensass and from the references in his letters to 'when we are together again' I think it is fair to assume that he hoped to meet Emilie there (we must remember that her parents knew nothing of her feelings for Ibsen).

In September, he broke his silence to write to Emilie a letter of sympathy on the bereavement of her father, with some news of himself and his family, but no more. On 30th December, he wrote briefly to thank her for a Christmas present:

> I have duly received your dear letter, as well as the bell with the beautiful picture. I thank you for them, straight from the heart. My wife finds the picture very pretty. But I beg you, for the time being, not to write to me again. When conditions have changed, I will let you know. I shall soon send you my new play. Accept it in friendship—but in silence. How I should love to see you and talk with you again! A Happy New Year to you and to Madame your mother. Your always devoted H.I.

She did not write to him again, nor did the meeting to which they had both looked forward so eagerly ever take

---

HEDDA: What was this little village called?

TESMAN: What? Let me think. Oh, that's Gossensass, on the Brenner Pass. We stayed a day there—

But when he revised the play Ibsen struck out all mention of Gossensass, so that the dialogue reads:

HEDDA: Do you remember this little village?

TESMAN: Oh, that one down by the Brenner Pass? We stayed a night there—

place. For seven years, there was no contact between them.
Then, on his seventieth birthday, an occasion of great celebration in Scandinavia, she sent him a telegram of congratu-
lation. His letter of reply was the last message that passed
between them:

Christiania, 15th March 1898.

Herzlich liebes Fräulein!

Accept my most deeply felt thanks for your message. The summer in Gossensass was the happiest, the
most beautiful, in my whole life.

I scarcely dare to think of it—and yet I must think of
it always. Always!

Your truly devoted H.I.

It is against this background that we must read *The Master
Builder*. Other influences, of course, intrude into it. He had
returned to Norway by the time he began to write it, and
took pains to make Hilde almost ostentatiously Norwegian
in her speech and manners. He had by this time struck up a
friendship with a young Norwegian pianist, Hildur Andersen, the daughter of old friends from his Bergen days; she
seems to have possessed many of the qualities which he admired in Emilie, notably the combination of eagerness and
sensitivity, and it may be that her name, Hildur, caused him
to remember the Hilde whom he had created as a minor
character in *The Lady from the Sea* and whom he now resur-
rected, ten years older, to play a more important role. Aline
Solness is plainly based on Ibsen's own wife, and the relationship between the Solnesses bears an uncomfortable re-
semblance to that which appears to have existed at this time
in the Ibsen household. Shortly after their return to Norway,
Ibsen's mother-in-law, Magdalene Thoresen (the original of
Ellida in *The Lady from the Sea*), wrote: 'They live splen-

didly, and have an elegant home, though all is pretty much in Philistine style. They are two lonely people—each for himself—each absolutely for himself.'

Ibsen destroyed his preliminary notes for *The Master Builder* and whatever work he may have done on the play in the spring of 1892, apart from a curious rhymed poem of twelve lines. As William Archer pointed out, 'It is said to have been his habit, before setting to work on a play, to crystallize in a poem the mood which then possessed him', and this is the only one of these poems which has survived. It is dated 16th March 1892. I quote it in A. G. Chater's translation:

> They dwelt, those two, in so cosy a house
> In autumn and winter weather.
> Then came the fire—and the house was gone.
> They must search the ashes together.
>
> For down in the ashes a jewel lies hid
> Whose brightness the flames could not smother,
> And search they but faithfully, he and she,
> 'Twill be found by one or the other.
>
> But e'en though they find it, the gem they lost,
> The enduring jewel they cherished—
> She ne'er will recover her vanished faith
> Nor he the joy that has perished.*

A few months before Ibsen began work on *The Master Builder,* the young novelist Knut Hamsun had delivered

---

*Ibsen in fact incorporated this poem in his first draft of *Little Eyolf,* which he wrote two years after *The Master Builder;* Allmers reads it to Rita in the third act. It contained one amendment: the penultimate line ends with the word peace *(ro)* instead of faith *(tro).* But he deleted the poem in revision.

three lectures in Christiania on the decadence of modern literature, in the course of which he had particularly attacked the 'big four' of Norwegian letters, Ibsen, Bjœrnson, Alexander Kielland and Jonas Lie. An invitation was sent to Ibsen, and to the consternation of those present, he attended all three lectures, sitting in seat number one in the front row. He is reported to have sat 'quiet and serious, with unmoved countenance. . . His strong blue eyes did not leave the speaker for a minute'. It may well have been the memory of Hamsun's invective that suggested Solness's fear of 'youth banging on the door'. In passing, one may note that in his lectures Hamsun had insisted on the necessity of probing into the dark and unconscious corners of the human mind, and that Ibsen, in *The Master Builder* and the three plays which followed, was to do this; though he had already made a beginning in *The Lady from the Sea*.

The character of Solness was the nearest thing to a self-portrait that Ibsen had yet attempted, though he was to follow it with two equally merciless likenesses in *John Gabriel Borkman* and *When We Dead Awaken*. He admitted in a speech a few years later that 'Solness is a man who is somewhat related to me'. Ibsen had long regarded himself as a builder and his plays as works of architecture. As early as 1858, in a poem entitled *Building Plans,** he had compared

---

*BUILDING PLANS (1858)

I remember as well as if it were yesterday
The evening when, in the paper, I saw my first poem in print.
I sat there in my garret puffing my pipe
And dreaming dreams of blest complacency.

'I shall build a cloud-castle. It shall shine over the North.
Two wings shall it have; one little and one great.
The great wing shall shelter an immortal poet;
The small wing shall be a young girl's bower.'

the artist to a master builder; and when Erik Werenskiold, seeing him looking at some new buildings in Christiania, asked him: 'You are interested in architecture?' Ibsen replied: 'Yes; it is, as you know, my own trade.' Ibsen, like Solness, had always had a fear of looking down from a great height, or into a deep chasm, and this had become worse as he had grown older. Solness's ruthlessness, his readiness to sacrifice the happiness of those nearest to him for the sake of his ambition, his longing for and fear of youth, and the conflict in him between aesthetic and ethical demands—all these were Ibsen's too. Moreover, during Ibsen's last years in Munich he continually raised the subject of hypnotism, of how one human being could gain power over the mind of another, and how unexpressed wishes sometimes translated themselves into actions. This curiosity, too, had already manifested itself in *The Lady from the Sea*.

Two drafts of the play survive, written one after the other in the autumn of 1892. The second of these corresponds more or less exactly with the final printed version, and the first, unlike most of Ibsen's early drafts, contains no very significant variations. One sentence, however, deleted in revision, reveals how closely Ibsen identified himself with Solness. In the second act, when Solness is telling Hilde how success came to him, Ibsen originally made him conclude with the words: 'And now, at last, they have begun to talk of me abroad.' Viewed with this in mind, the theory propounded soon after the publication of the play that, to quote Archer, 'the churches which Solness sets out by building doubtless represent Ibsen's early romantic plays, the "homes for human beings" his social dramas, while the

---

I thought this a noble and harmonious plan.
But then confusion entered into it.
As the master grew sane, the castle went all crazy.
The great wing shrank; the small fell into ruins.

(Translation: Michael Meyer)

273

houses with high towers, merging into "castles in the air", stand for those spiritual dramas, with a wide outlook over the metaphysical environment of humanity, on which he was henceforth to be engaged' seems less fanciful than might at first appear.

Ever since childhood, Ibsen had been fascinated by towers. In the memoirs of his childhood and youth which he had compiled a few years previously to help Henrik Jæger in the writing of his authorized biography, Ibsen had mentioned that the house in which he was born 'stood exactly opposite the front of the church, with its high flight of steps and its conspicuous tower' from which the watchman used to proclaim the hour at night. A poodle also lived in the tower; 'it had fiery red eyes, but was rarely visible. Indeed, so far as I know, he was never seen but once'. One New Year's morning, just as the watchman shouted 'One' through the opening in the front of the tower, the poodle appeared behind him and looked at him with his fiery eyes, whereupon the watchman fell down into the market place and was killed. 'From that night, the watchman never calls "One" from the church tower at Skien.' It was from the opening in this tower, Ibsen continues, that he received 'the first conscious and permanent impression on my mind. My nurse one day took me up the tower and allowed me to sit on the ledge outside . . . I perfectly recollect how amazed I was at looking down on the tops of the hats of the people below.' His mother happened to look up from her window, saw him there, shrieked and fainted 'as people used to do in those days . . . As a boy, I never went across the market place without looking up at the tower window. I always felt as though the opening and the church poodle were some special concern of mine.'

In a letter written to his sister Hedvig on 13th March 1891, when he was already planning *The Master Builder,* Ibsen recalled that 'the house where I was born and lived the first years of my childhood, and the church, the old church with its christening-angel under the roof, are now burned down. All that my earliest memories are associated with—it was all burned.' These feelings are strongly echoed in Solness's account of the burning of his wife's ancestral home; and the christening-angel (which was lowered when a child was to be christened) may possibly be the original of Aline's dolls.

Shortly before he left Munich that summer, Ibsen heard the legend of the master builder who had built St. Michael's Church there and had thrown himself down from the tower of the church because he was afraid the roof would not hold. Ibsen said he thought the legend must have arisen in Scandinavia, and when Helene Raff observed that every famous cathedral in Germany had the same legend he replied that this must be because people felt instinctively that a man could not build so high without paying the penalty for his hubris.

The publication of *The Master Builder* was eagerly awaited throughout Europe. Elizabeth Robins, the American actress who did so much during the eighteen-nineties to promote Ibsen's cause in England, has described the atmosphere in her book, *Theatre and Friendship* (1932). 'Months before *The Master Builder* reached these shores, the excitement that was set up by mere anticipation will never be credited in these times . . . Impatience for the play to come was exacerbated by the darkness that shrouded it . . . Neither the man who had committed himself to publishing it [William Heinemann] nor anybody else had even now the faintest idea what the play would be about. People lived on supposition, and were as hot over it as though they knew what it was they were contending for.' Among the enthusiasts who visited Miss Robins 'up those seventy-four steps' for news of the play—the list of names reveals the extent to which the literary world of London had rallied to William

Archer's call—were Henry James, Sidney Colvin, Sir Frederick Pollock, Mrs. Humphrey Ward, Rhoda Broughton, Bernard Shaw, Gertrude Bell, Herbert Beerbohm Tree, Hubert Crackanthorpe, Arthur Symons and Oscar Wilde. Three pulls of the play (as yet unnamed) were sent from Norway as fast as they were printed. 'These,' wrote Miss Robins, 'ultimately arrived in small, in very small, violently agitating spurts—or, as one might say, in volts, projected across the North Sea in a series of electric shocks.' As a result, the English, French and German translations appeared almost simultaneously with the original, the German translation being by Ibsen's son, Sigurd. Translations into Russian, Dutch, Polish and Bohemian followed shortly afterwards.

At first even the most ardent Ibsenites were puzzled. 'The interest certainly hangs fire,' wrote William Archer to Elizabeth Robins; and she herself added: *'I* fear the whole thing is hopeless.' Henry James confessed himself 'utterly bewildered and mystified . . . It is all most strange, most curious, most vague, most horrid, most "middle-classy" in the peculiar ugly Ibsen sense—and alas most *un*promising for Miss Elizabeth or for any *woman*. What is already clear is that a man is the central figure . . . and the man, alas, an elderly white-haired architect, or Baumeister, is, although a strange and interesting, a fearfully charmless figure.'

The Master Builder received its first performance at the Lessing Theatre in Berlin on 19th January 1893, after the usual public reading in London (in Norwegian) to secure performing copyright. Before the end of the month it had also been staged in Bergen, Copenhagen, Gothenburg, Trondhjem, Stockholm, Åbo and Helsingfors. London and Chicago saw it in February, and Rome in April. The London newspapers greeted it, as they greeted the early productions of most of Ibsen's plays, with a chorus of vituperation:

'Dense mist enshrouds characters, words, actions and motives . . . One may compare it . . . to the sensations of a man who witnesses a play written, rehearsed and acted by lunatics.'—*The Daily Telegraph*

'Platitudes and inanities . . . The play is hopeless and indefensible.'—*The Globe*

'A feast of dull dialogue and acute dementia . . . The most dreary and purposeless drivel we have ever heard in an English theatre . . . A pointless, incoherent and absolutely silly piece.'—*The Evening News*

'Assuredly no one may fathom the mysteries of the play, so far as it can be called a play . . . It is not for a moment to be understood that we personally recommend anyone to go and see it.'—*The Standard*

'Rigmarole of an Oracle Delphic in obscurity and Gamplike in garrulity . . . Pulseless and purposeless play, which has idiocy written on every lineament . . . Three acts of gibberish.'—*The Stage*

'Sensuality . . . irreverence . . . unwholesome . . . simply blasphemous.'—*The Morning Post*

'Dull, mysterious, unchaste.'—*The Daily Graphic*

London was, of course (as usual where theatrical matters are concerned) particularly behind the times; but *The Master Builder,* like all of Ibsen's plays from *The Wild Duck* onwards, bewildered readers in every country. Great arguments developed as to the meaning of the play. As a contemporary put it: 'While one person sees Solness as Ibsen himself, another sees him as Bjœrnson, a third as a symbol of the right wing party, a fourth as a symbol of the left and its leader; a fifth sees Solness as a symbol of Man rising in rebellion against God; a sixth sees the play as a conflict between youth and the older generation.' Some sought to identify Solness with Bismarck, while *The Saturday Review* in London decided that he was meant as a portrait of Mr. Gladstone, and that the play was full of references to the Irish question. Ibsen, when asked which of these interpretations was true, replied that the play merely portrayed people whom he had known and that he could not understand what everyone was arguing about.

To date London has seen no less than sixteen separate professional productions of *The Master Builder,* a number exceeded among Ibsen's other plays only by *A Doll's House, Ghosts* and *Hedda Gabler.* The many distinguished actors who have essayed the role of Solness include Herbert Waring (1893), Lewis Waller (1893), Lugné-Poe (1895, in French), Norman McKinnel (1911), Donald Wolfit (1934, 1943, and 1948), Frederick Valk (1947), Andrew Cruickshank (1962), Michael Redgrave (1964) and Laurence Olivier (1964). Of these, the greatest in modern times and, I have little doubt, the greatest of all, was Frederick Valk, an extraordinary interpreter of Ibsen, as he was of Shakespeare. *The Times* wrote of his performance:

'Mr. Frederick Valk's superbly flamboyant playing of Halvard Solness reminds us that the necessary basis of the Master Builder's destructive genius is a super-abundant vitality. As much by this uncomfortable power as by untoward circumstance has he destroyed himself and others for his art, and it is the same power which has led him to misuse that art himself. It is upon the drab side of the character that most English actors concentrate. So concerned are they to reproduce the fear and remorse that are overtaking the sick and ageing artist that they are always in danger of belittling the spirit struggling to the last against retribution. And a moribund man makes a poor stage figure. Mr. Valk brings Solness completely to life . . . His Solness is a man in whose genius and reckless charm we can believe; the remnants of those qualities are there along with the remorse bred of age and introspection and the fantastic fear of youth, and the still more fantastic craving for it.'

The most admired English Hildes have been Elizabeth Robins (1893), Octavia Kenmore (1907 and 1918) whom C. E. Montague rated the finest he had seen, Lillah McCarthy (1911), Beatrix Lehmann (1936) and Mary Miller (1962). Of Octavia Kenmore, Montague wrote: 'She gave the part all that it wanted—the high vitality, the childlike candour, the non-morality rather than immorality, the troubled ecstasy of a mind exhilarated with the exercise of a new sense and ranging through its own emotions with the delight and the fears of an explorer. A less fine artist might have laboured to work up a more-is-meant-than-meets-the-ear effect, wherever Hilde uses language out of its literal meaning; Miss Kenmore preserved in the character a girlish simplicity direct enough to wreck whole civilizations, and yet she was "like them that dream"; she spoke like a natural person in a state of unnatural exaltation; the highly figured language, with its charge of symbolic values, came tumbling out of her mouth like indiscretions from a terrible child in its hours of most flowing inspiration.' Of Beatrix Lehmann's performance, Ivor Brown commented: '[She] is perfectly cast as Hilde Wangel, for, with her sharp, expressive profile, and her eyes all eloquence, she can be at once the ecstatic worshipper and remorseless bird of prey. Many Hildes have been industriously "fey"; none, in my experience, so essentially the falcon, a thing of air as well as of fire, demonic, taloned, soaring.' And of Mary Miller's interpretation, T.C. Worsley wrote: 'The dangers that lie in wait for the actress playing Hilde are gush and archness. In Miss Miller's performance there is not one touch of either. The note of spontaneity is held clear and pure throughout.'

In 1908 Emilie Bardach saw *The Master Builder* for the first time, in Munich. After the performance, she said: 'I didn't see myself; but I saw him. There is something of me in Hilde; but in Solness, there is little that is not Ibsen.'

MICHAEL MEYER

CHARACTERS

HALVARD SOLNESS, master builder
ALINE SOLNESS, his wife
DOCTOR HERDAL, a family physician
KNUT BROVIK, sometime architect, now assistant to Solness
RAGNAR BROVIK, his son, a draughtsman
KAJA FOSLI, book-keeper, niece to Knut Brovik
HILDE WANGEL
LADIES
PEOPLE IN THE STREET

Act 1. The office
Act 2. The sitting-room
Act 3. The verandah

The action takes place in Solness's house.

This translation of *The Master Builder* was first performed on 19 November 1962 at the Ashcroft Theatre, Croydon. The cast was:

HALVARD SOLNESS	Andrew Cruickshank
ALINE SOLNESS	Viola Keats
DOCTOR HERDAL	Derek Tansley
KNUT BROVIK	Keith Pyott
RAGNAR BROVIK	Michael Culver
KAJA FOSLI	Carole Mowlam
HILDE WANGEL	Mary Miller

Directed by Terence Kilburn

On 4 December 1962 the production transferred to the Arts Theatre, London. The cast was unchanged.

ACT ONE

A plainly furnished office in SOLNESS's *house. In the left-hand wall, double doors lead out to the hall. To the right is a door leading to the inner rooms of the house. In the rear wall, an open door leading to the drawing office. Downstage left, a high desk with books, papers and writing materials. Upstage of the door, a stove. In the right-hand corner, a sofa with a table and two or three chairs. On the table, a water carafe and glasses. Downstage right, a smaller table, with a rocking chair and an armchair. Lighted lamps are on the table in the drawing office, and also on the table in the corner and on the desk.*

Inside the drawing office sit KNUT BROVIK *and his son,* RAGNAR, *busy with plans and calculations.* KAJA FOSLI *stands at the desk in the office, writing in the ledger.* KNUT BROVIK *is a thin old man with white hair and beard, dressed in a somewhat worn but carefully preserved black tail coat. He wears spectacles and a white cravat, which has turned rather yellow.* RAGNAR BROVIK *is in his thirties, well dressed, fair haired, with a slight stoop.* KAJA FOSLI *is a slender girl in her early twenties, neatly dressed but of sickly appearance. She wears a green shade over her eyes. For a while, all three work in silence.*

BROVIK (*gets up suddenly from the drawing table, as though in distress, and breathes heavily and with difficulty as he comes forward into the doorway*): No, I can't go on with this much longer.

KAJA (*goes over to him*): It's really bad tonight, isn't it, uncle?

BROVIK: Yes, it seems to grow worse every day.

RAGNAR (*has got up, and comes closer*): You'd better go home, father. Try to get a little sleep—

BROVIK (*impatiently*): Go to bed? Do you want me to suffocate?

KAJA: Take a little walk, anyway.

RAGNAR: Yes, do that. I'll come with you.

BROVIK: I'm not going before he comes! This evening I'm going to have it out with— (*Bitterly.*) —with *him*. The master builder!

KAJA (*anxiously*): Oh, no, uncle, let that wait.

RAGNAR: Yes, better wait, father.

BROVIK (*laughs with difficulty*): I can't afford to wait very long.

KAJA (*listens*): Ssh! I can hear him coming up the steps.

All three go back to their work again. Short pause. HALVARD SOLNESS, *master builder, enters through the hall door. He is an oldish man, strong and vigorous, with close-cut, curly hair, dark moustache, and dark, thick eyebrows. He is dressed in a grey-green jacket, buttoned up, with high collar and broad lapels. He has a soft grey hat on his head, and two or three portfolios under his arm.*

SOLNESS (*in the doorway, points towards the drawing office and asks in a whisper*): Have they gone?

KAJA (*softly, shakes her head*): No.

She takes off her eyeshade. SOLNESS *walks across the room, throws his hat on a chair, puts the portfolios on*

the table by the sofa and comes back towards the desk.
KAJA *continues writing, but seems nervous and ill at
ease.*

SOLNESS *(aloud):* What's that you're entering there, Miss
Fosli?

KAJA *(starts):* Oh, just something that—

SOLNESS: Let me see. *(Leans over her, pretending to look at
the ledger, and whispers.)* Kaja?

KAJA *(softly as she writes):* Yes?

SOLNESS: Why do you always take off that eyeshade when I
come in?

KAJA: It makes me look so ugly.

SOLNESS *(smiles):* And you don't want to look ugly, Kaja?

KAJA *(half glances up at him):* Not for anything! Not to you!

SOLNESS *(strokes her hair gently):* Poor, poor little Kaja!

KAJA *(moves her head away):* Ssh! They can hear you!

SOLNESS *strolls across the room to the right, turns, and
stands by the door to the drawing office.*

SOLNESS: Has anyone been asking for me?

RAGNAR *(stands up):* Yes, that young couple who want the
villa built out at Lœvstrand.

SOLNESS *(growls):* Oh, them? Well, they'll have to wait.
The plan's not come clear in my mind yet.

RAGNAR *(comes closer, a little diffidently):* They were very
anxious to get the drawings as soon as possible.

SOLNESS: Yes, that's what they all say.

BROVIK *(looks up):* They're longing to get into a place of
their own.

SOLNESS: Oh, yes, yes. I know that sort. They'll take anything with four walls and a roof over it. Anywhere to lay
their heads. That's not what I call a home. If that's what
they want, let them go to someone else. Tell them that
next time they come.

BROVIK (*pushes his spectacles up on to his forehead and stares amazed*): Someone else? Would you let the contract go?

SOLNESS (*impatiently*): Yes, damn it, yes! If it comes to the point. I'd rather that than build rubbish. Anyway, I don't know these people.

BROVIK: Oh, they're sound enough. Ragnar knows them. He's a friend of the family. Very sound people.

SOLNESS: Oh, sound, sound! That's not what I mean. Great God, don't you understand me either? (*Angrily.*) I don't want to have anything to do with people I don't know. As far as I'm concerned, they can go to anyone they like.

BROVIK (*gets up*): Are you serious?

SOLNESS: Yes. For once.

He walks across the room. BROVIK *glances at* RAGNAR, *who makes a warning gesture, then goes into the other room.*

BROVIK: May I have a few words with you?

SOLNESS: Certainly.

BROVIK: Go inside for a moment, Kaja.

KAJA (*uneasy*): But, uncle—

BROVIK: Do as I say, child. And close the door after you.

KAJA *goes unwillingly into the drawing office, glances anxiously and pleadingly at* SOLNESS, *and closes the door.*

BROVIK (*lowers his voice*): I don't want the children to know how seriously ill I am.

SOLNESS: Yes, you look rather poorly these days.

BROVIK: I haven't much longer. My strength gets less every day.

SOLNESS: Sit down for a moment.

BROVIK: Thank you, may I?

SOLNESS (*moves the armchair a little*): Here. Well?

BROVIK *(sits down with difficulty):* It's this question of Ragnar. That's what weighs most on my mind. What's to become of him?

SOLNESS: Your son? He'll stay here with me, for as long as
he wants to.

BROVIK: But that's just it. He doesn't want to. He doesn't
feel he can—now.

SOLNESS: Well, he's doing quite well for himself, I should
have thought. Still, if he wants a little more, I wouldn't be
unwilling to—

BROVIK: No, no, that's not it. *(Impatiently.)* It's time he was
given the chance to do something on his own.

SOLNESS *(not looking at him):* Do you think he's got the ability?

BROVIK: That's what's so dreadful. I've begun to have
doubts about the boy. In all these years you've never uttered so much as a single word of encouragement about
him. But it must be there. I can't believe he hasn't got the
ability.

SOLNESS: But he doesn't know anything. Not really. Except
how to draw.

BROVIK *(with suppressed hatred):* You didn't know much
either, when you were working for me. But you managed
to get started all right. *(Breathes heavily.)* Fought your
way up. Put me out of business—and plenty of others.

SOLNESS: Yes—things worked out for me.

BROVIK: That's right. Everything worked out nicely for you.
But surely you won't let me die without seeing what Ragnar can do? And I would like to see them married before I
go.

SOLNESS *(sharply):* Does she want that?

BROVIK: Not Kaja so much. It's Ragnar—he talks about it
every day. *(Pleadingly.)* You must—you *must* help him to
stand on his own feet now! I must see the lad do something on his own! Do you hear?

SOLNESS *(angrily):* But damn it, I can't conjure contracts out of the air for him.

BROVIK: He could get a commission right away. A nice big job.

SOLNESS: *(startled, uneasy):* Could he?

BROVIK: If you agree.

SOLNESS: What kind of a job would that be?

BROVIK *(a little diffidently):* He could build that villa out at Lœvstrand.

SOLNESS: That! But I'm going to build that myself.

BROVIK: Oh, you don't really want to do that.

SOLNESS: Don't want to? Who dared to say that?

BROVIK: You said so yourself, just now.

SOLNESS: Oh, never mind what I *say*. Could Ragnar get the contract?

BROVIK: Yes. He knows the family, you see. And then, he's—just for the fun of it, you know—he's made drawings and estimates and so on—

SOLNESS: And these drawings—are they satisfied with them? These people who are going to live there?

BROVIK: Yes. If only you'd just look through them and approve them, they—

SOLNESS: They'd like Ragnar to build their home for them?

BROVIK: They were very taken with his idea. They thought it was so new and original.

SOLNESS: Oh! New. Not the old-fashioned junk I build?

BROVIK: They thought this was—different.

SOLNESS: So it was Ragnar they came to see—while I was out.

BROVIK: They came to talk to you. And to ask if you'd be willing to give way—

SOLNESS: I? Give way for your son!

BROVIK: Rescind the contract, they meant.

SOLNESS: What's the difference? *(Laughs bitterly.)* So that's it! Halvard Solness is to retire! Retire to make way for

younger men! For apprentices! Make way for the young!
Make way! Make way!

BROVIK: Good heavens, there's room in this town for more
than one—

SOLNESS: Oh, there's not so much room round here either.
But that's not the point. I shall never give way. I shall
never make way for anyone! Not of my own free-will.
Never, never!

BROVIK *(gets up with difficulty):* Won't you let me die in
peace? Happy—believing in my son? Won't you let me
see him do one thing on his own?

SOLNESS *(turns half aside and mutters):* Don't ask me that
now.

BROVIK: Yes, answer me! Must I die so poor?

SOLNESS *(seems to fight with himself, then says, quietly but
firmly):* You must die as best you can.

BROVIK: So be it. *(Walks away.)*

SOLNESS *(follows him, almost desperately):* I can't do otherwise, don't you understand? I am what I am. And I can't
create myself anew.

BROVIK: No, no. You can't do that. *(Stumbles and stops by
the sofa table.)* May I have a glass of water?

SOLNESS: Of course. *(Pours one out and hands it to him.)*

BROVIK: Thank you.

BROVIK *drinks and puts the glass down.* SOLNESS *goes
over to the door of the drawing office and opens it.*

SOLNESS: Ragnar, you'd better take your father home.

RAGNAR *gets up quickly. He and* KAJA *come into the office.*

RAGNAR: What is it, father?

BROVIK: Take my arm. Let's go.

RAGNAR: All right. Put your coat on, Kaja.

SOLNESS: Miss Fosli must stay. For a few minutes. I have a letter to write.

BROVIK (*looks at* SOLNESS): Good night. Sleep well—if you can.

SOLNESS: Good night.

> BROVIK *and* RAGNAR *go out through the front door.* KAJA *goes across to her desk.* SOLNESS *stands with bowed head near the armchair on the right.*

KAJA (*uncertainly*): Have you got a letter—?

SOLNESS (*curtly*): No, no, of course not. (*Looks sharply at her.*) Kaja!

KAJA (*quietly, frightened*): Yes?

SOLNESS (*points commandingly with a finger towards the floor*): Come here. At once!

KAJA (*unwillingly*): Yes.

SOLNESS (*still in the same tone*): Closer!

KAJA (*obeying him*): What do you want me to do?

SOLNESS (*looks at her for a moment*): Is it you I have to thank for this?

KAJA: No, no, please don't think that.

SOLNESS: So you want to get married now.

KAJA (*quietly*): Ragnar and I have been engaged for nearly five years, so—

SOLNESS: So you think it's time something happened. That's it, isn't it?

KAJA: Ragnar and uncle say I must. So I suppose I shall.

SOLNESS (*more gently*): You're quite fond of Ragnar too, aren't you, Kaja?

KAJA: I was very fond of Ragnar. Before I came here.

SOLNESS: But not any longer?

KAJA (*passionately*): Oh, you know there's only one person now. There's no one else in all the world. I'll never be fond of anyone else.

SOLNESS: Yes, you say that. But you're going to leave me,

all the same. Leave me here to put up with everything
alone.

KAJA: But couldn't I stay here with you even if Ragnar—?

SOLNESS: No, no, that's quite impossible. If Ragnar leaves
me and sets up on his own account, he'll want to have you
with him.

KAJA: Oh, I don't feel I can leave you! I can't, possibly—I
can't!

SOLNESS: Then try to get Ragnar to put these foolish ideas
out of his head. Marry him as much as you like—
(*Changes his tone.*) Yes, yes, I mean, persuade him to
stay on in this good position he's got with me. Because
then I can keep you too, Kaja dear.

KAJA: Oh, yes, how wonderful! If only it could work out
like that!

SOLNESS (*takes her face between his hands and whispers*): I
can't be without you, you see. I must have you here with
me, every day.

KAJA: God! Oh God!

SOLNESS (*kisses her hair*): Kaja, Kaja!

KAJA (*drops on her knees*): Oh, you're so kind to me! So
wonderfully kind!

SOLNESS (*sharply*): Get up! Get up, for heaven's sake! I
think I can hear someone.

He helps her up. She falters over towards the desk.
MRS. SOLNESS comes in through the door on the right.
She looks thin and haggard, but retains traces of
former beauty. Fair hair hanging in ringlets. She is el-
egantly dressed, all in black. She speaks rather slowly
and plaintively.

MRS. SOLNESS (*in the doorway*): Halvard!

SOLNESS (*turns*): Oh, is it you, my dear?

MRS. SOLNESS (*glances at* KAJA): I've come at an inconvenient moment, I see.

SOLNESS: Not at all. Miss Fosli is just writing a short letter for me.

MRS. SOLNESS: So I see.

SOLNESS: What was it you wanted, Aline?

MRS. SOLNESS: I only wanted to tell you that Dr. Herdal is in the drawing room. Would you like to come in and join us, Halvard?

SOLNESS (*looks at her suspiciously*): Mm. Has he something special to say to me?

MRS. SOLNESS: No, nothing special. He came to visit me, and he'd like to see you while he's here.

SOLNESS (*laughs quietly*): Yes, I'm sure he would. Well, ask him to wait a moment.

MRS. SOLNESS: You'll come and talk to him later, then?

SOLNESS: Perhaps. Later, my dear—later. In a little while.

MRS. SOLNESS (*with another look at* KAJA): Yes, well, don't forget now, Halvard.

MRS. SOLNESS *goes out, closing the door behind her.*

KAJA (*quietly*): Oh, God, oh, God—I'm sure she thinks something dreadful about me!

SOLNESS: Nonsense. Well, not more than usual, anyway. I think you'd better go now though, Kaja.

KAJA: Yes, yes, I *must* go now.

SOLNESS (*sternly*): And get this other thing settled for me. Do you hear?

KAJA: Oh God, if it were only up to me—

SOLNESS: I want it settled, do you hear? And by tomorrow.

KAJA: If there's no other way, I'll break it off with him.

SOLNESS: Break it off? Have you gone mad? Do you want to break it off?

KAJA: Yes—I'd rather that than—! I must—I must stay here with you! I can't leave you! I can't—possibly!

SOLNESS: But for Christ's sake, what about Ragnar?

KAJA: Is it Ragnar you—?

SOLNESS: Oh no, no, of course not. You don't understand me. *(Gently, quietly.)* Of course it's you I want, Kaja. Above all else. And it's just because of that that you must persuade Ragnar to stay. Now then, run along home.

KAJA: Yes, yes. Good night, then.

SOLNESS: Good night. *(As she turns to go.)* Oh, by the way—are Ragnar's drawings in there?

KAJA: Yes. I didn't see him take them.

SOLNESS: Go in and find them for me. I might have a glance at them after all.

KAJA *(happily):* Oh, yes, please do.

SOLNESS: I'll do it for your sake, Kaja. Well, hurry up and find them for me, then!

> KAJA *runs into the drawing office, searches anxiously in the drawer of the desk, finds a portfolio and brings it out.*

KAJA: All the drawings are here.

SOLNESS: Good. Put them over there on the table.

KAJA *(puts down the portfolio):* Good night, then. *(Pleadingly.)* Think kindly of me, won't you?

SOLNESS: I always do. Good night, my dear little Kaja. *(Glances right.)* Hurry up, now, run off.

> MRS. SOLNESS *and* DR. HERDAL *enter through the door on the right. He is a stout, elderly man with a round, genial face, clean-shaven, with sparse, fair hair and gold-rimmed spectacles.*

MRS. SOLNESS *(in the doorway):* Halvard, I couldn't keep the doctor waiting any longer.

SOLNESS: Well, come in, then.

MRS. SOLNESS *(to KAJA, who is turning down the lamp on the desk):* Quite finished your letter, Miss Fosli?

KAJA *(confused):* Letter?

SOLNESS: Yes, it was just a short one.

MRS. SOLNESS: It must have been very short.

SOLNESS: You may go, Miss Fosli. Be sure you're here punctually tomorrow.

KAJA: Why, of course. Good night, Mrs. Solness.

She goes out through the hall door.

MRS. SOLNESS: You must be very pleased, Halvard, to have got hold of this young lady.

SOLNESS: Yes, indeed. She's useful in all sorts of ways.

MRS. SOLNESS: I'm sure she is.

HERDAL: Good at book-keeping too?

SOLNESS: Well—she's picked up a little in these two years. And she's always cheerful and willing, whatever one asks her to do.

MRS. SOLNESS: Yes, that must be a great advantage—

SOLNESS: It is. Especially when one isn't used to that kind of thing.

MRS. SOLNESS *(gently reproachful):* Halvard, how can you say that?

SOLNESS: Oh no, no, Aline dear. I apologize.

MRS. SOLNESS: There's no need. Well, Doctor, you'll come back later and take tea with us?

HERDAL: As soon as I've seen that patient, I'll be back.

MRS. SOLNESS: Good.

She goes out through door, right.

SOLNESS: Are you in a hurry, Doctor?

HERDAL: No, not at all.

SOLNESS: May I have a word with you?

HERDAL: By all means.

SOLNESS: Let's sit down, then.

He indicates the rocking chair to the DOCTOR, and seats himself in the armchair.

SOLNESS *(looks searchingly at him):* Tell me—did you notice anything about Aline?

HERDAL: Just now, you mean?

SOLNESS: Yes. In her attitude towards me. Did you notice anything?

HERDAL *(smiles):* Yes, well, damn it—one couldn't very well help noticing that your wife—er—

SOLNESS: Yes?

HERDAL: That your wife doesn't altogether approve of this Miss Fosli.

SOLNESS: Oh, that? I'd noticed that myself.

HERDAL: Well, it's not really surprising, is it?

SOLNESS: What isn't?

HERDAL: That she doesn't exactly like your having another woman with you in the house every day.

SOLNESS: No, no, you may be right. But there's nothing to be done about that.

HERDAL: Couldn't you get yourself a male clerk?

SOLNESS: The first man-jack who put his head through the door? No, thank you, that's not the way I work.

HERDAL: But if your wife—? She's very frail, you know. If she can't stand this arrangement—

SOLNESS: Well, she'll have to put up with it. I don't mean it like that, but I have to keep Kaja Fosli. She's the only one who'll do.

HERDAL: The only one?

SOLNESS *(curtly):* Yes, the only one.

HERDAL *(pushes his chair closer):* Listen, Mr. Solness. May I ask you a question—in strict confidence?

SOLNESS: By all means?

HERDAL: Women, you know—they've a damnably sharp nose for some things—

SOLNESS: They have. That's quite true. But—

HERDAL: Well, now, listen a moment. If your wife can't stand the sight of this Kaja Fosli—

SOLNESS: Yes, what then?

HERDAL: Isn't it possible that she may have some—some grounds for this instinctive dislike?

SOLNESS (*looks at him, and gets up*): Oh-ho!

HERDAL: Please don't take this amiss. But am I right?

SOLNESS (*curtly, firmly*): No.

HERDAL: No grounds whatever?

SOLNESS: None other than her own suspiciousness.

HERDAL: You've—known a few women in your time.

SOLNESS: I have.

HERDAL: And been fairly fond of one or two of them?

SOLNESS: Oh, yes, that too.

HERDAL: But this Miss Fosli—there's nothing like that between you?

SOLNESS: Nothing whatever. As far as I'm concerned.

HERDAL: And what about her?

SOLNESS: I don't think you have a right to ask that, Doctor.

HERDAL: We were talking about your wife's instinct, remember.

SOLNESS: So we were. Well, as a matter of fact— (*He lowers his voice.*) —that sharp nose of Aline's that you were talking about hasn't altogether misled her.

HERDAL: Well—there we are!

SOLNESS (*sits*): Dr. Herdal—I'm going to tell you a strange story. If you care to listen to it.

HERDAL: I like listening to strange stories.

SOLNESS: Good. Well, you remember, I dare say, some time ago I took Knut Brovik and his son into my employ—when things were going badly for the old man.

HERDAL: Yes, I know something about that.

SOLNESS: They're clever fellows, you know, those two. They've both got ability, in different ways. But then the son went and got himself engaged; and then, of course, he wanted to marry the girl, and start out on his own. That's what they all want nowadays, these young people.

HERDAL *(laughs):* Yes, they've all got this bad habit of wanting to get married.

SOLNESS: Mm. Well, I didn't like it. I needed Ragnar. And the old man too. He's so damned clever at working out stresses and cubic content and all that bloody nonsense, you know.

HERDAL: Ah, well, that's part of the job, I suppose.

SOLNESS: So it is. But Ragnar—he wanted to go off and start on his own. He wouldn't listen to me.

HERDAL: But he's stayed with you.

SOLNESS: Well, that's just it. One day this girl, Kaja Fosli, came to see them on some errand or other. She'd never been here before. Well, when I saw how infatuated they were with each other, the idea struck me that if I could get her to come and work here in the office, Ragnar might stay too.

HERDAL: A reasonable supposition.

SOLNESS: Yes, but I didn't mention a word of all this. I just stood and looked at her—and kept wishing from the bottom of my heart that I had her here. Well, I chatted to her in a friendly way about one thing and another. And then she went.

HERDAL: Well?

SOLNESS: But the next day, in the evening, after old Brovik and Ragnar had gone home, she came back and acted just as though we'd come to some kind of an agreement.

HERDAL: What kind of agreement?

SOLNESS: The very one I'd been wanting to suggest. But which I hadn't mentioned a word about.

HERDAL: That was very strange.

SOLNESS: Yes. And now she wanted to know what kind of work she'd be doing. Whether she could begin at once the next morning. And so on.

HERDAL: Don't you think she did this to be near her young man?

SOLNESS: That was what I thought at first. But no, that wasn't it. She seemed to drift away from him—once she was here with me.

HERDAL: Drifted—over to you?

SOLNESS: Yes, completely. I've noticed that she knows I'm looking at her, even when her back's turned. She trembles and shivers if I even go near her. What do you make of that?

HERDAL: I suppose that could be explained.

SOLNESS: But what about this other business—that she thought I'd told her what I'd only wished for? Silently; inwardly, secretly. What do you make of that? Can you explain such a thing to me, Dr. Herdal?

HERDAL: No, that's outside my field.

SOLNESS: That's what I thought; and that's why I haven't wanted to talk to you about it before. But in the long run, it's been a confounded nuisance to me, you know. I have to walk round here day after day pretending I— And it's not fair to her, poor girl. *(Violently.)* But what else can I do? If she leaves me, Ragnar will go too.

HERDAL: And you haven't told your wife all this?

SOLNESS: No.

HERDAL: Why on earth don't you, then?

SOLNESS: Because somehow I feel it does me good to suffer Aline to do me an injustice.

HERDAL *(shakes his head)*: I'm damned if I understand a word of that.

SOLNESS: Oh, yes. You see it's like paying a minute instalment on a great debt—a debt so vast it can never be settled.

HERDAL: A debt to your wife?

SOLNESS: Yes. And that—eases my mind a little. I can breathe more freely—for a while, you understand.

HERDAL: No, I'm damned if I understand a word—

SOLNESS (*breaks off and gets up again*): No, no—well, we won't talk about it any more.

He wanders across the room, comes back and stops beside the table. He looks at the DOCTOR with a quiet smile.

SOLNESS: I suppose you think you're drawing me out pretty successfully, eh, Doctor?

HERDAL (*somewhat vexed*): Drawing you out? I really don't know what you mean, Mr. Solness.

SOLNESS: Oh, stop pretending. I've noticed it clearly enough.

HERDAL: Noticed what?

SOLNESS: That you came here to keep an eye on me.

HERDAL: *I?* Why on earth should I do that?

SOLNESS: Because you think I'm—(*Flares up.*) Damn it—you think the same about me as Aline does!

HERDAL: And what does she think about you?

SOLNESS (*in control of himself again*): She's begun to think I'm—well—you know—ill.

HERDAL: Ill? You? She's never mentioned a word about this to me. What could be the matter with you, my dear fellow?

SOLNESS (*leans over the back of the chair, and whispers*): Aline thinks I'm mad. Oh yes, she does.

HERDAL (*gets up*): But, my dear Mr. Solness—

SOLNESS: Yes, by God, she does! That's what she thinks; and she's got you to believe it too! Oh, I know it, Doctor, I can see it in your behaviour. I'm not that easily deceived, I promise you.

HERDAL (*stares amazed*): Never, Mr. Solness—never has such a thought entered my head.

SOLNESS (*with a distrustful smile*): Indeed? Hasn't it really?

HERDAL: Never. Nor your wife's either—I think I could swear to that.

SOLNESS: Well, I wouldn't if I were you. In a way, you see, she might not be altogether wrong.

HERDAL: No, really, this is going too far!

SOLNESS: Well, well, my dear Doctor—let's not pursue the matter. It's better left as it is. (*Quietly gleeful.*) But now, listen, Doctor—hm—

HERDAL: Yes?

SOLNESS: As you don't think I'm—hm—ill—deranged—mad—or anything like that—

HERDAL: Well? What do you mean?

SOLNESS: Then you must be labouring under the illusion that I am an exceedingly lucky man.

HERDAL: Would that be an illusion?

SOLNESS (*laughs*): No, no—of course not! God forbid! Just think—to be a master builder, *the* master builder, Halvard Solness! Oh, yes, that's not to be sniffed at.

HERDAL: Yes, I really must say you seem to have been unbelievably lucky all your life.

SOLNESS (*represses an ironic smile*): That's right. I can't complain.

HERDAL: First of all that crazy old castle of yours burned down. And you'll admit that was a great stroke of luck.

SOLNESS: It was Aline's ancestral home. Remember that.

HERDAL: Yes, it must have been a terrible blow to her.

SOLNESS: She has never got over it, to this day. Not in all these twelve—thirteen—years.

HERDAL: What followed must have been the heaviest blow for her.

SOLNESS: The one with the other.

HERDAL: But it was that that gave you your start. You began as a poor country lad, and here you are, the top man in your profession. Oh, yes, Mr. Solness, you've had the luck on your side all right.

SOLNESS (*glances nervously at him*): I know. That's what makes me so afraid.

HERDAL: Afraid? Because you've been lucky?

SOLNESS: Day and night—I'm afraid. Because some time my luck must change.

HERDAL: Nonsense. What should make it change?

SOLNESS *(swiftly, with conviction)*: Youth.

HERDAL: Rubbish! Youth? You're not past it yet. Oh no— your position's stronger now than it's ever been.

SOLNESS: My luck will change. I know it. And I feel it will happen soon. Someone will stand up and demand: 'Make way for me!' And then all the others will storm after him shaking their fists and shouting: 'Make way! Make way!' Just you wait, Doctor. One fine day, youth will come and bang on that door—

HERDAL *(laughs)*: Well, for heaven's sake, what of it?

SOLNESS: What of it? Why, that will be the end for master builder Solness.

There is a banging on the door to the left.

SOLNESS *(starts)*: What was that? Did you hear something?

HERDAL: It's someone banging on the door.

SOLNESS *(loudly)*: Come in!

HILDE WANGEL *comes in through the hall door. She is of medium height and slender and supple build. A little sun-tanned. She is wearing walking clothes, with a caught-up skirt, an open sailor collar and a small sailor hat on her head. She has a rucksack on her back, a plaid in a strap and a long alpenstock.*

HILDE *(goes over to SOLNESS, her eyes alight and happy)*: Good evening!

SOLNESS *(looks at her uncertainly)*: Good evening.

HILDE *(laughs)*: I believe you don't recognize me.

SOLNESS: No—to be honest, just for a moment I—

HERDAL *(goes closer to her)*: But I recognize you, Miss—

HILDE *(delighted)*: Oh, no! Is it you?

HERDAL: Indeed it's me. *(To* SOLNESS.*)* We met up in one of the mountain huts this summer. *(To* HILDE.*)* What happened to the other ladies?

HILDE: Oh, they went on to the west coast.

HERDAL: They didn't like all that noise in the evenings.

HILDE: No, they didn't.

HERDAL *(wags his finger):* And you must confess you flirted a little with us!

HILDE: Well, it was more fun than knitting socks with all those old ladies.

HERDAL *(laughs):* I quite agree with you.

SOLNESS: Did you come to town this evening?

HILDE: Yes, I've just arrived.

HERDAL: All alone, Miss Wangel?

HILDE: Why, yes!

SOLNESS: Wangel? Is your name Wangel?

HILDE *(looks at him in merry surprise):* Yes, of course.

SOLNESS: Then—could it be that you are the daughter of the district physician up at Lysanger?

HILDE *(in the same tone as before):* Yes, who else would I be the daughter of?

SOLNESS: Oh, then we must have met up there. That summer when I went up to build the tower on the old church.

HILDE *(more earnestly):* Yes, that was it.

SOLNESS: Well, that's a long time ago.

HILDE *(gazes hard at him):* It was exactly ten years ago.

SOLNESS: You can only have been a child at the time.

HILDE *(carelessly):* I was nearly thirteen.

HERDAL: Is this the first time you've visited this town, Miss Wangel?

HILDE: Yes.

SOLNESS: So you—don't know anyone here, I suppose?

HILDE: No one except you. Oh, and your wife.

SOLNESS: Really? You know her too?

HILDE: Only slightly. We stayed in the same place up in the mountains. For a few days.

SOLNESS: Oh, up there.

HILDE: She said I might visit her if I ever came this way. *(Smiles.)* Not that there was any need.

SOLNESS: I wonder why she didn't mention it to me—

> HILDE *puts down her alpenstock by the stove, takes off her rucksack and puts it and her plaid on the sofa.* DR. HERDAL *tries to help her;* SOLNESS *stands looking at her.*

HILDE *(goes towards him):* Can I stay the night here?

SOLNESS: I think that could be arranged.

HILDE: I haven't any clothes apart from what I'm wearing, you see. Oh, and a set of underclothes in my rucksack. I'll have to get them washed, though. They're filthy.

SOLNESS: Oh, well, that can be taken care of. I'd better tell my wife—

HERDAL: And I'll go and see my patient.

SOLNESS: Yes, do. And come back when you've finished.

HERDAL *(merrily, with a glance at HILDE):* Yes, you can be damn sure I will! *(Laughs.)* Well, you're a true prophet after all, Mr. Solness.

SOLNESS: How do you mean?

HERDAL: Why, youth *has* come and banged on your door.

SOLNESS *(cheerfully):* Yes, but not quite the way I meant.

HERDAL: I should say not.

> *He goes out through the hall door.* SOLNESS *opens the door to the right and speaks into the side room.*

SOLNESS: Aline! Will you come in here, please? There's a Miss Wangel here, whom you know.

MRS. SOLNESS *(appears in the doorway):* Who is it, do you say? *(Sees HILDE.)* Oh, is it you, my dear?

She goes over to her and holds out her hand.

MRS. SOLNESS: So you came this way after all?

SOLNESS: Miss Wangel has just arrived. She asks if she may stay the night.

MRS. SOLNESS: With us? Yes, with pleasure.

SOLNESS: You know, to get her clothes in order.

MRS. SOLNESS: I'll look after you as well as I can. It's my simple duty. Your luggage will be coming on later, of course?

HILDE: I haven't any.

MRS. SOLNESS: Oh. Well, I'm sure you'll manage. Just make yourself at home with my husband while I get a room ready for you.

SOLNESS: Can't we use one of the nurseries? They're all ready.

MRS. SOLNESS: Oh, yes. We've plenty of room *there*. *(To* HILDE.*)* Sit down now, and rest a little.

She goes out to the right. HILDE *wanders round the room with her hands behind her back, looking at this and that.* SOLNESS *stands by the table downstage, also with his hands behind his back, watching her.*

HILDE *(stops and looks at him):* Have you got more than one nursery, then?

SOLNESS: There are three nurseries in this house.

HILDE: That's a lot. You must have heaps of children.

SOLNESS: No. We have no children. But now you can be the child here for a while.

HILDE: For tonight, yes. I won't cry. I intend to sleep like a log.

SOLNESS: Yes, I suppose you must be very tired.

HILDE: Not me! I'll sleep all right, though. I think it's absolutely marvellous to lie in bed and dream.

SOLNESS: Do you often dream at night?

HILDE: Gosh, yes. Nearly every night.

SOLNESS: What do you mostly dream about?

HILDE: I shan't tell you tonight. Some other time—perhaps.

She wanders across the room again, stops by the desk, and fingers among the books and papers.

SOLNESS *(goes over to her):* Are you looking for something?

HILDE: No, I'm just looking around. *(Turns.)* Perhaps I mustn't?

SOLNESS: No, please do.

HILDE: Do you write in this big ledger?

SOLNESS: No, my book-keeper does. I leave that to her.

HILDE: A woman?

SOLNESS *(smiles):* Yes.

HILDE: And she works here with you?

SOLNESS: Yes.

HILDE: Is it a married woman?

SOLNESS: No, it isn't.

HILDE: I see.

SOLNESS: But she's going to get married soon.

HILDE: How very nice for her.

SOLNESS: But not so nice for me. Because then I'll have no one to help me.

HILDE: Can't you find another one who'd do as well?

SOLNESS: Perhaps you'd like to stay here and—and write in the ledger?

HILDE *(looks at him scornfully):* What an idea! No, thank you. None of that.

She wanders across the room again and sits in the rocking chair. SOLNESS *comes to the table beside her.*

HILDE *(as though continuing):* There are better things here for me to do than that. *(Looks at him with a smile.)* Don't you think so?

SOLNESS: I understand. You want to go shopping and get yourself something smart to wear.

HILDE *(gaily):* No. I think I'll give that a miss.

SOLNESS: Oh?

HILDE: I've spent all my money, you see.

SOLNESS *(laughs):* No luggage, and no money!

HILDE: No. Oh, hell, what do I care?

SOLNESS: You know, I like you for that.

HILDE: Just for that?

SOLNESS: Among other things.

He sits in the armchair.

SOLNESS: Is your father still alive?

HILDE: Yes, he's alive.

SOLNESS: And now you're thinking of studying here, perhaps?

HILDE: No, I hadn't thought of that.

SOLNESS: But you'll be staying for some time?

HILDE: That depends.

She sits for a few moments rocking herself and looking at him with a half smile. Then she takes off her hat and puts it on the table in front of her.

HILDE: Mr. Solness?

SOLNESS: Yes?

HILDE: Have you a bad memory?

SOLNESS: A bad memory? No, not that I'm aware of.

HILDE: Don't you want to talk to me about what happened up there?

SOLNESS *(starts, momentarily):* Up at Lysanger? *(Casually.)* Well, there isn't much to talk about, is there?

HILDE *(looks at him reproachfully):* How can you say such a thing?

SOLNESS: All right, you talk to me about it, then.

306

HILDE: The day the tower was ready was a great day for our little town.

SOLNESS: Yes, I shan't forget that day in a hurry.

HILDE *(smiles):* Won't you? That's nice of you.

SOLNESS: Nice?

HILDE: There was music in the churchyard. And hundreds and hundreds of people. We schoolgirls were dressed in white. And we all had flags.

SOLNESS: Ah, yes. Those flags! I remember them.

HILDE: Then you climbed up the scaffolding. Up to the very top. You carried a big wreath with you. And you hung that wreath right up on the weathercock.

SOLNESS *(curtly, interrupting her):* I used to do that in those days. It's an old custom.

HILDE: It was so marvellously exciting to stand down there and stare up at you. Think—if he should fall now! The great master builder himself!

SOLNESS *(as though trying to deflect her train of thought):* Yes, yes, and it could very easily have happened. One of those little white devils suddenly waved and shouted up at me—

HILDE *(glowing and excited):* 'Hurrah for Solness! Hurrah for the master builder!' Yes!

SOLNESS: And waved her flag and swung it about so that I—I almost turned giddy watching it.

HILDE *(quiet, serious):* That little devil was me.

SOLNESS *(stares hard at her):* Of course. It must have been you.

HILDE *(full of life again):* It was so frightfully exciting and marvellous! I'd never imagined there could be a master builder anywhere in the world who could build such an enormously high tower! And then to see you standing there yourself, right up at the top! And you weren't at all giddy. That was the thing that—that made me feel giddy.

SOLNESS: What made you so sure I wasn't—?

HILDE: Don't be silly! I knew it—in here. Otherwise, how could you have stood up there singing?

SOLNESS (*stares at her, amazed*): Singing? Did I sing?

HILDE: You certainly did.

SOLNESS (*shakes his head*): I've never sung a note in my life.

HILDE: Well, you sang then. It sounded like harps in the air.

SOLNESS (*thoughtfully*): This is most extraordinary.

HILDE (*looks at him silently for a moment, then says softly*): But it was afterwards that the real thing happened.

SOLNESS: The real thing?

HILDE: Yes. I don't have to remind you about that?

SOLNESS: Yes, remind me a little about that, too.

HILDE: Don't you remember they gave a great banquet for you at the Club?

SOLNESS: Oh yes. That must have been the same evening. I left next morning.

HILDE: When it ended we invited you home for supper.

SOLNESS: You're quite right, Miss Wangel. It's remarkable how clearly you remember all these little details.

HILDE: Little details! You're a fine one! Was it just a little detail that I happened to be alone in the room when you came in?

SOLNESS: Were you?

HILDE: You didn't call me a little devil then.

SOLNESS: No, I don't suppose I did.

HILDE: You said I looked beautiful in my white dress. Like a little princess.

SOLNESS: So you did, Miss Wangel. And besides—I felt so happy and free that evening—

HILDE: And then you said that when I grew up, I would be *your* princess.

SOLNESS (*with a short laugh*): Well, well! Did I say that, too?

HILDE: Yes, you did. And then, when I asked how long I should have to wait, you said you'd come back in ten years—like a troll—and carry me off. To Spain or somewhere like that. And you promised that when we got there, you'd buy me a kingdom.

SOLNESS (*in the same tone as before*): Yes, after a good dinner one doesn't count the shillings. But did I really say all this?

HILDE (*laughs quietly*): Yes. And you told me what this kingdom was to be called, too.

SOLNESS: Oh, what?

HILDE: You said it was to be called Orangia.

SOLNESS: Well, that's a nice appetizing name.

HILDE: I didn't like it. It sounded as though you were making fun of me.

SOLNESS: I'm sure I didn't mean that.

HILDE: I can well believe you didn't. Considering what you did next—

SOLNESS: And what on earth did I do next?

HILDE: No, that's the last straw! Have you forgotten that, too? I really think you might have remembered that.

SOLNESS: Well, give me a hint, and perhaps— Well?

HILDE: You took me in your arms and kissed me, Mr. Solness.

SOLNESS (*gets up from his chair, his mouth open*): I did?

HILDE: Yes, you did. You took me in both your arms and bent me backwards and kissed me. Many, many times.

SOLNESS: Oh, but my dear, good Miss Wangel—

HILDE (*gets up*): You're not going to deny it?

SOLNESS: I certainly am!

HILDE (*looks at him scornfully*): Oh. I see.

She turns and walks slowly across to near the stove, where she stands motionless with her back towards him and her hands behind her. Short pause.

SOLNESS (*goes diffidently up behind her*): Miss Wangel—!

HILDE *remains silent and motionless.*

SOLNESS: Don't stand there like a statue. All this that you've just told me must have been something you've dreamed. *(He touches her arm.)* Now, listen—

HILDE *makes an impatient gesture with her arm. A thought strikes* SOLNESS.

SOLNESS: Or—wait a moment! No, there's more to it than that.

HILDE *does not move.* SOLNESS *speaks softly, but with emphasis.*

SOLNESS: I must have thought all this. I must have wanted it—wished it—desired it. So that— Couldn't that be an explanation?

HILDE *remains silent.* SOLNESS *bursts out impatiently.*

SOLNESS: Oh, damn it. Have it your own way—say I *did* it!

HILDE *(turns her head slightly, but does not look at him):* You confess?

SOLNESS: Yes. Anything you say.

HILDE: That you put your arms around me?

SOLNESS: Yes, yes.

HILDE: And bent me over backwards?

SOLNESS: Yes, right back.

HILDE: And kissed me?

SOLNESS: Yes, I kissed you.

HILDE: Many times?

SOLNESS: As many as you like.

HILDE *(turns quickly towards him, her eyes again glowing and excited):* You see! I wormed it out of you in the end!

SOLNESS *(smiles wryly):* Yes, just fancy—that I could forget a thing like that!

HILDE *(walks away from him, a little sulky again):* Oh, you've kissed so many women in your time, I suppose.

SOLNESS: No, you mustn't think I'm that sort.

> HILDE *sits in the armchair.* SOLNESS *stands, leaning against the rocking chair.*

SOLNESS *(looks searchingly at her)*: Miss Wangel?

HILDE: Yes?

SOLNESS: What happened? What more happened between you and me?

HILDE: Nothing more happened. You know that. The other guests arrived, and then—well—

SOLNESS: Yes, of course! The others arrived, and—fancy my forgetting that too!

HILDE: Oh, you haven't forgotten anything. You're just a bit ashamed. One doesn't forget things like that. I know.

SOLNESS: No, one would think not.

HILDE *(alive again, looks at him)*: Perhaps you've also forgotten what day it was.

SOLNESS: What day?

HILDE: Yes, what day was it when you hung the wreath on the tower? Well? Tell me! At once!

SOLNESS: Hm—I've forgotten the actual day, I must confess. I know it was ten years ago. Some time in the autumn.

HILDE *(nods slowly several times)*: It was ten years ago. The nineteenth of September.

SOLNESS: Yes, about then, I suppose. So you remember that, too! *(Pause.)* But wait a moment—! Today is the nineteenth of September!

HILDE: Exactly. And the ten years are up. And you didn't come—as you'd promised you would.

SOLNESS: Promised? I only said it to frighten you.

HILDE: I didn't find it frightening.

SOLNESS: Well, to tease you.

HILDE: Was that all you wanted to do? Tease me?

SOLNESS: Oh, I don't remember—for fun, if you like. It

can't have been anything else, you were only a child at the time.

HILDE: Oh, maybe I wasn't such a child. Not such a little innocent as you think.

SOLNESS *(looks searchingly at her):* Did you really and seriously think I'd come back?

HILDE *(suppressing a half-teasing smile):* Oh, yes! I'd expected no less of you.

SOLNESS: That I'd come to your home and take you away with me?

HILDE: Yes. Like a troll.

SOLNESS: And make you a princess?

HILDE: That's what you promised.

SOLNESS: And give you a kingdom, too?

HILDE *(looks up at the ceiling):* Why not? It didn't have to be an ordinary kingdom.

SOLNESS: But—something else, just as good?

HILDE: Yes, at least as good. *(Looks at him for a moment.)* If you could build the highest church tower in the world, I thought you would be able to find your way to a kingdom too. Of some kind.

SOLNESS *(shakes his head):* I can't quite make you out, Miss Wangel.

HILDE: You can't? To me it's all so simple.

SOLNESS: No, I can't make out whether you mean what you say. Or whether you're simply having me on—

HILDE *(smiles):* Making fun of you?

SOLNESS: Yes, exactly. Making fun of me. Of us both. *(Looks at her.)* Have you known for long that I'm married?

HILDE: I've known all along. Why do you ask that?

SOLNESS *(casually):* No, no, I just wondered. *(He looks earnestly at her and says quietly)* Why have you come?

HILDE: Because I want my kingdom. The time's up now.

SOLNESS *(laughs involuntarily):* That's a good one!

HILDE *(merrily):* Stump up my kingdom, master builder! *(Taps with her finger.)* On the table!

SOLNESS *(pushes the rocking chair closer, and sits down):* Seriously, why have you come? What do you want here?

HILDE: Well, to begin with, I want to go round and look at everything you've built.

SOLNESS: Then you'll have a lot of walking to do.

HILDE: Yes, you've built such a frightful lot.

SOLNESS: I have. Especially these last years.

HILDE: Lots of church spires too? As high as the sky?

SOLNESS: No. I don't build church spires any more. Nor churches, neither.

HILDE: What do you build now, then?

SOLNESS: Homes for people to live in.

HILDE *(thoughtfully):* Couldn't you put little spires on them, too?

SOLNESS *(starts):* What do you mean?

HILDE: I mean—something that points—straight up in the air. With a weathercock high up at the top—so high it makes you giddy!

SOLNESS *(musingly):* It's strange you should say that. That's just what I'd like to do—most of all.

HILDE *(impatiently):* Why don't you, then?

SOLNESS *(shakes his head):* No, people don't want that.

HILDE: Really? They don't want that?

SOLNESS *(more lightly):* But now I'm building a new home for myself. Here, just opposite.

HILDE: For yourself?

SOLNESS: Yes. It's almost ready. And on that there's a spire.

HILDE: A high spire?

SOLNESS: Yes.

HILDE: Very high?

SOLNESS: People are sure to say it's too high. For a home.

HILDE: I'm going out to see that spire first thing tomorrow morning.

SOLNESS (*sits leaning his cheek on his hand, staring at her*): Tell me, Miss Wangel, what's your name? Your first name, I mean?

HILDE: Hilde, of course.

SOLNESS (*as before*): Hilde? Really?

HILDE: Don't you remember? You called me Hilde. The day you misbehaved.

SOLNESS: I called you Hilde?

HILDE: Yes, but then you said 'little Hilde'. And I didn't like that.

SOLNESS: So you didn't like that, Miss Hilde?

HILDE: No. Not just then. But—Princess Hilde—that'll sound quite nice. I think.

SOLNESS: Yes, indeed. Princess Hilde of—what was our kingdom to be called?

HILDE: Ugh! I don't want any of that stupid kingdom. I want a quite different kind of kingdom.

SOLNESS (*has leant back in his chair, still staring at her*): Isn't it strange—? The more I think about it now—the more it seems to me as though for years I've been torturing myself—hm—

HILDE: Go on.

SOLNESS: Trying to remember something—something that had happened to me, and that I must have forgotten. But I could never discover what it was.

HILDE: You ought to have tied a knot in your handkerchief, master builder.

SOLNESS: Then I'd only have gone round wondering what the knot stood for.

HILDE: Oh, well. I suppose it takes trolls like you to make a world.

SOLNESS (*gets up slowly*): I'm glad you've come to me just at this time.

HILDE (*looks into his eyes*): Are you glad?

SOLNESS: I've been so alone. Staring at it all. So helpless.

(Lowers his voice.) You see—I've begun to be so afraid—so terribly afraid—of youth.

HILDE *(scornfully):* Youth? Is youth something to be afraid of?

SOLNESS: Yes, it is. That's why I've shut myself up here. *(Secretively.)* Some day, youth will come here and thunder on my door, and force its way in to me.

HILDE: Then I think you ought to go out and open the door.

SOLNESS: Open the door?

HILDE: Yes. And let youth in. As a friend.

SOLNESS: No, no! Youth means retribution. It marches at the head of a rebel army. Under a new banner.

HILDE *(gets up, looks at him and says, her mouth trembling):* Can you use me, master builder?

SOLNESS: Yes! Yes, now I can use you! For you, too, march under a new banner. Youth against youth—!

DR. HERDAL *comes in through the hall door.*

HERDAL: Hullo! Are you and our young friend still here?

SOLNESS: Yes. We two have found many things to talk about.

HILDE: Both old and new.

HERDAL: Oh, have you indeed!

HILDE: It's been great fun. The master builder has a quite incredible memory. Every little detail—just like that!

MRS. SOLNESS *enters through the door on the right.*

MRS. SOLNESS: Well, Miss Wangel, your room's ready now.

HILDE: Oh, how kind you are!

SOLNESS *(to MRS. SOLNESS):* The nursery?

MRS. SOLNESS: Yes. The middle one. But let's have supper first.

SOLNESS *(nods to HILDE):* Hilde shall sleep in the nursery tonight.

MRS. SOLNESS *(looks at him):* Hilde?

315

SOLNESS: Yes, Miss Wangel's name is Hilde. I used to know her when she was a child.

MRS. SOLNESS: No, did you really, Halvard? Well, please come in. Supper's on the table.

She takes DR. HERDAL's *arm and goes out with him to the right. Meanwhile,* HILDE *has gathered her things together.*

HILDE (*swiftly, quietly, to* SOLNESS): Was it true, what you said? Can you find some use for me?

SOLNESS (*takes her things from her*): You are the one I've been wanting.

HILDE (*looks at him, joyful and amazed, and clasps her hands*): Oh, master builder—!

SOLNESS (*tensely*): Yes?

HILDE: Then I have my kingdom!

SOLNESS (*involuntarily*): Hilde!

HILDE (*her mouth trembling again*): Almost—I was going to say.

She goes out right. SOLNESS *follows her.*

ACT TWO

A pleasantly furnished little sitting-room in SOLNESS's
*house. In the rear wall is a glass door leading to the veran-
dah and garden. The right-hand corner is broken by a bay
containing stands for plants and a large window. A similar
bay in the left-hand corner contains a small door covered
with wallpaper. In each of the side walls is an ordinary
door. Downstage right, a console table with a large mirror.
A rich profusion of flowers and plants. Downstage left, a
sofa, with a table and chairs. Further back, a bookcase. In
the middle of the room, in front of the bay, a small table and
one or two chairs. It is early morning.*

SOLNESS *is seated at the small table, with* RAGNAR
BROVIK's *portfolio open in front of him. He leafs
through the drawings, examining some of them closely.*
MRS. SOLNESS *is going round silently with a small can,
watering the flowers. She is dressed in black, as before. Her hat, overcoat and parasol lie on a chair by
the mirror.* SOLNESS *looks at her once or twice without
her noticing. Neither of them speaks.* KAJA FOSLI *comes
quietly in through the door on the left.*

SOLNESS *(turns his head and says casually):* Oh, it's you.
KAJA: I just wanted to tell you I'm here.
SOLNESS: Yes, good. Is Ragnar there, too?

KAJA: No, not yet. He had to stay behind to wait for the doctor. He won't be long, he wants to come and ask you how you feel about the—

SOLNESS: How's the old man feeling today?

KAJA: Bad. He says will you please excuse him, but he'll have to stay in bed today.

SOLNESS: By all means let him. You go along and start work, though.

KAJA: Yes. *(Stops at the door.)* Perhaps you'd like to speak to Ragnar when he comes?

SOLNESS: No, not particularly.

KAJA *goes out again to the left.* SOLNESS *continues to look through the drawings.*

MRS. SOLNESS *(over by the plants):* It wouldn't surprise me if he died too.

SOLNESS *(looks at her):* Too? Who else?

MRS. SOLNESS *(not replying):* Yes, yes; old Brovik—he'll die too now, Halvard. You'll see.

SOLNESS: Aline dear, don't you think you should go out and get a little fresh air?

MRS. SOLNESS: Yes, I should, shouldn't I?

She continues attending to the flowers.

SOLNESS *(bent over the drawings):* Is she still asleep?

MRS. SOLNESS *(looks at him):* Is it Miss Wangel you're sitting there thinking about?

SOLNESS *(indifferently):* Just happened to think of her.

MRS. SOLNESS: Miss Wangel's been up a long time.

SOLNESS: Oh, has she?

MRS. SOLNESS: When I looked in she was seeing to her clothes.

She goes to the mirror and begins slowly to put on her hat.

318

SOLNESS *(after a short pause):* Well, we've found a use for one of the nurseries after all, haven't we, Aline?

MRS. SOLNESS: Yes, we have.

SOLNESS: I think that's better than that they should all stand empty.

MRS. SOLNESS: Yes, that emptiness is horrible. You're right there.

SOLNESS *(closes the portfolio, gets up and goes over to her):* From now on things will be better, Aline. You'll see. Much more satisfactory. Life will be easier to bear. Especially for you.

MRS. SOLNESS *(looks at him):* From now on?

SOLNESS: Yes, Aline, believe me—

MRS. SOLNESS: You mean—because she's come?

SOLNESS *(controls himself):* I mean, of course, once we've moved into the new house.

MRS. SOLNESS *(takes her overcoat):* Do you really think so, Halvard? Things will be better?

SOLNESS: I'm sure they will. You believe that too, don't you?

MRS. SOLNESS: I don't believe anything where that new house is concerned.

SOLNESS *(vexed):* I'm sorry to hear that, my dear. It was mainly for your sake I built it.

He tries to help her on with her coat.

MRS. SOLNESS *(moves away):* You do much too much for me.

SOLNESS *(almost violently):* No, no, you mustn't talk like that, Aline. I can't bear to hear you say such things.

MRS. SOLNESS: Very well, Halvard, I won't say them.

SOLNESS: I'm right, though. You'll be happy in that new house. You'll see.

MRS. SOLNESS: God! *I*—happy—?

SOLNESS: Yes! Yes! I promise you! Don't you see, there'll be so much there that'll remind you of your own home—

319

MRS. SOLNESS: Father's and mother's home. And it was burnt. All burnt.

SOLNESS *(subdued):* Yes, my poor Aline. That was a terrible blow for you.

MRS. SOLNESS: You can build as much as you like, Halvard—you'll never be able to build a real home for me again.

SOLNESS *(turns and walks away across the room):* Well, in that case for God's sake let's not talk about it any more.

MRS. SOLNESS: Well, we don't usually talk about it, anyway. You always avoid the subject—

SOLNESS *(stops abruptly and looks at her):* I do? And why should I avoid the subject?

MRS. SOLNESS: Oh, I understand you so well, Halvard. You want to spare me. And stop me feeling guilty. As far as you can.

SOLNESS *(stares amazed):* Stop *you* feeling guilty! Are you—are you talking about yourself, Aline?

MRS. SOLNESS: Yes, who else would I be talking about?

SOLNESS *(involuntarily, to himself):* That too!

MRS. SOLNESS: It's not so much what happened to the old house. I think I could resign myself to that. After all, that was an accident—

SOLNESS: Yes, you're right. Accidents will happen, and it's no use blaming oneself for them.

MRS. SOLNESS: But the dreadful thing that happened after the fire. That's what I can't forget. I can't, I can't, I can't!

SOLNESS *(violently):* Don't think about it, Aline.

MRS. SOLNESS: I have to think about it. And I must talk about it some time. I don't think I can endure it any longer. And I never *can* forgive myself—

SOLNESS: Forgive *yourself*—?

MRS. SOLNESS: Yes—because I had a duty to all of you. To you, and the children. I should have hardened myself, I

320

shouldn't have let fear weaken me. Or grief—for my burnt home. Oh, if only I'd had the strength, Halvard!

SOLNESS (*quiet, shaken, comes towards her*): Aline, you must promise me you'll never let these thoughts enter your head again. Promise me that, my dear.

MRS. SOLNESS: God—promise, promise! It's easy to promise anything—

SOLNESS (*walks across the room*): Oh, this is hopeless, hopeless! Not a ray of light ever enters this home. Not a glimmer.

MRS. SOLNESS: This is no home, Halvard.

SOLNESS: No, you're right. And, God knows, you may be right too when you say it won't be any better in the new house.

MRS. SOLNESS: Never. It'll be just as empty and just as desolate there as it is here.

SOLNESS (*violently*): Why in God's name have we built it, then? Can you tell me that?

MRS. SOLNESS: No. That you must answer yourself.

SOLNESS (*looks at her suspiciously*): What do you mean by that, Aline?

MRS. SOLNESS: What do I mean?

SOLNESS: Yes, damn it! You said it so strangely. As though you meant something else.

MRS. SOLNESS: No. I assure you—

SOLNESS (*goes closer*): Oh, thank you very much—I know what I know. I've got eyes and ears, Aline. You can be sure of that.

MRS. SOLNESS: What do you mean? What do you mean?

SOLNESS (*stands in front of her*): You find some cunning, hidden meaning in every harmless little thing I say, don't you, eh?

MRS. SOLNESS: I, Halvard. Do *I* do that?

SOLNESS (*laughs*): Oh, it's very understandable, Aline. When you've a sick man on your hands, well—

321

MRS. SOLNESS *(alarmed):* Sick? Are you sick, Halvard?

SOLNESS: An idiot, then. A lunatic. Call me what you like.

MRS. SOLNESS *(gropes for the back of the chair and sits down):* Halvard—for God's sake—!

SOLNESS: But you're wrong, both of you. You and your doctor. There's nothing the matter with me.

He walks up and down the room. MRS. SOLNESS *watches him anxiously. At length he comes over to her, and says calmly:*

SOLNESS: There's nothing the matter with me at all.

MRS. SOLNESS: No, of course not. But—what's worrying you, then?

SOLNESS: It's this dreadful burden of debt that's crushing me—

MRS. SOLNESS: Debt? But you're not in debt to anyone, Halvard.

SOLNESS *(quietly):* I owe a boundless debt to you. To you, Aline.

MRS. SOLNESS *(rises slowly):* What is behind all this?

SOLNESS: There's nothing *behind* it. I've never done you any harm. Not wittingly, anyway. And yet—it feels as though a huge stone of guilt lay on me, weighing me down, crushing me.

MRS. SOLNESS: Guilt? Towards me, you mean?

SOLNESS: Towards you, most of all.

MRS. SOLNESS: Then you really are—sick, Halvard.

SOLNESS: I suppose I must be. Sick—or something.

He glances towards the door on the right, as it is opened.

SOLNESS: Ah! Now it grows lighter!

HILDE WANGEL *enters. She has made one or two changes in her dress, and has let down her skirt so that it reaches to her ankles.*

HILDE: Good morning, master builder!

SOLNESS (*nods*): Slept well?

HILDE: Marvellously! Just as though I was in a cradle. Oh, I lay there and stretched myself like a—like a princess.

SOLNESS (*with a little smile*): Really comfortable?

HILDE: I should say so!

SOLNESS: And you dreamed too, I suppose?

HILDE: Yes. Ugh—beastly!

SOLNESS: Oh?

HILDE: Yes, I dreamed I'd fallen over a frightfully high, steep cliff. Do you ever have that dream?

SOLNESS: Er—yes—now and then—

HILDE: It's so exciting! As you fall and fall—

SOLNESS: It makes me go cold as ice.

HILDE: Do you hug your knees up under you as you fall?

SOLNESS: Yes, as high as I can.

HILDE: So do I.

MRS. SOLNESS (*takes her parasol*): Well, I'd better be going into town now, Halvard. (*To* HILDE.) I'll see if I can bring back one or two things you might need.

HILDE (*tries to embrace her*): Oh, darling, beautiful Mrs. Solness! You're really too sweet. Frightfully sweet—

MRS. SOLNESS (*freeing herself*): Not at all. It's my simple duty. And I'm only too glad to do it.

HILDE (*pouts, piqued*): Actually, I think I'm all right to go into town as I am, now that I've made myself smart. Or perhaps I'm not?

MRS. SOLNESS: To speak frankly, I think one or two people might raise their eyebrows.

HILDE: Pooh! Is that all? That'd be rather a lark.

SOLNESS (*concealing his mood*): Yes, but people might think you were mad, too, you see.

HILDE: Mad? Are there so many mad people in this town?

SOLNESS (*points to his forehead*): Here you see one, anyway.

HILDE: *You*—master builder?

MRS. SOLNESS: Oh, but my dear Halvard, really!

SOLNESS: Haven't you noticed yet?

HILDE: No, I certainly haven't. *(Thinks and gives a little laugh.)* Yes, perhaps in just one little thing, now I think of it.

SOLNESS: You hear that, Aline?

MRS. SOLNESS: In what thing, Miss Wangel?

HILDE: No, I'm not telling.

SOLNESS: Yes, do tell us.

HILDE: No, thanks—I'm not *that* mad.

MRS. SOLNESS: When you and Miss Wangel are alone, she'll tell you, Halvard.

SOLNESS: Oh, do you think so?

MRS. SOLNESS: Why, yes. You and she have been such good friends; ever since she was a child, you say. *(She goes out through the door on the left).*

HILDE *(after a moment):* Do you think your wife doesn't like me?

SOLNESS: Why, did you notice anything?

HILDE: Didn't you?

SOLNESS *(avoiding the question):* Aline's become very shy of people these last years.

HILDE: That too?

SOLNESS: But if only you could get to know her properly—she's very good and kind—a really good woman—

HILDE *(impatiently):* If she is, why did she have to talk like that about duty?

SOLNESS: About duty?

HILDE: Yes, she said she'd go out and buy something for me because it was her duty. Oh, I can't stand that nasty beastly word.

SOLNESS: Why not?

HILDE: It sounds so cold and sharp, like a knife. Duty, duty, duty! Don't you feel that, too? That it—somehow—pierces you?

SOLNESS: Hm—I haven't given it much thought.

HILDE: Oh yes! And if she's as good and kind as you pretend, why should she say a thing like that?

SOLNESS: Well, good Lord, what should she have said?

HILDE: She could have said she wanted to do it because she liked me so much. Or something like that, she could have said. Something really warm and kind, don't you think?

SOLNESS *(looks at her)*: So that's what you want?

HILDE: Yes.

She walks round the room, stops in front of the bookcase and looks at the books.

HILDE: You've an awful lot of books.

SOLNESS: Oh, I've collected a few.

HILDE: Do you read them all?

SOLNESS: I used to try. Do you read?

HILDE: No. Not any more. It all seems so meaningless.

SOLNESS: That's exactly how I feel.

HILDE *wanders round for a few moments, stops by the small table, opens the portfolio and glances through it.*

HILDE: Have you done all these drawings?

SOLNESS: No, a young man I have here to help me.

HILDE: A pupil of yours?

SOLNESS: Oh, yes, I dare say he's learned something from me, too.

HILDE *(sits)*: He must be awfully clever, then. *(She looks at a drawing for a moment.)* Isn't he?

SOLNESS: Oh, not so bad. For my purposes—

HILDE: Oh, *yes*. He must be frightfully clever.

SOLNESS: You can tell that from his drawings, can you?

HILDE: What, this stuff? Oh, no. But if he's been studying with *you*—

SOLNESS: Oh, that? There are plenty of people round here who've studied under me. And nothing's become of them.

HILDE (*looks at him and shakes her head*): Upon my soul, I don't understand how you can be so stupid.

SOLNESS: Stupid? Do you think I'm so very stupid, then?

HILDE: Yes, indeed I do. Letting these young men come here and pick your brains—

SOLNESS (*starts*): Well? And why not?

HILDE (*gets up, half in earnest, half laughing*): Oh, no, master builder, that's no good. No one but you should be allowed to build. Only you. Do it all yourself. Now you know.

SOLNESS (*unwillingly*): Hilde—

HILDE: Yes?

SOLNESS: What on earth made you say that?

HILDE: Why—*that's* not such a wicked idea, is it?

SOLNESS: No, I didn't mean that. But—I'll tell you something.

HILDE: Well, what?

SOLNESS: I walk up and down in this house—incessantly—in silence—and loneliness—turning that very idea over in my mind.

HILDE: Yes, well, that's very reasonable.

SOLNESS (*glances searchingly at her*): I dare say you've noticed this?

HILDE: No, I haven't *noticed* anything.

SOLNESS: But just now—when you said you thought I was—wrong in the head—on one point of the compass. Did you mean—?

HILDE: Oh, I was thinking of something quite different then.

SOLNESS: What were you thinking of?

HILDE: Never you mind, master builder.

SOLNESS (*walks across the room*): As you please. (*He stops by the bay.*) Come here, and I'll show you something.

HILDE (*goes closer*): What is it?

SOLNESS (*points*): Just beyond that big stone-pit—

HILDE: That new house?

SOLNESS: That one that's being built, yes. Almost finished now.

HILDE: It's got a very high tower, hasn't it?

SOLNESS: The scaffolding's still round it.

HILDE: Is that your new house?

SOLNESS: Yes.

HILDE: The house you're going to move into soon?

SOLNESS: Yes.

HILDE *(looks at him):* Are there nurseries in that house, too?

SOLNESS: Three, the same as here.

HILDE: And no children?

SOLNESS: There won't be any, either.

HILDE *(with a half smile):* Well, wasn't I right?

SOLNESS: What do you mean?

HILDE: You are a little—mad—after all.

SOLNESS: Was *that* what you were thinking?

HILDE: Yes—all those empty nurseries, where I was sleeping.

SOLNESS *(quietly):* We have had children—Aline and I.

HILDE *(looks at him tensely):* Have you?

SOLNESS: Two little boys. Both the same age.

HILDE: Twins?

SOLNESS: Yes, twins. It's nearly twelve years ago, now.

HILDE *(gently):* You mean they're both—? You haven't got these twins any longer?

SOLNESS *(quiet, moved):* We only had them three weeks. Hardly that. *(Bursts out.)* Oh, Hilde, I can't tell you how glad I am that you've come! Now at last I've found someone I can talk to.

HILDE: Can't you talk to—to her, too?

SOLNESS: Not about this. Not the way I want to—and need to. *(Sadly.)* Nor about much else, either.

HILDE: Was that all you meant when you said you needed me?

SOLNESS: Must have been—I suppose. Yesterday, at least. Today, I'm no longer so sure.

He breaks off; takes her by the hand and leads her to the sofa.

SOLNESS: There. You can see the garden from there.

She sits in the corner of the sofa. He brings a chair nearer to her.

SOLNESS: Would you like to hear about it?

HILDE: Yes, I love sitting and listening to you.

SOLNESS *(sits):* Well, I'll tell you all about it.

HILDE: Now I can see you *and* the garden, master builder. Now then, tell me! Come on!

SOLNESS *(points through the bay window):* Up there—where you see that new house—

HILDE: Yes?

SOLNESS: That's where Aline and I lived during the first years of our marriage. In those days there used to be an old house up there which had belonged to her mother. She left it to us. And all the grounds with it.

HILDE: Was there a spire on that house, too?

SOLNESS: No, nothing of the kind. To look at from the outside, it was a great, dark ugly crate. But indoors it was nice and cosy enough.

HILDE: Did you pull the old thing down?

SOLNESS: No, it was burned down.

HILDE: The whole thing?

SOLNESS: Yes.

HILDE: Was that a terrible blow to you?

SOLNESS: It depends which way you look at it. It was that fire that made me a master builder.

HILDE: Oh? But—?

SOLNESS: Our two little boys had just been born—

HILDE: The poor little twins.

SOLNESS: They were so healthy and strong when they were born. And you could see them growing from day to day—

HILDE: Babies grow frightfully quickly the first few days.

SOLNESS: It was the prettiest sight you could wish to see, Aline lying there with the two of them. But then there came the night of the fire—

HILDE: What happened? Tell me! Was anyone burned alive?

SOLNESS: No, not that. Everyone got safely out of the house—

HILDE: Well, then, what—?

SOLNESS: It was a terrible shock for Aline. The alarm, and being rushed out of the house, into the ice-cold night— they had to be carried out, just as they were—she and the little boys.

HILDE: And they couldn't stand the cold?

SOLNESS: Oh, they stood up to that all right. But Aline caught a fever. And it infected her milk. She had to feed them herself. It was her duty, she said. And both our little boys—both of them—

HILDE: They didn't get over *that?*

SOLNESS: No, they didn't get over that. It—took them from us.

HILDE: That must have been a great loss for you.

SOLNESS: It was great enough for me. But ten times greater for her. *(Clenches his hands in quiet fury.)* How can such a thing be allowed to happen in this world? *(Curtly.)* From that day on, I lost interest in building churches.

HILDE: Then you didn't enjoy building the steeple on our church?

SOLNESS: I didn't. How relieved and glad I was when it was finished.

HILDE: I know that.

SOLNESS: And now I shall never build anything like that again. Neither churches, nor steeples.

HILDE *(nods slowly):* Just houses, for people to live in.

SOLNESS: Homes, Hilde. Homes for men and women and children.

HILDE: But homes with high towers and spires on top.

SOLNESS: Yes, if possible. *(Speaks more lightly.)* Well, you see—as I said—that fire started me on my way. As a master builder.

HILDE: Why don't you call yourself an architect, like all the others?

SOLNESS: I've never really studied it properly. Most of what I know I've found out for myself.

HILDE: But you got to the top, master builder.

SOLNESS: Yes; fanned by those flames. I cut up nearly all the grounds into building plots. And *there* I was able to build, just the way I wanted. And from then on things went well for me.

HILDE *(looks searchingly at him):* You must be a very happy man, then. With all the success you've had.

SOLNESS: Happy? You say that, too. Like all the others.

HILDE: Yes, I think you should be. If you could only stop thinking about those two little boys—

SOLNESS *(slowly):* Those two little boys—are not so easy to forget, Hilde.

HILDE *(a little uncertain):* So they still stand in your way? After so many years?

SOLNESS *(stares at her, without replying):* A happy man, you said—

HILDE: Yes, well, aren't you—apart from this?

SOLNESS *(still staring at her):* When I told you about the fire—

HILDE: Go on.

SOLNESS: Didn't anything particular strike you?

HILDE: No. I can't think of anything.

SOLNESS: If it hadn't been for that fire, I wouldn't have been able to build homes. Bright, peaceful, comfortable homes, where mothers and fathers could live with their children secure and happy in the knowledge that it is good to be

330

alive. And, above all, to belong to each other—in great things and in small.

HILDE: Yes, doesn't it bring you great happiness to know that you can build such wonderful homes for them?

SOLNESS: But the price, Hilde. The terrible price I had to pay.

HILDE: Is there no way to put all that behind you?

SOLNESS: No. Because—to be able to build homes for other people, I had to renounce for ever all hope of having a home of my own. I mean a home with children. And for their father and mother.

HILDE: For ever, you say? Was that absolutely necessary?

SOLNESS *(nods slowly):* That was the price I had to pay for this 'happiness' people talk so much about. *(Takes a deep breath.)* That happiness—hm—that happiness wasn't to be had at a lesser price, Hilde.

HILDE: But perhaps things may still work out?

SOLNESS: No, they never can. Never. That is another consequence of the fire. And of Aline's illness which resulted from it.

HILDE *(looks at him with an enigmatic expression):* And yet you are building all these nurseries?

SOLNESS: Haven't you noticed, Hilde, that the impossible—beckons and calls to us?

HILDE *(thinks):* The impossible? *(Excitedly.)* Why, yes! Is it like that with you as well?

SOLNESS: It is.

HILDE: Then you have something of the troll in you, too.

SOLNESS: Why troll?

HILDE: Well, what would you call it?

SOLNESS *(gets up):* No, no, you may be right. *(Violently.)* But please God I may never become a troll like the one who mocks me in everything I do! Everything!

HILDE: What do you mean?

SOLNESS: Mark my words, Hilde. Everything that I have

created, beautiful, secure and friendly—yes, and magnificent too!—I must sit here and expiate. Pay for it. Not with money. But with human happiness. And not only with my happiness, but with the happiness of others, too. You see, Hilde! That's the price that my success as an artist has cost me—and others. And every day of my life I have to sit here and see that price being paid for me—day after day after day!

HILDE *(gets up and looks steadily at him):* You're thinking of *her*—aren't you?

SOLNESS: Yes. Aline had her calling in life. Just as I had mine. But she had to be destroyed and annihilated so that I could follow my calling and gain a—kind of triumph. Yes—you see, Aline had a—a talent for building, too.

HILDE: She? For building?

SOLNESS *(shakes his head):* Not houses and towers and steeples. Not the kind of things I bother with—

HILDE: Well, what, then?

SOLNESS *(softly, moved):* Children, Hilde. The souls of children. So that they might grow into something noble, harmonious and beautiful. So that they might become worthy human beings. That was where her talent lay. And it lies there, unused—and unusable; waste and barren, like the charred ruins left after a fire.

HILDE: Yes, but even if this were true—

SOLNESS: It is! I know it!

HILDE: Well, anyway, it's not your fault. You're not guilty.

SOLNESS: Aren't I? That's the terrible doubt that gnaws me night and day.

HILDE: This?

SOLNESS: Yes—suppose it is true. Suppose I am guilty? In a kind of way.

HILDE: You? You mean—the fire?

SOLNESS: Everything. Everything. And on the other hand—I may be quite innocent.

HILDE: Oh, master builder! If you can talk like that, you must be—well—ill, anyway.

SOLNESS: Hm—incurably, I'm afraid. Where this is concerned.

RAGNAR BROVIK *cautiously opens the small door in the corner on the left.* HILDE *walks across the room.*

RAGNAR *(as he sees* HILDE*):* Oh—I beg your pardon, Mr. Solness— *(He is about to go.)*

SOLNESS: No, no, come in. Let's get this matter settled.

RAGNAR: Oh, yes—if we could!

SOLNESS: Your father's no better, I hear.

RAGNAR: He's sinking fast. So—please—I beg you—write a few kind words about one of the drawings. Something he can read before he—

SOLNESS *(violently):* You mustn't ask me any more questions about those drawings of yours.

RAGNAR: Have you looked at them?

SOLNESS: Yes—I have.

RAGNAR: And—they're no good? And I suppose I'm no good either?

SOLNESS: You stay here with me, Ragnar. You shall have whatever you want. Then you can marry Kaja, and all your cares will be over. You might even be happy. Only don't think of building by yourself.

RAGNAR: Very well. I'd better go home and tell father that. I promised him I would. Shall I tell father this—before he dies?

SOLNESS *(distressed):* Oh, tell him—tell him what you like. Better not tell him anything. *(Violently.)* I can't help it, Ragnar. I have no choice.

RAGNAR: In that case, may I have the drawings?

SOLNESS: Yes, take them—take them away. They're on the table.

RAGNAR *(goes across):* Thank you.

HILDE *(puts her hand on the portfolio):* No, no, leave them.

SOLNESS: Why?

HILDE: I'd like to look at them, too.

SOLNESS: But you've already—*(To* RAGNAR.*)* All right, then. Leave them there.

RAGNAR: By all means.

SOLNESS: And now go home to your father.

RAGNAR: I suppose I must.

SOLNESS *(as though desperate):* Ragnar—you mustn't ask of me something I cannot do! Do you hear, Ragnar? You mustn't do that!

RAGNAR: No, no. I'm sorry.

He bows and goes out through the corner door. HILDE *goes and sits on a chair by the mirror.*

HILDE *(looks angrily at* SOLNESS*):* That was beastly of you.

SOLNESS: You think so, too?

HILDE: Yes, really beastly. Hard and vicious and cruel.

SOLNESS: Oh, you don't understand.

HILDE: All the same—no, you shouldn't be like that. Not you.

SOLNESS: You said yourself just now that I was the only person who should be allowed to build.

HILDE: I can say that. Not you.

SOLNESS: If anyone can, I can. I paid dearly enough for my position.

HILDE: Oh, yes. Domestic bliss, and all that.

SOLNESS: Peace of mind.

HILDE *(gets up):* Peace of mind! *(With feelings.)* Yes, of course! Poor master builder! You fancy that—

SOLNESS *(chuckles):* You sit down again, Hilde, and I'll tell you a funny story.

HILDE *(sits):* Well?

SOLNESS: It sounds so ludicrously trivial. You see, it all turns on a crack in a chimney pipe.

HILDE: That all?

SOLNESS: Yes, to begin with.

He moves a chair closer to HILDE, *and sits.*

HILDE *(impatient, slaps her knee):* So there was a crack in the chimney?

SOLNESS: I'd noticed that crack for a long time, long before the fire. Each time I went up to the loft, I looked to see if it was still there.

HILDE: And it was?

SOLNESS: Yes. No one else knew about it.

HILDE: And you didn't say anything?

SOLNESS: No, I didn't.

HILDE: And you didn't think of getting it mended?

SOLNESS: Oh, I thought about it, but I didn't do anything. Each time I decided to get down to it, it was just as though a hand reached out and held me back. Not today, I thought. Tomorrow. So nothing ever came of it.

HILDE: Why did you always put it off?

SOLNESS: Because a thought had occurred to me. *(Slow, quiet.)* 'Through this little black crack in this chimney pipe, I might climb my way to the top. Become a master builder.'

HILDE *(to herself):* That must have been exciting.

SOLNESS: It was irresistible—almost. Utterly irresistible! At the time, it all seemed so unimportant and trivial. I wanted it to happen some time in winter. Shortly before dinner. I would be out, driving Aline in the sleigh. The servants would have built up great fires in all the rooms—

HILDE: It'd be frightfully cold that day, wouldn't it?

SOLNESS: Pretty sharp, yes. And they'd want it to be good and warm for Aline when she came back.

HILDE: Yes, she suffers from the cold, doesn't she?

SOLNESS: She does. And then, it'd be on the way home that we'd see the smoke.

HILDE: Just the smoke?

SOLNESS: First of all the smoke. But then, when we reached the drive, the old crate was just a surging mass of flames! That's the way I wanted it to happen.

HILDE: Oh, why couldn't it have happened like that? *(Pause.)* But, wait a moment, master builder. Are you quite sure that the fire was caused by this little crack in the chimney?

SOLNESS: No, on the contrary. I'm quite sure the crack in the chimney had nothing whatever to do with the fire.

HILDE: What!

SOLNESS: It's been established that the fire broke out in the linen room, on the other side of the house.

HILDE: Then why on earth are you sitting here drivelling about this cracked chimney?

SOLNESS: May I go on talking to you for a little, Hilde?

HILDE: Yes, but only if you talk sensibly.

SOLNESS: I'll do my best. *(He moves his chair closer.)*

HILDE: Well! Out with it, master builder!

SOLNESS *(confidentially):* Don't you think, Hilde, that there are people singled out by fate who have been endowed with grace and power to wish for something, desire it so passionately, *will* it so inexorably that, ultimately, they must be granted it? Don't you think so?

HILDE *(with an enigmatic expression in her eyes):* If that is so, the time will come when we shall see if I am one of them.

SOLNESS: No man can achieve such things alone. Oh, no. There are—helpers and servers—who must be at our side if we are to succeed. But they never come of their own accord. One must call on them with all one's strength. Silently, you understand.

HILDE: Who are these helpers and servers?

SOLNESS: Oh, let's talk about that some other time. For the moment, let's concentrate on the fire.

HILDE: Don't you think there would have been a fire even if you hadn't wished for it?

SOLNESS: If that house had been owned by old Knut Brovik, it would never have burned down at such an opportune moment. I'm sure of that. Because he doesn't understand how to call on the helpers, or to summon those who serve him. *(Gets up restlessly.)* So you see, Hilde—it *is* I who am guilty, and both those little boys had to pay with their lives. And is it not also true that it is my fault that Aline has not become what she should and could have become? And what she so longed to become.

HILDE: Yes, but if it's these helpers and servers who—

SOLNESS: Who called to the helpers and to the servers? I did! And they came and bowed to my will. *(In increasing turmoil.)* This is what people call being lucky. But I'll tell you how it feels to be lucky! It feels as though the skin had been flayed from my breast. And the helpers and servers go round taking the skin from other people's bodies to cover the wound. But it can't be healed. Never, never! Oh, if you only knew how it burns sometimes.

HILDE: You are ill, master builder. Very ill, I think.

SOLNESS: Say mad. That's what you mean.

HILDE: No, I don't think there's anything wrong with your head.

SOLNESS: What, then? Out with it!

HILDE: I'm wondering if you weren't born with an under-developed conscience.

SOLNESS: Under-developed conscience? What the devil do you mean?

HILDE: I mean that your conscience is very frail. Over-sensitive; won't get to grips with things. Can't carry a heavy burden.

SOLNESS *(growls)*: Hm! How ought a conscience to be, if I may ask?

HILDE: In your case I wish it were a little more—well—robust.

SOLNESS: Indeed? Robust? Well! And have you a robust conscience?

HILDE: Yes, I think so. I haven't noticed anything to the contrary.

SOLNESS: I don't suppose you've had much opportunity to test it, have you?

HILDE *(with a tremble round her mouth):* Oh, it wasn't all that easy to leave father. I'm frightfully fond of him.

SOLNESS: Oh, just for a month or two—

HILDE: I don't think I shall ever go back.

SOLNESS: What, never? Why did you leave him, then?

HILDE *(half serious, half teasing):* Have you forgotten again? The ten years are up!

SOLNESS: Nonsense. Was there anything wrong at home? Mm?

HILDE *(earnestly):* This thing inside me drove me to come here. Tempted and drove me.

SOLNESS *(eagerly):* That's it! That's it, Hilde! There's troll in you, too; the same as in me. And it's the troll, you see, that calls to the powers outside! And we have to submit whether we like it or not.

HILDE: I begin to think you're right, master builder.

SOLNESS *(paces the floor):* Oh, there are so many invisible demons in the world, Hilde. *(Stops.)* Good demons and evil demons. Fair demons and dark. If only one always knew whether it was the fair that had hold of one, or the dark! *(Starts walking again.)* Ha, ha! It would all be so simple.

HILDE *(watches him as he walks):* Or if only one had a really brash and hearty conscience! So that one dared to do what one wanted.

SOLNESS *(stops by the console table):* Oh, I think most people are as cowardly as I, in that respect.

HILDE: That may well be.

SOLNESS *(leans against the table):* In the sagas—have you read any of those old sagas?

HILDE: Oh, yes! In the days when I used to read—

SOLNESS: Those sagas tell about vikings, who sailed to foreign lands and plundered and burned and killed—

HILDE: And carried away women—

SOLNESS: And kept them—

HILDE: Took them home with them in their ships—

SOLNESS: And used them like—like the worst kind of trolls.

HILDE *(to herself, with her eyes half closed):* I think that must be so exciting!

SOLNESS *(with a short, gruff laugh):* To take a woman, you mean?

HILDE: To be taken.

SOLNESS *(looks at her for a moment):* I see.

HILDE *(as though changing the subject):* But what were you going to say about these vikings, master builder?

SOLNESS: Oh, yes—well, those fellows, their consciences were robust enough. When they came home, they ate and drank, and were as merry as children. And what about the women! Quite often they didn't want to leave these men! Can you understand that, Hilde?

HILDE: I can understand the women frightfully well.

SOLNESS: Ah! Perhaps you would do the same yourself?

HILDE: Why not?

SOLNESS: Live—willingly—with a brute like that?

HILDE: If he was a brute I'd come to grow really fond of—

SOLNESS: *Could* you grow fond of a man like that?

HILDE: Oh, God, one can't help whom one grows fond of, can one?

SOLNESS *(looks at her thoughtfully):* No, no—I suppose it's the troll in us that decides that.

HILDE *(with a little laugh):* And all these blessed demons you know so much about. The fair and the dark.

339

SOLNESS (*warmly and quietly*): I hope the demons choose kindly for you, Hilde.

HILDE: They have chosen for me. Once and for all.

SOLNESS (*looks deep into her eyes*): Hilde—you are like a wild bird of the forest.

HILDE: Far from it. I'm not shy.

SOLNESS: No, no. There's more of the falcon in you.

HILDE: Yes—perhaps. (*Violently.*) And why not a falcon? Why shouldn't I go hunting, too? Get the prey I want? If only I can get my claws into it! Bring it to the ground!

SOLNESS: Hilde—do you know what you are?

HILDE: Yes, I'm a strange kind of bird.

SOLNESS: No. You are like a new dawn. When I look at you, it is as though I were watching the sunrise.

HILDE: Tell me, master builder—are you sure you've never called to me? Silently?

SOLNESS (*quietly*): I think I must have done.

HILDE: What do you want from me?

SOLNESS: Your youth, Hilde.

HILDE (*smiles*): Youth, which you are so frightened of?

SOLNESS (*nods slowly*): And which, in my heart, I long for.

> HILDE *gets up, goes over to the small table, and fetches* RAGNAR BROVIK's *portfolio.*

HILDE (*holds out the portfolio towards him*): What about these drawings, now?

SOLNESS (*curtly*): Put those things away. I've seen enough of them.

HILDE: Quite, but you're going to approve them.

SOLNESS: Approve them? I'm damned if I will.

HILDE: Can't you do this little thing for him? The poor old man's dying. And then perhaps his son might get the chance to build the house, too.

SOLNESS: Yes, that's just it. He can. He's made sure of that, that young gentleman.

HILDE: Well, for goodness sake, if he has, can't you bring yourself to lie a tiny little bit?

SOLNESS: Lie? *(Furiously.)* Hilde, take those damned drawings away from me!

HILDE *(draws the portfolio a little towards her)*: Now, now, now, don't snap at me. You talk about trolls. I think you behave like one yourself. *(Looks round.)* Where do you keep your pen and ink?

SOLNESS: I haven't any in here.

HILDE *(goes towards the door)*: Well, that girl'll have some—

SOLNESS: Stay where you are, Hilde! I must tell a lie, you said. Oh, I wouldn't mind doing it for his old father. A man I once ruined.

HILDE: You ruined him too?

SOLNESS: I needed room. But this young Ragnar—he mustn't on any account be allowed to come to the front.

HILDE: He won't, either, will he, poor boy? If he's no good—

SOLNESS *(comes closer, looks at her and whispers)*: If Ragnar Brovik gets started, he will break me. Just as I broke his father.

HILDE: Break *you?* He is some good, then?

SOLNESS: Yes, he's good, make no mistake. He is the youth who is waiting ready to bang upon my door. And make an end of master builder Solness.

HILDE: And yet you wanted to shut him out? For shame, master builder!

SOLNESS: This struggle has cost me enough. Besides, I'm afraid the helpers and the servers won't obey me any longer.

HILDE: Then you'll have to manage on your own. There's nothing for it.

SOLNESS: Hopeless, Hilde. The tide will turn. Sooner or later. Retribution will come.

HILDE *(frightened, puts her hands over her ears)*: Don't talk

like that! Do you want to take away from me what I value
more than my life?

SOLNESS: And what's that?

HILDE: To see you great! See you with a wreath in your
hand! High, high up on a church tower! *(Calm again.)*
Well, at least you must have a pencil. Give it to me.

SOLNESS *(takes out his notebook):* Yes, I've got one here.

HILDE *(puts the portfolio on the table by the sofa):* Right.
And now we'll sit down here, master builder.

SOLNESS *sits at the table.*

HILDE *(behind him, leaning over the back of his chair):* And
then we'll write on the drawings. Really, really nicely and
kindly, we'll write. For this beastly Ragnvald or whatever
his name is.

SOLNESS *(writes a few lines, turns and looks up at her):* Tell
me something, Hilde.

HILDE: Yes?

SOLNESS: If you've really been waiting for me for ten years—

HILDE: Well?

SOLNESS: Why didn't you write to me?

HILDE *(quickly):* No, no, no! That was just what I didn't
want!

SOLNESS: Why not?

HILDE: I was afraid that then it might all go wrong. But we
were going to write on the drawings, master builder.

SOLNESS: So we were.

HILDE *(leans over him and watches while he writes):*
How good and kind. Oh, how I hate—how I hate this
Ragnvald—

SOLNESS *(as he writes):* Have you never been—really fond
of anyone, Hilde?

HILDE *(in a hard voice):* What did you say?

SOLNESS: I asked if you had ever been really fond of anyone.

HILDE: Anyone else, you mean?

342

SOLNESS *(looks up at her):* Yes, of course—anyone else.
Haven't you? In all these years? Ever?

HILDE: Oh, yes, once in a while. When I was really mad
with you for not coming.

SOLNESS: Then you—cared about others too?

HILDE: A little. For a week or two. Oh, God, master builder,
you know how it is.

SOLNESS: Hilde—why have you come?

HILDE: Don't waste time. That poor old man may be dying
while you talk.

SOLNESS: Answer me, Hilde. What is it you want from me?

HILDE: I want my kingdom.

SOLNESS: Hm—

> *He glances quickly towards the door on the left, and
> continues writing on the drawings.* MRS. SOLNESS *en-
> ters, carrying some parcels.*

MRS. SOLNESS: I've brought you a few things, Miss Wangel.
There are some big parcels being sent on later.

HILDE: Oh, how very sweet of you!

MRS. SOLNESS: It's my simple duty. That's all.

SOLNESS *(reading through what he has written):* Aline!

MRS. SOLNESS: Yes?

SOLNESS: Did you see if she—if the book-keeper was out
there?

MRS. SOLNESS: Yes, of course she was there.

SOLNESS *(replacing the drawings in the portfolio):* Hm—

MRS. SOLNESS: She was standing at the desk, as she always
does—when I'm in the room.

SOLNESS *(gets up):* I'll give this to her, then, and tell her
that—

HILDE *(taking the portfolio from him):* Oh, no, let me,
please! *(She goes to the door, then turns.)* What's her
name?

SOLNESS: Her name's Miss Fosli.

HILDE: Ugh, that sounds so formal. What's her first name, I mean?

SOLNESS: Kaja, I think.

HILDE *(opens the door and calls):* Kaja! Come in here. Hurry! The master builder wants to speak to you.

KAJA *comes inside the door.*

KAJA *(looks at him, frightened):* Here I am—?

HILDE *(holds out the portfolio to her):* Look, Kaja! You can take this, now. The master builder's written on them.

KAJA: Oh—at last!

SOLNESS: Give them to the old man as soon as you can.

KAJA: I'll take them home at once.

SOLNESS: Yes, do that. And then Ragnar can begin to build.

KAJA: Oh, may he come and thank you for everything—?

SOLNESS: I want no thanks. Tell him so from me.

KAJA: Yes, I'll—

SOLNESS: And tell him at the same time that from now on I've no use for him. Nor for you.

KAJA *(quietly trembling):* Nor for me?

SOLNESS: You'll have other things to think about now. And someone else to look after. And that's as it should be. All right, go home now with your drawings, Miss Fosli. Quickly! Do you hear?

KAJA: Yes, Mr. Solness. *(She goes out.)*

MRS. SOLNESS: Oh, what sly eyes she has!

SOLNESS: That poor little creature?

MRS. SOLNESS: Oh, I'm not blind, Halvard. Are you really dismissing them?

SOLNESS: Yes.

MRS. SOLNESS: Her too?

SOLNESS: Well, wasn't that what you wanted?

MRS. SOLNESS: But how can you manage without her? Oh, I see. You've someone else up your sleeve, haven't you, Halvard?

HILDE *(gaily)*: Well, I'm no good for standing at desks, anyway.

SOLNESS: I shall manage somehow, Aline. You must make arrangements for moving into our new home as soon as possible. This evening we shall hoist the wreath— *(Turns to* HILDE.*)* —to the top of the spire. What do you say to that, Miss Hilde?

HILDE *(looks at him excitedly)*: It'll be so marvellous to see you standing high up there again!

SOLNESS: Me!

MRS. SOLNESS: Oh God, Miss Wangel, you mustn't think of it! My husband gets dizzy. He has no head for heights.

HILDE: Dizzy? I don't believe it.

MRS. SOLNESS: Oh, yes, he's always been like that.

HILDE: But I've seen him myself high up on the top of a church steeple.

MRS. SOLNESS: Yes, I've heard people talk about that. But it's impossible.

SOLNESS *(violently)*: Impossible, yes! But nevertheless, I stood up there!

MRS. SOLNESS: How can you say that, Halvard? You hardly even dare to go out on to the balcony on the second floor. You've always been like that.

SOLNESS: You may think otherwise this evening.

MRS. SOLNESS *(frightened)*: No, no, no! God will help me to prevent that! I'll write a message to the doctor at once. He'll talk you out of it.

SOLNESS: But Aline—

MRS. SOLNESS: Yes, you're ill, Halvard! That's what it is, you're ill! Oh God, oh God—! *(She hurries out to the right.)*

HILDE *(looks at him tensely)*: Is it true?

SOLNESS: That I have no head for heights?

HILDE: That *my* master builder dare not—cannot—rise as high as he can build?

SOLNESS: That is how you see it?

HILDE: Yes.

SOLNESS: I begin to think there is nothing in me that is safe from you.

HILDE (*looks towards the bay window*): Up there! Right up there!

SOLNESS (*goes closer*): You could live up there, Hilde. In the highest room in the tower. You could live there like a princess.

HILDE (*enigmatically, half-serious, half-jesting*): Yes, that's what you promised me.

SOLNESS: Did I?

HILDE: For shame, master builder! You said you'd make me a princess, and that you would give me a kingdom. And then you took me and— Well?

SOLNESS (*gently*): Are you quite sure it wasn't a dream? Something you just imagined?

HILDE (*sharply*): You think you didn't do it?

SOLNESS: I hardly know myself— (*More quietly.*) But I know one thing—that I—

HILDE: That you—? Say it!

SOLNESS: That I should have done it.

HILDE (*suddenly laughs*): You—dizzy!

SOLNESS: Tonight we shall hang up our wreath, Princess Hilde.

HILDE (*with a touch of bitterness*): Over your new home.

SOLNESS: Over the new house. It will never be a home for me. (*He goes out through the garden door.*)

HILDE (*with half closed eyes, whispers to herself. Only two words can be heard*): . . . frightfully exciting . . .

ACT THREE

A large, broad verandah belonging to SOLNESS's *house. Part of the house, with a door leading to the verandah, can be seen on the left. In front, to the right, a railing. Backstage, at one end of the verandah, a flight of steps leads down to the garden below. Large old trees stretch their branches over the verandah towards the house. On the extreme right, through the trees, can be glimpsed the lower part of the new villa, with scaffolding round the base of the tower. Backstage, the garden is bounded by an old fence. Beyond the fence is a street, with low, tumbledown cottages. Evening sky, with clouds irradiated by the sun.*

On the verandah, against the wall of the house, stands a garden seat, and in front of the seat is a long table. On the other side of the table, an armchair and some stools. All the furniture is of wicker.

> MRS. SOLNESS, *wrapped in a large, white crepe shawl, is resting in the armchair, gazing over towards the right. After a few moments,* HILDE WANGEL *comes up the steps from the garden. She is dressed as before, and is wearing her hat. On her breast is pinned a little bouquet of common flowers.*

MRS. SOLNESS *(turns her head slightly):* Have you been in the garden, Miss Wangel?

HILDE: Yes, I've been having a look round.

MRS. SOLNESS: You've found some flowers too, I see.

HILDE: Oh, yes. There are heaps of them. Among the bushes.

MRS. SOLNESS: No, are there really? Still? I hardly ever go down there.

HILDE *(comes closer):* What? I should have thought you'd skip down there every day.

MRS. SOLNESS *(smiles wanly):* I don't skip anywhere, I'm afraid. Not any longer.

HILDE: But don't you go down now and then to say hullo to all the beautiful things there?

MRS. SOLNESS: It's all become so foreign to me. I'm almost afraid to look at it again.

HILDE: Your own garden?

MRS. SOLNESS: I don't feel it's mine any longer.

HILDE: Oh, what rubbish!

MRS. SOLNESS: No, no, it isn't. It's not like it was in mother's and father's time. They've taken such a dreadful lot of it away, Miss Wangel. Can you imagine? They've broken it up, and built houses in it, for strangers! People I don't know. They can look at me from their windows.

HILDE *(with a sunny expression):* Mrs. Solness?

MRS. SOLNESS: Yes?

HILDE: May I sit here with you for a little?

MRS. SOLNESS: Yes, please do, if you'd really like to.

> HILDE *moves a stool close to the armchair and sits on it.*

HILDE: Ah, one can sit and sun oneself here. Like a cat.

MRS. SOLNESS *(puts her hand gently on* HILDE's *neck):* It's very sweet of you to want to sit with me. I thought you were going inside to my husband.

HILDE: What would I want with him?

MRS. SOLNESS: I thought you'd want to help him.

HILDE: No, thank you. Anyway, he's not in. He's over there among the workmen. But he looked so fierce I didn't dare to talk to him.

MRS. SOLNESS: Oh, he's very soft and gentle really.

HILDE: *He?*

MRS. SOLNESS: You don't know him well enough yet, Miss Wangel.

HILDE *(looks affectionately at her):* Are you happy to be moving over to the new house?

MRS. SOLNESS: I should be happy. That's what Halvard wants.

HILDE: Oh, I didn't mean just because of that.

MRS. SOLNESS: Yes, Miss Wangel, yes. That's my duty, don't you see, to do what he wants. But it's often so difficult to force oneself to be obedient.

HILDE: Yes, that must be difficult.

MRS. SOLNESS: Yes, indeed. When one's as weak a person as I am—

HILDE: When one has suffered as much as you have—

MRS. SOLNESS: How do you know that?

HILDE: Your husband told me.

MRS. SOLNESS: He so seldom speaks to me about these things. Yes, I've had more than my share of suffering in my lifetime, Miss Wangel.

HILDE *(looks at her sympathetically, and nods slowly):* Poor Mrs. Solness. First there was the fire—

MRS. SOLNESS *(sighs):* Yes. Everything I had was burned.

HILDE: And then there was worse to follow.

MRS. SOLNESS: Worse?

HILDE: The worst thing of all.

MRS. SOLNESS: What do you mean?

HILDE *(quietly):* You lost both your little boys.

MRS. SOLNESS: Oh, them, yes. Well, that was different. That was an Act of God. One must resign oneself to such things. And be thankful.

HILDE: Are you?

MRS. SOLNESS: Not always, I'm afraid. I know so well that it's my duty. But I can't.

HILDE: No, well, I think that's very understandable.

MRS. SOLNESS: Time and again I have to remind myself that I've been justly punished—

HILDE: Why?

MRS. SOLNESS: Because I wasn't resolute enough in the face of adversity.

HILDE: But I don't see that—

MRS. SOLNESS: No, no, Miss Wangel—don't talk to me any more about the two little boys. We should be happy for them. They're so much, much better off where they are. No, it's the little losses which leave the deepest wound. Things which other people would regard as unimportant.

HILDE (*puts her arms on* MRS. SOLNESS'*s knee and looks up at her warmly*): Dear Mrs. Solness, tell me—what kind of things?

MRS. SOLNESS: Just little things. All the old portraits on the walls were burned. And all the old silk dresses, that had been in our family for generations. And all mama's and grandmama's lace. That was burned too. And think of the jewels! (*Sadly.*) And—all the dolls.

HILDE: The dolls?

MRS. SOLNESS (*tearfully*): I had nine beautiful dolls.

HILDE: And they were burned too?

MRS. SOLNESS: All of them. Oh, it was so hard for me—so hard.

HILDE: Had you kept those dolls, then? Ever since you'd been a child?

MRS. SOLNESS: I didn't just keep them. They lived with me.

HILDE: After you'd grown up?

MRS. SOLNESS: Yes, long after.

HILDE: After you were married?

MRS. SOLNESS: Oh, yes. As long as he didn't see them— But

then they were burned, poor dears. No one thought of saving them. Oh, it makes me so sad to think about it. Now you mustn't laugh at me, Miss Wangel.

HILDE: I'm not laughing.

MRS. SOLNESS: They were alive, too, in a way, you see. I carried them under my heart. Like little unborn children.

> DR. HERDAL, *hat in hand, comes out through the door and catches sight of* MRS. SOLNESS *and* HILDE.

HERDAL: Giving yourself a cold, I see, Mrs. Solness!

MRS. SOLNESS: I think it's so nice and warm out here today.

HERDAL: Yes, yes. But is something the matter? I got a note—

MRS. SOLNESS *(gets up):* Yes, there's something I have to talk to you about.

HERDAL: By all means. Perhaps we'd better go inside. *(To* HILDE.*)* Still wearing your climbing outfit, young lady?

HILDE *(gaily, as she gets up):* Rather! Dressed to kill! No climbing for me today, though. You and I will stay down here and watch like good little children.

HERDAL: Watch what?

MRS. SOLNESS *(quietly, frightened, to* HILDE*):* Ssh, please, for heaven's sake! He's coming! Try to dissuade him from this idea! And—do let us be friends, Miss Wangel. Can't we?

HILDE *(throws her arms impetuously round* MRS. SOLNESS's *neck):* Oh, if only we could!

MRS. SOLNESS *(frees herself, gently):* Now, now, now. Here he comes, Doctor. Let me talk to you for a moment.

HERDAL: Is it about him?

MRS. SOLNESS: Yes, it's about him. Come inside.

> *She and the* DOCTOR *go into the house. The next moment,* SOLNESS *comes up the steps from the garden. A serious expression comes over* HILDE's *face.*

SOLNESS *(glances at the door as it is carefully shut from inside):* Have you noticed, Hilde? As soon as I come, she goes.

HILDE: I've noticed that when you come that makes her go.

SOLNESS: Possibly. But I can't help that.

He looks closely at her.

SOLNESS: Are you cold, Hilde? You look as if you were.

HILDE: I've just come up out of a tomb.

SOLNESS: What does that mean?

HILDE: The frost's got into me, master builder.

SOLNESS *(slowly):* I think I understand—

HILDE: Why have you come up here?

SOLNESS: I saw you.

HILDE: You must have seen her, too.

SOLNESS: I knew she'd go as soon as I came.

HILDE: Does it hurt you that she always avoids you?

SOLNESS: In a way it's a kind of relief.

HILDE: That you don't always have to be looking at her?

SOLNESS: Yes.

HILDE: That you don't have to be reminded the whole time of how much she grieves for her little boys?

SOLNESS: Yes. That above all.

HILDE *wanders along the verandah with her hands behind her back, stops by the railing and gazes out across the garden.*

SOLNESS: How long did you talk to her?

HILDE *does not move or reply.*

SOLNESS: How long, I asked?

HILDE *remains silent.*

SOLNESS: What did she talk about, then?

HILDE *still does not speak.*

SOLNESS: Poor Aline! About the children, I suppose.

HILDE *shivers nervously, then nods twice rapidly.*

SOLNESS: She can't get over it. She will never get over it. *(He goes closer.)* Now you're standing there like a statue again. You stood like that last night.

HILDE *(turns and looks at him, large-eyed, serious):* I want to go.

SOLNESS *(sharply):* Go?

HILDE: Yes.

SOLNESS: No. I won't allow it.

HILDE: What can I do here now?

SOLNESS: Just—stay here, Hilde.

HILDE *(looks at him scornfully):* Thank you very much. But it wouldn't end there.

SOLNESS *(impulsively):* So much the better!

HILDE *(violently):* I can't hurt someone I *know*. I can't take what belongs to her.

SOLNESS: Who says you will?

HILDE: From a stranger, yes. That's different. Someone I've never set eyes on. But someone I've got close to—! No! No! Ugh!

SOLNESS: But I haven't suggested that you should.

HILDE: Oh, master builder, you know very well how it would end. That's why I'm leaving.

SOLNESS: And what's to become of me when you've gone? What shall I have to live for? Afterwards?

HILDE *(with the enigmatic expression in her eyes):* It's easy for you. You have your duty to her. You must live for that duty.

SOLNESS: Too late. These powers—these—

HILDE: Demons—

SOLNESS: Yes, demons. And the troll in me. They've sucked

353

her blood. *(Laughs desperately.)* It was done for my happiness. *(Heavily.)* And for my sake she died. And I am chained to the corpse. *(In anguish.)* I—I, who cannot live without joy!

> HILDE *walks round the table and sits down on the seat with her elbows on the table, leaning her head on her hands.*

HILDE *(sits for a moment, looking at him):* What are you going to build next?

SOLNESS *(shakes his head):* I don't think I shall build much more.

HILDE: No more happy homes for mummy and daddy? And all the little children?

SOLNESS: God knows whether people will want that kind of thing any more.

HILDE: Poor master builder! And you've spent ten years thinking of nothing else? You've given your life to it.

SOLNESS: I have, haven't I, Hilde?

HILDE *(bursts out):* Oh, I think it's all so wrong, so wrong!

SOLNESS: What?

HILDE: That one should be afraid to seize happiness! To seize hold of life! Just because someone stands in the way. Someone one knows.

SOLNESS: Someone one has no right to pass by.

HILDE: Haven't we that right, I wonder? But even so— Oh, if one could only sleep and forget it all!

> She lays her arms flat on the table, rests her left cheek on her hands and closes her eyes.

SOLNESS *(turns the armchair round and sits down by the table):* Did you have a happy home with your father, Hilde?

HILDE *(without moving, replies as though half asleep):* I only had a cage.

354

SOLNESS: And you don't want to go back into it?

HILDE *(as before):* Wild birds don't fly into cages.

SOLNESS: They want to chase the free air—

HILDE *(still in the same tone):* Eagles love the chase.

SOLNESS *(resting his eyes on her):* If only one were a viking. They had hunting in their blood.

HILDE *(opens her eyes, but does not move, and says in her normal voice):* What else did they have? Tell me!

SOLNESS: A robust conscience.

> HILDE *sits up, alive. Her eyes are again excited and aflame.*

HILDE *(nodding):* I know what you're going to build next!

SOLNESS: Then you know more than I do, Hilde.

HILDE: Yes. Master builders are very stupid people.

SOLNESS: What is it to be, then?

HILDE *(nods again):* The castle.

SOLNESS: What castle?

HILDE: *My* castle, of course.

SOLNESS: You want a castle, now?

HILDE: You owe me a kingdom, don't you?

SOLNESS: So you tell me.

HILDE: Well, then! You owe me this kingdom. And a kingdom's got to have a castle, hasn't it?

SOLNESS *(more and more exhilarated):* Yes, they usually do.

HILDE: Good. Build it for me then! At once!

SOLNESS *(laughs):* Within the hour?

HILDE: Yes! The ten years are up now. And I don't intend to wait any longer. I want my castle, master builder!

SOLNESS: It's no joke to have you as a creditor, Hilde.

HILDE: You should have thought of that before. Now it's too late. Now then! *(Thumps on the table.)* Where's my castle? It's *my* castle!

SOLNESS *(more earnestly, leans closer to her, with his arms*

355

on the table): What does it look like, this castle of yours, Hilde?

HILDE *(slowly):* My castle must stand high up. High above everything. Open and free on every side. So that I can see for miles around.

SOLNESS: It's got a tower, I suppose?

HILDE: A frightfully high tower. And right up on the top of the tower there'll be a balcony. And that's where I shall stand—

SOLNESS *(involuntarily clutches his head):* How can you want to stand so high? Doesn't it make you giddy—?

HILDE: I want to stand up there and look down at the others—the ones who build churches. And homes for mothers and fathers and children. And you can come up there and look down too.

SOLNESS *(humbly):* Has the master builder leave to climb up to the princess?

HILDE: If the master builder wishes.

SOLNESS *(whispers):* Then—I think the master builder will come.

HILDE *(nods):* The master builder—he will come.

SOLNESS: But he will never build again. Poor master builder!

HILDE *(alive):* Oh, yes he will! We'll do it together! And we'll build the most beautiful thing—the most beautiful thing in the world!

SOLNESS: Hilde—tell me. What is that?

HILDE *(looks at him with a smile, gives a little shake of her head, pouts and says, as though to a child):* Master builders—they are vewy—vewy stupid people.

SOLNESS: Yes, they're stupid, I know. But tell me—what is the most beautiful thing in the world? The thing we two are going to build together?

HILDE *(is silent for a moment, then says, with the enigmatic expression in her eyes):* A castle in the air.

SOLNESS: A castle in the air.

HILDE *(nods):* A castle in the air, yes. Do you know what a castle in the air is?

SOLNESS: It's the most beautiful thing in the world, you say.

HILDE *(jumps up angrily and makes a contemptuous gesture with her hand):* Yes, of course! Castles in the air are so safe to hide in. And easy to build. *(Looks at him scornfully.)* Especially for master builders with a—a giddy conscience.

SOLNESS *(gets up):* From now on we two shall build together, Hilde.

HILDE *(with a doubting smile):* A real castle in the air?

SOLNESS: Yes. Built on a true foundation.

> RAGNAR BROVIK *comes out of the house. He is carrying a big, green wreath with flowers and silk ribbons.*

HILDE *(exclaims joyfully):* The wreath! Oh, it's going to be absolutely marvellous!

SOLNESS *(amazed):* Have you brought the wreath, Ragnar?

RAGNAR: I promised the foreman I would.

SOLNESS *(relieved):* Your father's better, then?

RAGNAR: No.

SOLNESS: Didn't it cheer him up, what I wrote?

RAGNAR: It came too late.

SOLNESS: Too late!

RAGNAR: By the time she came with it, he'd lost consciousness. He'd had a stroke.

SOLNESS: Get back home to him, then. Look after your father.

RAGNAR: He doesn't need me any more.

SOLNESS: But surely you ought to be with him?

RAGNAR: She's sitting with him.

SOLNESS *(a little uncertainly):* Kaja?

RAGNAR *(looks darkly at him):* Yes. Kaja.

SOLNESS: Go home, Ragnar. Go home to them. Give me the wreath.

RAGNAR *(represses a scornful smile):* Surely *you're* not going to—?

SOLNESS: I'll take it down there myself. *(He takes the wreath from him.)* Go home, now. We won't need you today.

RAGNAR: I know you won't. But today, I'm staying.

SOLNESS: Oh, stay—stay, by all means.

HILDE *(at the railing):* Master builder—I shall stand here and watch you.

SOLNESS: Watch me?

HILDE: It'll be frightfully exciting.

SOLNESS *(subdued):* We'll—talk about that later, Hilde. *(He descends the steps with the wreath and goes out through the garden.)*

HILDE *(watches him go, then turns to* RAGNAR*):* You might at least have thanked him.

RAGNAR: Thanked him? Should I have thanked *him?*

HILDE: Yes, you should.

RAGNAR: I ought to thank you, if anyone.

HILDE: How can you say such a thing?

RAGNAR: But you watch out. You don't know him yet.

HILDE *(angrily):* I know him better than anyone.

RAGNAR *(laughs bitterly):* Thank *him,* who's kept me back year after year? Who made my father lose his belief in me? Made me lose belief in myself. And all just so that he could—

HILDE *(as though sensing his meaning):* So that he could—what? Tell me.

RAGNAR: So that he could keep *her.*

HILDE *(with a movement towards him):* The girl at the desk?

RAGNAR: Yes.

HILDE *(clenches her fists):* It's not true! You're lying!

RAGNAR: I didn't want to believe it either, until today. When she told me.

HILDE: What did she tell you? I want to know! Now! Now!

RAGNAR: She said he'd taken possession of her mind. That

358

he'd directed all her thoughts towards himself. She says she'll never be able to free herself from him. That she'll stay wherever he is—

HILDE: She won't!

RAGNAR: Who's going to stop her? Are you?

HILDE *(quickly):* I won't be the only one.

RAGNAR: Oh yes. I see. Now she'd only be a nuisance to him.

HILDE: You don't understand anything, if you talk like that. No, I'll tell you why he kept her on.

RAGNAR: Why?

HILDE: To keep you.

RAGNAR: Did he tell you that?

HILDE: No, but it's true! It *must* be! *(Wildly.)* It is, it is, I want it to be!

RAGNAR: And the moment *you* came he let her go.

HILDE: It was *you* he let go! What do you think he cares about girls like her?

RAGNAR *(thoughtfully):* You mean he's been afraid of me all these years?

HILDE: Afraid of you? You fancy yourself!

RAGNAR: Oh, he must have realized a long time ago that I've got something in me. Besides—afraid—that's just what he is, don't you see?

HILDE: Try to make me believe that!

RAGNAR: In some ways he's afraid. The great master builder! Oh, he's not afraid to destroy people's happiness, the way he has father's and mine. But ask him to climb up a few feet of scaffolding, and he'll go down on his knees and pray to God to be delivered.

HILDE: Oh, if only you'd seen him high up there! As giddily high as I once saw him!

RAGNAR: Have you seen that?

HILDE: Yes, I've seen it. Oh, so proud and free he stood up there as he tied the wreath to the church weathercock!

RAGNAR: I know he dared to do it once in his life. Just once. We've often talked about it. But no power on earth will persuade him to do it again.

HILDE: He'll do it today.

RAGNAR: Don't you believe it.

HILDE: You'll see.

RAGNAR: I won't, and neither will you.

HILDE (*violently, uncontrollably*): I will! I will—I *must* see it!

RAGNAR: But he won't do it. He just daren't. He's got this yellow streak—the great master builder!

MRS. SOLNESS *comes out of the house on to the verandah.*

MRS. SOLNESS (*looking round*): Isn't he here? Where's he gone?

RAGNAR: The master builder is over there with the workmen.

HILDE: He took the wreath.

MRS. SOLNESS (*in terror*): Took the wreath? Oh, my God, my God! Brovik—you must go down to him! Get him to come back here!

RAGNAR: Shall I say you want to speak to him?

MRS. SOLNESS: Oh, yes, my dear boy, please do. No, no—don't tell him I want him. Tell him there's someone here. That he must come at once.

RAGNAR: Very well. I'll tell him that, Mrs. Solness. (*He goes down the steps and out through the garden.*)

MRS. SOLNESS: Oh, Miss Wangel, you can't imagine how frightened I am for him.

HILDE: But what is there to be so frightened about?

MRS. SOLNESS: Suppose he's serious! Suppose he takes it into his head to climb up the scaffolding!

HILDE (*tensely*): Do you think he will?

360

MRS. SOLNESS: Oh, one can never be sure what he might do. He's quite capable of doing anything.

HILDE: Oh, so you, too, think he's a bit—er—?

MRS. SOLNESS: I no longer know what to think. The doctor's been telling me so many strange things. And when I think of some of the things I've heard him say—

DR. HERDAL *looks out through the door.*

HERDAL: Not here yet?

MRS. SOLNESS: He'll be back soon. I've sent him a message.

HERDAL *(closer):* You'd better go inside, Mrs. Solness.

MRS. SOLNESS: No, no. I want to stay out here and wait for Halvard.

HERDAL: Yes, but some ladies have come to see you—

MRS. SOLNESS: Oh, my God—no, not now!

HERDAL: They say they simply must watch the ceremony.

MRS. SOLNESS: Oh, well, I suppose I'll have to go in to them. It's my duty.

HILDE: Can't you ask them to go away?

MRS. SOLNESS: No, no, that's impossible. Since they've come, it's my duty to receive them. You stay out here, though, and talk to him when he gets back.

HERDAL: Yes, talk to him and keep him here as long as possible.

MRS. SOLNESS: Yes, do that, please, dear Miss Wangel. Keep him as long as you can.

HILDE: Hadn't you better do it yourself?

MRS. SOLNESS: Oh dear, yes—it's *my* duty, really. But one has so many duties—

HERDAL *(looking towards the garden):* Here he is.

MRS. SOLNESS: Oh dear, just as I have to go inside!

HERDAL *(to HILDE):* Don't tell him I'm here.

HILDE: Oh, no. I'll find other things to talk about with the master builder.

MRS. SOLNESS: And keep him here. I think you can do that better than anyone.

> MRS. SOLNESS *and* DR. HERDAL *go into the house.* HILDE *remains standing on the verandah.* SOLNESS *comes up the steps from the garden.*

SOLNESS: I'm told there's someone here who wants to speak to me.

HILDE: Yes, master builder. I want to speak to you.

SOLNESS: Oh, it's you, Hilde. I was afraid it might be Aline and the doctor.

HILDE: You scare very easily, don't you?

SOLNESS: You think so, do you?

HILDE: Yes. People say you're scared of clambering round on the scaffolding.

SOLNESS: That's different.

HILDE: Then you are afraid of it?

SOLNESS: Yes, I am.

HILDE: Afraid you might fall down and kill yourself?

SOLNESS: No, not that.

HILDE: What then?

SOLNESS: I am afraid of retribution, Hilde.

HILDE: Of retribution? *(Shakes her head.)* I don't understand.

SOLNESS: Sit down, and I'll tell you something.

HILDE: Yes, tell me. Out with it! *(She sits down on a stool by the railing and looks at him expectantly.)*

SOLNESS *(throws his hat on the table):* As you know, I began by building churches.

HILDE *(nods):* Yes, I know that.

SOLNESS: When I was a boy, you see, my parents were pious, country people. So I thought building churches was the finest work that a man could choose to do.

HILDE: Yes, yes.

SOLNESS: And I think I may say that I built these humble

little churches with such honesty and tenderness and devotion that—that—

HILDE: That—? Well?

SOLNESS: Yes—that I think He ought to have been pleased with me.

HILDE: He? Which He?

SOLNESS: He whom the churches were meant for, of course. Whose honour and glory they were meant to proclaim.

HILDE: I see. But are you so sure that—that He wasn't—well—pleased with you?

SOLNESS *(scornfully)*: He pleased with me? How can you talk so foolishly, Hilde? He who let the troll in me cut loose? He who bade them wait on me day and night, these—these—

HILDE: Demons?

SOLNESS: Yes. And the others. Oh, no, I was made to realize He wasn't pleased with me. *(Secretively.)* That's why He let the old house be burned down, you see.

HILDE: Was that why?

SOLNESS: Yes, don't you understand? He wanted to give me the chance to be a real master in my own field, and build greater churches to His glory. At first I didn't realize what He wanted. But then, suddenly, it all became clear to me.

HILDE: When was that?

SOLNESS: When I built the church tower up at Lysanger.

HILDE: I thought so.

SOLNESS: You see, Hilde, up there, where I was a stranger, I spent so much time by myself, brooding and puzzling. Then I saw so clearly why He had taken my little children from me. It was so that I should have nothing to bind me. No love or happiness or anything, you see. I was to be a master builder—nothing else. And all my life was to be spent building for Him. *(Laughs.)* But that wasn't the way it worked out.

HILDE: What did you do?

SOLNESS: First, I examined and tried myself—

HILDE: And then—?

SOLNESS: Then, like Him, I did the impossible.

HILDE: The impossible?

SOLNESS: I could never bear to climb up high before. But that day, I did it.

HILDE *(jumps up)*: Yes, yes, you did!

SOLNESS: And as I stood high up there, right at the top, and placed the wreath over the weathercock, I said to Him: 'Listen to me, mighty One! Henceforth I, too, want to be a free master builder. Free in my field, as You are in Yours. I never want to build churches for You again. Only homes, for people to live in.'

HILDE *(her eyes wide and glittering)*: That was the song I heard in the air.

SOLNESS: But He took His revenge later.

HILDE: What do you mean by that?

SOLNESS *(looks at her dejectedly)*: Building homes for people isn't worth twopence, Hilde.

HILDE: How can you say that now?

SOLNESS: Because I realize now that people have no use for the homes they live in. They can't be happy in them. And a home wouldn't have been any use to me—even if I'd had one. *(Laughs quietly and savagely.)* So when all the accounts are closed, I have built nothing really. And sacrificed nothing. It all adds up to nothing. Nothing. Nothing.

HILDE: And are you never going to build again?

SOLNESS: Yes, now I shall begin!

HILDE: What will you build? What? Tell me! Quickly!

SOLNESS: Now I shall build the only place where I believe that happiness can exist.

HILDE *(looks at him)*: Master builder—you mean our castles in the air.

SOLNESS: Yes. Castles in the air.

364

HILDE: I'm afraid you'll get giddy before we've climbed halfway.

SOLNESS: Not when I can go hand in hand with you, Hilde.

HILDE: Just with me? Won't there be others?

SOLNESS: What others? What do you mean?

HILDE: Oh—that Kaja at the desk. Poor thing, aren't you going to take her along too?

SOLNESS: Oh. So that's what Aline and you were sitting here talking about!

HILDE: Is it true or isn't it?

SOLNESS (*angrily*): I won't answer that. You must believe in me unquestioningly.

HILDE: I have believed in you for ten years. Unquestioningly.

SOLNESS: You must go on believing in me.

HILDE: Then let me see you stand up there, high and free!

SOLNESS (*heavily*): Oh, Hilde. One can't do things like that every day.

HILDE (*passionately*): But I want you to! I want you to! (*Pleadingly.*) Just once more, master builder! Do the impossible again!

SOLNESS (*looks deeply into her eyes*): If I try it, Hilde, I shall stand up there and speak to Him the way I spoke to Him before.

HILDE (*with mounting excitement*): What will you tell Him?

SOLNESS: I shall say to Him: 'Hear me, mighty Master! Judge me as You will. But from now on I shall build only one thing—the most beautiful thing in the world—'

HILDE: Yes, yes, yes!

SOLNESS: 'I shall build it together with a princess, whom I love—'

HILDE: Yes, tell Him that! Tell Him that!

SOLNESS: I will. And then I shall say to Him: 'Now I go down, to take her in my arms and kiss her—'

HILDE: Many times! Tell Him that!

SOLNESS: 'Many, many times,' I shall tell Him.

HILDE: And then—?

SOLNESS: Then I shall wave my hat—and come down to the ground—and do as I told Him.

HILDE *(flings her arms wide)*: Now I see you again as you were when I heard that song in the air!

SOLNESS *(looks at her with bowed head)*: How have you come to be what you are, Hilde?

HILDE: How did you make me what I am?

SOLNESS *(curtly, decisively)*: The princess shall have her castle.

HILDE *(jubilant, claps her hands)*: Oh, master builder! My beautiful, beautiful castle! Our castle in the air!

SOLNESS: Built on a true foundation.

In the street, a crowd of people has gathered; they can be indistinctly glimpsed through the trees. A brass band can be distantly heard from behind the new house. MRS. SOLNESS, *with a fur collar round her neck,* DR. HERDAL, *carrying her white shawl on his arm, and several* LADIES *come out on to the verandah. At the same moment,* RAGNAR BROVIK *comes up from the garden.*

MRS. SOLNESS *(to* RAGNAR*)*: Are we going to have music, too?

RAGNAR: Yes. It's the Builders' Association. *(To* SOLNESS.*)* The foreman asked me to tell you he's ready to go up with the wreath.

SOLNESS *(takes his hat)*: Good. I'll go down there myself.

MRS. SOLNESS *(anxiously)*: What are you going to do down there, Halvard?

SOLNESS *(curtly)*: I must be down below with the men.

MRS. SOLNESS: Yes—down below, of course. Down below.

SOLNESS: I always do it. It's my everyday custom. *(He goes down the steps and out through the garden.)*

MRS. SOLNESS *(shouts over the railing after him):* Do tell the
man to be careful when he climbs up! Promise me that,
Halvard!

HERDAL *(to* MRS. SOLNESS*):* There, you see, I was right.
He's put these mad ideas out of his head.

MRS. SOLNESS: Oh, what a relief! Two of our men have
fallen. And they were both killed instantaneously. *(Turns
to* HILDE.*)* Thank you so much for holding on to him,
Miss Wangel. I'd never have been able to budge him.

HERDAL: Yes, yes, Miss Wangel, I'm sure you know how to
hold on to someone when you really want to.

> MRS. SOLNESS *and* DR. HERDAL *go over to the* LADIES,
> *who are standing by the steps looking out across the
> garden.* HILDE *remains standing downstage by the
> railing.* RAGNAR *goes across to her.*

RAGNAR *(quietly, trying not to laugh):* Do you see all those
young men down in the street, Miss—er—?

HILDE: Yes.

RAGNAR: They're my fellow apprentices, come to watch the
master.

HILDE: What do they want to watch him for?

RAGNAR: They want to see him not dare to climb up his own
house.

HILDE: Is that what the little boys want?

RAGNAR: He's kept us down for so long. Now we want to
see him keeping himself down, for a change.

HILDE: You won't. Not this time.

RAGNAR *(smiles):* Oh? Where shall we see him, then?

HILDE: High, high up by the weathercock! That's where
you'll see him!

RAGNAR *(laughs):* Him? Not likely!

HILDE: He intends to climb to the top. And you'll see him
there.

RAGNAR: Oh, he intends to, I'm sure. But he can't, he just

can't. He'd get giddy long before he'd climbed halfway. He'd have to crawl down again on his hands and knees.

HERDAL (*pointing*): Look. There's the foreman climbing up.

MRS. SOLNESS: He's got the wreath too. Oh, I do hope he takes care.

RAGNAR (*stares incredulously, then shouts*): But that's not—!

HILDE (*cries ecstatically*): It's the master builder himself!

MRS. SOLNESS (*screams in terror*): Yes, it's Halvard! Oh, my God, my God! Halvard! Halvard!

HERDAL: Ssh! Don't shout to him!

MRS. SOLNESS (*almost out of her mind*): I must go to him! I must make him come down!

HERDAL (*restraining her*): Stand still, all of you! Don't make a sound!

HILDE (*standing motionless, follows* SOLNESS *with her eyes*): He's climbing and climbing! Higher—higher! Look! Just look!

RAGNAR (*breathlessly*): He must turn back now! He must!

HILDE: He's climbing, climbing! Soon he'll be up!

MRS. SOLNESS: Oh, I shall die of fright. I can't bear to look.

HERDAL: Don't look up at him, then.

HILDE: There he is on top of the scaffolding! Right at the top!

HERDAL: Don't move, anyone! Do you hear?

HILDE (*quiet, but jubilant*): At last! At last! Now I see him great and free again!

RAGNAR (*almost speechless*): But this is—

HILDE: That's how I've seen him all these ten years. How squarely he stands! Frightfully exciting, though! Look at him! Now he's hanging the wreath over the spire!

RAGNAR: But—I can't believe it! This is impossible!

HILDE: Yes! That's what he's doing now! The impossible! (*With the enigmatic expression in her eyes.*) Can you see anyone else up there with him?

RAGNAR: There's no one else.

HILDE: Oh, yes. There's someone he's arguing with.

RAGNAR: You're mistaken.

HILDE: Perhaps you can't hear a song in the air, either?

RAGNAR: It must be the wind in the treetops.

HILDE: I hear a song. A mighty song! *(Cries in jubilant ecstasy)* Look, look! Now he's waving his hat! He's waving to us down here! Oh, wave back to him! He's done it at last, he's done it! *(She tears the white shawl from the* DOCTOR, *waves it and cries up)* Hurrah for Solness! Hurrah for the master builder!

HERDAL: Stop it! Stop it, for God's sake—!

The LADIES *on the verandah wave their handkerchiefs, and the shouting is taken up in the street. Suddenly there is a silence; then the crowd utters a shriek of terror. A human body and some planks and poles can be indistinctly glimpsed falling through the trees.*

MRS. SOLNESS, LADIES *(simultaneously):* He's falling! He's falling!

MRS. SOLNESS *staggers and falls back unconscious. The* LADIES *pick her up amid noise and confusion. The* PEOPLE IN THE STREET *break down the fence and storm into the garden.* DR. HERDAL *hurries down. Short pause.*

HILDE *(still staring upwards, as though turned to stone):* My master builder!

RAGNAR *(supports himself, trembling, against the railing):* He must have been smashed to pieces. Killed outright.

ONE OF THE LADIES *(while* MRS. SOLNESS *is carried into the house):* Run down to the doctor—

RAGNAR: I can't move a step—

ANOTHER LADY: Call down to someone, then.

RAGNAR *(tries to shout):* How is he? Is he alive?

A VOICE *(from down in the garden):* The master builder is
dead.

OTHER VOICES *(nearer):* His head was crushed. He fell into
the stone-pit.

HILDE *(turns to* RAGNAR, *and says quietly):* Now I can't see
him up there any longer.

RAGNAR: This is terrible. He hadn't the strength after all.

HILDE *(in quiet, crazed triumph):* But he climbed right to the
top! And I heard harps in the air! *(She waves her shawl
upwards and cries wildly and ecstatically) My—my* master builder!

Note on the Translation

The Master Builder is, with the possible exception of *Hedda Gabler*, the most tautly written of all Ibsen's plays, and the main problem for a translator, apart from that of conveying the sub-text, is Solness's style of speech. He is a self-made man of humble country upbringing who normally speaks with a gruff abruptness; but in the long dialogues with Hilde he finds himself groping in unfamiliar territory and achieving a rough and slightly awkward eloquence. Hilde speaks in the unfamiliar idiom of the new generation; and I would ask anyone who suspects that I have allowed her too many modernisms to remember that *The Master Builder* was written in the same year as *Charley's Aunt*. I have in fact, as in all my translations, taken pains to use no word or phrase that was not current in England when Ibsen wrote the play.

A word about trolls. Solness's repeated references to them are confusing unless one has a clear idea of what the word means. Professor Francis Bull, the greatest of Ibsen scholars (his father was Ibsen's doctor during the dramatist's last years) defined them admirably in a lecture given at Oxford in 1954:

> Trolls—what are they? The word cannot be translated at all! The trolls are supernatural beings, akin to the enemies of the gods in the heathen world, and very well known in Norwegian fairy-tales and folk lore.

371

They are supposed to live in the woods and mountains, and you must not imagine them in the shape of little goblins; they look more like Polyphemus and Cyclops in the *Odyssey*—huge, clumsy and ugly. . . . [They] may be said to represent the evil forces in Nature, at first only as incarnations of frightening sounds and visions from without, but in more recent literature gradually taken in a wider sense, embodying or symbolizing those powers of evil, hidden in the soul of man, which may at times suddenly suppress his conscious will and dominate his actions. A great Norwegian novelist and friend of Ibsen* has written two volumes of short stories and fairy-tales, simply called *Trolls,* starting with this declaration: "That there are trolls in Man, everybody knows who has any insight into such things. . . ." In . . . *The Master Builder,* which is very much the author's personal confession, Solness, half in joke and half in earnest and remorse, tells about his devils or trolls; in a way they serve him, but by ever pandering to his evil instincts and desires, they have come to be really his rulers—mysterious powers that make him afraid of himself.

I again gladly acknowledge my thanks to Mr. Casper Wrede for much invaluable criticism and more shrewd suggestions than I can enumerate.

---

*Jonas Lie.

An Enemy of the People

Introduction

Ibsen wrote *An Enemy of the People* in Rome between March and June 1882, less than six months after completing *Ghosts*. It is probable that he had begun to plan it as early as 1880, for on 26 November of that year he wrote to Edmund Gosse that he was 'busy pondering a new play which I hope to complete during the summer', and both Lorentz Dietrichson and Kristofer Janson report conversations that they had with Ibsen around this time in which he expressed many of the opinions which he was later to put into Dr. Stockmann's mouth. But he had put this project aside in order to write *Ghosts*, 'a theme' (he wrote to his publisher, Hegel of Gyldendal) 'which has long occupied my thoughts and which at length forced itself upon me so insistently that I could no longer ignore it.'

The extremely hostile reception which *Ghosts* had received in Scandinavia on its appearance in December 1881 drove Ibsen into a fury. 'What is one to say of the attitude taken by the so-called liberal press?' he wrote to Georg Brandes on 3 January 1882. 'These leaders who talk and write of freedom and progressiveness and at the same time allow themselves to be the slaves of the supposed opinions of their subscribers! I become more and more convinced that there is something demoralising about involving oneself in politics and attaching oneself to a party. Under no circumstances will I ever link myself with any party that has the majority behind it. Bjœrnson says: "The majority is always right." As a practising politician I suppose he has to say that. But I say: "The minority is always right." I am of course not thinking of the minority of reactionaries who have been left astern by the big central party which we call liberal; I mean the minority which forges ahead in territory which the majority has not yet reached. I believe that he is right who is most closely attuned to the future . . . For me liberty is the first condition of life, and the highest. At home people don't bother much about liberty but only about liberties—a few more or a few less, according to the party standpoint. I feel most painfully affected by this vulgarity, this plebeianism in our public discussion. In the course of their undeniably worthy efforts to turn our country into a democratic community, people have unwittingly gone a good way towards turning us into a mob community. The aristocracy of the intellect seems to be in short supply in Norway.'

Later the same month (24 January 1882) he wrote to Olaf Skavlan: 'I myself am responsible for what I write, and I alone. I cannot possibly embarrass any party, for I belong to none. I want to act as a lone *franc-tireur* in the outposts and operate on my own . . . Is it only in the political field that men are to be allowed to work for freedom in Norway? Is it not first and foremost man's spirit that needs to be set free? Such spiritual slaves as we are cannot even use the freedoms we already have. Norway is a free country inhabited by serfs.'

Normally, Ibsen allowed eighteen months to elapse between completing one play and beginning another;* but on

---

*Between 1877, when he finished *The Pillars of Society*, and 1896, when he wrote *John Gabriel Borkman*, *An Enemy of the People* provides the only exception to this rule. *When We Dead Awaken*, Ibsen's last play, came three years after *John Gabriel Borkman*, but this was largely because 1898 was much taken up with preparations for the celebration of Ibsen's seventieth birthday.

16 March he surprised Hegel by writing: 'I am able to tell you that I am now fully occupied with preparations for my new play. This time it will be a peaceful work which can be read by cabinet ministers and wholesale merchants and their ladies, and from which the theatres will not need to shrink. I should have no difficulty in polishing it off, and I will try to have it ready quite early in the autumn.' For once he found himself ahead of schedule, for on 21 June he was able to write to Hegel, still from Rome: 'Yesterday I completed my new play. It is entitled *An Enemy of the People,* and is in five acts. I am still a little uncertain whether to call it a comedy or simply a play; it has much of the character of a comedy, but there is also a serious basic theme . . . In a few days I shall start on the fair copy, which should be ready at the latest by the end of July. I will send you the manuscript in stages, as usual.'

Unfortunately no working notes or preliminary draft of *An Enemy of the People* have survived, so that we do not know, as we do with most of his other plays, exactly how long he took to write each act and what alterations he made from his original conception.

At the beginning of August he left Rome for Gossensass in the Tyrol, and from there, on 28 August, he sent Hegel the fair copy of the first four acts. 'The fifth,' he explained, 'will follow in a few days, as I have already done half of it. The reason the manuscript is arriving somewhat later than I implied in my previous letter is that I have fair-copied the whole play twice to achieve the maximum perfection in the dialogue.' On 9 September he posted the final act. 'It has been fun', he wrote, 'working on this play, and I feel a sense of deprivation and emptiness at being parted from it. Dr. Stockmann and I got on most excellently; we agree about so many things; but the Doctor has a more muddled head on his shoulders than I have, and he has besides certain characteristics which will permit people to tolerate various things from his lips which they might not accept so readily if they had issued from mine. If you have begun to read the manuscript, I think you will share this opinion.'

An Enemy of the People was published by Gyldendal of Copenhagen on 28 November 1882, in an edition (despite the calamitous sales of *Ghosts)* of 10,000 copies. Its reception was mixed; not surprisingly, Dr. Stockmann's hard remarks about political parties offended all the reviewers who belonged to either. Liberal circles were particularly cool; Strindberg dismissed it as 'insufferably aesthetic' (the modern word would be 'uncommitted'). The theatres, however, seized eagerly on the play. The Christiania Theatre and the Royal Theatres of Copenhagen and Stockholm, all of which had rejected *Ghosts* as unfit for public presentation, immediately acquired the production rights of *An Enemy of the People,* apparently insensitive to the fact that the theme of the latter play was the unworthiness of those who 'do not dare,' and its conclusion: 'The strongest man is he who stands most alone.' It was performed at the Christiania Theatre on 13 January 1883; at Bergen on 24 January; at Gothenburg in February, and in Stockholm and Copenhagen in March. In all three countries it was cordially, but not over-enthusiastically received. Strangely, in view of the popularity of *The Pillars of Society* and *A Doll's House,* and the sensation caused by the publication of *Ghosts,* it was not performed in Germany until 1887.

In 1892, *An Enemy of the People* was acted in New York, in German;* and the following year Lugné-Poe staged it in Paris at the Théâtre de L'Œuvre. 'On the first night,' writes Archer, 'it was preceded by a lecture by M. Laurent Tail-

---

*Several of the first American performances of Ibsen were in a language other than English, owing to the high proportion, in those days, of first-generation European immigrants. The world première of *Ghosts* took place in Chicago in Norwegian (or in a mixture of Norwegian and Danish).

hade, which consisted not so much of an exposition of the play, as of a violent attack upon all the "leading men" in French literature and politics. Beside it, Dr. Stockmann's harangue in the fourth act seems moderate and almost mealy-mouthed . . . The audience listened, not without protest, to M. Tailhade's diatribe, until he thought fit to describe the recent Franco-Russian fêtes as an act of collective insanity. At this point a storm of indignation burst forth, which lasted without pause for a quarter of an hour, and was not allayed by an attempt at intervention on the part of M. Lugné-Poe. The lecture closed amid wild confusion, and altogether the preliminary scene in the auditorium was like a spirited rehearsal of the meeting at Captain Horster's.'

In 1893 *An Enemy of the People* was produced in England by Herbert Beerbohm Tree at the Haymarket Theatre—the first Ibsen play to attract the attention of a fashionable actor-manager and receive the full West End treatment. Archer found the text 'monstrously mutilated' and the production 'distinctly below the level of the so-called "scratch" performances to which we have been accustomed'. Bernard Shaw thought that Tree's own performance 'though humorous and entertaining in its way, was, as a character creation, the polar opposite of Ibsen's Stockmann'. But the production was a success; Tree revived it several times, and in 1895 took it to America, where its success was repeated. Yet, for reasons which will be discussed later, apart from a single matinée in 1928 to celebrate the centenary of Ibsen's birth, central London has seen only one production of *An Enemy of the People* since Tree's, in 1939, when Tyrone Guthrie directed it at the Old Vic with Roger Livesey as Stockmann and Edward Chapman as the Mayor. Joan Littlewood staged it at Stratford East in 1954, with Howard Goorney as Stockmann and Harry Corbett as the Mayor, setting the action in Lancashire; but, as T. C. Worsley commented, the Theatre Workshop company was 'less happy in the naturalistic mode than in some others'.

In 1905 *An Enemy of the People* was the instance of a demonstration even more remarkable than that which it had caused in Paris. The venue was the Moscow Arts Theatre, and Konstantin Stanislavsky, who was playing Dr. Stockmann, has described the occasion vividly in his autobiography, *My Life and Art:*

'In that time of political unrest—it was but a little while before the first revolution—the feeling of protest was very strong in all spheres of society. They waited for the hero who could tell the truth strongly and bravely in the very teeth of the government. It is not to be wondered at that the image of Dr. Stockmann became popular at once in Moscow, and especially so in Petrograd. *An Enemy of the People* became the favourite play of the revolutionists, notwithstanding the fact that Stockmann himself despised the solid majority and believed in individuals to whom he would entrust the conduct of life. But Stockmann protested, Stockmann told the truth, and that was considered enough.

'On the day of the well-known massacre in Kazansky Square, *An Enemy of the People* was on the boards of our theatre. The average run of spectators that night was from the intelligentsia, the professors and learned men of Petrograd. I remember that the orchestra was filled almost entirely with grey heads. Thanks to the sad events of the day, the auditorium was very excited and answered even the slightest hints about liberty in every word of Stockmann's protest. In the most unexpected places in the play the thunder of applause would break in on the performance. . . . The atmosphere in the theatre was such that we expected arrests at any minute and a stop to the performance. Censors, who sat at all the performances of *An Enemy of the People* and saw to it that I, who played Dr. Stockmann, should use only the censored text, and raised trouble over every syllable that was not admitted by the censorship, were on this evening even more watchful than on other occasions. I had to be doubly careful. When the text of a role is cut and re-cut many times it is not hard to make a mistake and say too much or too little. In the last act of the play, Dr. Stockmann, putting into order his room which has been stoned by the crowd, finds in the general chaos his black coat,* in which he appeared at the meeting the day before. Seeing a rent in the cloth, Stockmann says to his wife: "One must never put on a new coat when one goes to fight for freedom and truth."

'The spectators in the theatre connected this sentence with the massacre in Kazansky Square, where more than one new coat must have been torn in the name of freedom and truth. Unexpectedly, my words aroused such a pandemonium that it was necessary to stop the performance, into which a real mob scene was interpolated by impromptu. There had taken place the unification of the actor and the spectators, who took on themselves the role of chief actor in the theatre, that same mob action of which so much is said by the theoreticians of art. The entire audience rose from its seats and threw itself towards the footlights. Thanks to the fact that the stage was very low and there was no orchestra before it, I saw hundreds of hands stretched towards me, all of which I was forced to shake. The younger people in the audience jumped on to the stage and embraced Dr. Stockmann. It was not easy to establish order and to continue with the play. That evening I found out through my own experience what power the theatre could exercise'.†

---

*More accurately, his trousers.

†Similarly, on the occasion of the Paris premiere, which occurred at the time of the Dreyfus affair, everyone, according to Lugné-Poe, identified Stockmann with Emile Zola. The play was deliberately chosen for the first

Although the public reception of *Ghosts* was the immediate inspiration of *An Enemy of the People*, the opinions to which Ibsen gave expression in the latter play were not new to him; we find them continually cropping up in his earlier correspondence, especially in his letters to the Danish critic Georg Brandes. As early as 1871, eleven years before he began *An Enemy of the People*, he had declared to Brandes: 'I shall never be able to regard liberty as synonymous with political liberty. What you call liberty I call liberties, and what I call the fight for freedom is nothing but the eternal and living quest for the idea of freedom. He who possesses freedom otherwise than as an object to be sought possesses something dead and soulless. For the quintessence of freedom is the fact that, as one acquires it, it grows, so that if anyone stops during the battle and says: "Now I have it!" he reveals, by this very statement, that he has lost it.'

On 21 March 1872, he asserted to Fredrik Gjertsen his 'fundamental principle, in every context and situation, namely, that the minority is always right.' And the following month he wrote to Brandes: 'My dear friend, the liberals are the worst enemies of freedom. Spiritual and intellectual freedom flourish best under absolutism; that has been proved in France, and later in Germany, and it is now being proved in Russia . . . As regards this agitation which is being worked up against you, with its lies and back-biting and so forth, let me give you a piece of advice which from my own experience I know to be sovereign. Be an aristocrat [*fornem*]! Aristocracy is the only weapon against this kind of thing. Appear indifferent; never write a word of reply in the newspapers; if you polemise in your writings, never direct

---

Ibsen production in Spain (in Barcelona on 14 April 1893) to help organized opposition to the established order in government and industry, and for the first Japanese production (in Tokyo in 1898) as a protest against dangerous effusion from a chemical factory.

your polemic against this or that specific attack; never write a single word which could make it seem that your enemies have found their mark; in short, act as though you had no idea that anyone was opposed to you.'

On 19 December 1879, a fortnight after the publication of *A Doll's House,* he wrote to Lorentz Dietrichson: 'It seems to me doubtful whether it is practicable to obtain better artistic conditions in our country before the intellectual soil has been thoroughly turned up, and cleansed and drained of all its swamp-like filth.' This was a metaphor to which he was to return in *An Enemy of the People.* And Kristofer Janson, the writer who was a part-original of Hjalmar Ekdal in *The Wild Duck,* reports a conversation he had with Ibsen on New Year's Eve, 1880, when Ibsen is thought to have been making his first plans for *An Enemy of the People.* 'Ibsen flared up. "The majority? What is the majority? The ignorant mass! The intelligence is always in the minority. How many of the majority do you think are qualified to hold an opinion? Most of them are just sheepdogs!" '*

'When my new play reaches you,' Ibsen wrote to Brandes on 21 September 1882, shortly after he had finished *An Enemy of the People,* 'you will perhaps be able to understand what interest and, I may add, fun it has given me to recall the many scattered and casual remarks I have made in my letters to you.' Nine months later, to the same correspondent, he added a provocative postscript to the play. 'An intellectual pioneer', he declared, 'can never gather a majority about him. In ten years the majority may have reached

---

*He also once remarked to Janson: 'The only people with whom I really have any sympathy are the nihilists and the socialists. They want something wholeheartedly, and they are consistent.' Ibsen did not object when, in 1890, Bernard Shaw identified 'Ibsenism' with socialism—indeed, he protested when some newspapers asserted that he had nothing to do with socialism.

the point where Dr. Stockmann stood when the people held their meeting. But during those ten years the Doctor has not remained stationary; he is still at least ten years ahead of the others. The majority, the masses, the mob, will never catch him up; he can never rally them behind him. I myself feel a similarly unrelenting compulsion to keep pressing forward. A crowd now stands where I stood when I wrote my earlier books. But I myself am there no longer. I am somewhere else—far ahead of them—or so I hope. At present I am struggling with the draft of a new play in four acts . . .' This new play, the successor to *An Enemy of the People*, was to be *The Wild Duck*.

The plot of *An Enemy of the People* had its origin in two actual incidents to which Ibsen's attention had been drawn. Alfred Meissner, a young German poet whom he knew in Munich, told him how, when his father had been medical officer at the spa of Teiplitz in the eighteen-thirties, there had occurred an outbreak of cholera which the latter felt it his duty to make public. As a result, the season was ruined, and the citizens of Teiplitz became so enraged that they stoned the Doctor's house and forced him to flee the town.

Then there had been the case in Norway of a chemist named Harald Thaulow. For nearly ten years Thaulow had furiously attacked the Christiania Steam Kitchens for neglecting their duty towards the city's poor. He had delivered a violent speech on the subject in 1874, when Ibsen was revisiting Norway; and on 23 February 1881, only two weeks before he died, Thaulow had attempted to read a prepared speech at the annual general meeting of the Steam Kitchens. The chairman of the meeting tried to prevent him from speaking, and eventually the audience forced him, amid commotion, to remain silent. Ibsen read a report of this meeting in *Aftenposten* just at the time when his indignation at the reception of *Ghosts* was reaching its climax, and he must have recognised in the eccentric old chemist a spirit very kindred to his own. The newspaper account is worth quoting:

THAULOW: I will not stop, you have no right to stop me, Mr. Chairman.

(Continues): Point number ten—

CONSUL HEFTYE: Mr. Thaulow must be stopped!

> THAULOW *continues. Several of the public show their displeasure by walking about the hall.* THE CHAIRMAN *asks the meeting whether they recognize his right to bar* MR. THAULOW *from the floor. Unanimous 'Ayes'.* THE CHAIRMAN *again asks* MR. THAULOW *to stop reading.*

THAULOW: I will not be silenced.

THE CHAIRMAN: In that case, I shall—

THAULOW: I'll keep it quite short. *(Reads on.)*

CONSUL HEFTYE: Is he to be allowed to continue?

THAULOW *(continues reading):* The glorious achievements of the Christiania Steam Kitchens— I'll soon be through—

CONSUL HEFTYE: If this goes on the meeting can't continue.

CHAIRMAN: I regret that I must interrupt Mr. Thaulow. You have not the floor—

> THAULOW *reads on.*

CONSUL HEFTYE: Be quiet, or you'll be thrown out.

THAULOW: Oh, very well.

> THAULOW *sits down at last. After* THE CHAIRMAN *had read his report for some minutes—*

THAULOW: . . . It's too much. It's no use trying to oppose the mob—

CONSUL HEFTYE: Did the Chairman hear Mr. Thaulow
refer to us as the mob? . . .
At length MR. THAULOW *left the meeting in a rage,*
saying: I'll have no more to do with you. I won't cast
my pearls into the sand. This is a damned insult
being inflicted on a free people in a free society.
Now I'll go! Stand in the dunce's corner and be
ashamed of yourselves!

An English Member of Parliament may also have contrib-
uted something to the play. Charles Bradlaugh, having nar-
rowly escaped imprisonment for his part in a pamphlet
advocating birth control (he had actually been sentenced,
but had escaped on appeal), had been elected Radical M.P.
for Northampton in 1880, but had been barred from taking
his seat on the ground that, since he was a confessed freethinker, the oath would not bind him. New elections were
held in Northampton, and he was returned each time, but
was still excluded; in 1881, he was forcibly removed from
the House by ten policemen, and it was not until 1886 that a
new Speaker granted him the right to take the oath and sit.
'You should hear Ibsen on Bradlaugh—he has the most vivid
sympathy for him', wrote William Archer to his brother
Charles on 14 March 1882, when Ibsen was about to start
writing *An Enemy of the People;* and Bradlaugh has an obvious deal in common with Dr. Stockmann.

Stockmann himself, however, was primarily based on
two old acquaintances of Ibsen, both distinguished writers—
Jonas Lie and Bjœrnstjerne Bjœrnson. Ibsen had re-
encountered Lie in Berchtesgaden the previous summer
(1880) and had found him as confused, warm-hearted, inconsistent and impatient as ever. Bjœrnson shared the same
warm-heartedness and impatience, plus eloquence, a strong

family feeling, and an infinite capacity for moral indignation. But one must not forget, when considering the origins of Stockmann, that Ibsen himself had, as a younger man, been a fiery and eloquent speaker on causes that touched him. Lorentz Dietrichson has described him addressing a gathering of the Scandinavian community in Rome in 1864, on the subject of the Danish–German war. 'All the bitterness which had for so long been stored up within him, all the fiery indignation and passion for the Scandinavian cause which he had bottled up for so long, found an outlet. His voice began to ring, and in the evening dusk one saw only his burning eyes. When he had finished, no one cried bravo or raised his glass, but I think we all felt that that evening the Marseillaise of the North had rung out into the Roman night air'. That is not very far from the Dr. Stockmann of Act Four; and it is worth remembering that the house in Skien in which Ibsen had been born was called Stockmannsgaarden.

One of the characters in *An Enemy of the People*, Aslaksen the printer, had already appeared in *The League of Youth*, completed in 1869. There he had been a sad little drunk; in the later play he has become a pillar of respectability and moderation. Morten Kiil, 'the Badger,' had been planned as a character for *The Pillars of Society*. He appears in the rough notes for that play, but never got into the final draft. Ibsen, like the Button Moulder's description of The Master in *Peer Gynt*, was

> a thrifty man . . .
> He never rejects as worthless anything
> Which he can use again as raw material.

As recently as October 1964 a number of previously unpublished letters of Ibsen were privately printed in a limited edition,* and among them are three of particular interest in which Ibsen discusses in detail the characters of *An Enemy of the People*. Hans Schrœder, the director of the Christiania Theatre who had rejected *Ghosts*—a memory which the unfortunate man was to carry with him for the rest of his days—had telegraphed Ibsen in Rome for permission to give the first public performance of *An Enemy of the People*. Ibsen agreed, stinging them for a lump payment of 4,000 crowns (he had let them have *A Doll's House* for 2,500), and a week later, on 14 December 1882, he wrote to Schrœder from Rome:

Permit me to address to you a few lines concerning the forthcoming production of *An Enemy of the People*. It is not my intention or wish to attempt to influence *in absentio* either the staging or the casting; but the expression of certain feelings which I hold regarding various aspects of the play can do no harm. I trust I may assume that Mrs. Wolf will play Mrs. Stockmann. . . . If for the role of Hovstad you have an otherwise suitable actor of not too heroic build, that is the kind of man you should choose. Hovstad is the son of poor people, has grown up in a dirty home on wretched and inadequate food, has frozen and toiled horribly throughout his childhood, and subsequently, as a poverty-stricken young man, has continued to undergo considerable privation. Such living conditions leave their mark not only on a man's spirit but also on his outward appearance. Men of heroic exterior are an exception among the plebs. Whatever the circumstances Hovstad must always wear a depressed appearance,

---

Henrik Ibsens Brevveksling med Christiania Theater 1878–1899, edited with a commentary by Œyvind Anker (Gyldendal Norsk Forlag, Oslo, 1964).

somewhat shrunken and stooping, and uncertain in his movements; all, of course, portrayed with complete naturalism. Billing's lines are so worded that they require an east-coast and not, e.g., a Bergen dialect. He is, essentially, an east-coast character. Captain Horster has been ridiculously misunderstood by a Danish critic. He characterizes Horster as an old man, Dr. Stockmann's old friend, etc. This is, of course, utterly wrong. Horster is a young man, one of the young people whose healthy appetite delights the Doctor, though he is an infrequent visitor at the house because he dislikes the company of Hovstad and Billing. Already in Act One, Horster's interest in Petra must subtly and delicately be indicated, and during the brief exchanges between him and her in Act Five we must sense that they now stand at the threshold of a deep and passionate relationship.

Both the boys must be carefully instructed so that the difference in their characters is clearly established. And I must beg that in Act Four every possible actor at your disposal be used. The stage director must here enjoin the greatest possible naturalism and strictly forbid any caricaturing or exaggeration. The more realistic characters you can work into the crowd the better.

Throughout the play the stage director must inexorably insist that none of the players alter his or her lines. They must be spoken exactly as they stand in the text. A lively tempo is desirable. When I was last at the Christiania Theatre the speech seemed to me very slow. But above all, truthfulness to nature—the illusion that everything is real and that one is sitting and watching something that is actually taking place in real life. *An Enemy of the People* is not easy to stage. It demands exceptionally well-drilled ensemble playing, i.e., protracted and meticulously supervised rehearsals. But I rely upon the good will of all concerned. . . .

Ten days later, on Christmas Eve, Ibsen had occasion to write again to Schrœder: '*Morgenbladet* has published an announcement about the casting for *An Enemy of the People,* in consequence of which I must further inconvenience you with a few lines. I see that Gundersen is to play the Mayor. This actor's appearance hardly suggests a man who cannot bear to eat hot food in the evening, has a bad stomach and an uncertain digestion, and lives on weak tea. Nor is it well suited to a man who is characterized as neat, refined, and fastidious. But these shortcomings can partly be countered by the right clothes and make-up. Mr. Gundersen must therefore pay careful attention to these two points. Nor does Mr. Reimers's physique fit such a temperament as Dr. Stockmann's; hot-headed people are in general more slightly built. The same advice accordingly applies to Mr. Reimers as that which I have suggested for Mr. Gundersen. He must make himself as thin and small as possible.'

On 31 December 1882, Ibsen wrote again: 'I fear I must once again trouble you with a few lines. From your kind letter which reached me yesterday I gather it is intended to have both the boys in my play acted by girls. This has somewhat disturbed me, since it seems to imply that sufficient attention has not been paid to the spirit in which this play was written and in which it requires to be staged. To allow boys' parts to be taken by women may sometimes be excusable in operetta, vaudeville, or the so-called romantic drama; for in these the prime requirement is unqualified illusion; every member of the audience is fully conscious throughout the evening that he is merely sitting in a theatre and watching a theatrical performance. But this should not be the case when *An Enemy of the People* is being acted. The spectator must feel as though he were invisibly present in Dr. Stockmann's living-room; everything here must seem real; the two boys included. Consequently they cannot be played by actresses dressed up in wigs and stays; their feminine figures will not be able to be concealed by their costume of shirt and trousers, and they will never make any spectator believe that he is looking at two real schoolboys from some small town. How in any case can a grown woman make herself look like a ten-year-old child? Both parts must therefore be played by children, or at worst by a couple of small girls whose figures are not yet fully developed; and then damn the corsets and let them have big boys' boots on their legs. They must also, of course, be taught the way boys behave.

'It is stated in the play that at the public meeting Dr. Stockmann is to be dressed in black; but his clothes must not be new or elegant, and his white cravat should sit a little crooked.'

Of all the roles, by any author, that Konstantin Stanislavsky played, Dr. Stockmann was his favourite. 'I felt myself more at home on the stage in the role of Stockmann', he wrote in *My Life and Art,* 'than in any other role of my repertoire . . . For me Stockmann was not a politician, not an orator at meetings, not a *raisonneur,* but a man of ideals, the true friend of his country and his people. He was the best and purest citizen of his motherland.' Stanislavsky goes on to speak of: 'the inner image with all its peculiarities and details; the short-sighted eyes which spoke so eloquently of his inner blindness to human faults, the childlike and youthful manner of movement, the friendly relations with his children and family, the happiness, the love of joking and play, the gregariousness and attractiveness which forced all who came in touch with him to become purer and better, and to show the best sides of their natures in his presence . . . I had only to think of the thoughts and cares of Stockmann and the signs of short sight would come of themselves, together with the forward stoop of the body, the quick step, the eyes that looked trustfully into the soul of the man or object on the stage with me, the index and middle fingers of the hand stretched forward of themselves for the sake of greater persuasiveness, as if to push my own thoughts, feelings and words, into the soul of my listener'.*

An Enemy of the People is less frequently performed today than most of Ibsen's mature plays, for two principal reasons. One is, simply, the size of the cast. A crowd costs money, and without a crowd the great fourth act loses much of its impact (Shakespeare's *Julius Caesar* presents a similar problem). The other difficulty is ideological. Some of the opinions expressed by Dr. Stockmann, especially his demands for 'aristocrats', his contempt for the masses, and his assertion that 'the minority is always right', strike an illiberal note in modern ears. On these points Ibsen was in fact expressing a commonly shared attitude; Mill, Tocqueville, Dickens and most liberal thinkers of the time distrusted the tyranny of the commonplace majority. 'Those whose opinions go by the name of public opinion . . . are always a mass, that is to say, collective mediocrity', wrote Mill in his great essay *On Liberty*. 'No government by a democracy or a numerous aristocracy, either in its political acts or in the opinions, qualities, and tone of mind which it fosters, ever did or could rise above mediocrity, except in so far as the sovereign Many have let themselves be guided (which in their best times they always have done) by the counsels and influence of a more highly gifted and instructed One or Few. The initiation of all wise or noble things comes and must come from individuals; generally at first from some one individual'. That is precisely Dr. Stockmann's message. But it

---

*Stanislavsky based his physical appearance in the role on that of Rimsky-Korsakov, and borrowed several gestures and characteristics from Gorki. The actor L. M. Leonidov observed that 'Stockmann's loneliness was of the same nature as Stanislavsky's loneliness'.

is an unfashionable viewpoint to put forward in an age of universal suffrage.

The play has, also, suffered worse than most from the dead hand of academic criticism. The kind of commentator that dismisses *Emperor and Galilean* as 'stone-cold', *Brand* as 'ambiguous', and *Little Eyolf* as 'a falling-off' (to quote from a recent and embarrassing English book intended as a vindication of Ibsen), has tended to reject *An Enemy of the People* as 'thin'. It lacks, indeed, the extra density and overtones of Ibsen's later works; but there are precious few other plays outside the Greeks, Shakespeare and Chekhov with which it need fear comparison. Nor can it be glibly dismissed as a *jeu d'esprit*. Even adequately performed, it is one of the most accessible and compulsive of Ibsen's plays, and Dr. Stockmann is one of the half-dozen greatest male parts he wrote. The truths it expresses have not dated, and are not likely to as long as there are town councils and politicians. There will always, somewhere in the world, be a Kazansky Square.

MICHAEL MEYER

CHARACTERS

DR. THOMAS STOCKMANN, medical officer at the Baths
MRS. STOCKMANN, his wife
PETRA, their daughter, a schoolteacher
EILIF, their son, aged 13
MORTEN, their son, aged 10
PETER STOCKMANN, the doctor's elder brother, Mayor and
    Chief Constable, Chairman of the Baths Committee, etc.
MORTEN KIIL, master tanner, foster-father to Mrs. Stock-
    mann
HOVSTAD, editor of the *People's Tribune*
BILLING, an employee on the newspaper
HORSTER, a sea captain
ASLAKSEN, a printer
PEOPLE AT A PUBLIC MEETING: MEN of all classes, a few
    WOMEN and a bunch of SCHOOLBOYS

The action takes place in a coastal town in southern Norway.

This translation of *An Enemy of the People* was first performed on 3 April 1962 at the Playhouse, Nottingham, with
the following cast:

DR. THOMAS STOCKMANN	John Stratton
MRS. STOCKMANN	Dorothy Primrose
PETRA	Anne Stallybrass
EILIF	Terry Smith
MORTEN	Paul Nugent
PETER STOCKMANN	Alan MacNaughtan
MORTEN KIIL	Stafford Byrne
HOVSTAD	Roland Curram
BILLING	Roger Jerome
HORSTER	Ronald Magill
ASLAKSEN	Bartlett Mullins

Other parts were played by: Vanessa Forsyth, Pauline
Mason, Ethel Farrugia, Michael Colefax, Paul Silber,
John Tordoff, Roy Greenwood, Christopher Ackhurst,
Roger Dyason, Edmund Thomas, Herbert Simpson

Directed by Allan Davis

ACT ONE

Evening in DR. STOCKMANN'S *living-roo̶m̶ ̶ ̶t̶ is humbly but neatly furnished and decorated. In the wall to the right are two doors, of which the further leads out to the hall and the nearer to the* DOCTOR'S *study. In the opposite wall, facing the hall door, is a door that leads to the other rooms occupied by the family. In the middle of this wall stands a tiled stove; further downstage is a sofa with a mirror above it. In front of the sofa is an oval table with a cloth on it. Upon this table stands a lighted lamp with a shade. Upstage, an open door to the dining-room, in which can be seen a table laid for the evening meal, with a lamp on it.*

At this table BILLING *is seated, a napkin tucked beneath his chin.* MRS. STOCKMANN *is standing by the table, offering him a plate with a large joint of beef on it. The other places around the table are empty, and the table is in the disorder of a meal that has been finished.*

MRS. STOCKMANN: There, Mr. Billing! But if you will come an hour late, you'll have to put up with cold.

BILLING *(eating):* Oh, but this is capital. Absolutely capital!

MRS. STOCKMANN: Well you know how punctually my husband always likes to eat—

BILLING: It doesn't bother me. I enjoy eating alone, without having to talk to anyone.

MRS. STOCKMANN: Oh. Well, as long as you're *enjoying* it, that's—*(Listens towards the hall.)* Ah, this must be Mr. Hovstad.

BILLING: Very likely.

MAYOR PETER STOCKMANN *enters wearing an overcoat and his official hat, and carrying a stick.*

MAYOR: Good evening to you, my dear sister-in-law.

MRS. STOCKMANN *(goes into the living-room):* Why, good evening! Fancy seeing you here! How nice of you to come and call on us!

MAYOR: I just happened to be passing, so— *(Glances towards the dining-room.)* But I hear you have company.

MRS. STOCKMANN *(a little embarrassed):* Oh, no, no, that's no one. *(Quickly.)* Won't you have something, too?

MAYOR: I? No, thank you! Good heavens, a cooked meal at night! My digestion would never stand that!

MRS. STOCKMANN: Oh, but surely just for once—

MAYOR: No, no! It's very kind of you, but I'll stick to my tea and sandwiches. It's healthier in the long run; and a little less expensive.

MRS. STOCKMANN *(smiles):* You speak as though Thomas and I were spendthrifts!

MAYOR: Not you, my dear sister-in-law. Such a thought was far from my mind. *(Points towards the* DOCTOR's *study.)* Isn't he at home?

MRS. STOCKMANN: No, he's gone for a little walk with the boys.

MAYOR: I wonder if that's wise so soon after a meal? *(Listens.)* Ah, this must be he.

MRS. STOCKMANN: No, I don't think it can be, yet. *(A knock on the door.)* Come in!

HOVSTAD, *the editor of the local newspaper, enters from the hall.*

MRS. STOCKMANN: Oh—Mr. Hovstad—?

HOVSTAD: Yes. Please excuse me, I was detained down at the printer's. Good evening, Your Worship.

MAYOR (*greets him somewhat stiffly*): Good evening. I suppose you are here on business?

HOVSTAD: Partly. About an article for my newspaper—

MAYOR: I guessed as much. I hear my brother is a regular contributor to the *People's Tribune*.

HOVSTAD: Yes, he usually drops us a line when he thinks the truth needs to be told about something.

MRS. STOCKMANN (*to* HOVSTAD, *pointing towards the dining-room*): But—won't you—?

MAYOR: Great heavens, you mustn't think I blame him for writing for the kind of public he's most likely to find sympathetic to his ideas. Besides, I have no reason to bear your newspaper any ill will, Mr. Hovstad—

HOVSTAD: I should hope not.

MAYOR: On the whole I think I may say that an admirable spirit of tolerance reigns in our town. A fine communal spirit! And the reason for this is that we have this great common interest that binds us together—an interest which is the close concern of every right-minded citizen—

HOVSTAD: You mean the Baths?

MAYOR: Exactly! Our magnificent new Baths! Mark my words, sir! These Baths will prove the very heart and essence of our life! There can be no doubt about it.

MRS. STOCKMANN: Yes, that's just what Thomas says.

MAYOR: It's really astounding the strides this place has made during the past two or three years! The town is becoming prosperous. People are waking up and beginning to live. Buildings and ground rents are increasing in value every day.

HOVSTAD: And unemployment is going down.

MAYOR: Yes, there's that too. The burden upon the propertied classes of poor relief has been most gratifyingly

reduced—and will be still more if only we have a really
good summer this year, with plenty of visitors. What we
want most is invalids. They'll give the Baths a good
name.

HOVSTAD: And I hear the indications are promising.

MAYOR: They are indeed. Enquiries about accommodation
are pouring in every day.

HOVSTAD: Well then, the Doctor's article will be most opportune.

MAYOR: Oh, has he written something new?

HOVSTAD: No, it's something he wrote last winter; a eulogy
of the Baths and the excellent health facilities of the town.
But I decided to hold it over.

MAYOR: Ah, there was a snag somewhere?

HOVSTAD: No, it wasn't that. I just thought it would be better to wait till the spring. Now people are thinking about
where to spend their summer holidays—

MAYOR: Quite right! Quite right, Mr. Hovstad!

MRS. STOCKMANN: Thomas never stops thinking about those
Baths.

MAYOR: Well, he *is* employed there.

HOVSTAD: Yes, and he was the one who really created it all,
wasn't he?

MAYOR: Was he? Really? Yes, I have heard that certain people do hold that opinion. I must say I was labouring under
the delusion that I had had some modest share in promot-
ing the enterprise.

MRS. STOCKMANN: That's what Thomas is always telling
people.

HOVSTAD: No one denies that, Your Worship. You got it
going and saw to all the practical details—we all know
that. I only meant that the idea originated with the Doctor.

MAYOR: Yes, my brother's always been full of ideas—
unfortunately. But when things have to be done, another

kind of man is needed, Mr. Hovstad. And I should have thought that least of all in this house would—

MRS. STOCKMANN: But my dear brother-in-law—!

HOVSTAD: Surely Your Worship doesn't—?

MRS. STOCKMANN: Do go inside and get yourself something to eat, Mr. Hovstad. My husband will be here any moment.

HOVSTAD: Thank you—just a bite, perhaps. *(Goes into the dining-room.)*

MAYOR *(lowers his voice slightly):* It's extraordinary about people of peasant stock. They never learn the meaning of tact.

MRS. STOCKMANN: But is it really anything to bother about? Can't you and Thomas share the honour as brothers?

MAYOR: Well, I should have thought so. But it seems not everyone is content to share.

MRS. STOCKMANN: Oh, nonsense! You and Thomas always get on so well together. Ah, this sounds like him.

Goes over and opens the door leading to the hall.

DR. STOCKMANN *(laughing and boisterous):* Hullo, Catherine! I've another guest for you here! The more the merrier, what? Come in, Captain Horster! Hang your overcoat up there on the hook. No, of course, you don't wear an overcoat, do you? Fancy, Catherine, I bumped into him in the street! Had the devil of a job persuading him to come back with me!

CAPTAIN HORSTER *enters and shakes hands with* MRS. STOCKMANN.

DR. STOCKMANN *(in the doorway):* Run along in now, lads. *(To* MRS. STOCKMANN.*)* They're hungry again already! This way, Captain Horster, you're going to have the finest roast beef you ever—!

Drives HORSTER *into the dining-room.* EILIF *and*
MORTEN *go in too.*

MRS. STOCKMANN: Thomas! Don't you see who's—?

DR. STOCKMANN (*turns in the doorway*): Oh, hullo, Peter!
(*Goes over and shakes his hand.*) Well, it's good to see
you!

MAYOR: I'm afraid I can only spare a few minutes—

DR. STOCKMANN: Rubbish! We'll be having some hot toddy
soon. You haven't forgotten the toddy, Catherine?

MRS. STOCKMANN: No, of course not. I've got the kettle
on— (*Goes into the dining-room.*)

MAYOR: Hot toddy too—!

DR. STOCKMANN: Yes. Now sit down, and we'll have a good
time.

MAYOR: Thank you. I never partake in drinking parties.

DR. STOCKMANN: But this isn't a party.

MAYOR: Well, but—! (*Glances towards the dining-room.*)
It's really extraordinary the amount they eat!

DR. STOCKMANN (*rubs his hands*): Yes, there's nothing better than to see young people tuck in, is there? Always
hungry! That's the way it should be! They've got to have
food! Gives them strength! They're the ones who've got
to ginger up the future, Peter.

MAYOR: May one ask what it is that needs to be 'gingered
up', as you put it?

DR. STOCKMANN: You must ask the young ones that—when
the time comes. We can't see it, of course. Obviously—a
couple of old fogeys like you and me—

MAYOR: Well, really! That's a most extraordinary way to describe us—

DR. STOCKMANN: Oh, you mustn't take me too seriously,
Peter. I feel so happy and exhilarated, you see! It's so
wonderful to be alive at a time like this, with everything
germinating and bursting out all around us! Oh, it's a glo-

diff. uses of change
than Mayor p. 398

rious age we live in! It's as though a whole new world were coming to birth before our eyes!

MAYOR: Do you really feel that?

DR. STOCKMANN: Yes. Of course, you can't see it as clearly as I do. You've spent your life in this background, so it doesn't make the same impression on you as it does on me. But I've had to spend all these years sitting up there in that damned northern backwater, hardly ever seeing a new face that had a stimulating word to say to me. To me it's as though I had moved into the heart of some pulsing metropolis—

MAYOR: Hm; metropolis—!

DR. STOCKMANN: Oh, I know it must seem small in comparison with lots of other cities. But there's life here— promise—so many things to work and fight for! And that's what matters. (*Shouts.*) Catherine, hasn't the post come yet?

MRS. STOCKMANN (*from the dining-room*): No, not yet.

DR. STOCKMANN: And to be making a decent living, Peter! That's something one learns to appreciate when one's been living on the edge of starvation, as we have—

MAYOR: Oh, surely—!

DR. STOCKMANN: Oh yes, I can tell you we were often pretty hard pressed up there. But now, we can live like lords! Today, for instance, we had roast beef for dinner! *And* there was enough left over for supper! Won't you have a bit? Let me show it to you anyway. Come on, have a look—

MAYOR: No, really—

DR. STOCKMANN: Well, look at this, then! Do you see? We've got a tablecloth!

MAYOR: Yes, I've noticed it.

DR. STOCKMANN: And a lampshade too! See? All from what Catherine's managed to save! It makes the room so cosy, don't you think? Come and stand here—no, no, no, not there! There, now! Look! See how the light sort of concentrates downwards? I really think it looks very elegant, don't you?

MAYOR: Well, if one can indulge in that kind of luxury—

DR. STOCKMANN: Oh, I think I can permit myself that now. Catherine says I earn almost as much as we spend.

MAYOR: Almost!

DR. STOCKMANN: Well, a man of science ought to live in a little style. I'm sure any magistrate spends far more in a year than I do.

MAYOR: Yes, I should think so! After all, a magistrate is an important public official—

DR. STOCKMANN: Well, a wholesale merchant, then. A man like that spends much more—

MAYOR: His circumstances are different.

DR. STOCKMANN: Oh, it isn't that I'm wasteful, Peter. I just can't deny myself the pleasure of having people around me! I need that, you know. I've been living outside the world for so long, and for me it's a necessity to be with people who are young, bold and cheerful, and have lively, liberal minds—and that's what they are, all the men who are sitting in there enjoying a good meal! I wish you knew Hovstad a little better—

MAYOR: That reminds me, Hovstad told me he's going to print another article by you.

DR. STOCKMANN: An article by me?

MAYOR: Yes, about the Baths. Something you wrote last winter.

DR. STOCKMANN: Oh, that. No, I don't want them to print that now.

MAYOR: No? But I should have thought now would be the most suitable time.

DR. STOCKMANN: I dare say it would under ordinary circumstances. *(Walks across the room.)*

MAYOR *(watches him):* And what is extraordinary about the circumstances now?

DR. STOCKMANN *(stops):* I'm sorry, Peter, I can't tell you that yet. Not this evening, anyway. There may be a great deal that's extraordinary; or there may be nothing at all. It may be my imagination—

MAYOR: I must say you're making it all sound very mysterious. Is there something the matter? Something I mustn't be told about? I should have thought that I, as Chairman of the Baths Committee—

DR. STOCKMANN: And I should have thought that I, as—well, let's not start flying off the handle.

MAYOR: Heaven forbid. I'm not in the habit of flying off the handle, as you phrase it. But I must absolutely insist that all arrangements be made and executed through the proper channels [and through the authorities legally appointed for that purpose].* I cannot permit any underhand or backdoor methods.

DR. STOCKMANN: Have I ever used underhand or backdoor methods?

MAYOR: You will always insist on going your own way. And that's almost equally inadmissible in a well-ordered community. The individual must learn to fall in line with the general will—or, to be more accurate, with that of the authorities whose business it is to watch over the common good.

DR. STOCKMANN: I dare say. But what the hell has that to do with me?

MAYOR: Because that, my dear Thomas, is what you seem never to be willing to learn. But take care. You'll pay for it some time. Well, I've warned you. Good-bye.

DR. STOCKMANN: Are you raving mad? You're barking completely up the wrong tree—

---

*Square brackets in the text indicate suggested cuts for performance.

MAYOR: I'm not in the habit of doing that. Well, if you'll excuse me— *(Bows towards the dining-room.)* Good-bye, sister-in-law. Good day, gentlemen. *(Goes.)*

MRS. STOCKMANN *(comes back into the living-room):* Has he gone?

DR. STOCKMANN: Yes, Catherine, and in a damned bad temper.

MRS. STOCKMANN: Oh, Thomas, what have you done to him now?

DR. STOCKMANN: Absolutely nothing. He can't expect me to account to him until the time comes.

MRS. STOCKMANN: Account to him? For what?

DR. STOCKMANN: Hm; never mind, Catherine. Why the devil doesn't the post come?

> HOVSTAD, BILLING *and* HORSTER *have got up from the dining table and come into the living-room.* EILIF *and* MORTEN *follow a few moments later.*

BILLING *(stretches his arms):* Ah, a meal like that makes one feel like a new man! By Jingo, yes!

HOVSTAD: His Worship wasn't in a very cheerful mood tonight.

DR. STOCKMANN: Oh, that's his stomach. He's got a bad digestion.

HOVSTAD: I expect we radical journalists stuck in his gullet.

MRS. STOCKMANN: I thought you were getting on rather well with him.

HOVSTAD: Oh, it's only an armistice.

BILLING: That's it! The word epitomizes the situation in a nutshell!

DR. STOCKMANN: Peter's a lonely man, poor fellow. We must remember that. He has no home where he can relax; only business, business. And all that damned tea he pours into himself! Well, lads, pull up your chairs! Catherine, where's that toddy?

MRS. STOCKMANN *(goes into the dining-room):* It's just coming.

DR. STOCKMANN: You sit down here on the sofa with me, Captain Horster. You're too rare a guest in this house! Sit, sit, gentlemen!

THE GENTLEMEN *sit at the table.* MRS. STOCKMANN *brings a tray with a kettle, decanters, glasses, etc.*

MRS. STOCKMANN: Here you are. This is arrack, and this is rum; and there's the brandy. Now everyone must help himself.

DR. STOCKMANN *(takes a glass):* Don't you worry about that! *(As the toddy is mixed.)* But where are the cigars? Eilif, you know where the box is. Morten, you can bring me my pipe. *(The* BOYS *go into the room on the right.)* I've a suspicion Eilif pinches a cigar once in a while, but I pretend I don't know! *(Shouts.)* And my smoking cap, Morten! Catherine, can't you tell him where I've put it? Oh, good, he's found it. *(The* BOYS *return with the things he asked for.)* Help yourselves, my friends! I stick to my pipe, you know; this old friend's been my companion on many a stormy round up there in the north. *(Clinks his glass with theirs.)* Skoal! Ah, I must say it's better to be sitting here, warm and relaxed.

MRS. STOCKMANN *(who is sitting, knitting):* Will you be sailing soon, Captain Horster?

HORSTER: I expect to be off next week.

MRS. STOCKMANN: It's America this time, isn't it?

HORSTER: That's the idea.

BILLING: But then you won't be able to vote in the next council elections!

[HORSTER: Is there going to be a new election?

BILLING: Didn't you know?

HORSTER: No, such things don't interest me.

BILLING: But you must care about public affairs?]

will bevly supporter at end

HORSTER: No, I don't understand these matters.

BILLING: All the same, one ought at least to vote.

HORSTER: Even if one doesn't understand what it's about?

BILLING: Understand? What's that got to do with it? Society's like a ship. Everyone's got to lend a hand at the rudder.

HORSTER: Not in my ship!

[HOVSTAD: It's curious how little sailors bother about what goes on in their own country.

BILLING: Most abnormal.]

DR. STOCKMANN: Sailors are like birds of passage; wherever they happen to be, they regard that as home. Which means the rest of us must be all the more active, Mr. Hovstad. Have you anything salutary to offer us in the *People's Tribune* tomorrow?

HOVSTAD: Nothing of local interest. But the day after, I thought of printing your article—

DR. STOCKMANN: Oh God, yes, that article! No, look, you'll have to sit on that.

HOVSTAD: Oh? We've plenty of space just now; and I thought this would be the most suitable time—

DR. STOCKMANN: Yes, yes, I dare say you're right, but you'll have to wait all the same. I'll explain later—

> PETRA, *in hat and cloak, with a pile of exercise books under her arm, enters from the hall.*

PETRA: Good evening.

DR. STOCKMANN: Hullo, Petra, is that you?

> *The* OTHERS *greet her, and she them. She puts down her cloak, hat and books on a chair by the door.*

PETRA: And you're all sitting here having a party while I've been out working!

DR. STOCKMANN: Well, come and have a party too.

BILLING: May I mix you a tiny glass?

He is a familiar visitor

PETRA *(comes over to the table):* Thanks, I'll do it myself; you always make it too strong. Oh, by the way, father, I've a letter for you.

Goes over to the chair on which her things are lying.

DR. STOCKMANN: A letter? Who from?

PETRA *(looks in her coat pocket):* The postman gave it to me just as I was going out—

DR. STOCKMANN *(gets up and goes over to her):* Why on earth didn't you let me have it before?

PETRA: I really didn't have time to run up again. Here it is.

DR. STOCKMANN *(seizes the letter):* Let me see it, child, let me see it! *(Looks at the envelope.)* Yes, this is it!

MRS. STOCKMANN: Is this what you've been waiting for so anxiously, Thomas?

DR. STOCKMANN: It is indeed. I must go and read it at once. Where can I find a light, Catherine? Is there no lamp in my room again?

MRS. STOCKMANN: Yes, there's one burning on your desk.

DR. STOCKMANN: Good, good. Excuse me a moment—

Goes into the room on the right.

PETRA: What on earth can that be, Mother?

MRS. STOCKMANN: I don't know. These last few days he's done nothing but ask about the post.

BILLING: Probably some patient out of town—

PETRA: Poor father! He'll soon find he's bitten off more than he can chew. *(Mixes herself a glass.)* Ah, that tastes good!

HOVSTAD: Have you been at evening classes tonight, too?

PETRA *(sips her drink):* Two hours.

BILLING: And four hours this morning at the technical college—

PETRA *(sits at the table):* Five hours.

MRS. STOCKMANN: And you've got exercises to correct tonight, I see.

PETRA: Yes, lots.

HORSTER: You seem to have bitten off more than you can
chew too, by the sound of it.

PETRA: Yes, but I like it. It makes you feel so wonderfully
tired.

BILLING: Wonderfully?

PETRA: Yes. One sleeps so soundly afterwards.

MORTEN: You must be very wicked, Petra.

PETRA: Wicked?

MORTEN: Yes, if you work so much. Dr. Rœrlund says work
is a punishment for our sins.

EILIF *(sniffs):* Silly! Fancy believing stuff like that!

MRS. STOCKMANN: Now, now, Eilif!

BILLING *(laughs):* Ha! Very good!

HOVSTAD: Don't you want to work hard too, Morten?

MORTEN: No! Not me!

HOVSTAD: But surely you want to become something?

MORTEN: I want to be a Viking!

EILIF: But then you'll have to be a heathen.

MORTEN: All right, I'll be a heathen!

BILLING: I'm with you there, Morten! That's just the way I
feel!

MRS. STOCKMANN *(makes a sign):* I'm sure you don't really,
Mr. Billing.

BILLING: By Jingo, I do! I *am* a heathen and I'm proud of it!
Before long we'll all be heathens. Just you wait and see!

MORTEN: Shall we be able to do anything we like then?

BILLING: Yes, Morten! You see—

MRS. STOCKMANN: Hurry off now, boys. I'm sure you've
some homework to do.

EILIF: I can stay a few minutes longer—

MRS. STOCKMANN: No, you can't. Be off, the pair of you!

The BOYS *say good night and go into the room on the left.*

HOVSTAD: Do you really think it can do the boys any harm to hear this kind of thing?

MRS. STOCKMANN: Well, I don't know. I just don't like it.

PETRA: Oh, really, mother! I think you're being very stupid.

MRS. STOCKMANN: Perhaps I am; but I don't like it. Not here in the home.

PETRA: Oh, there's so much fear of the truth everywhere! At home and at school. Here we've got to keep our mouths shut, and at school we have to stand up and tell lies to the children.

HORSTER: Lie to them?

PETRA: Yes, surely you realize we have to teach them all kinds of things we don't believe in ourselves.

BILLING: I fear that is all too true!

PETRA: If only I had the money, I'd start a school of my own. And there things would be different.

BILLING: Ah! Money!

HORSTER: If you mean that seriously, Miss Stockmann, I could gladly let you have a room at my place. My father's old house is almost empty; there's a great big dining-room downstairs—

PETRA *(laughs):* Thank you! But I don't suppose it'll ever come to anything.

HOVSTAD: No, I think Miss Petra will probably turn to journalism. By the way, have you found time to look at that English novel you promised to translate for us?

PETRA: Not yet. But I'll see you get it in time.

DR. STOCKMANN *enters from his room with the letter open in his hand.*

DR. STOCKMANN *(waves the letter):* Here's news that's going to set this town by the ears, believe you me!

410

BILLING: News?

MRS. STOCKMANN: Why, what's happened?

DR. STOCKMANN: A great discovery has been made, Catherine!

HOVSTAD: Really?

MRS. STOCKMANN: By you?

DR. STOCKMANN: Precisely! By me! *(Walks up and down.)* Now let them come as usual and say it's all madman's talk and I'm imagining things! But they'll have to watch their step this time! *(Laughs.)* Yes, I fancy they'll have to watch their step!

PETRA: Father, for Heaven's sake tell us what it is!

DR. STOCKMANN: Yes, yes, just give me time and you'll hear everything. Oh, if only I had Peter here now! Well, it only goes to show how blindly we mortals can form our judgments—

HOVSTAD: What do you mean by that, Doctor?

DR. STOCKMANN *(stops by the table):* Is it not popularly supposed that our town is a healthy place?

HOVSTAD: Yes, of course.

DR. STOCKMANN: A quite unusually healthy place? A place which deserves to be recommended in the warmest possible terms both for the sick and for their more fortunate brethren?

MRS. STOCKMANN: Yes, but my dear Thomas—!

DR. STOCKMANN: And we ourselves have praised and recommended it, have we not? I have written thousands of words of eulogy both in the *People's Tribune*, and in pamphlets—

HOVSTAD: Yes, well, what of it?

DR. STOCKMANN: These Baths, which have been called the artery of the town, and its central nerve and—and God knows what else—

BILLING: 'The pulsing heart of our city' is a phrase I once, in a festive moment, ventured to—

411

DR. STOCKMANN: No doubt. But do you know what they really are, these beloved Baths of ours which have been so puffed up and which ~~have cost so~~ much money? Do you know what they are?

HOVSTAD: No, what are they?

DR. STOCKMANN: Nothing but a damned cesspit!

PETRA: The Baths, father?

MRS. STOCKMANN *(simultaneously)*: Our Baths!

HOVSTAD *(simultaneously)*: But, Doctor—!

BILLING: Absolutely incredible!

DR. STOCKMANN: These Baths are a whited sepulchre—and a poisoned one at that. Dangerous to health in the highest degree! All that filth up at Mœlledal—you know, that stinking refuse from the tanneries—has infected the water in the pipes that feed the Pump Room. And that's not all. This damnable muck has even seeped out on to the beach—

HORSTER: Where the sea baths are?

DR. STOCKMANN: Exactly!

HOVSTAD: But how can you be so sure about all this, Doctor?

DR. STOCKMANN: I've investigated the whole thing most thoroughly. Oh, I've long suspected something of the kind. Last year there were a lot of curious complaints among visitors who'd come for the bathing—typhoid, and gastric troubles—

MRS. STOCKMANN: Yes, so there were.

DR. STOCKMANN: At the time we thought these people had brought the disease with them. But later, during the winter, I began to have other thoughts. So I set to work to analyse the water as closely as I was able.

MRS. STOCKMANN: So that's what you've been toiling so hard at!

DR. STOCKMANN: Yes, you may well say I have toiled, Catherine. But of course I lacked the proper scientific facilities. So I sent specimens of both the drinking water and the sea water to the University to have them analysed by a chemist.

HOVSTAD: And now you have that analysis?

DR. STOCKMANN *(shows the letter)*: Here it is! It establishes conclusively that the water here contains putrid organic matter—millions of bacteria! It is definitely noxious to the health even for external use.

MRS. STOCKMANN: What a miracle you found this out in time!

DR. STOCKMANN: You may well say that, Catherine.

HOVSTAD: And what do you intend to do now, Doctor?

DR. STOCKMANN: Put the matter right, of course.

HOVSTAD: Can that be done?

DR. STOCKMANN: It must be done! Otherwise the Baths are unusable—and all our work has been wasted. But don't worry. I'm pretty sure I know what needs to be done.

MRS. STOCKMANN: But, my dear Thomas, why have you kept all this so secret?

DR. STOCKMANN: Did you expect me to go round the town talking about it before I was certain? No, thank you, I'm not that mad.

PETRA: You might have told us—

DR. STOCKMANN: I wasn't going to tell anyone. But tomorrow you can run along to the Badger and—

MRS. STOCKMANN: Thomas, really!

DR. STOCKMANN: Sorry, I mean your grandfather. It'll shock the old boy out of his skin. He thinks I'm a bit gone in the head anyway—oh, and there are plenty of others who think the same! I know! But now these good people shall see! Now they shall see! *(Walks around and rubs his hands.)* There's going to be such a to-do in this town, Catherine! You've no idea! The whole water system will have to be relaid.

HOVSTAD *(gets up)*: The whole of the water system—?

DR. STOCKMANN: Of course. The intake is too low. It'll have to be raised much higher up.

PETRA: Then you were right after all! *Neg daughter*

DR. STOCKMANN: Yes, Petra, do you remember? I wrote protesting against the plans when they were about to start laying it. But no one would listen to me then. Well, now I'll give them a real broadside. Of course, I've written a full report to the Baths Committee; it's been ready for a whole week, I've only been waiting to receive this. *(Shows the letter.)* But now I shall send it to them at once! *(Goes into his room and returns with a sheaf of papers.)* Look at this! Ten foolscap pages—closely written! I'm sending the analysis with it. A newspaper, Catherine! Get me something to wrap these up in. Good! There, now! Give it to—to—! *(Stamps his foot.)* What the devil's her name? You know, the maid! Tell her to take it straight down to the Mayor.

MRS. STOCKMANN *goes out through the dining-room with the parcel.*

PETRA: What do you think Uncle Peter will say, father?

DR. STOCKMANN: What can he say? He must be grateful that so important a fact has been brought to light.

HOVSTAD: May I have your permission to print a short piece about your discovery in the *People's Tribune?*

DR. STOCKMANN: I'd be very grateful if you would.

HOVSTAD: I think it's desirable that the community should be informed as quickly as possible.

DR. STOCKMANN: Yes, yes, of course.

MRS. STOCKMANN *(comes back):* She's gone with it now.

BILLING: You'll be the first citizen in the town, Doctor, by Jingo, you will!

DR. STOCKMANN *(walks round contentedly):* Oh, nonsense, I've really done nothing except my duty. I dug for treasure and struck lucky, that's all. All the same—!

414

BILLING: Hovstad, don't you think the town ought to organize a torchlight procession in honour of Dr. Stockmann?

HOVSTAD: I'll suggest it, certainly.

BILLING: And I'll have a word with Aslaksen.

DR. STOCKMANN: No, my dear friends, please don't bother with that nonsense. I don't want any fuss made. And if the Baths Committee should decide to raise my salary, I won't accept it! It's no good, Catherine, I won't accept it!

MRS. STOCKMANN: Quite right, Thomas.

PETRA *(raises her glass):* Skoal, father!

HOVSTAD
BILLING } Skoal, skoal, Doctor!

HORSTER *(clinks his glass with the* DOCTOR's*):* Here's hoping your discovery will bring you nothing but joy!

DR. STOCKMANN: Thank you, my dear friends, thank you! I'm so deeply happy! Oh, it's good to know that one has the respect of one's fellow-citizens! Hurrah, Catherine!

Seizes her round the neck with both hands and whirls round with her. MRS. STOCKMANN *screams and struggles. Laughter, applause, and cheers for the* DOCTOR. *The* BOYS *stick their heads in through the door.*

ACT TWO

The DOCTOR's *living-room. The door to the dining-room is shut. Morning.*

MRS. STOCKMANN *(enters from the dining-room with a sealed letter in her hand, goes over to the door downstage right and peeps in):* Are you at home, Thomas?

DR. STOCKMANN *(offstage):* Yes, I've just come in. *(Enters.)* What is it?

MRS. STOCKMANN: A letter from your brother. *(Hands it to him.)*

DR. STOCKMANN: Aha, let's see what he says. *(Opens the envelope and reads):* 'I return herewith the manuscript you sent me—' *(Reads on, mumbling.)* Hm—!

MRS. STOCKMANN: Well, what does he say?

DR. STOCKMANN *(puts the papers in his pocket):* No, he just writes that he'll be coming up here to see me towards noon.

MRS. STOCKMANN: You must remember to stay at home, then.

DR. STOCKMANN: Oh, that'll be all right. I've finished my round for today.

MRS. STOCKMANN: I'm very curious to know how he's taken it.

DR. STOCKMANN: You'll see. He won't like the fact that I made this discovery and not he.

416

MRS. STOCKMANN: Doesn't it worry you? It does me.

DR. STOCKMANN: Well, he'll be happy at heart, of course. The trouble is, Peter gets so damned angry at the idea of anyone but himself doing anything for the good of the town.

MRS. STOCKMANN: You know, Thomas, I really think you ought to share the honour with him. Couldn't you say it was he who started you thinking along these lines—?

DR. STOCKMANN: Gladly, as far as I'm concerned. As long as I get the matter put right, I—

OLD MORTEN KIIL (*puts his head in through the door leading from the hall, looks around inquiringly, chuckles to himself and asks slyly*): Is it—is it true?

MRS. STOCKMANN: Why, father!

DR. STOCKMANN: Hullo, father-in-law! Good morning, good morning!

MRS. STOCKMANN: Well, aren't you going to come in?

MORTEN KIIL: I will if it's true. If not, I'll be off—

DR. STOCKMANN: If what's true?

MORTEN KIIL: This nonsense about the water system. Is it true, eh?

DR. STOCKMANN: Of course it's true. But how did you hear about it?

MORTEN KIIL (*comes in*): Petra looked in on her way to school—

DR. STOCKMANN: Oh, did she?

MORTEN KIIL: Mm. And she told me. I thought she was just pulling my leg. But that's not like Petra.

DR. STOCKMANN: How could you think she'd do a thing like that?

MORTEN KIIL: Never trust anyone. That's my motto. You get made a fool of before you know where you are. So it is true, then?

DR. STOCKMANN: Absolutely true. Sit down now, father.

417

(Coaxes him down on to the sofa.) Isn't it a stroke of luck for the town?

MORTEN KIIL *(stifles a laugh):* Stroke of luck for the town?

DR. STOCKMANN: That I made this discovery in time—

MORTEN KIIL *(as before):* Oh, yes, yes, yes! But I never thought you'd start playing monkey tricks with your own flesh and blood!

DR. STOCKMANN: Monkey tricks?

MRS. STOCKMANN: Father dear—?

MORTEN KIIL *(rests his hands and chin on the handle of his stick and winks slyly at the* DOCTOR*):* What was it, now? Didn't you say some animals had got into the water pipes?

DR. STOCKMANN: Yes, bacteria.

MORTEN KIIL: Quite a number of them, so Petra told me. Regular army!

DR. STOCKMANN: Millions, probably.

MORTEN KIIL: But no one can see them. Isn't that right?

DR. STOCKMANN: Of course one can't *see* them.

MORTEN KIIL *(chuckles silently):* Devil take me if this isn't the best I've heard from you yet!

DR. STOCKMANN: What do you mean?

MORTEN KIIL: But you'll never get the Mayor to believe a tale like that.

DR. STOCKMANN: We'll see.

MORTEN KIIL: Do you think he's that daft?

DR. STOCKMANN: I hope the whole town will be that daft.

MORTEN KIIL: The whole town? That's perfectly possible! Serve them right, it'll teach them a lesson! They hounded me out of the Council—yes, that's what I call it, for they drove me out like a dog, they did! But now they're going to pay for it! You make fools of them, Stockmann!

DR. STOCKMANN: But, father—

MORTEN KIIL: You make fools of them, my boy! *(Gets up.)* If you can put the Mayor and his friends out of countenance, I'll give a hundred crowns to the poor immediately!

DR. STOCKMANN: That's very generous of you.

MORTEN KIIL: I'm not a rich man, mind! But if you do that, I'll remember the poor to the tune of fifty crowns; at Christmas.

HOVSTAD *enters from the hall.*

HOVSTAD: Good morning! *(Stops.)* Oh, am I intruding?

DR. STOCKMANN: No, come in, come in!

MORTEN KIIL *(chuckles again):* Him! Is he in with you on this?

HOVSTAD: What do you mean?

DR. STOCKMANN: Indeed he is.

MORTEN KIIL: I might have guessed it! So it's to be in the papers! Yes, you're a card all right, Stockmann! Well, you two put your heads together. I'm off.

DR. STOCKMANN: Oh, father, stay a little longer.

MORTEN KIIL: No, I'm off. Pull out all the tricks you know! By God, I'll see you don't lose by it! *(Goes.* MRS STOCKMANN *accompanies them out.)*

DR. STOCKMANN *(laughs):* Imagine, Hovstad, the old man doesn't believe a word I say about the water system!

HOVSTAD: Oh, so *that* was—?

DR. STOCKMANN: Yes, that's what we were talking about. I suppose that's why you've come too?

HOVSTAD: Yes. Can you spare me a moment or two, Doctor?

DR. STOCKMANN: As long as you want, my dear fellow.

HOVSTAD: Have you heard anything from the Mayor?

DR. STOCKMANN: Not yet. He'll be along shortly.

HOVSTAD: I've been thinking a lot about this since last night.

DR. STOCKMANN: Yes?

HOVSTAD: You're a doctor and a man of science, and to you this business of the water is something to be considered in isolation. I ~~think you don't perhaps~~ realize how it's tied up with a lot of other things.

DR. STOCKMANN: I don't quite understand you. [Let's sit down, my dear chap. No, over there on the sofa.]

HOVSTAD *sits on the sofa,* DR. STOCKMANN *in an arm-chair on the other side of the table.*

DR. STOCKMANN: Well?

HOVSTAD: You said yesterday that the pollution of the water was the result of impurities in the soil.

DR. STOCKMANN: Yes, we're pretty certain that filthy swamp up at Mœlledal is the cause of the evil.

HOVSTAD: Forgive me, Doctor, but I believe the real cause of all the evil is to be found in quite a different swamp.

DR. STOCKMANN: Which one?

HOVSTAD: The swamp in which our whole communal life is slowly rotting.

DR. STOCKMANN: Damn it, Mr. Hovstad, what kind of talk is this?

HOVSTAD: Little by little all the affairs of this town have fallen into the hands of a small clique of bureaucrats.

DR. STOCKMANN: Oh, come, you can't group them all under that description.

HOVSTAD: No, but the ones who don't belong to it are the friends and hangers-on of the ones who do. It's the rich men, the ones with names—they're the people who rule our life.

DR. STOCKMANN: They're shrewd and intelligent men.

HOVSTAD: Did they show shrewdness or intelligence when they laid the water pipes where they are now?

DR. STOCKMANN: No, that was very stupid, of course. But it's going to be put right now.

HOVSTAD: You think they'll enjoy doing that?

DR. STOCKMANN: Enjoy it or not, they'll be forced to do it.

HOVSTAD: If the press is allowed to use its influence.

DR. STOCKMANN: That won't be necessary, my dear fellow. I'm sure my brother will—

HOVSTAD: I'm sorry, Doctor, but I intend to take this matter up myself.

DR. STOCKMANN: In the newspaper?

HOVSTAD: When I took over the *People's Tribune* I did so with the fixed purpose of breaking up this ring of obstinate bigots who hold all the power in their hands.

DR. STOCKMANN: But you told me yourself what happened as a result. The paper almost had to close down.

HOVSTAD: We had to play it easy then, that's true. There was a risk that if these men fell, the Baths might not be built. But now we have them, and these fine gentlemen have become dispensable.

DR. STOCKMANN: Dispensable, perhaps. But we owe them a debt all the same.

HOVSTAD: Oh, that'll be handsomely acknowledged. But a radical writer like me can't let an opportunity like this pass unused. We must destroy the myth of these men's infallibility. It must be rooted out like any other kind of superstition.

DR. STOCKMANN: Ah, I'm with you there! If it is a superstition, then away with it!

HOVSTAD: I'd prefer not to attack the Mayor, since he's your brother. But I know you feel as strongly as I do that truth must precede all other considerations.

DR. STOCKMANN: Of course. *(Bursts out.)* But—! But—!

HOVSTAD: You mustn't think ill of me. I'm not more ambitious or self-seeking than most men.

DR. STOCKMANN: But my dear fellow, who suggests you are?

HOVSTAD: I'm the son of poor people, as you know, and I've had the chance to see what's needed most in the lower strata of society. It's to have a share in the control of pub-

lic affairs. That's what develops ability, and knowledge
and human dignity.

DR. STOCKMANN: I appreciate that.

HOVSTAD: And then I think a journalist has a lot to answer
for if he neglects an opportunity to achieve emancipation
for the masses—[—the small and the oppressed]. Oh, I
know—the big boys will call me a demagogue and all
that—but I don't care. As long as my conscience is clear.
I—

DR. STOCKMANN: That's the point, yes! That's exactly it,
Mr. Hovstad! All the same—damn it— *(A knock at the
door.)* Come in!

> ASLAKSEN, *the printer, appears in the doorway leading
> from the hall. He is humbly but decently dressed in
> black, with a white and somewhat crumpled cravat,
> gloves, and a silk hat in his hand.*

ASLAKSEN *(bows):* I trust you'll forgive me for being so
bold, Doctor—

DR. STOCKMANN *(gets up):* Why, hullo! Aren't you Aslaksen the printer?

ASLAKSEN: I am indeed, Doctor.

HOVSTAD *(gets up):* Are you looking for me, Aslaksen?

ASLAKSEN: No, I'd no idea I'd see you here. It was the Doctor himself I—

DR. STOCKMANN: Well, what can I do for you?

ASLAKSEN: Is it true what Mr. Billing tells me, that you're
thinking of getting us a better water system?

DR. STOCKMANN: Yes, for the Baths.

ASLAKSEN: Ah, yes, I see. Well, I just came to say that I'm
right behind you!

HOVSTAD *(to DR. STOCKMANN):* You see!

DR. STOCKMANN: I'm most grateful; but—

ASLAKSEN: You might find it useful to have us tradespeople
behind you. We form a pretty solid majority in this

town—when we choose to, mind! And it's always good to have the majority behind you, Doctor.

DR. STOCKMANN: True enough. But I don't see that any special effort is necessary here. Surely it's a perfectly straightforward matter—

ASLAKSEN: Yes, but you might be glad of us all the same. I know these local authorities. The boys in power don't like accepting suggestions from outside. So I thought it might not be out of place if we organized a little demonstration.

HOVSTAD: That's just what I feel.

DR. STOCKMANN: Demonstration? In what way will you demonstrate?

ASLAKSEN: Oh, with restraint, Doctor. I always insist on restraint. Restraint is the primary virtue of every citizen. That's my opinion, anyway.

DR. STOCKMANN: Yes, yes, Mr. Aslaksen. Your views are well known—

ASLAKSEN: Yes, I fancy they are. Now this business of the water system is very important to us tradespeople. It looks as though the Baths are going to prove as you might say a little goldmine for the town. We'll all be depending on the Baths for our livelihood, especially us property owners. That's why we want to give the project every support we can. And seeing as I'm Chairman of the Property Owners' Association—

DR. STOCKMANN: Yes?

ASLAKSEN: And seeing as I'm also on the Council of the Temperance Society—you do know I'm a temperance worker—?

DR. STOCKMANN: Yes, yes.

ASLAKSEN: Well, so it stands to reason I come into contact with a lot of people. And seeing as I'm known to be a level-headed and law-abiding citizen, as you said yourself, it means I have a certain influence in the town—I wield a little power—though I say it myself.

define "liberal"

DR. STOCKMANN: I'm well aware of that, Mr. Aslaksen.

ASLAKSEN: Yes, well—so it'd be an easy matter for me to arrange an address, if the occasion should arise.

DR. STOCKMANN: An address?

ASLAKSEN: Yes, a kind of vote of thanks from the citizens of this town to you for having carried this important matter to a successful conclusion. Of course, it stands to reason the wording's got to be restrained, so it won't offend the authorities and the other people as has the power. And so long as we're careful about that, I don't think anyone can take offence, can they?

HOVSTAD: Well, even if they don't particularly like it, they—

ASLAKSEN: No, no, no! We mustn't offend authority, Mr. Hovstad! We can't afford to defy the people on whom our lives depend. I've seen plenty of that in my time, and no good ever came out of it. But the sober expression of liberal sentiments can cause no affront.

DR. STOCKMANN *(shakes his hand):* My dear Aslaksen, I can't tell you how deeply happy I am to find all this support among my fellow citizens. I am most moved, most moved. Well, now! What about a small glass of sherry?

ASLAKSEN: No, thank you! I never touch spirits.

DR. STOCKMANN: A glass of beer, then? What do you say to that?

ASLAKSEN: No, thank you, not that either, Doctor. I never touch anything so early in the day. And now I must be getting back to town to talk to some of the other property owners and prepare the atmosphere.

DR. STOCKMANN: It's really most kind of you, Mr. Aslaksen. But I simply cannot get it into my head that all this fuss is really necessary. I should have thought the matter would solve itself.

ASLAKSEN: The authorities move somewhat ponderously,

Doctor. Heaven knows I don't intend any reflection on them—!

HOVSTAD: We'll give them a drubbing in print tomorrow, Mr. Aslaksen.

ASLAKSEN: But no violence, Mr. Hovstad! Proceed with restraint! Otherwise you'll get nowhere with them. You can rely on my judgement, for I have culled my knowledge in the school of life. Yes, well, I must say good-bye. You know now that we tradespeople stand behind you like a wall, Doctor. You have the solid majority on your side, whatever else may happen.

DR. STOCKMANN: Thank you, my dear Mr. Aslaksen. *(Shakes his hand.)* Good-bye, good-bye!

ASLAKSEN: Are you coming down to the press too, Mr. Hovstad?

HOVSTAD: I'll follow later. I've a few things to arrange first.

ASLAKSEN: Yes, yes.

Bows and goes out. DR. STOCKMANN *accompanies him out into the hall.*

HOVSTAD *(as the* DOCTOR *returns):* Well, what do you say to that, Doctor? Don't you think it's time this town was shaken out of its torpidity and its weak-kneed half-heartedness?

DR. STOCKMANN: You mean Aslaksen?

HOVSTAD: Yes, I do. Oh, he's honest enough in some respects, but he's stuck in the swamp. And most of the others are the same. They swing this way and that, and spend so much time looking at every side of the question that they never make a move in any direction.

DR. STOCKMANN: But Aslaksen seemed very well-meaning, I thought.

HOVSTAD: There's something I regard as more important than that. To know your own mind and have the courage of your convictions.

DR. STOCKMANN: Yes, you're right there.

HOVSTAD: That's why I'm so keen to seize this opportunity and see if I can't get these well-meaning idiots to act like men for once. All this grovelling to authority has got to be stopped. This blunder they've made about the water system is quite indefensible, and that fact's got to be drummed into the ears of every citizen who's got the right to vote.

DR. STOCKMANN: Very well. If you think it's for the communal good, go ahead. But not till I've talked with my brother.

HOVSTAD: I'll get my editorial written anyway. And if the Mayor refuses to take action, then—

DR. STOCKMANN: Oh, but that's unthinkable.

HOVSTAD: It's a possibility. And if it should happen—?

DR. STOCKMANN: If it does, I promise you that—yes, you can print my report. Print the whole damned thing!

HOVSTAD: Is that a promise?

DR. STOCKMANN *(hands him the manuscript):* Here it is. Take it with you. It won't do any harm for you to read through it; and you can give it back to me afterwards.

HOVSTAD: Right, I'll do that. Well, good-bye, Doctor.

DR. STOCKMANN: Good-bye, good-bye! Don't you worry, Mr. Hovstad—everything's going to go quite smoothly. Quite smoothly!

HOVSTAD: Hm. We shall see.

Nods and goes out through the hall.

DR. STOCKMANN *(goes over to the dining-room and looks in):* Catherine—! Oh, hullo, Petra, are you here?

PETRA *(enters):* Hasn't he come yet?

DR. STOCKMANN: Peter? No. But I've been having a long talk with Hovstad. He's quite excited about this discovery of mine. It seems it has a much wider significance than

I'd supposed. So he's placed his newspaper at my disposal, if I should need it.

MRS. STOCKMANN: But do you think you will?

DR. STOCKMANN: Oh no, I'm sure I won't. But it's good to know that one has the free press on one's side—the mouthpiece of liberal opinion. And what do you think? I've had a visit from the Chairman of the Property Owners' Association!

MRS. STOCKMANN: Oh? And what did he want?

DR. STOCKMANN: He's going to support me too. They're all going to support me, if there's any trouble. Catherine, do you know what I have behind me?

MRS. STOCKMANN: Behind you? No, what have you behind you?

DR. STOCKMANN: The solid majority.

MRS. STOCKMANN: I see. And that's a good thing, is it?

DR. STOCKMANN: Of course it's a good thing! *(Rubs his hands and walks up and down.)* How splendid to feel that one stands shoulder to shoulder with one's fellow citizens in brotherly concord!

PETRA: And that one's doing so much that's good and useful, father.

DR. STOCKMANN: Yes, and for one's home town too!

MRS. STOCKMANN: There's the doorbell.

DR. STOCKMANN: Ah, this must be him! *(A knock on the inner door.)* Come in!

MAYOR *(enters from the hall):* Good morning.

DR. STOCKMANN *(warmly):* Hullo, Peter!

MRS. STOCKMANN: Good morning, brother-in-law. How are you?

MAYOR: Oh, thank you; so-so. *(To the DOCTOR.)* Last night, after office hours, I received a thesis from you regarding the state of the water at the Baths.

DR. STOCKMANN: Yes. Have you read it?

MAYOR: I have.

DR. STOCKMANN: Well! What do you think?

MAYOR *(glances at the others):* Hm—

MRS. STOCKMANN: Come, Petra.

She and PETRA *go into the room on the left.*

MAYOR *(after a pause):* Was it necessary to conduct all these investigations behind my back?

DR. STOCKMANN: Well, until I was absolutely certain, I—

MAYOR: And now you are?

DR. STOCKMANN: Yes. Surely you must be convinced—?

MAYOR: Is it your intention to place this document before the Baths Committee as an official statement?

DR. STOCKMANN: Of course! Something must be done. And quickly.

MAYOR: I find your phraseology in this document, as usual, somewhat extravagant. Amongst other things, you say that all we have to offer our visitors at present is a permanent state of ill-health.

DR. STOCKMANN: Peter, how else can you describe it? Just think! That water's poisonous even if you bathe in it, let alone drink it! And we're offering this to unfortunate people who are ill and who have turned to us in good faith, and are paying us good money, in order to get their health back!

MAYOR: And your conclusion is that we must build a sewer to drain away these aforesaid impurities from the swamp at Mœlledal, and that the whole water system must be relaid.

DR. STOCKMANN: Can you think of any other solution? I can't.

MAYOR: This morning I called upon the town engineer. In the course of our discussion I half jokingly mentioned these proposals as a thing we might possibly undertake some time in the future.

DR. STOCKMANN: Some time in the future?

MAYOR: He smiled at what he obviously regarded as my extravagance—as I knew he would. Have you ever troubled to consider what these alterations you suggest would <u>cost</u>? According to the information I received, the expense would probably run into several hundred thousand crowns.

DR. STOCKMANN: Would it be that much?

MAYOR: Yes. But that's not the worst. The work would take at least two years.

DR. STOCKMANN: Two years, did you say? Two whole years?

MAYOR: At least. And what do we do with the Baths in the meantime? Close them? Yes, we'd be forced to. You don't imagine anyone would come here once the rumour got around that the water was impure?

DR. STOCKMANN: But, Peter, it is!

MAYOR: [And for this to happen just now, when the whole enterprise is coming to fruition!] There are other towns around with qualifications to be regarded as health resorts. Do you think they won't start trying to attract the market? Of course they will! And there we shall be! We'll probably have to abandon the whole expensive scheme, and you will have ruined the town [that gave you birth].

DR. STOCKMANN: I—ruined—!

MAYOR: It's only as a health resort—a Spa—that this town has any future worth speaking of. Surely you realize that as well as I do.

DR. STOCKMANN: But what do you propose we do?

MAYOR: Your report has not completely convinced me that the situation is as dangerous as you imply.

DR. STOCKMANN: Oh, Peter, if anything it's worse! Or at least it will be in the summer, once the hot weather starts.

MAYOR: As I said, I believe that you are exaggerating the danger. [A capable medical officer must be able to take measures. He must know how to forestall such unpleasantnesses, and how to remedy them if they should become obvious.

DR. STOCKMANN: Go on.]

MAYOR: The existing water system at the Baths is a fact, and must be accepted as such. However, in due course I dare say the Committee might not be inflexibly opposed to considering whether, without unreasonable pecuniary sacrifice, it might not be possible to introduce certain improvements.

DR. STOCKMANN: And you think I'd lend my name to such chicanery?

MAYOR: Chicanery!

DR. STOCKMANN: That's what it would be! A fraud, a lie, a crime against the community, against the whole of society!

MAYOR: As I have already pointed out, I have not succeeded in convincing myself that any immediate or critical danger exists.

DR. STOCKMANN: Oh, yes you have! [You must have! My arguments are irrefutable—I know they are! And you know that as well as I do, Peter!] But you won't admit it, because it was you who forced through the proposal that the Baths and the water pipes should be sited where they are, and you refuse to admit that you made a gross blunder. Don't be such a fool, do you think I don't see through you?

MAYOR: And suppose you were right? If I do guard my reputation with a certain anxiety, it is because I have the welfare of our town at heart. Without moral authority I cannot guide and direct affairs as I deem most fit for the general good. For this, and diverse other reasons, it is vital to me that your report should not be placed before the Baths Committee. It must be suppressed for the general good. At a later date I shall bring the matter up for discussion, and we shall discreetly do the best we can. But noth-

430

ing, not a single word, about this unfortunate matter must
come to the public ear.

DR. STOCKMANN: Well, it can't be stopped now, my dear
Peter.

MAYOR: It must and shall be stopped.

DR. STOCKMANN: It can't, I tell you. Too many people
know.

MAYOR: Know? Who knows? You don't mean those fellows
from the *People's Tribune*—?

DR. STOCKMANN: [Oh, yes, they too.] The free press of our
country will see to it that you do your duty.

MAYOR *(after a short pause):* You're an exceedingly foolish
man, Thomas. Haven't you considered what the consequences of this action may be for you?

DR. STOCKMANN: Consequences? Consequences for me?

MAYOR: Yes. For you and for your family.

DR. STOCKMANN: What the devil do you mean by that?

MAYOR: I think I have always shown myself a good brother
to you, whenever you've needed help.

DR. STOCKMANN: You have, and I thank you for it.

MAYOR: I'm not asking for thanks. To a certain extent I've
been forced to do it—for my own sake. [I always hoped I
might be able to curb you a little if I could help to improve
your economic position.

DR. STOCKMANN: What! So it was only for your own sake
that you—

MAYOR: Partly, I said.] It's painful for a public servant to see
his next-of-kin spend his entire time compromising himself.

DR. STOCKMANN: And you think I do that?

MAYOR: Unfortunately you do, without knowing it. You
have a restless, combative, rebellious nature. And then
you've this unfortunate passion for rushing into print
upon every possible—and impossible—subject. The mo-

431

ment you get an idea you have to sit down and write a newspaper article or a whole pamphlet about it.

DR. STOCKMANN: Surely if a man gets hold of a new idea it's his duty as a citizen to tell it to the public?

MAYOR: People don't want new ideas. They're best served by the good old accepted ideas they have already.

DR. STOCKMANN: And you can say that to my face!

[MAYOR: Yes, Thomas. I'm going to speak bluntly to you for once. Up to now I've tried to avoid it, because I know how hasty you are; but now I've got to tell you the truth. You've no idea how much harm you do yourself by this impulsiveness of yours. You abuse the authorities, and even the government—you throw mud at them, you claim you've been cold-shouldered and persecuted. But what else can you expect, when you're such a difficult person?

DR. STOCKMANN: Oh, so I'm difficult too, am I?]

MAYOR: Oh, Thomas, you're impossible to work with. [I've discovered that for myself.] You never consider anyone else's feelings. You even seem to forget it's me you have to thank for getting you your job at the Baths—

DR. STOCKMANN: It was mine by right! I was the first person to see that this town could become a flourishing watering place! [And I was the only person who did see it at that time!] For many years I fought alone for this idea! I wrote, and wrote—

MAYOR: No one denies that. But the time wasn't ripe then. [Of course you weren't to know that, tucked away in your northern backwater.] But as soon as the right moment arrived, I—and others—took the matter up—

DR. STOCKMANN: Yes, and made a mess of my wonderful plan! Oh yes, it's becoming very clear now what brilliant fellows you were!

MAYOR: As far as I can see, all you're looking for now is just another excuse for a fight. You've always got to pick a quarrel with your superiors—it's your old failing. You

432

can't bear to have anyone in authority over you. [You look askance at anyone who occupies a position higher than yours. You regard him as a personal enemy—and then, as far as you're concerned, one weapon of attack is as good as another.] But now I've shown you what's at stake, for the whole town, and for myself too. And I'm not prepared to compromise.

DR. STOCKMANN: What do you mean?

MAYOR: Since you have been so indiscreet as to discuss this delicate matter, which you ought to have kept a professional secret, the affair obviously cannot be hushed up. All kinds of rumours will spread around, and the malicious elements among us will feed these rumours with details of their own invention. It is therefore necessary that you publicly deny these rumours.

DR. STOCKMANN: I don't understand you.

MAYOR: I feel sure that on further investigation you will convince yourself that the situation is not nearly as critical as you had at first supposed.

DR. STOCKMANN: Aha; you feel sure, do you?

MAYOR: I also feel sure you will publicly express your confidence that the Committee will [painstakingly and conscientiously take all necessary measures to] remedy any possible defects which may exist.

DR. STOCKMANN: But you can't remedy the defect by just patching things up! I'm telling you, Peter, unless you start again from scratch, it's my absolute conviction that—

MAYOR: As an employee you have no right to any independent conviction.

DR. STOCKMANN (*starts*): No right!

MAYOR: As an employee. As a private person—well, heaven knows that's another matter. But as a subordinate official at the Baths, you have no right to express any opinion which conflicts with that of your superiors.

433

DR. STOCKMANN: This is going too far! I, a doctor, a man of science, have no right—!

MAYOR: The question is not merely one of science. [The problem is complex.] The issues involved are both technical and economical.

DR. STOCKMANN: I don't care how you define the bloody thing! I must be free to say what I think about anything!

MAYOR: Go ahead. As long as it isn't anything connected with the Baths. That we forbid you.

DR. STOCKMANN (shouts): You forbid—! You—! Why, you're just a—

MAYOR: I forbid you—! Your chief! And when I forbid you to do something, you must obey!

DR. STOCKMANN (controls himself): Peter—if you weren't my brother—!

PETRA (throws open the door): Father, don't put up with this!

MRS. STOCKMANN (follows her): Petra, Petra!

MAYOR: Ha! Eavesdroppers!

MRS. STOCKMANN: You were talking so loud—we couldn't help hearing—

PETRA: I was listening.

MAYOR: Well, I'm not altogether sorry—

DR. STOCKMANN (goes closer to him): You spoke to me of forbidding and obeying?

MAYOR: You forced me to use that tone.

DR. STOCKMANN: And you expect me to publicly swallow my own words?

MAYOR: We regard it as an unavoidable necessity that you issue a statement on the lines I have indicated.

DR. STOCKMANN: And if I don't—obey?

MAYOR: Then we shall be forced to issue an explanation, to calm the public.

DR. STOCKMANN: All right! But I shall write and refute you.

I stick to my views. I shall prove that I am right and you are wrong. And what will you do then?

MAYOR: Then I shall be unable to prevent your dismissal.

DR. STOCKMANN: What—!

PETRA: Father! Dismissal!

MRS. STOCKMANN: Dismissal!

MAYOR: Dismissal from your post as public medical officer. I shall feel compelled to apply for immediate notice to be served on you, barring you from any further connection with the Baths.

DR. STOCKMANN: You'd have the impudence to do that?

MAYOR: You're the one who's being impudent.

PETRA: Uncle, this is a disgraceful way to treat a man like father!

MRS. STOCKMANN: Be quiet, Petra.

MAYOR (*looks at* PETRA): So we've opinions of our own already, have we? But of course! (*To* MRS. STOCKMANN.) Sister-in-law, you seem to be the most sensible person in this house. Use what influence you have over your husband. Make him realize the consequences this will have both for his family and—

DR. STOCKMANN: My family concerns no one but myself.

MAYOR: —both for his family, and for the town he lives in.

DR. STOCKMANN: I'm the one who has the town's real interests at heart! I want to expose the evils that sooner or later must come to light. I'm going to prove to people that I love this town where I was born.

MAYOR: Oh, you're blind! All you're trying to do is to stop up the source of the town's prosperity.

DR. STOCKMANN: That source is poisoned, man! Are you mad? We live by hawking filth and disease! And all this communal life you boast so much about is based upon a lie!

MAYOR: That's pure imagination—if nothing worse. The

man who casts such foul aspersions against the town he
lives in is an enemy of society.

DR. STOCKMANN *(goes towards him):* You dare to—!

MRS. STOCKMANN *(throws herself between them):* Thomas!

PETRA *(grasps her father by the arm):* Keep calm, father!

MAYOR: I shall not expose myself to violence. You've been
warned. Consider what is your duty to yourself and your
family. Good-bye. *(Goes.)*

DR. STOCKMANN *(walks up and down):* And in my own
house too, Catherine!

MRS. STOCKMANN: Yes, Thomas. It's a shame and a
scandal—

PETRA: I'd like to get my hands on him—!

DR. STOCKMANN: It's my own fault. I ought to have exposed
them long ago! I should have bared my teeth; and used
them! Calling me an enemy of society! By God, I'm not
going to take that lying down!

MRS. STOCKMANN: But, Thomas dear, might is right—

DR. STOCKMANN: I'm the one who's right!

MRS. STOCKMANN: What's the good of being right if you
don't have the might?

PETRA: Mother, how can you speak like that?

DR. STOCKMANN: So it's no use in a free society to have
right on one's side? Don't be absurd, Catherine.
Besides—don't I have the free press in front of me—and
the solid majority behind me? That's might enough, I
should have thought!

MRS. STOCKMANN: For heaven's sake, Thomas, surely
you're not thinking of setting yourself up against your
brother?

DR. STOCKMANN: What the devil else do you expect me to
do? Don't you want me to stand up for what I believe to
be right?

PETRA: Yes, father, you must!

436

MRS. STOCKMANN: It'll do you no good. If they won't, they won't.]

DR. STOCKMANN *(laughs):* Oh, Catherine, just give me time. You'll see! I'm going to fight this war to the end.

MRS. STOCKMANN: Yes, and the end will be that you'll lose your job. [You'll see.

DR. STOCKMANN: At least I shall have done my duty to the community; my duty to society. And they call me an enemy of society—!]

MRS. STOCKMANN: What about your family, Thomas? [And your home? Do you think you'll be doing your duty to the ones who depend on you?]

PETRA: Oh, mother, don't always think only of us.

MRS. STOCKMANN: It's easy for you to talk. You can stand on your own feet, if need be. But think of the boys, Thomas! [And think of yourself too—and me—

DR. STOCKMANN: You must be mad, Catherine! If I give in like a coward to Peter and his wretched gang, do you think I'd ever have another moment of happiness in my life?

MRS. STOCKMANN: I don't know about that. But God preserve us from the happiness we're likely to enjoy if you go on digging your heels in. You'll have no means of livelihood, no regular income. Didn't we have enough of that in the old days? Remember that, Thomas. Think what it'll mean.

DR. STOCKMANN *(writhes, fighting with himself, and clenches his fists):* And these office lackeys can do this to a free and honourable man! Isn't it monstrous, Catherine?

MRS. STOCKMANN: Yes, they've behaved very wickedly to you, that's true. But heaven knows, there's so much injustice one has to put up with in this world. There are the boys, Thomas.] Look at them! What's to become of them? [No, no, you can't have the heart.]

437

EILIF *and* MORTEN *have meanwhile entered, carrying their schoolbooks.*

DR. STOCKMANN: My sons! *(Suddenly stands erect, his mind made up.)* Even if my whole world crashes about me, I shall never bow my head. *(Goes towards his room.)*

MRS. STOCKMANN: Thomas, what are you going to do?

DR. STOCKMANN *(in the doorway):* I want to have the right to look my sons in the eyes when they grow up into free men! *(Goes into his room.)*

MRS. STOCKMANN *(bursts into tears):* Oh, God help us!

[PETRA: Father's right, mother! He'll never give in.]

The BOYS *ask in bewilderment what is the matter.* PETRA *signs to them to go.*

438

ACT THREE

The editorial office of the People's Tribune. *On the left in the background is the entrance door; to the right in the same wall is another door with glass panes through which the composing room is visible. Another door is in the wall on the right. In the middle of the room is a big table covered with papers, newspapers and books. Downstage left is a window; by it is a writing desk with a high stool. Two armchairs stand by the table, and there are other chairs along the walls. The room is gloomy and uncomfortable; the furniture is old, the armchairs dirty and torn. In the composing room one or two* COMPOSITORS *are at work. Beyond them, a hand-press is being operated.*

HOVSTAD *sits writing at the desk. After a few moments,* BILLING *enters right, with the* DOCTOR's *manuscript in his hand.*

BILLING: I say, I say, I say!

HOVSTAD *(writing):* Have you read it?

BILLING *(puts the manuscript on the desk):* I should say I have!

HOVSTAD: Pretty forceful, isn't it?

BILLING: Forceful? He'll butcher them, by Jingo! Every paragraph's a knock-out!

439

HOVSTAD: Those fellows won't give in at the first blow, though.

BILLING: That's true. But we'll go on bashing them, punch after punch, till their whole damned oligarchy falls to the ground! As I sat in there reading this, it was as though I saw the revolution dawning from afar!

HOVSTAD (turns): Hush, don't let Aslaksen hear.

BILLING (lowers his voice): Aslaksen's a coward, a jellyfish! He hasn't the guts of a man! But you'll have your way? You will publish the Doctor's article?

HOVSTAD: Yes, unless the Mayor backs down—

BILLING: That'd be a damned nuisance!

HOVSTAD: Whichever way it turns out we can exploit the situation. If the Mayor doesn't agree to the Doctor's proposal, he'll have all the tradespeople down on him—the Property Owners' Association, and the rest. And if he does agree to it he'll antagonize all the big shareholders in the Baths who up to now have been his chief supporters—

BILLING: Of course! They'll have to fork out a pile of money—

HOVSTAD: You bet they will. And then the clique will be broken, and day after day we'll drum it into the public that the Mayor's incompetent in more respects than one, and that [all the responsible offices in the town,] the whole municipal authority, ought to be handed over to people of liberal opinions.

BILLING: By Jingo, that's the truth! I see it! I see it! We stand on the threshold of a revolution!

A knock on the door.

HOVSTAD: Quiet! (Shouts) Come in.

DR. STOCKMANN enters through the door upstage left.

HOVSTAD (goes to greet him): Ah, here is the Doctor! Well?

DR. STOCKMANN: Print away, Mr. Hovstad!

HOVSTAD: So it's come to that?

440

BILLING: Hurrah!

DR. STOCKMANN: Print away, I say! Yes, it's come to that all right. Well, now they shall have it the way they want it. It's war now, Mr. Billing!

BILLING: War to the death, I hope! Give it to them, Doctor!

DR. STOCKMANN: This report is only the beginning. My head's already teeming with ideas for four or five other articles. Where's Aslaksen?

BILLING *(calls into the composing-room):* Aslaksen, come here a moment!

HOVSTAD: Four or five other articles, did you say? On the same theme?

DR. STOCKMANN: No—oh, good heavens no, my dear fellow! No, they'll be about quite different things. But it all stems from this business of the water system and the sewer. One thing leads to another, you know. It's like when you start to pull down an old building. Exactly like that.

BILLING: By Jingo, that's true! You suddenly realize you'll never be finished till you've pulled down the whole rotten structure!

ASLAKSEN *(from the composing-room):* Pulled down! You're surely not thinking of pulling the Baths down, Doctor?

HOVSTAD: No, no, don't get frightened.

DR. STOCKMANN: No, we were talking about something else. Well, Mr. Hovstad, what do you think of my report?

HOVSTAD: I think it's an absolute masterpiece—

DR. STOCKMANN: Do you think so? That makes me very happy—very happy.

HOVSTAD: It's so clear and to the point; you don't have to be a specialist to follow the argument. I'm sure you'll have every enlightened person on your side.

ASLAKSEN: Every discriminating one too, I trust?

441

BILLING: Discriminating or not—you'll have the whole town behind you.

ASLAKSEN: Well then, I don't think we need be afraid to print it.

DR. STOCKMANN: I should damn well hope not.

HOVSTAD: It'll be in tomorrow morning.

DR. STOCKMANN: Good God, yes, we can't afford to waste a single day. Oh, Mr. Aslaksen, there was one thing I wanted to ask you. You must take charge of this manuscript yourself.

ASLAKSEN: If you wish.

DR. STOCKMANN: Treat it as though it was gold. No misprints! Every word is important. I'll drop back later; perhaps you'd let me look at a proof. I can't tell you how eager I am to see this thing in print—launched—!

BILLING: Launched, yes! Like a thunderbolt!

DR. STOCKMANN: —and submitted to the judgment of every intelligent citizen. Oh, you'd never guess what I've had to put up with today! I've been threatened with God knows what. They want to rob me of my elementary rights as a human being—

BILLING: Your rights as a human being!

DR. STOCKMANN: [They want to degrade me, reduce me to the level of a beggar.] They demand that I put my private interests above my most sacred and innermost convictions—

BILLING: By Jingo, that's going too far!

HOVSTAD: You can expect anything from that lot.

DR. STOCKMANN: [But they won't get far with me!] I'll give it to them in black and white! I'll grapple with them every day in the *People's Tribune!* I'll sweep them with one broadside after another—!

ASLAKSEN: Yes, but remember—

BILLING: Hurrah! It's war, it's war!

DR. STOCKMANN: I'll beat them to the ground, [I'll crush

442

Right, but...

them,] I'll flatten their defences for every honest man to
see! [By God I will!]

ASLAKSEN: But do it soberly, Doctor. Act with restraint—

BILLING: No, no! Don't spare your powder!

DR. STOCKMANN (continues imperturbably): You see, it isn't
just a question of the water system and the sewer. This
whole community's got to be cleansed and decontami-
nated—

BILLING: That's the very word!

DR. STOCKMANN: All these skimpers and compromisers
have got to be thrown out! There's got to be a clean
sweep! [Oh, such endless vistas have been opened up before my eyes today! I don't see my way quite clearly yet.
But I will!] We need fresh standard-bearers, my friends!
Young men! Our advance posts must be manned by new
captains!

BILLING: Hear, hear!

DR. STOCKMANN: As long as we stick together, [it'll all happen so easily!—] the whole revolution will glide into existence like a ship from the stocks! Don't you agree?

HOVSTAD: I think we've every prospect now of getting the
helm into the right hands.

ASLAKSEN: As long as we proceed with restraint, I don't
think there can be any danger.

DR. STOCKMANN: Who the hell cares about danger? I'm
doing this in the name of truth and of my conscience!

HOVSTAD: You're a man who deserves support, Doctor.

ASLAKSEN: Yes, the Doctor's a true friend of the town,
that's certain. I'll go further; he's a friend of society!

BILLING: By Jingo, Mr. Aslaksen, Dr. Stockmann is a friend
of the people!

[ASLAKSEN: I think the Property Owners' Association might
be able to use that phrase.]

DR. STOCKMANN (moved, presses their hands): Thank you,
my dear, good friends—thank you! It's so refreshing for

443

me to hear this. My brother described me in vastly different terms. By God, I'll give it back to him with interest! Now I must go and see a poor devil of a patient. But I'll be back! Take good care of that manuscript, Mr. Aslaksen. And for heaven's sake don't cut out any of the exclamation marks! If anything, put in a few more! Good, good! Well, good-bye! Good-bye, good-bye!

He shakes hands with them as they accompany him to the door and he goes out.

HOVSTAD: He's going to be bloody useful to us.

ASLAKSEN: As long as he sticks to the Baths. But if he tries to go further, we'd be unwise to stay with him.

HOVSTAD: Hm; that all depends—

BILLING: You're such a damned coward, Aslaksen!

ASLAKSEN: Coward? Yes, when it's a question of fighting local authorities, I am a coward, Mr. Billing. That's a lesson I have learned in the school of life. But elevate me into the field of high politics, confront me with the Government, and then see if I am a coward!

HOVSTAD: No, no, I'm sure you're not. But that's just where you're so inconsistent.

ASLAKSEN: Because I know my responsibilities as a citizen! Throwing stones at the government can't harm society. It doesn't bother those fellows—they stay put. But local authorities can be overthrown, and then you may get inexperience at the helm. [With disastrous results for property owners and the like.]

HOVSTAD: But what about the education of people through self-government?

ASLAKSEN: When a man has interests to protect he can't think of everything, Mr. Hovstad.

HOVSTAD: Then I hope to God I never have any interests to protect.

BILLING: Hear, hear!

HOVSTAD: I'm not a trimmer, and I never will be.

ASLAKSEN: A politician should never commit himself, Mr. Hovstad. And you, Mr. Billing, you ought to put a reef or two in your sails if you want that job of clerk to the council.

BILLING: I—!

HOVSTAD: *You*, Billing?

BILLING: Of course I only applied for it to put their backs up, you understand.

ASLAKSEN: Well, it's no business of mine. But since I'm being accused of cowardice and inconsistency, I'd like to make this clear. My political record is open for anyone to investigate. I've never changed my standpoint—apart from having learned more restraint. My heart still belongs with the people; but I don't deny that my head keeps one ear cocked towards the authorities. The local ones, anyway. *(Goes into the composing-room.)*

BILLING: Couldn't we change to some other printer, Hovstad?

HOVSTAD: Do you know anyone else who'd give us credit [for printing and paper]?

BILLING: It's a damned nuisance not having any capital!

HOVSTAD *(sits at the desk)*: Yes, if we only had *that*—

BILLING: Ever thought of trying Dr. Stockmann?

HOVSTAD *(glancing through his papers)*: What'd be the use of that? He hasn't a bean.

BILLING: No; but he's got a good man behind him. Old Morten Kiil—the fellow they call the Badger—

HOVSTAD *(writing)*: Do you really think he's got much?

BILLING: By Jingo, of course he has! And part of it must go to the Stockmanns. He's bound to provide for—well, the children, anyway.

HOVSTAD *(half turns)*: Are you banking on that?

BILLING: Banking? I never bank on anything.

HOVSTAD: You'd better not. And don't bank on becoming

clerk to the council either, because I can promise you you won't.

BILLING: Do you think I don't know? *Not* to get it is just what I want! A snub like that puts you on your mettle. It gives you a fresh supply of gall, and you need that in a backwater like this, where hardly anything really infuriating ever happens.

HOVSTAD *(writing):* Yes, yes.

BILLING: Well, they'll soon hear from me! I'll go and write that appeal for funds to the Property Owners' Association. *(Goes into the room on the right.)*

HOVSTAD *(sitting at the desk, chews his pen and says slowly):* Hm! So that's the way the wind blows! *(There is a knock on the door.)* Come in!

PETRA *enters through the door upstage left.*

HOVSTAD *(gets up):* Why, hullo! Fancy seeing you here!

PETRA: Please forgive me—

HOVSTAD *(pushes forward an armchair):* Won't you sit down?

PETRA: No, thank you. I'm only staying a moment.

HOVSTAD: Is it something from your father—?

PETRA: No, something from me. *(Takes a book from her coat pocket.)* Here's that English novel.

HOVSTAD: Why are you giving it back to me?

PETRA: I don't want to translate it.

HOVSTAD: But you promised—

PETRA: I hadn't read it then. You can't have, either!

HOVSTAD: No—you know I don't understand English. But—

PETRA: Exactly. That's why I wanted to tell you—you'll have to find something else to serialize. *(Puts the book on the table.)* You can't possibly print this in the *People's Tribune.*

HOVSTAD: Why not?

dignity in rel. to God?

PETRA: Because it's diametrically opposed to what you believe.

HOVSTAD: Oh, that's the reason?

PETRA: I don't think you understand. Its theme is that there's a supernatural power which takes care of all the so-called good people in this world, and works things so that in the end everything turns out well for them and all the so-called bad people get punished.

HOVSTAD: Yes, well, that's all right. That's just what people want to read.

PETRA: But do you want to be the one who provides it for them? You don't believe a word of that! You know quite well it doesn't happen like that in real life.

HOVSTAD: Of course not. But an editor can't always do as he wishes. One often has to bow to people's feelings in minor matters. After all, politics are the most important things in life—for a newspaper, anyway. And if I want to win people over to my views about freedom and progress, I mustn't frighten them away. If they find a moral story like this in the back pages of the newspaper they're more likely to go along with what we print on the front page. It reassures them.

PETRA: Oh, really! You're not as crafty as that. I don't see you as a spider spinning webs to catch your readers!

HOVSTAD *(smiles):* Thank you for holding such a high opinion of me. No, actually this was Billing's idea, not mine.

PETRA: Billing's!

HOVSTAD: Yes. He was talking on those lines here the other day. He's the one who's so keen that we should publish this novel. I'd never heard of the book.

PETRA: But Billing holds such progressive views—

HOVSTAD: Oh, there's more in Billing than meets the eye. I've just heard he's applied for the post of clerk to the council.

PETRA: I don't believe that, Mr. Hovstad. How could he reconcile himself to doing a thing like that?

HOVSTAD: You'd better ask him.

PETRA: I'd never have thought that of Billing.

HOVSTAD *(looks more closely at her):* Wouldn't you? Does it so surprise you?

PETRA: Yes. Perhaps not, though. I don't really know—

HOVSTAD: We journalists aren't worth much, Miss Stockmann.

PETRA: How can you say that?

HOVSTAD: I sometimes think it.

PETRA: In the ordinary run of events, perhaps not—that I can understand. But now, when you've taken up such an important cause—

[HOVSTAD: This business with your father, you mean?

PETRA: Yes, that.] Now surely you must feel you're worth more than most men.

HOVSTAD: Yes, today I do feel a bit like that.

PETRA: It's true, isn't it! You do! Oh, it's a wonderful vocation you've chosen! To be able to pioneer neglected truths and brave new doctrines—the mere fact of standing fearlessly forth to defend a man who's been wronged—

HOVSTAD: Especially when this man who's been wronged is—hm—how shall I say—?

PETRA: When he is a man of such honour and integrity?

HOVSTAD *(more quietly):* I was about to say: especially when he is your father.

PETRA *(astounded):* Mr. Hovstad!

HOVSTAD: Yes, Petra—Miss Petra—

PETRA: Is that what seems important to you? Not the issue itself. Not the truth—or the fact that this means everything to Father—

HOVSTAD: Yes—yes, of course—those things too—

PETRA: No, thank you. You let the cat out of the bag there,

Mr. Hovstad. Now I shall never believe you again. About anything.

HOVSTAD: Does it make you so angry that I've done this for your sake?

PETRA: I'm angry because you haven't been honest with Father. You've been talking to him as though truth and the good of the people were what mattered most to you. You've been fooling both of us. You're not the man you've been pretending you are. And that I'll never forgive you—never!

HOVSTAD: You shouldn't speak so sharply to me, Miss Petra. Least of all just now.

PETRA: Why not now?

HOVSTAD: Because your father needs my help.

PETRA: So that's the sort of man you are!

HOVSTAD: No, no, I didn't mean that. Please believe me—!

PETRA: I know what to believe. Good-bye.

ASLAKSEN (*hurries in furtively from the composing-room*): For God's sake, Mr. Hovstad—! (*Sees* PETRA.) Oh, dear, that's unlucky—!

PETRA: There's the book. You can give it to someone else. (*Goes towards the door.*)

HOVSTAD (*goes after her*): But, Miss Petra—!

PETRA: Good-bye. (*Goes.*)

ASLAKSEN: Mr. Hovstad, listen, please!

HOVSTAD: Yes, yes, what is it?

ASLAKSEN: The Mayor's standing outside there in the composing-room!

HOVSTAD: The Mayor?

ASLAKSEN: Yes. He wants to talk to you. He came in the back way—didn't want to be seen, I suppose.

HOVSTAD: What can he want? No, wait, I'd better— (*Goes to the door of the composing-room, opens it, bows and invites the* MAYOR *to enter.*)

HOVSTAD: Keep a look out, Aslaksen, and make sure no one—

ASLAKSEN: Of course. *(Goes into the composing-room.)*

MAYOR: You weren't expecting to see me here.

HOVSTAD: No, frankly, I wasn't.

MAYOR *(looks round):* You've done this up quite nicely. Very pleasant.

HOVSTAD: Oh—

MAYOR: And here I am, coming along and making demands on your time.

HOVSTAD: Not at all, sir. What can I do for you? Please allow me— *(Takes the* MAYOR's *hat and stick and puts them on a chair.)* Won't you sit down?

MAYOR *(sits at the table):* Thank you.

HOVSTAD *also sits at the table.*

MAYOR: Something—something extremely irritating has happened to me today, Mr. Hovstad.

HOVSTAD: Really? Of course, Your Worship has so many responsibilities—

MAYOR: This particular matter concerns the medical officer at the Baths.

HOVSTAD: Oh—the Doctor—?

MAYOR: He's written a sort of—report to the Baths Committee regarding some supposed defects in the Baths.

HOVSTAD: You amaze me.

MAYOR: Hasn't he told you? I thought he said—

HOVSTAD: Oh yes, that's true, he did say something—

ASLAKSEN *(from the composing-room):* I'd better have that manuscript—

HOVSTAD *(irritated):* Hm—it's there on the desk—

ASLAKSEN *(finds it):* Good.

MAYOR: Why, surely that's it!

ASLAKSEN: Yes, this is the Doctor's article, Your Worship.

HOVSTAD: Oh, is this what you were talking about?

MAYOR: The very thing. What do you think of it?

HOVSTAD: Of course I'm not a specialist, and I've only glanced through it—

MAYOR: But you're going to print it?

HOVSTAD: I can't very well refuse a signed contribution—

ASLAKSEN: I have no say in the contents of the paper, Your Worship—

MAYOR: Of course not.

ASLAKSEN: I only print what's put into my hands.

MAYOR: Absolutely.

ASLAKSEN: So if you'll excuse me— *(Goes towards the composing-room.)*

MAYOR: No, wait a moment, Mr. Aslaksen. With your permission, Mr. Hovstad—

HOVSTAD: Of course, Your Worship.

MAYOR: You're an intelligent and discriminating man, Mr. Aslaksen.

ASLAKSEN: I'm glad Your Worship thinks so.

MAYOR: And a man of wide influence in more circles than one.

ASLAKSEN: Oh—mostly among humble people—

MAYOR: The small taxpayers are the most numerous, here as elsewhere.

ASLAKSEN: Yes, that's true.

MAYOR: And I've no doubt you know how most of them feel. Don't you?

ASLAKSEN: Yes, I think I may say I do, Your Worship.

MAYOR: Well then, since the less affluent of the citizens of this town are so laudably disposed to make this sacrifice, I—

ASLAKSEN: What!

HOVSTAD: Sacrifice—?

MAYOR: It's a fine token of public spirit. A remarkably fine token. I was about to confess I hadn't expected it. But you know the mood of the people better than I do.

ASLAKSEN: But, Your Worship—

MAYOR: And it will probably be no mean sacrifice that the ratepayers will be called upon to make.

HOVSTAD: The ratepayers?

ASLAKSEN: But I don't understand—surely the shareholders—?

MAYOR: According to a provisional estimate, the alterations that the medical officer at the Baths regards as desirable will cost some two to three hundred thousand crowns.

ASLAKSEN: That's a lot of money; but—

MAYOR: We shall of course be forced to raise a municipal loan.

HOVSTAD (gets up): You surely don't mean that the ordinary citizens—?

ASLAKSEN: You mean you'd charge it on the rates! Empty the pockets of the tradespeople—?

MAYOR: Well, my dear Mr. Aslaksen, where else is the money to come from?

ASLAKSEN: That's the business of the gentlemen who own the Baths.

MAYOR: The Committee cannot see their way towards authorizing any further expenditure.

ASLAKSEN: Is that quite definite, Your Worship?

MAYOR: I have gone into the matter very thoroughly. If the people want all these comprehensive alterations, then the people themselves will have to pay for them.

ASLAKSEN: But good God Almighty—oh, I beg Your Worship's pardon!—but this puts a completely different face on the situation, Mr. Hovstad.

HOVSTAD: It certainly does.

MAYOR: The worst of the matter is that we shall be compelled to close the Baths for two to three years.

HOVSTAD: Close them? You mean—close them completely?

ASLAKSEN: For two years?

MAYOR: That's how long the work will take, at the lowest calculation.

ASLAKSEN: But, good heavens, we'll never be able to stand that, Your Worship! How are we property owners to live in the meantime?

MAYOR: I'm afraid that's a very difficult question to answer, Mr. Aslaksen. But what do you expect us to do? Do you imagine we shall get a single visitor here if we start spreading the idea that the water is contaminated, that we are living over a cesspit, that the whole town—?

ASLAKSEN: And all this is just pure speculation?

MAYOR: With the best will in the world I have been unable to convince myself that it is anything else.

ASLAKSEN: But if that's the case it's monstrous of Dr. Stockmann to have—I beg Your Worship's pardon, but—

MAYOR: I deplore your observation, Mr. Aslaksen, but I'm afraid it represents the truth. My brother has unfortunately always been an impulsive man.

ASLAKSEN: And you still want to support him in this action, Mr. Hovstad?

HOVSTAD: But who could have possibly guessed that—?

MAYOR: I have written a brief *résumé* of the situation as it appears to an impartial observer; and in it I have suggested how any possible flaws in the existing arrangements could safely be remedied by measures within the financial resources at present possessed by the Baths.

HOVSTAD: Have you that document with you, Your Worship?

MAYOR *(feels in his pocket):* Yes, I brought it with me just in case you—

ASLAKSEN *(quickly):* Oh, my goodness, there he is!

MAYOR: Who? My brother?

HOVSTAD: Where—where?

ASLAKSEN: He's just coming through the composing-room.

MAYOR: Most unfortunate! I don't want to meet him here, and I've something else I wanted to speak to you about.

HOVSTAD *(points towards the door, right):* Go in there till he's gone.

MAYOR: But—?

HOVSTAD: There's only Billing there.

ASLAKSEN: Quick, quick, Your Worship! He's coming now!

MAYOR: Very well. But get rid of him as soon as you can.

Goes out through the door on the right, which ASLAKSEN *opens and closes for him.*

HOVSTAD: Find something to do, Aslaksen.

He sits down and writes. ASLAKSEN *starts looking through a pile of newspapers on a chair to the right.*

DR. STOCKMANN *(enters from the composing-room):* Well, here I am again! *(Puts down his hat and stick.)*

HOVSTAD *(writing):* Already, Doctor? Aslaksen, hurry up with that thing we were talking about. We're badly behindhand today.

DR. STOCKMANN *(to* ASLAKSEN*):* No proofs yet, by the sound of it?

ASLAKSEN *(without turning):* No, surely you didn't think they'd be ready yet.

DR. STOCKMANN: That's all right. I'm just impatient, as I know you'll appreciate. I can't rest till I've seen that thing in print.

HOVSTAD: Hm—it'll be a good time yet. Won't it, Aslaksen?

ASLAKSEN: I'm afraid so.

DR. STOCKMANN: Very well, my dear friends. I'll be back later. I don't mind making the journey twice if need be! [In such a vital matter, with the welfare of the whole town at stake, one mustn't grudge a little extra effort!] *(Is about to go, but stops and comes back.)* Oh, by the way, there's one more thing I must speak to you about.

HOVSTAD: I'm sorry, but couldn't it wait till another time—?

DR. STOCKMANN: I can tell you in two words. It's just this— [when people read my article in the paper tomorrow and discover I've been racking my brains all winter working silently for the welfare of the town—

HOVSTAD: But, Doctor—

DR. STOCKMANN: I know what you're going to say! You think it was no more than my damned duty—my job as a citizen. Yes, of course—I know that as well as you do. But] my fellow citizens, you see—oh dear, those good people, they're so fond of me—

ASLAKSEN: Yes, the people of this town have been very fond of you, Doctor, up to today.

[DR. STOCKMANN: Yes, and that's exactly why I'm frightened that—what I mean is—when they read this—especially the poorer people—as a clarion call bidding them take the government of their town into their own hands—

HOVSTAD *(gets up):* Look, Doctor, I don't want to hide anything from you—

DR. STOCKMANN: Ah, something's already afoot! I might have guessed! But I don't want it! If anything like that's being organized, I—

HOVSTAD: Like what?]

DR. STOCKMANN: Well, if anything like a torchlight procession or a banquet or—a subscription for some little token of thanks is being organized, you must promise me solemnly you'll squash the idea. And you too, Mr. Aslaksen! You hear?

HOVSTAD: I'm sorry, Doctor, but we might as well tell you the truth now as later—

MRS. STOCKMANN, *in hat and cloak, enters through the door upstage, left.*

MRS. STOCKMANN *(sees the* DOCTOR*):* I knew it!

HOVSTAD *(goes towards her):* You here too, Mrs. Stockmann?

DR. STOCKMANN: What the devil do you want here, Catherine?

MRS. STOCKMANN: Surely you can guess.

HOVSTAD: Won't you sit down? [Or perhaps—?]

MRS. STOCKMANN: Thank you, you needn't bother. And you mustn't take offence at my coming here to fetch my husband, for I'm the mother of three children, I'd have you realize.

DR. STOCKMANN: Oh really, Catherine, we know all this.

MRS. STOCKMANN: Well, it doesn't seem you've much thought for your wife and children today, or you wouldn't have come here to cause all of us misery.

DR. STOCKMANN: Are you quite mad, Catherine? Simply because a man has a wife and children, is he to be forbidden to proclaim the truth—to be a useful and active citizen—to serve the town he lives in?

MRS. STOCKMANN: Oh, Thomas, if only you'd use some restraint.

ASLAKSEN: That's exactly what I say. Restraint in all things.

MRS. STOCKMANN: And as for you, Mr. Hovstad, it's not right for you to persuade my husband to leave his house and home and trick him into involving himself in all this—

HOVSTAD: I haven't tricked anyone—

DR. STOCKMANN: Tricked! You think *I* allow myself to be tricked?

MRS. STOCKMANN: Yes, you do. Oh, I know you're the cleverest man in the town, but you're so dreadfully easy to fool, Thomas. *(To* HOVSTAD.*)* And don't forget he'll lose his job at the Baths if you print that thing he's written—

ASLAKSEN: What!

456

HOVSTAD: But Doctor—I—

DR. STOCKMANN *(laughs):* Just let them try! Oh no, Catherine—they'll watch their step! You see, I have the majority behind me!

MRS. STOCKMANN: Yes, that's just the trouble. They're an ugly thing to have behind you.

DR. STOCKMANN: Rubbish, Catherine! You go home now and take care of the house, and let me take care of society. How can you be frightened when I feel so calm and happy? *(Rubs his hands and walks up and down.)* Truth and the people will win this battle, never you fear! Oh, I can see every liberal-minded citizen in this town marching forward in an unconquerable army—! *(Stops by a chair.)* What—the devil is *this?*

ASLAKSEN *(looks at it):* Oh dear!

DR. STOCKMANN: The crown of authority! *(Takes the MAYOR's hat carefully in his fingers and holds it in the air.)*

MRS. STOCKMANN: The Mayor's hat!

DR. STOCKMANN: And his marshal's baton too. How in the name of hell—?

HOVSTAD: Well—

DR. STOCKMANN: Ah, I see! He's been here to talk you over! *(Laughs.)* He came to the wrong men! And then he saw me in the composing-room—*(Roars with laughter.)* Did he run away, Mr. Aslaksen?

ASLAKSEN *(quickly):* Oh yes, Doctor, he ran away.

DR. STOCKMANN: Ran away leaving his stick and—? Rubbish! Peter never left anything behind in his life! But where the devil have you put him? Ah, yes, of course—in there! Now, Catherine, you watch!

MRS. STOCKMANN: Thomas, I beg you—!

ASLAKSEN: Don't do anything rash, Doctor!

DR. STOCKMANN *has put the* MAYOR's *hat on his head and taken his stick. Then he goes across, throws the door open and brings his hand up to the hat in salute. The* MAYOR *enters, red with anger.* BILLING *follows him.*

MAYOR: What is the meaning of this disorderly scene?

DR. STOCKMANN: A little more respect if you please, my dear Peter. I am the supreme authority in this town now. *(He walks up and down.)*

MRS. STOCKMANN *(almost in tears):* Thomas, please!

MAYOR *(follows him):* Give me my hat and stick!

DR. STOCKMANN *(as before):* You may be Chief of Police, but I'm the Mayor! I'm master of this whole town, I am!

MAYOR: Take off that hat, I tell you! Remember that that hat is an official emblem—

DR. STOCKMANN: Rubbish! Do you think the awakening lion of public opinion is going to let itself be frightened by a hat? We're starting a revolution tomorrow, I'd have you know! You threatened to sack me, but now I'm going to sack you—sack you from all your positions of responsibility! You think I can't? You're wrong, Peter! I have as my allies the conquering forces of social revolution! Hovstad and Billing will thunder in the *People's Tribune,* and Mr. Aslaksen will march forth at the head of the entire Property Owners' Association—

ASLAKSEN: No, Doctor, I won't.

DR. STOCKMANN: Indeed you will!

MAYOR: Aha! But perhaps Mr. Hovstad will support this uprising!

HOVSTAD: No, Your Worship.

ASLAKSEN: Mr. Hovstad isn't so mad as to ruin himself and his newspaper for the sake of an hallucination.

DR. STOCKMANN *(looks around):* What the devil—?

HOVSTAD: You have presented your case in a false light, Doctor; and therefore I cannot support you.

458

BILLING: No, after what His Worship has had the grace to tell me in there, I shouldn't—

DR. STOCKMANN: Lies! I'll answer for the truth of my report! You just print it. I shan't be frightened to defend it.

HOVSTAD: I'm not printing it. I can't and I won't and I dare not print it.

DR. STOCKMANN: Dare not? What nonsense is this? You're the editor, and it's the editors who rule the press.

ASLAKSEN: No, Doctor. It's the subscribers.

MAYOR: Fortunately.

ASLAKSEN: It's public opinion, the educated reader, the property owners and so forth—they're the ones who rule the press.

DR. STOCKMANN *(calmly):* And all these forces are ranged against me?

ASLAKSEN: They are. If your report got printed, it would mean ruin for the entire community.

DR. STOCKMANN: I see.

MAYOR: My hat and stick!

> DR. STOCKMANN *takes off the hat and puts it on the table together with the stick.*

MAYOR *(takes them both):* Your little reign didn't last long.

DR. STOCKMANN: It isn't over yet. *(To* HOVSTAD.*)* You refuse absolutely, then, to print my report in the *People's Tribune?*

HOVSTAD: Absolutely. Out of consideration for your family, if for no other reason.

MRS. STOCKMANN: Never you mind his family, Mr. Hovstad.

MAYOR *(takes a paper from his pocket):* This will give the public full possession of the facts. It's an official statement. Mr. Hovstad—

HOVSTAD *(takes the paper):* Right. I'll see it's set up at once.

DR. STOCKMANN: But not mine! You think you can gag me

and stifle the truth! But it won't be as easy as you think. Mr. Aslaksen, take this manuscript of mine and print it immediately as a pamphlet—at my own expense! I'll publish it myself! I want four hundred copies—five—no, make it six hundred copies!

ASLAKSEN: I wouldn't give you the use of my press if you offered me gold, Doctor. I daren't. Public opinion wouldn't allow me. You won't find a printer to take it anywhere in this town.

DR. STOCKMANN: Give it back to me then.

HOVSTAD *hands him the manuscript.*

DR. STOCKMANN *(takes his hat and stick):* I'll see the contents are made known all the same. I'll summon a public meeting and read it! All my fellow citizens shall know the truth!

MAYOR: You won't find anyone in this town who'll lease you a hall for such a purpose.

ASLAKSEN: Not one. I'm sure of that.

BILLING: By Jingo, you won't.

MRS. STOCKMANN: This is too disgraceful! Why are they all against you?

DR. STOCKMANN *(hotly):* I'll tell you why! It's because in this town all the men are old women! Like you, they just think of their families and not of the community.

MRS. STOCKMANN *(grasps his arm):* Then I'll show them that an—an old woman can be a man—for once. I'm sticking with you, Thomas.

DR. STOCKMANN: Well said, Catherine! The truth shall be told—by God it will! If I can't lease a hall, I'll hire a drummer to march through the town with me, and I'll read it out at every street corner!

MAYOR: You can't be so crazy as to do that!

DR. STOCKMANN: I am!

460

ASLAKSEN: You won't find a single man in the whole town who'll go with you.

BILLING: No, by Jingo!

MRS. STOCKMANN: Don't you give in, Thomas! I'll ask the boys to go with you.

DR. STOCKMANN: That's a splendid idea!

MRS. STOCKMANN: Morten will love to do it. And so will Eilif, I'm sure.

DR. STOCKMANN: Yes, and Petra, too! And you, Catherine!

MRS. STOCKMANN: No, no, not me. But I'll stand at the window and watch you. I'll do that.

DR. STOCKMANN (*throws his arms around her and kisses her*): Thank you! Well, my fine gentlemen, let the trumpets sound! Let's see whether meanness and mediocrity have the power to gag a man who wants to clean up society!

DR. *and* MRS. STOCKMANN *go out through the door upstage left.*

MAYOR (*shakes his head thoughtfully*): Now he's driven her mad, too!

ACT FOUR

A big, old-fashioned room in CAPTAIN HORSTER's *house. In the background an open double-leaved door leads to a lobby. In the left-hand wall are three windows. Against the middle of the opposite wall has been placed a dais, on which stands a small table with two candles, a water carafe, a glass and a bell. The room is further illuminated by bracket lamps between the windows. Downstage left stands a table with a candle on it, and a chair. Downstage right is a door, with a few chairs by it.*

A large gathering of CITIZENS, *of all classes. Here and there,* WOMEN *can be seen among the crowd, and there are a few* SCHOOLBOYS. *More and more people gradually stream in from the back, filling the room.*

A CITIZEN *(to another, as he bumps against him):* Hullo, Lamstad! You here too this evening?

SECOND CITIZEN: I never miss a public meeting.

THIRD CITIZEN *(standing near them):* Brought your whistle, I hope?

SECOND CITIZEN: Course I have. Haven't you?

THIRD CITIZEN: You bet! And Skipper Evensen said he'd bring a darned great horn!

SECOND CITIZEN: He's a card, old Evensen!

Laughter among the CROWD.

FOURTH CITIZEN *(joins them):* I say, what's this meeting about?

SECOND CITIZEN: Dr. Stockmann's going to deliver a lecture attacking the Mayor.

FOURTH CITIZEN: But the Mayor's his brother.

FIRST CITIZEN: That don't matter. Dr. Stockmann ain't afraid of no one.

THIRD CITIZEN: But he's in the wrong. It said so in the *People's Tribune.*

SECOND CITIZEN: Yes, he must be in the wrong this time. The Property Owners wouldn't let him use their hall, nor the People's Club neither.

FIRST CITIZEN: He couldn't even get the hall at the Baths.

SECOND CITIZEN: Well, what do you expect?

FIRST CITIZEN: Which one do you think we ought to support?

FOURTH CITIZEN: Just keep your eye on old Aslaksen, and do as he does.

BILLING *(with a portfolio under his arm, pushes his way through the* CROWD*):* Excuse me, please, gentlemen! Can I get through, please? I'm reporting the meeting for the *People's Tribune.* Thank you! *(Sits down at the table, left.)*

[A WORKER: Who was that?

ANOTHER WORKER: Don't you know? It's that chap Billing, who works on Aslaksen's paper.]

CAPTAIN HORSTER *escorts* MRS. STOCKMANN *and* PETRA *in through the door downstage right.* EILIF *and* MORTEN *are with them.*

CAPTAIN HORSTER: I thought you might sit here. You can slip out easily if anything should happen.

MRS. STOCKMANN: Do you think there'll be trouble?

CAPTAIN HORSTER: One never knows, with a crowd like this. But sit down, and don't worry.

MRS. STOCKMANN *(sits):* It was very kind of you to offer my husband this room.

CAPTAIN HORSTER: Well, no one else would, so I—

PETRA *(who has sat down too):* It was brave of you, too, Captain Horster.

CAPTAIN HORSTER: Oh, that didn't call for much courage.

> HOVSTAD *and* ASLAKSEN *come through the crowd, at the same time but separately.*

ASLAKSEN *(goes over to* CAPTAIN HORSTER*):* Hasn't the Doctor come yet?

CAPTAIN HORSTER: He's waiting in there.

> *There is a stir among the* CROWD *near the door backstage.*

HOVSTAD *(to* BILLING*):* There's the Mayor! See?

BILLING: Yes, by Jingo! So he's come after all!

> *The* MAYOR *gently pushes his way through the* CROWD, *greeting people politely, and stations himself against the wall on the left. A few moments later* DR. STOCKMANN *enters through the door downstage right. He is dressed in black, with a frock-coat and a white cravat. A few people clap uncertainly, but are countered by subdued hissing. Silence falls.*

DR. STOCKMANN *(in a low voice):* How do you feel, Catherine?

MRS. STOCKMANN: I'm all right. *(More quietly.)* Now don't lose your temper, Thomas!

DR. STOCKMANN: Oh, I'll control myself, don't you worry. *(Looks at his watch, steps up on to the dais and bows.)* It's a quarter past, so I'll begin— *(Takes out his manuscript.)*

ASLAKSEN: Surely a Chairman ought to be elected first?

DR. STOCKMANN: No, no, there's no need for that.

464

SEVERAL MEN *(shout)*: Yes, yes!

MAYOR: I really think we should have someone in the chair.

DR. STOCKMANN: But, Peter, I've called this meeting to deliver a lecture!

MAYOR: The Doctor's lecture may possibly give rise to divergent expressions of opinion.

SEVERAL VOICES FROM THE CROWD: A Chairman! A Chairman!

HOVSTAD: Public opinion seems to demand a Chairman.

DR. STOCKMANN *(controlling himself)*: Very well. Let public opinion have its way.

ASLAKSEN: Would His Worship the Mayor be willing to undertake that function?

THREE MEN *(clap)*: Bravo! Hear, hear!

MAYOR: For reasons which I'm sure you will appreciate, I must decline that honour. But fortunately we have among us a man whom I think we can all accept. I refer to the Chairman of the Property Owners' Association, Mr. Aslaksen.

MANY VOICES: Yes, yes! Good old Aslaksen! Hurrah for Aslaksen.

> DR. STOCKMANN *picks up his manuscript and descends from the dais.*

ASLAKSEN: If my fellow citizens want to express their trust in me, I won't refuse their call.

> *Applause and cheers.* ASLAKSEN *steps up on to the dais.*

BILLING *(writes)*: 'Mr. Aslaksen was chosen amid acclamation . . .'

ASLAKSEN: Now that I stand here, may I crave permission to say a few brief words? I'm a mild and peace-loving man who believes in sensible discretion, and in—and in—and in discreet good sense. Everyone who knows me knows that.

MANY VOICES: Yes! That's right, Aslaksen!

ASLAKSEN: Experience in the school of life has taught me that the most valuable virtue for any citizen is restraint—

MAYOR: Hear, hear!

ASLAKSEN: [And that discretion and restraint are the best servants of society.] I would therefore suggest to our respected fellow-citizen who has summoned this meeting that he endeavour to keep himself within the bounds of temperance.

DRUNKEN MAN *(by the entrance door):* Three cheers for the Temperance Society! Jolly good health!

A VOICE: Shut your darned trap.

MANY VOICES: Hush, hush!

ASLAKSEN: No interruptions, gentlemen, please! Does anyone wish to say anything before I—?

MAYOR: Mr. Chairman!

ASLAKSEN: Your Worship!

MAYOR: As everyone here is doubtless aware, I have close ties of relationship with the present medical officer at the Baths, and would consequently have preferred not to speak this evening. But my official position on the Committee of that organization, and my anxiety for the best interests of the town, force me to table a resolution. I hope I may assume that no citizen here present would regard it as desirable that dubious and exaggerated allegations concerning the sanitary conditions at the Baths should circulate outside this town.

MANY VOICES: No, no, no! Certainly not! We protest!

MAYOR: I therefore move that this meeting refuse the aforesaid medical officer permission to read or dilate upon his theories concerning the matter in question.

DR. STOCKMANN *(explosively):* Refuse permission? What the devil—?

MRS. STOCKMANN *coughs.*

DR. STOCKMANN *(composes himself):* Very well. You refuse permission.

MAYOR: In my statement to the *People's Tribune* I have acquainted the public with the essential facts so that every intelligent citizen can form his own judgment. Amongst other things I pointed out that the medical officer's proposals—quite apart from the fact that they amount to a vote of no confidence in the leading citizens of this town—will burden the ratepayers with the unnecessary expenditure of at least a hundred thousand crowns.

Groans and a few whistles.

ASLAKSEN *(rings his bell):* Order please, gentlemen! I beg leave to second His Worship's motion. I would add that in my view the Doctor has had an ulterior motive, no doubt unconscious, in stirring up this agitation; [he talks about the Baths, but] what he's really aiming at is a revolution. He wants to transfer authority into other hands. No one doubts the honesty of the Doctor's intentions. [Heaven knows, there can be no two opinions about that!] I too believe in popular self-government, so long as it doesn't impose too heavy an expense upon the taxpayer. But that's just what would happen here; so I'm blowed, if you'll excuse the expression, if I can support Dr. Stockmann in this matter. One can pay too high a price for gold; that's my opinion.

Lively expressions of assent from all sides.

HOVSTAD: I too feel impelled to explain my position. Dr. Stockmann's agitation won considerable sympathy at first, and I myself supported it as impartially as I was able. But then we found we had allowed ourselves to be misled by a false picture of the facts—

DR. STOCKMANN: That's a lie!

467

HOVSTAD: A not completely reliable picture, then. His Worship's statement has proved that. I hope no one here doubts the liberality of my views. The *People's Tribune*'s attitude on major political questions is well known to you all. But I have learned from men of discretion and experience that in local matters it is the duty of a newspaper to observe a certain caution.

ASLAKSEN: Exactly my feelings.

HOVSTAD: Now in the matter under discussion it's quite clear that Dr. Stockmann has popular opinion against him. Well, I ask you, gentlemen, what is the primary duty of an editor? Is it not to reflect the opinions of his readers? Has he not been entrusted with what might be described as an unspoken mandate to advance the cause of those who hold the same views as himself, with all the eloquence of which he is capable? Or am I mistaken?

MANY VOICES: No, no, no! Mr. Hovstad is right!

HOVSTAD: It has caused me much heartsearching to break with a man under whose roof I have lately been a not infrequent guest—a man who has until this day rejoiced in the undivided affection of his fellow citizens—a man whose only, or anyway principal fault is that he follows his heart rather than his head.

SCATTERED VOICES: That's true. Hurrah for Dr. Stockmann!

HOVSTAD: But my duty towards society left me no alternative. And there's one further consideration which forces me to oppose him, in the hope of halting him on the inauspicious road he has now begun to tread—consideration for his family—

DR. STOCKMANN: Stick to the water system and the sewer!

HOVSTAD: —consideration for his wife and the children he has abandoned.

MORTEN: Does he mean us, Mother?

MRS. STOCKMANN: Hush!

ASLAKSEN: I shall now put His Worship's resolution to the vote.

DR. STOCKMANN: Don't bother! I won't say a word about those damned Baths. No. I've something else to tell you tonight.

MAYOR *(in a low voice)*: What the devil's this?

A DRUNKEN MAN *(near the entrance door)*: I pay my taxes! So I'm entitled to express my opinion! And it's my absolute 'n unintelligible opinion that—

SEVERAL VOICES: Keep quiet there!

OTHERS: He's drunk! Throw him out!

The DRUNK MAN *is removed.*

DR. STOCKMANN: Have I the floor?

ASLAKSEN *(rings his bell)*: Dr. Stockmann has the floor.

DR. STOCKMANN: A few days ago, if anyone had tried to gag me like this I'd have fought like a lion for my sacred human rights! But now that doesn't matter. Now I have more important things to talk about.

THE CROWD *moves closer around him.* MORTEN KIIL *can be seen among them.*

DR. STOCKMANN *(continues)*: I've been thinking a great deal these past few days. I've brooded so deeply that in the end my head began to spin—

MAYOR *(coughs)*: Hm—!

DR. STOCKMANN: But then everything began to fall into place. [I saw the whole picture of things quite clearly. And that's why I'm standing here this evening.] I'm going to make a mighty revelation to you, my friends! I'm going to tell you about a discovery that is infinitely more important than the fiddling little fact that our water system is poisoned and our health baths sited above a cesspit!

MANY VOICES *(shout)*: Leave the Baths alone! Don't talk about them! We won't listen!

469

DR. STOCKMANN: This great discovery that I have made during these last few days is that all our spiritual sources are
poisoned, and that the whole of our vaunted social system
is founded upon a cesspit of lies!

ASTONISHED VOICES *(mutter in low tones):* What's that?
What did he say?

MAYOR: These are ridiculous insinuations—

ASLAKSEN *(his hand on the bell):* I must request the speaker
to moderate his language.

DR. STOCKMANN: [I have loved this birthplace of mine as
dearly as any man can love the place where he spent his
youth.] I was young when I left home, and distance, hun-
ger and memory threw, as it were, a brighter lustre over
this place and the people who dwelt here.

Some applause and cheers are heard.

DR. STOCKMANN: For years I lived in a dreadful backwater
far up in the north. [As I wandered among those people
who lived scattered over the mountains, I often thought it
would have been better for those poor degraded creatures
if they'd had a vet instead of a man like me!

Murmurs.

BILLING *(puts down his pen):* By Jingo, I've never heard the
like of that—!

HOVSTAD: That's a filthy slander against a worthy community!

DR. STOCKMANN: Wait a moment! I don't think anyone
could say that I forgot my birthplace up there. I sat there
brooding like a duck on an egg; and the chick I hatched
was—the plan for these Baths.

Clapping, and murmurs of disapproval.

DR. STOCKMANN:] Then at long last fate smiled upon me and
allowed me to return. [And then, my fellow-citizens, then

I thought I had nothing left to wish for in this world.
No—] I had one ambition left—a burning desire to work
with all my heart and soul for the welfare of my home and
my community.

MAYOR *(gazing into space):* You've a strange way of showing it!

DR. STOCKMANN: I went around here revelling blindly in my
new-found happiness. But yesterday morning—no, it was
the previous night, actually—my eyes were opened, and
the first thing that greeted them was the stupendous imbe-
cility of the authorities—

Noise, shouting and laughter. MRS. STOCKMANN
coughs loudly.

MAYOR: Mr. Chairman!

ASLAKSEN *(rings his bell):* As Chairman of this meeting, I—

DR. STOCKMANN: Oh, let's not start quibbling about words,
Mr. Aslaksen. I only mean that I suddenly realized how
really revoltingly our politicians had behaved down there
at the Baths. I can't stand politicians! I've had all I can
take of them. They're like goats in a plantation of young
trees! They destroy everything! They block the way for a
free man, however much he may twist and turn—and I'd
like to see them rooted out and exterminated, like other
vermin—

meaning...?

Commotion in the hall.

MAYOR: Mr. Chairman, are such calumnies to be permitted?

ASLAKSEN *(his hand on the bell):* Dr. Stockmann—!

DR. STOCKMANN: I can't understand why I'd never had a
proper look at these gentlemen before. I'd had a prime example right in front of my eyes all the time—my brother
Peter—procrastinating and purblind—!

Laughter, confusion and whistling. MRS. STOCKMANN *sits and coughs.* ASLAKSEN *rings his bell loudly.*

THE DRUNK MAN *(who has come back):* Are you referring to me? My name's Petersen, but don't you darned well—

ANGRY VOICES: Throw that drunk out! Get rid of him!

The DRUNK MAN *is thrown out again.*

MAYOR: Who was that person?

A BYSTANDER: I don't know, Your Worship.

ASLAKSEN: The man was obviously intoxicated with German beer. Continue, Doctor; but please try to use restraint!

DR. STOCKMANN: Well, my fellow-citizens, I won't say anything more about our politicians. If anyone imagines from what I've just said that I've come here this evening to crucify these gentlemen, he's wrong—quite wrong. [For I cherish the comforting belief that these laggards, these survivors from a dying world, are studiously cutting their own throats. They need no doctor's help to hasten their demise. And anyway, it isn't they who are the chief danger to society!] They aren't the ones who are most active in poisoning the sources of our spiritual life [and contaminating the ground on which we tread]! It isn't they who are the most dangerous enemies of truth and freedom in our society!

SHOUTS FROM ALL SIDES: Who, then? Who is? Name them!

DR. STOCKMANN: Don't worry, I'll name them! Because this is the great discovery I've made today! *(Raises his voice.)* The most dangerous enemies of truth and freedom are the majority! Yes, the solid, liberal, darned majority—they're the ones we have to fear! Now you know!

Complete uproar. Nearly everyone is shouting, stamping and whistling. Some of the older men exchange covert glances and seem to be enjoying the situ-

ation. MRS. STOCKMANN *gets up anxiously.* EILIF *and* MORTEN *go threateningly over to the schoolboys, who are making a commotion.* ASLAKSEN *rings his bell and calls for silence.* HOVSTAD *and* BILLING *are both talking, but neither can be heard. At last silence is restored.*

ASLAKSEN: As Chairman I call upon the speaker to withdraw those mischievous observations.

DR. STOCKMANN: Never, Mr. Aslaksen! It's the majority in this community that is depriving me of my freedom and trying to forbid me to proclaim the truth.

HOVSTAD: The majority is always right.

BILLING: And speaks the truth, by Jingo!

DR. STOCKMANN: The majority is never right! Never, I tell you! That's one of those community lies that free, thinking men have got to rebel against! Who form the majority—in any country? The wise, or the fools? I think we'd all have to agree that the fools are in a terrifying, overwhelming majority all over the world! But in the name of God it can't be right that the fools should rule the wise! *(Uproar and shouting.)* Yes, yes, you can shout me down! But you can't say I'm wrong! The majority has the power—unfortunately—but the majority is not right! The ones who are right are a few isolated individuals like me! The minority is always right! *(Uproar again.)*

HOVSTAD: So Dr. Stockmann's turned aristocrat since the day before yesterday!

DR. STOCKMANN: I've already said I don't want to waste words on the little flock of short-winded sheep puffing along in the rear! Life has nothing exciting left to offer them. But I'm thinking of the few, the individuals amongst us, who have adopted the new, fresh, burgeoning truths as their watchword! These men stand at the outposts, so far forward that the compact majority hasn't

473

yet arrived—and there they are fighting for those truths which are still too new to man's conscious mind to have any majority behind them.

HOVSTAD: I see, so you've become a revolutionary!

DR. STOCKMANN: Yes, Mr. Hovstad, by God I have! I intend to start a revolution against the lie that truth is a monopoly of the majority! What are these truths to which the majority clings? They're the truths which are so old that they're on the way to becoming decrepit! But when a truth's as old as that, gentlemen, it's also well on the way to becoming a lie!

Laughter and jeers.

DR. STOCKMANN: Yes, yes, you can believe me or not, as you wish; but truths aren't such long-lived Methuselahs as people imagine. A normal truth lives for—what shall I say?—seventeen to eighteen years on an average—twenty years at the most—seldom longer. But truths as old as that are always dreadfully thin. [All the same, it isn't until then that the majority cottons on to them, and commends them to society as sound spiritual fodder. But] there's no great nourishment in that sort of food, I can promise you [that; and as a doctor, I know about these things.] All these majority truths are like last year's salt pork; they're hams that have gone sour and green and tainted. And they're the cause of all the moral scurvy that's rotting our society!

ASLAKSEN: It seems to me that the honourable speaker has strayed somewhat from his text.

MAYOR: I warmly endorse the Chairman's observation.

DR. STOCKMANN: Oh, really, Peter, I think you must be quite mad! I'm sticking as close to my text as any man could! My whole point is precisely this, that it's the masses, the mob, this damned majority—they're the thing that's poisoning the sources of our spiritual life and contaminating the ground we walk on!

HOVSTAD: And the great progressive majority does this simply by being sensible enough to believe in those truths which are indisputable and generally acknowledged?

DR. STOCKMANN: Oh, my good Mr. Hovstad, don't talk to me about indisputable truths. The truths that the masses and the mob acknowledge are the ones that were held by advanced thinkers in our grandparents' time. We outrunners of today don't acknowledge them any longer. I really believe there's only one indisputable truth. It is that no society can live a healthy life if it feeds on truths that are old and marrowless.

HOVSTAD: Instead of all this generalizing why don't you give us a few examples of these old and marrowless truths on which we're living?

Murmurs of agreement from several quarters.

DR. STOCKMANN: Oh, I could reel you off a whole list of the beastly things; but to start with I'll limit myself to one 'acknowledged' truth which is really a damned lie, but which Mr. Hovstad and the *People's Tribune* and all the hangers-on of the *People's Tribune* feed on all the same.

HOVSTAD: And that is—?

DR. STOCKMANN: That is the doctrine which you have inherited from your forefathers and which you continue thoughtlessly to proclaim far and wide—the doctrine that the plebs, the masses, the mob, are the living heart of the people—that they *are* the people—and that the common man, all those ignorant and incompetent millions, have the same right to sanction and condemn, to advise and to govern, as the few individuals who are intellectually aristocrats.

BILLING: Now, really, by Jingo—!

HOVSTAD *(simultaneously, shouts):* Mark that, fellow citizens!

FURIOUS VOICES: Oh-ho, so we're not the people, aren't we? So it's only the aristocrats who have the right to rule?

A WORKER: Throw him out if he talks like that!

OTHERS: Chuck him through the door!

A CITIZEN *(shouts):* Blow that horn, Evensen!

> *Loud blasts are heard. Whistles and furious uproar in the hall.*

DR. STOCKMANN *(when the noise has abated somewhat):* Can't you be reasonable? Can't you bear to hear the truth just for once? I'm not asking you all to agree with me immediately! But I did expect Mr. Hovstad would admit I was right once he'd given the matter a little thought. After all, Mr. Hovstad claims to be a freethinker—

SURPRISED VOICES *(murmur):* Freethinker, did he say? What? Is Mr. Hovstad a freethinker?

HOVSTAD *(shouts):* Prove that, Dr. Stockmann! When have I said so in print?

DR. STOCKMANN *(thinks):* No, by Jove, you're right! You've never had the guts to admit it publicly. Well, I won't corner you, Mr. Hovstad. Let me be the freethinker, then. From my knowledge of natural science I shall now reveal to you all that the *People's Tribune* is deceiving you most shamefully when it tells you that you, the common millions, the masses, the mob, are the true heart and core of the people! That's just a newspaper lie! The masses are nothing but raw material which may, some day, be refined into individuals!

> *Growls, laughter and disturbances in the hall.*

DR. STOCKMANN: Well, isn't that the way life works with the rest of creation? [Look at the enormous difference there is between a breed of animal that's cultivated and one that is uncultivated! Just look at a common farmyard hen. What is such a stunted piece of rubbish worth as flesh? Not much! And what kind of eggs does it lay? Any common rook or crow can lay eggs just as good. But take a cultivated Spanish or Japanese hen, or take a fine pheasant or turkey, and see the difference!] Consider dogs, with which we human beings have so much in common! Think first of a street dog—one of those filthy, ragged, common curs that lope along the streets and defile the walls of our houses. Now put that street dog next to a greyhound with a distinguished pedigree whose ancestors have been fed delicate meals for generations and have had the opportunity to listen to harmonious voices and music. Don't you think the brain of that greyhound is differently developed from that of the street dog? You bet your life it is! [It's the pups of these cultivated animals that trainers teach to perform the most amazing tricks. A common street dog couldn't learn to do such things if you stood it on its head!]

Noise and laughter.

A CITIZEN *(shouts):* So we're dogs too now, are we?

ANOTHER: We're not animals, Doctor!

DR. STOCKMANN: Yes, my friend, we are animals! But [there aren't many aristocratic animals among us. And there's a terrifying difference between men who are greyhounds and men who are street dogs. And that's what's so absurd, that Mr. Hovstad is quite at one with me as long as we're talking about four-legged animals—

HOVSTAD: Well, they're only beasts.

DR. STOCKMANN: All right! But as soon as I start to apply the law to the ones who are two-legged, Mr. Hovstad balks at the consequences; he turns his whole philosophy upside down, and proclaims in the *People's Tribune* that the street mongrel is the champion of the menagerie. But that's how it always is, as long as a man remains pos-

sessed by this blind worship of the mob and hasn't
worked his way out of spiritual bondage into aristocracy.

HOVSTAD: I don't want any kind of aristocracy. I come of
simple peasant stock; and I'm proud that I have my roots
deep down in the mob, whom you deride.

MANY WORKERS: Hurrah for Hovstad! Hurrah, hurrah!

DR. STOCKMANN: The kind of <u>mob I</u>'m talking about isn't
only to be found at the bottom of the barrel. It swarms and
mills all around us, even among the high peaks of society.
Just look at your own smug, sleek Mayor! My brother Peter's as good a <u>mobster</u> as ever walked in two shoes!

Laughter and hisses.

MAYOR: I protest against these personal insinuations.

[DR. STOCKMANN *(unperturbed)*: And that isn't because he
stems like me from a villainous old pirate from Pomerania
or somewhere down there—for we do—!

MAYOR: It's absurd, it's a myth! I deny it!]

DR. STOCKMANN: Because he thinks what his superiors
think, and his opinions are the opinions he's heard them
express. The men who do that are spiritually of the mob;
and that's why my noble brother Peter is so frighteningly
unaristocratic in all essentials—and consequently so
terrified of all things liberal.

MAYOR: Mr. Chairman—!

HOVSTAD: So it's the aristocrats who are the liberals in this
country? That really is a new discovery!

Laughter among the CROWD.

DR. STOCKMANN: Yes, that's part of my discovery too. [And
the reason is that liberality is almost exactly the same as
morality.] And I say it's quite indefensible of the *Tribune*
day after day to proclaim the false gospel that the masses,
[the mob, the solid majority,] have a monopoly on liberality and morality, and that vice and corruption and every

drikkehuse 11.

kind of spiritual filth are a kind of pus that oozes out of culture, just as all that beastly stuff in the Baths oozes down from the tanneries at Mœlledal!

Confusion and interruptions.

DR. STOCKMANN *(unperturbed, laughs in his excitement):* [And yet this same *People's Tribune* can preach that the masses and the mob must be elevated to a higher standard of living! Good God Almighty, if what the *People's Tribune* teaches were true, then to elevate the masses would simply be to start them on the road to ruin!] But luckily the idea that culture demoralizes is an old inherited fairy tale. No, it's stupidity, poverty and foul living conditions that do the Devil's work! In a house where the rooms aren't aired and the floors swept every day—my wife Catherine says they ought to be scrubbed too, but there can be two opinions on that—in such a house, I say, within two or three years people lose the capacity for moral thought and moral action. Lack of oxygen debilitates the conscience. And there's a shortage of oxygen in many, many houses in this town, from the sound of things, if the whole of this damned majority can be so devoid of conscience as to want to build the prosperity of their town on a quagmire of deceit and lies.

ASLAKSEN: You can't cast an accusation like that against a whole community!

A MAN: I appeal to the Chairman to order the speaker to stand down.

EXCITED VOICES: Yes, yes! That's right. Make him stand down!

DR. STOCKMANN *(explodes):* Then I'll shout the truth at every street corner! I'll write in the newspapers of other towns! The whole country shall be told what is happening here!

HOVSTAD: It sounds almost as though the Doctor wishes to destroy this town.

DR. STOCKMANN: Yes, I love this town where I was born so dearly that I would rather destroy it than see it flourish because of a lie!

ASLAKSEN: Those are strong words.

Shouts and whistling. MRS. STOCKMANN *coughs in vain; the* DOCTOR *no longer hears her.*

HOVSTAD *(shouts through the uproar):* The man who can want to destroy a whole community must be a public enemy!

DR. STOCKMANN *(with increasing excitement):* A community that lives on lies deserves to be destroyed! I say that the town that houses such a community should be levelled to the ground! All those who live by lies ought to be exterminated like vermin! You will end by contaminating the entire country! You will bring it to the pass where the whole land will deserve to be laid waste! And if things go that far, then I say with all my heart: 'Let the whole land be laid waste! Let the whole people be exterminated!'

A MAN: That's talking like an enemy of the people!

BILLING: There speaks the voice of the people, by Jingo!

THE WHOLE CROWD *(screams):* Yes, yes, yes! He's an enemy of the people! He hates his country! He hates the people!

ASLAKSEN: Both as a citizen and as a human being I am deeply shocked by what I have had to hear. Dr. Stockmann has shown himself in his true colours—[in a manner of which I should never have dreamed him capable. I fear I must support the view expressed a moment ago by respected citizens; and] I move that [we embody this opinion in a resolution. I suggest the following:] 'This meeting declares [that it regards] the medical officer at the Baths, Dr. Thomas Stockmann, an enemy of the people.'

Deafening cheers and applause. Many of the CROWD *form a circle around* DR. STOCKMANN *and whistle at him.* MRS. STOCKMANN *and* PETRA *have got to their feet.* MORTEN *and* EILIF *are fighting with the other* SCHOOLBOYS, *who have been whistling too. Some* ADULTS *part them.*

DR. STOCKMANN *(to the people who have been whistling):* You fools! I tell you—!

ASLAKSEN *(rings his bell):* The Doctor no longer has the floor. A formal ballot will take place; [but to protect personal feelings the voting should be done in writing and anonymously.] Have you any clean paper, Mr. Billing?

BILLING: I've both blue and white here—

ASLAKSEN *(descends from the dais):* Good, that'll save time. Tear it into squares; like that, yes. *(To the* CROWD.*)* Blue means no, white means yes. I'll collect the votes myself.

The MAYOR *leaves the hall.* ASLAKSEN *and a couple of other* CITIZENS *go around the* CROWD *with the pieces of paper in hats.*

FIRST CITIZEN *(to* HOVSTAD*):* What's come over the Doctor? What's one to think?

HOVSTAD: You know how impulsive he is.

SECOND CITIZEN *(to* BILLING*):* I say, you're a regular visitor in that house. Have you ever noticed—does the fellow drink?

BILLING: I don't know what to reply, by Jingo! There's always toddy on the table when anyone comes.

THIRD CITIZEN: I think he just goes off his head now and then.

FIRST MAN: Yes, don't they say there's madness in the family?

BILLING: Could be.

A FOURTH MAN: No, it's pure spite. Wants revenge for something or other.

BILLING: He did say something the other day about a rise in salary. But he didn't get it.

ALL THE MEN *(with one voice)*: Ah, that explains it!

THE DRUNK MAN *(in the thick of the* CROWD*)*: I want a blue one! And I want a white one too!

SHOUTS: There's the drunk man again! Throw him out!

MORTEN KIIL *(comes up to* DR. STOCKMANN*)*: Well, Stockmann, you see now what happens once you start playing monkey tricks?

DR. STOCKMANN: I have done my duty.

MORTEN KIIL: What was that you were saying about the tanneries at Mœlledal?

DR. STOCKMANN: You heard. I said that that's where all the filth comes from.

MORTEN KIIL: From my tannery too?

DR. STOCKMANN: I'm afraid your tannery is the worst of all.

MORTEN KIIL: Are you going to print that in the papers?

DR. STOCKMANN: I shall hide nothing.

MORTEN KIIL: That'll cost you dear, Stockmann. *(Goes.)*

A FAT MAN *(goes across to* CAPTAIN HORSTER, *without greeting the* LADIES*)*: Well, Captain, so you lend your house to enemies of the people?

CAPTAIN HORSTER: I reckon I can do what I like with my own property.

FAT MAN: Then you won't object if I do the same with mine?

CAPTAIN HORSTER: What do you mean?

FAT MAN: You'll hear from me tomorrow. *(Turns and goes.)*

PETRA: Isn't that the man who owns your ship, Captain Horster?

CAPTAIN HORSTER: Yes.

ASLAKSEN *(with the voting papers in his hand, steps up on to the dais and rings his bell)*: Gentlemen, allow me to in-

form you of the result. With only a single dissentient
vote—

A YOUNG MAN: That's the drunk man!

ASLAKSEN: With only one dissentient vote, and that of a man
not sober, this gathering of citizens unanimously declares
the medical officer of the Baths, Dr. Thomas Stockmann,
an enemy of the people! *(Shouts and gestures of approval.)* Long live our ancient and noble community!
(More cheers.) Long live our worthy and active Mayor,
who has so loyally ignored the ties of blood! *(Cheers.)*
The meeting is closed. *(He steps down.)*

BILLING: Three cheers for the Chairman!

WHOLE CROWD: Hurrah for Mr. Aslaksen! Hurrah! Hurrah!

DR. STOCKMANN: My hat and coat, Petra. Captain, have you
room in your ship for passengers to the new world?

CAPTAIN HORSTER: For you and yours, Doctor, I'll make
room.

DR. STOCKMANN *(as PETRA helps him on with his coat):*
Good! Come, Catherine! Come, boys! *(He takes his wife
by the arm.)*

MRS. STOCKMANN *(quietly):* Thomas dear, let's go out the
back way.

DR. STOCKMANN: No back way for me, Catherine! *(Raises
his voice.)* You'll hear from your enemy of the people before he shakes the dust of this town from his feet! I'm not
so forgiving as a certain person. I don't say: 'I forgive ye,
for ye know not what ye do!'

ASLAKSEN *(shouts):* That comparison's a blasphemy, Dr.
Stockmann!

BILLING: I'll say it is, by Go—! What a dreadful thing for respectable people to hear!

A COARSE VOICE: He's threatening us now!

EXCITED SHOUTS: Let's break his windows! Throw him in
the fjord!

A MAN *(in the* CROWD*)*: Blow your horn, Evensen! *(He imitates the sound of the horn twice.)*

> *Blasts on the horn, whistles and wild cries. The* DOCTOR *goes with his family towards the door.* CAPTAIN HORSTER *clears a way for them.*

THE WHOLE CROWD *(howls after them as they go)*: Enemy of the people! Enemy of the people! Enemy of the people!

BILLING *(as he puts his notes in order)*: I'm damned if I'll drink toddy with them tonight, by Jingo!

> *The* CROWD *swarms towards the door. The shouting spreads outside. From the street can be heard the cry: 'Enemy of the people! Enemy of the People! Enemy of the people!'*

ACT FIVE

DR. STOCKMANN's *study. Bookshelves and cupboards containing medicine bottles, along the walls. In the background is the exit to the hall; downstage left is the door to the living-room. In the wall on the right are two windows, all the panes of which are smashed. In the middle of the room stands the* DOCTOR's *desk, covered with books and papers. The room is in disorder. It is morning.*

> DR. STOCKMANN, *in dressing-gown and slippers and with his smoking-cap on his head, is crouched down raking under one of the cupboards with an umbrella. At length he pulls out a stone.*

DR. STOCKMANN (*speaks through the open door into the living-room*): Catherine, I've found another!

MRS. STOCKMANN (*from the living-room*): Oh, you'll find a lot more yet.

DR. STOCKMANN (*puts the stone among a heap of others on the table*): I shall keep these stones as sacred relics. Eilif and Morten shall see them every day, and when they're grown up they shall inherit them from me. (*Rakes under a bookshelf.*) Hasn't—what the devil's her name?—you know, the maid—hasn't she gone for the glazier yet?

MRS. STOCKMANN (*enters*): He said he didn't know if he'd be able to come today.

485

[DR. STOCKMANN: The truth is, he doesn't dare.

MRS. STOCKMANN: Yes.] Randine says he daren't because of the neighbours. *(Speaks into the living-room.)* What is it, Randine? Very well. *(Goes inside and returns immediately.)* Here's a letter for you, Thomas.

DR. STOCKMANN: Give it to me. *(Opens it and reads.)* I see.

MRS. STOCKMANN: Who's it from?

DR. STOCKMANN: The landlord. He's giving us notice to quit.

MRS. STOCKMANN: Is he really? He seems such a decent man—

DR. STOCKMANN *(looks at the letter):* [He daren't do otherwise, he says.] He's very sorry, but [he daren't do otherwise]—his fellow-citizens—respect for public opinion—certain obligations—dare not offend certain persons of influence—

MRS. STOCKMANN: There, Thomas, you see.

DR. STOCKMANN: Yes, yes, I see. They're all cowards in this town. None of them dares do anything for fear of the others. *(Throws the letter on the table.)* But we don't have to worry, Catherine. We're off to the new world now—

MRS. STOCKMANN: Thomas, do you really think it's a good idea, this going away?

DR. STOCKMANN: Am I to stay here when they've pilloried me as an enemy of the people, branded me, broken my windows? And just look at this, Catherine! They've torn my trousers, too!

MRS. STOCKMANN: Oh no! And they're your best!

DR. STOCKMANN: One should never wear one's best trousers when one goes out to fight for freedom and truth. [Oh, I don't mind so much about the trousers—you can always patch them up for me. It's the fact that these riff-raff dare to threaten me as though they were my equals—that's the thing I can't damned well stomach!

MRS. STOCKMANN: Yes, Thomas, they've behaved shock-

ingly to you in this town. But does that mean we have to
leave the country?

DR. STOCKMANN: Do you think the rabble aren't just as inso-
lent in other towns? Oh, yes, Catherine. There isn't twopence to choose between them. To hell with the curs, let
them yelp. That's not the worst. The worst is that
throughout this country all the people are just party
slaves. Mind you, they're probably not much better in
America. The majority's rampant there too, and liberal
public opinion and all the rest of the rubbish. But the context is larger there, you see. They may kill you, but they
won't torture you slowly; they don't pin a free man in a
vice like they do here. And if you want to, you can stay
independent outside it all.] *(Walks across the room.)* If
only I knew of some primeval forest or a little South Sea
island that was going cheap—

[MRS. STOCKMANN: But what about the boys, Thomas?

DR. STOCKMANN *(stops):* How extraordinary you are, Catherine! Would you rather they grew up in a society like
this? You saw for yourself last night that half the people
are raving lunatics; and if the other half haven't lost their
wits it's only because they're beasts that don't have any
wits to lose.

MRS. STOCKMANN: But, Thomas dear, you're so careless
about what you say.

DR. STOCKMANN: What! Don't I tell them the truth? Don't
they turn every idea upside down? Don't they merge right
and wrong so that they can't tell the difference? Don't
they call everything a lie which I know to be true? But the
maddest thing of all is that you get grown men of liberal
inclinations getting together in groups and convincing
themselves and other people that they're progressive
thinkers! Did you ever hear the like, Catherine?

MRS. STOCKMANN: Yes, yes, it's all very stupid, but—]

PETRA *enters from the living-room.*

MRS. STOCKMANN: Are you back from school already?

PETRA: I've got the sack.

MRS. STOCKMANN: The sack?

DR. STOCKMANN: You too!

PETRA: Mrs. Busk gave me notice. So I thought I'd better leave at once.

DR. STOCKMANN: Quite right, by heaven!

MRS. STOCKMANN: Who'd have thought Mrs. Busk was such a nasty woman?

PETRA: Oh, mother, she's not nasty. It was quite obvious she didn't like doing it. But she said she dared not do otherwise. So I got the sack.

DR. STOCKMANN *(laughs and rubs his hands):* [Dared not do otherwise!] She too! Oh, that's splendid!

MRS. STOCKMANN: Well, after those dreadful scenes last night, you can't—

PETRA: It wasn't only that. Listen to this, father.

DR. STOCKMANN: Yes?

PETRA: Mrs. Busk showed me no less than three letters she'd received this morning—

DR. STOCKMANN: Anonymous, of course?

PETRA: Yes.

DR. STOCKMANN: They daren't even sign their names, Catherine.

PETRA: Two of them stated that a gentleman who frequents this house announced in the Club last night that I held excessively free views on various subjects—

DR. STOCKMANN: I hope you didn't deny that.

PETRA: Not on your life! [Mrs. Busk expresses pretty free views herself when we're alone together; but now that this has come out about me, she didn't dare to keep me.]

MRS. STOCKMANN: [Fancy—'a gentleman who frequents this

house'!] You see what thanks you get for your hospitality, Thomas!

DR. STOCKMANN: We won't go on living in this jungle any longer. Pack the bags as quickly as you can, Catherine. The sooner we get away from here, the better.

MRS. STOCKMANN: Hush! I think there's someone in the hall. Go and look, Petra.

PETRA *(opens the door):* Oh, is it you, Captain Horster? Please come in.

CAPTAIN HORSTER *(from the hall):* Good morning. I felt I had to come along and see how everything was.

DR. STOCKMANN *(shakes his hand):* Thank you. It's extremely good of you.

MRS. STOCKMANN: And thank you for seeing us safely back last night, Captain Horster.

PETRA: How did you manage to get home again?

CAPTAIN HORSTER: Oh, I managed; [I'm pretty strong, and] those fellows bark worse than they bite.

DR. STOCKMANN: Yes, isn't it amazing what wretched cowards they are! [Come here, I'll show you something.] Look, here are all the stones they threw through our windows. Just look at them! Upon my soul, there aren't more than two decent rocks in the whole lot; the others are just pebbles—mere gravel! And yet they stood out there howling, and swearing they'd beat the life out of me—but action—action—no, you won't see much of that in this town.

CAPTAIN HORSTER: Just as well for you on this occasion, Doctor.

[DR. STOCKMANN: Of course! But it annoys me all the same; for if it ever comes to a serious fight, in defence of our country, you'll see, Captain Horster—public opinion'll be for safety first, and this sacred majority'll run for their lives like a flock of sheep. That's what's so sad—it really hurts me to think of it—no, damn it, I'm just being stupid!

They've said I'm an enemy of the people, so let me be an enemy of the people!

MRS. STOCKMANN: You'll never be that, Thomas.

DR. STOCKMANN: Don't be so sure, Catherine. An ugly word can be like the scratch of a needle on the lung. And that damned phrase—I can't forget it—it's got stuck down here in the pit of my stomach, and it's lying there chafing and corroding me like an acid. And there's no magnesia that will neutralize that.

PETRA: You must just laugh at them, father.

CAPTAIN HORSTER: People will think differently of you in time, Doctor.

MRS. STOCKMANN: Yes, Thomas, that's as sure as you're standing here.]

DR. STOCKMANN: [Perhaps, when it's too late.] Well, it's their funeral! [Let them live like beasts; they'll be sorry they drove a patriot into exile.] When do you sail, Captain Horster?

CAPTAIN HORSTER: Hm—that was what I came to talk to you about, as a matter of fact—

DR. STOCKMANN: Why, has something happened to the ship?

CAPTAIN HORSTER: No. It's just that I shan't be going with her.

PETRA: They surely haven't given you the sack?

CAPTAIN HORSTER (smiles): Indeed they have!

PETRA: You, too!

MRS. STOCKMANN: There, Thomas, you see!

DR. STOCKMANN: And just because I spoke the truth! Oh, if I'd ever dreamed that such a thing could happen—

CAPTAIN HORSTER: Don't worry about me. I'll find a job with a company somewhere else.

DR. STOCKMANN: But that boss of yours is a rich man, he's completely independent! Oh, damn, damn!

CAPTAIN HORSTER: He's fair enough in the ordinary way. He said himself, he'd have liked to have kept me, if only he'd dared—

DR. STOCKMANN *(laughs):* [But he didn't dare! No, of course not!]

CAPTAIN HORSTER: It isn't so easy, he said, when you belong to a party—

DR. STOCKMANN: That's the truest word he ever uttered! A party is like a mincing machine. It grinds everyone's brains into a pulp, and all you're left with is human sausages, all identical!

MRS. STOCKMANN: Thomas, really!

PETRA *(to CAPTAIN HORSTER):* If only you hadn't seen us home, this might never have happened.

CAPTAIN HORSTER: I don't regret it.

PETRA *(holds out her hand):* Thank you!

CAPTAIN HORSTER *(to DR. STOCKMANN):* What I wanted to say was, if you still want to go, I have thought of another way—

DR. STOCKMANN: Fine! As long as we can get away quickly—

MRS. STOCKMANN: Hush—wasn't that a knock at the door?

PETRA: I think it's Uncle.

DR. STOCKMANN: Aha! *(Shouts)* Come in!

MRS. STOCKMANN: Now, Thomas dear, do promise me—

The MAYOR enters from the hall.

MAYOR *(in the doorway):* Oh, you're engaged. I'll come back later—

DR. STOCKMANN: No, no. Please come in.

MAYOR: I wanted to speak to you privately.

MRS. STOCKMANN: We'll go into the living-room.

CAPTAIN HORSTER: And I'll come back later.

DR. STOCKMANN: No, you go in too. I want to know more about that—

CAPTAIN HORSTER: Right, I'll wait, then.

He goes with MRS. STOCKMANN *and* PETRA *into the living-room. The* MAYOR *says nothing but glances at the windows.*

DR. STOCKMANN: Do you find it draughty here today? Put your hat on.

MAYOR: Thank you, if I may. *(Does so.)* I think I caught a cold last night. [I stood there shivering—]

DR. STOCKMANN: Really? I found it warm enough.

MAYOR: I regret that it didn't lie within my power to prevent those nocturnal extravagances.

DR. STOCKMANN: Did you come out here to tell me that?

MAYOR *(takes out a large letter):* I have this document for you, from the Directors of the Baths.

DR. STOCKMANN: Am I dismissed?

MAYOR: From the date of writing. *(Puts the letter on the table.)* It distresses us; but, frankly, we had no choice. Public opinion being what it is, we didn't dare—

DR. STOCKMANN *(smiles):* [Didn't dare?] I've heard that word before today.

MAYOR: I beg you to realize your position. From now on you can't reckon on having any practice whatever in this town.

DR. STOCKMANN: To hell with the practice! But what makes you so sure?

MAYOR: The Property Owners' Association has drawn up a round robin which it is sending from house to house. All respectable citizens are being urged not to employ you; and I'll guarantee that not a single householder will dare refuse to sign it. They just won't dare.

DR. STOCKMANN: Yes, yes, I don't doubt that. But what then?

MAYOR: My advice would be that you should leave town for a while—

DR. STOCKMANN: Yes, I'm thinking of doing that.

MAYOR: Good. Then, when you've had six months to think

492

the matter over, you might, after mature consideration, possibly reconcile yourself to issuing a short statement admitting your error and expressing your regret—

DR. STOCKMANN: And then, you mean, I might get my job back?

MAYOR: It's not unthinkable.

DR. STOCKMANN: But what about public opinion? You daren't offend that.

MAYOR: Public opinion is very fickle. And, quite frankly, it's important to us that you should publish some such admission.

DR. STOCKMANN: Yes, that'd make you smack your lips, wouldn't it? But, damn it, haven't I told you already what I think of that kind of chicanery?

MAYOR: Your position was somewhat stronger then. You had reason to suppose that the whole town was behind you—

DR. STOCKMANN: And now they're rubbing my face in the dirt! *(Flares up.)* [I don't care if I've got the Devil himself and his great-grandmother on my back!] Never, I tell you, never!

MAYOR: A man with a family has no right to act as you're doing. You have no right, Thomas!

DR. STOCKMANN: No right! There's only one thing in the world that a free man has no right to do! Do you know what that is?

MAYOR: No.

DR. STOCKMANN: No, of course you don't. But I'll tell you. A free man has no right to befoul himself like a beast. He has no right to get himself into the position where he feels the need to spit in his own face!

MAYOR: That all sounds very plausible—if only there didn't happen to exist another explanation for your stubbornness. [But there does.]

DR. STOCKMANN: What do you mean by that?

MAYOR: You know perfectly well. But as your brother, and as a man of the world, I would advise you not to put too much trust in expectations that might so easily not be fulfilled.

DR. STOCKMANN: What on earth are you talking about?

MAYOR: Do you seriously expect me to believe that you don't know of the arrangements that Morten Kiil has made in his will?

DR. STOCKMANN: I know that what little he has is to go to a home for retired artisans. But what's that got to do with me?

MAYOR: To begin with, it's not so little. Morten Kiil is a pretty wealthy man.

DR. STOCKMANN: I had no idea—!

MAYOR: Hm—hadn't you really? Then I suppose you also have no idea that a considerable proportion of his money is earmarked for your children, and that you and your wife will be able to enjoy the interest for the rest of your lives. Hasn't he told you?

DR. STOCKMANN: Indeed he has not! On the contrary, he's done nothing but complain about how disgracefully overtaxed he is. But are you quite sure of this, Peter?

MAYOR: I have it from an impeccable source.

DR. STOCKMANN: But, good heavens—that means Catherine's future is secured—and the children's, too! I say, I must tell her! *(Shouts)* Catherine, Catherine!

MAYOR *(holds him back):* Hush, don't say anything yet.

MRS. STOCKMANN *(opens the door):* What is it?

DR. STOCKMANN: Nothing, my dear. Go back in again.

MRS. STOCKMANN *closes the door.*

DR. STOCKMANN *(paces up and down the room):* Their future secured! [I can't believe it! All of them—and for life! Oh, it's a wonderful feeling to know that one's future is secured.] For ever!

MAYOR: But that's just what it isn't. Morten Kiil can revoke that will any day or hour that he chooses.

DR. STOCKMANN: But he won't, my dear Peter. The Badger's much too delighted at the embarrassment I've caused to you and your worthy friends.

MAYOR *(starts and looks searchingly at him):* Aha! So that's the explanation!

DR. STOCKMANN: What do you mean?

MAYOR: This whole thing's been a conspiracy. These violent and unprincipled accusations which you've levelled against the authorities in the name of truth were simply your price for being remembered in that vindictive old idiot's will.

DR. STOCKMANN *(almost speechless):* Peter—you are the lowest bastard I have ever met in all my life!

MAYOR: Things are finished between us now. Your dismissal is final. Now we have a weapon against you. *(He goes.)*

DR. STOCKMANN: The filthy—damn, damn! *(Shouts)* Catherine! Scrub the floors behind him! Tell her to bring in a bucket—that girl—what the devil's her name?—the one who's always got a dirty nose—!

MRS. STOCKMANN *(in the doorway to the living-room):* Hush, hush, Thomas, please!

PETRA *(also in the doorway):* Father, grandfather's here and says, can he speak to you privately?

DR. STOCKMANN: Yes, of course. *(At the door.)* Come in, father.

> MORTEN KIIL *comes in.* DR. STOCKMANN *closes the door behind him.*

DR. STOCKMANN: Well, what is it? Sit down.

MORTEN KIIL: No, I won't sit. *(Looks around.)* Nice and cosy it looks here today, Stockmann.

DR. STOCKMANN: Yes, doesn't it?

MORTEN KIIL: Very nice. And fresh air too! You've got enough of that oxygen you were talking about last night! Your conscience feels pretty good today, I suppose?

DR. STOCKMANN: Yes, it does.

MORTEN KIIL: I thought it would. (*Thumps himself on the breast.*) But do you know what I've got here?

DR. STOCKMANN: A good conscience too, I hope.

MORTEN KIIL (*snorts*): No, something better than that.

> Takes out a thick pocket-book, opens it and shows a wad of papers.

DR. STOCKMANN (*looks at him in amazement*): Shares in the Baths?

MORTEN KIIL: They weren't hard to come by today.

DR. STOCKMANN: You mean you've been out and bought—?

MORTEN KIIL: As many as I could afford.

DR. STOCKMANN: But, my dear Mr. Kiil—the state those Baths are in now, you—!

MORTEN KIIL: If you act like a sensible man, you'll soon have them on their feet again.

DR. STOCKMANN: You see for yourself I'm doing all I can, but—! [The people of this town are quite mad!]

MORTEN KIIL: You said last night that the worst of the filth comes from my tannery. But if that were true, then my grandfather and my father before me, and I myself, have been polluting this town for generations like three angels of death. Do you think I'm going to let an imputation like that hang over my head?

DR. STOCKMANN: I'm afraid it looks as though you'll have to.

MORTEN KIIL: No, thank you! I value my name and reputation. People call me 'the Badger,' I'm told. A badger's a dirty beast, isn't it? Well, I'll prove them wrong. I intend to live and die clean.

DR. STOCKMANN: And how are you going to go about that?

MORTEN KIIL: You're going to make me clean, Stockmann.

DR. STOCKMANN: I—!

MORTEN KIIL: Do you know what money I've used to buy these shares with? No, you can't; but I'll tell you. It's the money Catherine and Petra and the boys are going to inherit when I'm gone. I've managed to put a little aside, you see.

DR. STOCKMANN *(flares up):* You mean you've spent Catherine's money on this?

MORTEN KIIL: Yes, now it's all invested in the Baths. So now we'll see if you're really as daft as you pretend, Stockmann. Every time you say there's vermin coming out of my tannery, it'll be as though you were cutting a pound of flesh from your wife's body, and Petra's and the children. But no self-respecting husband and father would do such a thing—unless he really was mad.

DR. STOCKMANN *(walks up and down):* Yes, but I *am* mad! I *am* mad!

MORTEN KIIL: You can't be that mad when your wife and children are at stake.

DR. STOCKMANN *(stops in front of him):* Why couldn't you have come and spoken to me before you went and bought all this waste paper?

MORTEN KIIL: Actions speak louder than words.

DR. STOCKMANN *(wanders around restlessly):* If only I weren't so sure—! But I *know* I'm right!

MORTEN KIIL *(weighs the pocketbook in his hand):* If you persist in this lunacy, these shares won't be worth much, you know.

He puts the pocketbook back in his pocket.

DR. STOCKMANN: But, damn it, science must be able to find some way. A preventative; or a purifier or something—

MORTEN KIIL: You mean something to kill these vermin?

DR. STOCKMANN: Yes, or render them harmless.

MORTEN KIIL: Couldn't you try rat poison?

DR. STOCKMANN: Oh, no, no! But everyone keeps saying it's just a fancy of mine. All right, then, let them have it that way. Those ignorant, narrow-minded curs denounced me as an enemy of the people, didn't they? And all but tore the clothes off my back!

MORTEN KIIL: And smashed your windows.

DR. STOCKMANN: Yes. And then this question of my duty towards my family. I must talk to Catherine. She knows about these things.

MORTEN KIIL: That's a good idea. She's a sensible woman. Follow her advice.

DR. STOCKMANN *(turns on him):* Why did you have to [do such a stupid thing? Hazard Catherine's money, and] put me in this frightful predicament! When I look at you, I feel as though I was looking at the Devil himself—

MORTEN KIIL: Then I'd best be off. But I want your answer by two o'clock. If it's no, I'm giving these shares to the Old Folks' Home—and I'll do it today.

DR. STOCKMANN: And what will Catherine get then?

MORTEN KIIL: Not a farthing!

The door to the hall is opened. HOVSTAD *and* ASLAKSEN *are seen there.*

MORTEN KIIL: Well! Look whom we have here!

DR. STOCKMANN *(stares at them):* What the devil—? Do you two still dare to visit me?

HOVSTAD: Indeed we do.

ASLAKSEN: We've something we want to talk to you about.

MORTEN KIIL *(whispers):* Yes or no—by two o'clock!

ASLAKSEN *(glances at* HOVSTAD*):* Aha!

MORTEN KIIL *goes.*

DR. STOCKMANN: Well, what do you want? Make it short.

HOVSTAD: I dare say you don't feel too kindly towards us in view of the stand we took at last night's meeting—

DR. STOCKMANN: Stand, you call it! A fine stand indeed! You just lay down like a couple of old women! Damn the pair of you!

HOVSTAD: Call it what you like; we *couldn't* do otherwise.

DR. STOCKMANN: You *dared* not do otherwise! Isn't that what you mean?

HOVSTAD: If you wish.

ASLAKSEN: But why didn't you tip us off? You only needed to drop a hint to Mr. Hovstad or me.

DR. STOCKMANN: Hint? About what?

ASLAKSEN: Why you were doing it.

DR. STOCKMANN: I don't understand.

ASLAKSEN (*nods conspiratorially*): Oh, yes you do, Dr. Stockmann.

HOVSTAD: There's no need to keep it secret any longer.

DR. STOCKMANN (*looks from one to the other*): What the devil—?

ASLAKSEN: Forgive the question, but isn't your father-in-law going round the town buying up all the shares in the Baths?

DR. STOCKMANN: He has bought some today. But—

ASLAKSEN: You'd have done wiser to employ someone else. Someone not quite so close to you.

HOVSTAD: And you shouldn't have done all this under your own name. Nobody need have known that the attack on the Baths came from you. You ought to have taken me into your confidence, Dr. Stockmann.

DR. STOCKMANN (*stares straight in front of him. A light seems to dawn on him, and he says as though thunderstruck*): Is it conceivable? Could such a thing really be *done?*

ASLAKSEN (*smiles*): Apparently. But it ought to be done with a certain subtlety, you know.

HOVSTAD: And there ought to be more than one person in on it. A man doesn't have so much responsibility to bear if he's in partnership.

DR. STOCKMANN (*composedly*): In brief, gentlemen, what do you want?

ASLAKSEN: Mr. Hovstad can explain better than—

HOVSTAD: No, you tell him, Aslaksen.

ASLAKSEN: Well, it's just this really, that now we know how the land lies, we think we might venture to put the *People's Tribune* at your disposal.

DR. STOCKMANN: You think you dare risk it? But what about public opinion? Aren't you afraid we might cause a storm?

HOVSTAD: We shall have to ride that storm.

ASLAKSEN: But you'll have to be quick on the trigger, Doctor. As soon as your campaign has done its job—

DR. STOCKMANN: As soon as my father-in-law and I have got all the shares cheaply, you mean—?

HOVSTAD: It is of course principally in the cause of science that you are seeking to gain control of the Baths.

DR. STOCKMANN: Of course. It was in the cause of science that I got the old Badger to come in with me on this. And then we'll tinker a bit with the water system and do a little digging on the beach and it won't cost the ratepayers half-a-crown. I think we'll get away with it, don't you! Eh?

HOVSTAD: I think so—if you have the *People's Tribune* behind you.

ASLAKSEN: In a <u>free</u> society the press is a power to be feared, Doctor.

DR. STOCKMANN: Quite. And public opinion, too. Mr. Aslaksen, you'll answer for the Property Owners' Association?

ASLAKSEN: The Property Owners' Association and the Temperance Society. Have no fear.

DR. STOCKMANN: But, gentlemen—I blush to mention the matter, but—what consideration—er—

HOVSTAD: Well, of course we'd like to help you absolutely gratis. But the *People's Tribune* is going through an awkward period; we're having an uphill struggle, and I'm very reluctant to wind things up just now, when there are such splendid causes that need our support.

DR. STOCKMANN: Of course. That'd be a bitter pill for a friend of the people like you to have to swallow. *(Flares up.)* But I—I am an enemy of the people! *(Strides around the room.)* Where's that stick of mine? Where the devil did I put my stick?

HOVSTAD: What do you mean?

ASLAKSEN: You surely aren't thinking of—?

DR. STOCKMANN *(stops):* And suppose I don't give you a penny of my shares? We rich men are pretty close with our money, you must remember.

HOVSTAD: And *you* must remember that this little business of the shares would bear more than one interpretation.

DR. STOCKMANN: Yes, that'd be right up your street, wouldn't it? If I don't come to the aid of the *People's Tribune,* you'll misrepresent my motives—you'll start a witch-hunt, drive me to ground, and throttle the life out of me as a hound throttles a hare!

HOVSTAD: That's the law of nature. Every animal has to fight for survival, you know.

ASLAKSEN: Bread doesn't grow on trees. You must take it where you can find it.

DR. STOCKMANN: Then see if you can find any in the gutter! *(Strides around the room.)* Now, by heaven, we'll see which is the strongest animal of us three! *(Finds his umbrella.)* Aha! *(Swings it.)* Now—!

HOVSTAD: You wouldn't dare to assault us!

ASLAKSEN: Be careful with that umbrella!

DR. STOCKMANN: Out of the window with you, Mr. Hovstad!

HOVSTAD *(at the doorway to the hall):* Are you out of your mind?

DR. STOCKMANN: Get through that window, Mr. Aslaksen! Jump, I tell you! Don't dally!

ASLAKSEN *(runs round the desk):* Doctor, Doctor, restrain yourself! I'm a weak man—I can't stand excitement—! *(Screams)* Help, help!

MRS. STOCKMANN, PETRA *and* CAPTAIN HORSTER *enter from the living-room.*

MRS. STOCKMANN: In heaven's name, Thomas, what's going on here?

DR. STOCKMANN *(brandishes the umbrella):* Jump out, I tell you! Down into the gutter!

HOVSTAD: An unprovoked assault! I call you to witness, Captain Horster—! *(Runs out through the hall.)*

MRS. STOCKMANN *(holds the* DOCTOR*):* Thomas, for mercy's sake control yourself!

ASLAKSEN *(desperate):* Restraint, Doctor! Restr—oh, dear! *(Scampers out through the living-room.)*

DR. STOCKMANN *(throws away the umbrella):* Damn it, they got away after all!

MRS. STOCKMANN: But what did they want?

DR. STOCKMANN: I'll tell you later. I've other things to think about just now. *(Goes to the table and writes on a visiting card.)* Look at this, Catherine. What do you see here?

MRS. STOCKMANN: 'No, no, no'—what does that mean?

DR. STOCKMANN: I'll explain that later, too. *(Holds out the card.)* Here, Petra, tell that smutty-nosed girl to run up to the Badger with this as quickly as she can. Hurry!

PETRA *goes out with the card through the hall.*

DR. STOCKMANN: If I haven't had all the devil's messengers after me today, I really don't know who's left! But now I'll sharpen my pen against them until it's like a dagger!

I'll dip it in gall and venom! I'll fling my inkstand against their stupid skulls! *Luttilrette Devil (?)*

MRS. STOCKMANN: But Thomas, we're leaving!

PETRA *returns.*

DR. STOCKMANN: Well?

PETRA: She's taken it.

DR. STOCKMANN: Good! Leaving, did you say? No, by God, we're not! We're staying here, Catherine!

PETRA: Staying?

MRS. STOCKMANN: In this town?

DR. STOCKMANN: Yes! This is the chosen battlefield, and it's here that the battle must be fought! And it's here that I shall win! As soon as you've sewn up those trousers of mine, I'll go into town and look for a house. We've got to have a roof over our heads [when winter comes].

CAPTAIN HORSTER: I can let you have my house.

DR. STOCKMANN: Would you?

CAPTAIN HORSTER: Of course. I've plenty of rooms, and I'm hardly ever there.

MRS. STOCKMANN: Oh, Captain Horster, how kind of you!

PETRA: Thank you!

DR. STOCKMANN (*presses his hand*): Thank you, thank you! [Well, that problem's behind us! I'll start my campaign this very day!] Oh, [Catherine,] there's so much to be done! But luckily I'll be able to devote my whole time to it. Look at this. I've been sacked from the Baths—

MRS. STOCKMANN (*sighs*): Ah, well, I was expecting that.

DR. STOCKMANN: And they want to take away my practice too! All right, let them! At least I'll keep my poor patients—they're the ones who can't pay—well, heaven knows they're the ones who need me most. But, by God, they'll have to listen to me! I'll preach to them morning, noon and night.

MRS. STOCKMANN: Oh, Thomas, Thomas! Surely you've seen what good preaching does!

DR. STOCKMANN: You really are absurd, Catherine! Am I to allow myself to be chased from the field by public opinion, and the majority, and such fiddle-faddle? No, thank you! [What I want is so simple and straightforward and easy! I only want to knock it into the heads of these curs that the Liberals are the most insidious enemies of freedom—that party programmes strangle every new truth that deserves to live—and that expediency and self-interest turn morality and justice upside down, so that in the end life here becomes intolerable. Well, Captain Horster, don't you think I ought to be able to get people to grasp that?

CAPTAIN HORSTER: I dare say. I don't really understand these things.

DR. STOCKMANN: Well, you see, the real point is this! It's the party bosses—they're the ones who've got to be rooted out! A party boss is like a hungry wolf—he needs a certain number of baby lambs to devour every year if he is to survive. Look at Hovstad and Aslaksen! How many innocent and vital young idealists have they knocked on the head! Or else they mangle and maul them till they're fit for nothing but to be property owners or subscribers to the *People's Tribune!* (*Half-sits on the table.*) Come here, Catherine! Look how beautifully the sun's shining in through the windows today! And smell this glorious, fresh spring air which is being wafted in to us.

MRS. STOCKMANN: Oh, my dear Thomas, if only we could live on sunshine and spring air!

DR. STOCKMANN: Well, you may have to pinch and scrape a little, but we'll manage. That's the least of my worries. No, the worst is that I don't know of anyone sufficiently free and—*unplebeian* to carry on my work after me.

504

PETRA: Oh, never mind that, father. You'll find someone in time. Look, here are the boys!

EILIF *and* MORTEN *enter from the living-room.*

MRS. STOCKMANN: Have you been given a holiday today?

MORTEN: No. But we had a fight with the other boys in the break, so—

EILIF: That's not true! It was the other boys who fought with us!

MORTEN: Yes. So I said to Dr. Rœrlund I thought it would be better if we stayed at home for a few days.

DR. STOCKMANN (*snaps his fingers and jumps from the table*): I've got it! By heaven, I've got it! Neither of you shall ever set foot in that school again!

THE BOYS: Not go to school?

MRS. STOCKMANN: But, Thomas—!

DR. STOCKMANN: Never, I say! I'll teach you myself! You won't learn a damned thing—

MORTEN: Hurrah!

DR. STOCKMANN: But I'll make you free men! Aristocrats! Petra, you'll have to help me.

PETRA: Yes, father, of course.

DR. STOCKMANN: And we'll hold the school in the room where they branded me as an enemy of the people. But we need more pupils. I must have at least twelve to begin with.

MRS. STOCKMANN: You won't find them in this town.

DR. STOCKMANN: We shall see. (*To the* BOYS.) Do you know any street urchins—real guttersnipes—?

EILIF: Oh yes, father, I know lots!

DR. STOCKMANN: That's fine! Get hold of a few for me. I'm going to experiment with street dogs for once. They have good heads on them sometimes.

EILIF: But what shall we do when we've become [free men and] aristocrats?

505

DR. STOCKMANN: Then, my boys, you'll chase all these damned politicians into the Atlantic Ocean!

EILIF *looks somewhat doubtful.* MORTEN *jumps and cheers.*

MRS. STOCKMANN: Let's hope it won't be the politicians who'll chase you out, Thomas.

DR. STOCKMANN: Are you quite mad, Catherine? Chase me out? Now, when I am the strongest man in town?

MRS. STOCKMANN: The strongest—now?

DR. STOCKMANN: Yes! I'll go further! I am now one of the strongest men in the whole world.

MORTEN: Hurrah!

DR. STOCKMANN (*lowers his voice*): Hush! You mustn't talk about it yet! But I've made a great discovery!

MRS. STOCKMANN: Not again!

DR. STOCKMANN: Yes—yes! (*Gathers them round him and whispers to them.*) The fact is, you see, that the strongest man in the world is he who stands most alone.

MRS. STOCKMANN (*smiles and shakes her head*): Oh, Thomas—!

PETRA (*warmly, clasps his hands*): Father!

And is reader meant to agree? Or the Dr. as proven to be wrong? Def. of "strongest"? form??

Note on the Translation

I have allowed myself a small amount of licence in translating one or two phrases. When Dr. Stockmann likens aristocrats of the intellect to pedigree dogs, Ibsen makes him name the poodle as an example of refinement and intelligence; but poodles, at any rate in England today, have rather the wrong kind of associations, and I have altered this to 'greyhound'. And when he speaks of his hatred of *ledende mænd* (literally 'leading men'—in the political, not the theatrical sense, though Ibsen knew a thing or two about the latter kind too), I have translated the phrase as 'politicians'. Ibsen means by *ledende mænd* anyone who leads other men by the nose, which is a pretty accurate definition of a politician.

I have indicated, by square brackets in the text, suggested cuts for performance. *An Enemy of the People* is, with the single exception of *The Wild Duck*, the longest of Ibsen's mature prose plays and, even when cut as here, still runs for nearly three hours. Stockmann's address in the fourth act contains a certain amount of red herringry which it is no great loss to shed; and the opening of the final act, with its repetitious insistence on 'not daring', and the closing minutes, both profit, in my opinion, from judicious thinning. But any director who uses this translation is free to follow his or her own judgement in this matter.

APPENDIX TO GHOSTS

The first English performance of *Ghosts* in 1891 was an event of exceptional importance in the history of the English theatre.

It was the opening production of the Independent Theatre Society, founded by a 29-year-old Dutchman, J. T. Grein, in emulation of Antoine's Théâtre Libre in Paris. The Independent Theatre Society was, to quote Charles Archer (*Life of William Archer,* London, 1931): 'a modest organization of most slender resources, intended to give the non-commercial drama, both native and foreign, a chance upon the stage, by means of occasional subscription performances in theatres hired for the purpose. Since no money was to be taken at the doors, the performances would be technically private, and it was believed that plays which, for one reason or another, the Censor could not be expected to pass for public performance, could be given without licence, as *The Cenci* had been given in 1886 under the auspices of the Shelley Society.'

The rest of the story is best told in Mrs. Alix Grein's biography of her husband, written under the pseudonym of 'Michael Orme' (London, 1936):

'Thomas Hardy and George Meredith both raised their voices in support of the new enterprise, and . . . J.T. proceeded to look about for a playhouse to harbour the initial performance of the Independent Theatre. Negotiations with the Novelty (now the Kingsway) fell through, and the Athenaeum Hall in Tottenham Court Road was selected. But it was soon evident that this small hall would not be able to accommodate all the people invited, particularly as J.T., in weak if friendly moments, extended invitations to everybody he met who expressed the slightest interest in Ibsen. There had been a reading by Dr. Aveling of *Ghosts* at the Playgoers' Club where J.T., in a burst of enthusiasm, convened the whole audience to his opening performance. It was a well-attended meeting and the response to this wholesale invitation was so great that the little Athenaeum Hall could not possibly have encompassed the swelling crowd.

'In this dilemma Miss Kate Santley, the proprietress of the Royalty, came to his assistance and offered her theatre at £15 for the evening of Friday, March 13th, 1891, braving the opposition that was increasing day by day. The *Daily Telegraph* hailed the forthcoming event with brimstone and hellfire and called upon the Lord Chamberlain to intervene. Miss Santley had a very pathetic interview with the Controller, fearing lest the licence granted to the Royalty itself might be in jeopardy. But the Lord Chamberlain's office pointed out that it had no official knowledge of any private performance—always provided such was legally private and did not infringe upon the domain of a public presentation. . . .

'The Royalty was filled from stalls to gallery. What with applications and invitations, this theatre in turn became too small to hold the audience. J.T. found a solution in a flash. That was the way he did things; brilliant flashes at times, impractical flashes at others. A swift decision to turn an ordinary dress rehearsal into the equivalent of the French *répétition générale* saved the situation. The many who were unable to secure seats for the actual performance flocked to this rehearsal two nights before. So well was it attended that the occasion assumed the air of a Society function. . . .

'On the evening of the performance it was intimated to him that there would possibly be a question asked in Parliament the next day, followed by a prosecution under Lord

Campbell's Act, an extremely pleasant prospect for a young man then earning his living in the City as a foreign correspondence clerk at the munificent remuneration of £180 per annum! . . . Yet the question in Parliament was never asked. . . . The Home Office had requested the Member to desist, as nothing was known in Government circles concerning *Ghosts,* and the question might put the House in an embarrassing position. . . .

'Mrs. Theodore Wright, who played Mrs. Alving . . . was a well-known amateur, and had occasionally played on the regular stage. One day she wandered into J.T.'s rooms and said she had heard of the intended production. He was immediately struck by the timbre of her voice, detecting in it his conception of the maternal accent to perfection. He asked her to read the third act and, when she had finished, said to her: "I know nothing about you, but you will play 'Mrs. Alving,' and you will be famous next morning." '

Of the reception of the play by the British press, William Archer noted: 'The shriek of execration with which this performance was received by the newspapers of the day has scarcely its counterpart in the history of criticism . . .'. Three weeks after the performance, on 8 April 1891, he published in the *Pall Mall Gazette* an anthology of the choicest comments, worth quoting in full:

'GHOSTS' AND GIBBERINGS

Descriptions of the Play

'An open drain; a loathsome sore unbandaged; a dirty act done publicly; a lazar-house with all its doors and windows open. . . . Candid foulness. . . . Kotzebue turned bestial and cynical. Offensive cynicism. . . . Ibsen's melancholy and malodorous world. . . . Absolutely loathsome and fetid. . . . Gross, almost putrid indecorum'— *Daily Telegraph* (leading article). 'This mass of vulgarity, egotism, coarseness, and absurdity'—*Daily Telegraph* (criticism). 'Unutterably offensive. . . . Prosecution under Lord Campbell's Act. . . . Abominable piece. . . . Scandalous'— *Standard*. 'Naked loathsomeness. . . . Most dismal and repulsive production'—*Daily News*. 'Revoltingly suggestive and blasphemous. . . . Characters either contradictory in themselves, uninteresting or abhorrent'—*Daily Chronicle*. 'A repulsive and degrading work'—*Queen*. 'Morbid, unhealthy, unwholesome and disgusting story. . . . A piece to bring the stage into disrepute and dishonour with every right-thinking man and woman'—*Lloyds's*. 'Merely dull dirt long drawn out'—*Hawk*. 'Morbid horrors of the hideous tale. . . . Ponderous dullness of the didactic talk. . . . If any repetition of this outrage be attempted, the authorities will doubtless wake from their lethargy'— *Sporting and Dramatic News*. 'Just a wicked nightmare'— *The Gentlewoman*. 'Lugubrious diagnosis of sordid impropriety. . . . Characters are prigs, pedants and profligates. . . . Morbid caricatures. . . . Maunderings of nook-shotten Norwegians. . . . It is no more of a play than an average Gaiety burlesque'—*Black and White*. 'Most loathsome of all Ibsen's plays. . . . Garbage and offal'—*Truth*. 'Ibsen's putrid play called *Ghosts*. . . . So loathsome an enterprise'—*Academy*. 'As foul and filthy a concoction as has ever been allowed to disgrace the boards of an English theatre. . . . Dull and disgusting. . . . Nastiness and malodorousness laid on thickly as with a trowel'— *Era*. 'Noisome corruption'—*Stage*.

511

Descriptions of Ibsen

'An egotist and a bungler'—*Daily Telegraph*. 'A crazy fanatic. . . . A crazy, cranky being. . . . Not only consistently dirty but deplorably dull'—*Truth*. 'The Norwegian pessimist *in petto* [*sic*]'—*Black and White*. 'Ugly, nasty, discordant, and downright dull. . . . A gloomy sort of ghoul, bent on groping for horrors by night, and blinking like a stupid old owl when the warm sunlight of the best of life dances into his wrinkled eyes'—*Gentlewoman*. 'A teacher of the aestheticism of the Lock Hospital'—*Saturday Review*.

Descriptions of Ibsen's Admirers

'Lovers of prurience and dabblers in impropriety who are eager to gratify their illicit tastes under the pretence of art'—*Evening Standard*. 'Ninety-seven per cent of the people who go to see *Ghosts* are nasty-minded people who find the discussion of nasty subjects to their taste in exact proportion to their nastiness'—*Sporting and Dramatic News*. 'The sexless. . . . The unwomanly woman, the unsexed females, the whole army of unprepossessing cranks in petticoats. . . . Educated and muck-ferreting dogs. . . . Effeminate men and male women. . . . They all of them—men and women alike—know that they are doing not only a nasty but an illegal thing. . . . The Lord Chamberlain left them alone to wallow in *Ghosts*. . . . Outside a silly clique, there is not the slightest interest in the Scandinavian humbug or all his works. . . . A wave of human folly'—*Truth*.

* * *

One of the few critics courageous enough to defend the play was A. B. Walkley. Writing in the *Star* over the pseudonym of 'Spectator,' he asked:

'Do these people really find nothing in *Ghosts* but a mere hospital ward play? Is it really for them nothing but a painful study of disease? Have they no eyes for what stares them in the face: the plain, simple fact that *Ghosts* is a great spiritual drama? Like nearly all other great masterpieces of the stage, it is a drama of revolt—the revolt of the 'joy of life' against the gloom of hide-bound, conventional morality, the revolt of the natural man against the law-made, law-bound puppet, the revolt of the individual against the oppression of social prejudice. . . . This is the spiritual drama which I see in *Ghosts*.'

Of Mrs. Theodore Wright, Walkley wrote: 'I have never heard of this lady before; she has never performed, I believe, on the regular stage: she knows little, I suspect, of the *technique* of acting—and her Mrs. Alving was quite admirable. The secret of her success was very simple. She had studied her part with perfect sympathy, she had thought out the meaning of her words before committing them to memory, and so she crept into the very skin of the character. A little wanting in distinction, perhaps? Yes, she is not a Madeleine Brohan. And in authority? Yes, she is not a Geneviève Ward. And in the final catastrophe, her histrionic means were scarcely adequate: one would have liked a little more power. But never mind that: she accomplished the chief thing. She made us understand the true significance of the part—hers was really modest, helpful interpretation, not that obtrusive nuisance which professional actors rather impudently call "creation". Mr. Leonard Outram's Pastor Manders, too, was a capital piece of quiet, sensible, honest work—no over-acting, no "character playing", no teasing elaboration of conventional stage "business"—the "great baby, Manders'' to the life. The Oswald of Mr. Frank Lindo was well-intended, but a little too hang-dog in expression and slouching in gait for my fancy; and the way he rolled his eyes in the fine frenzy of the third act struck me as rather farcical. . . . I am not sure, after all, that the Engstrand of Mr. Sydney Howard was not the best thing in the cast, a delightfully humorous, yet never overcharged, picture of Ibsen's greasy, sanctimonious hypocrite. So long as he was on the stage he kept the house in one continuous ripple of laughter, and laughter is a welcome relief in the ''inspissated'' gloom of this tragedy. There was great enthusiasm at the fall of the curtain.'

Subsequent Mrs. Alvings in London have included Janet Achurch, Eleonora Duse, Mrs. Patrick Campbell (in 1928, with the young John Gielgud as Oswald), Sybil Thorndike, Louise Hampton, Nancy Price, Marie Ney, Katina Paxinou, Beatrix Lehmann, Cathleen Nesbitt (on TV), Flora Robson, Catherine Lacey, Peggy Ashcroft and Celia Johnson (on TV); also, most memorably, Wendy Hiller in a production at Cambridge in 1972. Actors who have played Oswald include Lewis Waller, Courtenay Thorpe, Leon Quartermaine, Basil Sydney, Ernest Milton, John Gielgud, Emlyn Williams, Michael MacLiammoir, Michael Jayston and Tom Courtenay. Incomparably the best all-round production of the play in this writer's experience was that shown on BBC Television in 1968, details of which are given on page 24.

ABOUT THE AUTHOR

HENRIK IBSEN, widely regarded as the founder of modern drama, was born in Skien, Norway in 1828 into a family of prosperous merchants. His father's business failed suddenly while Ibsen was still a young boy, and Ibsen was forced to work as an apothecary's assistant. After six years of humiliating poverty, Ibsen entered the university, and in 1850 he was asked to join the new National Theater, where he wrote and directed plays and designed productions. His plays were not admired, the National Theater went bankrupt, and Ibsen, forced to live on the charity of friends and a government travel stipend, emigrated to Italy.

It was not until 1866, when *Brand* was published to critical acclaim and *Peer Gynt* to even greater praise, that Ibsen began to gain recognition as a playwright. The next decade was a fertile one. Ibsen's dramas of social and family life attracted more attention, and *A Doll's House* was produced to international admiration, though it aroused controversy for its unromantic portrayal of marriage and its realistic depiction of the tensions between husband and wife. Ibsen's next play, *Ghosts* (1881), which dealt frankly with free love and venereal disease, was violently attacked as indecent. His succeeding plays, among them such acknowledged masterpieces as *The Wild Duck* (1884) and *Hedda Gabler* (1890), were met with bafflement and disdain, the artistic establishment accusing Ibsen of being relentlessly pessimistic and unnecessarily obscure. In 1891, Ibsen returned to Norway, where he lived until his death from a stroke in 1906. He never lived to see the recognition that would one day place him among the greatest dramatists of Western Literature.

ABOUT THE TRANSLATOR

Michael Meyer is one of the leading Ibsen scholars of his generation. He was born in London in 1921 and educated at Oxford. He has lived extensively in the Scandinavian countries and taught English literature at Upsala University in Sweden. In addition to his translation of *The Plays of Ibsen*, available in four volumes from Washington Square Press, he has written a biography of Ibsen, translated the plays of Strindberg, and, most recently, written a biography of Strindberg. He currently resides in London.